A Treatise On the Law of Guarantees and of Principal and Surety

A

TREATISE

ON THE

LAW OF GUARANTEES

AND OF

𝔓𝔯𝔦𝔫𝔠𝔦𝔭𝔞𝔩 & 𝔖𝔲𝔯𝔢𝔱𝔶.

BY

HENRY ANSELM de COLYAR,

OF THE MIDDLE TEMPLE, ESQUIRE, BARRISTER-AT-LAW

From the Second English Edition.

NEW YORK AND ALBANY
BANKS & BROTHERS, LAW PUBLISHERS
1896

TO

THE RIGHT HONORABLE

JOHN DUKE, BARON COLERIDGE,

OF OTTERY ST. MARY, IN THE COUNTY OF DEVON,

Lord Chief Justice of England,

&c. &c. &c.

THIS TREATISE

IS,

WITH HIS LORDSHIP'S KIND PERMISSION,

MOST RESPECTFULLY

DEDICATED.

(1211)

(v)

PREFACE.

TO THE SECOND EDITION.

THE favourable reception accorded by the Profession to the First Edition of this Work has verified the opinion held by the Author, that there was room for a Treatise on the Law of Guarantees. Moreover, it is evident that the want of such a Treatise was not felt in this country alone; for, shortly after the publication of the Author's Work in England, there appeared, but without his knowledge or permission, an American Edition.

Since this Work was first issued, many important decisions have been given on the subject to which it relates. These, it is believed, are all referred to in the present Edition, which embraces altogether upwards of 1140 authorities. This number not only comprises all the *English* decisions on the law of guarantees which have been pronounced since the publication of the First Edition, but, likewise, includes the principal IRISH and AMERICAN cases on the same subject which have been determined during the past ten years.

An endeavor has been made, in the present Edition, to simplify the arrangement of one or two of the Chapters into which the Treatise is divided; and it is hoped that the introduction of *marginal notes* throughout the text will prove of some assistance to the reader.

That most important part of every legal text book—the Index—has received special attention from the Author, and no pains have been spared by him to render it as complete as possible.

The present Volume is necessarily somewhat larger than the original Edition of the Work, but it is believed that only essential additions have been made.

The very great difficulty of the subject discussed in this Work will be generally admitted. The Author therefore hopes that this will be remembered by those to whom the present Treatise may appear to be, in some respects, defective.

H. A. de C.

4, PAPER BUILDINGS, TEMPLE, E. C.
      31st October, 1885.

PREFACE.

TO THE FIRST EDITION.

As a branch of Mercantile Law, the subject of Guarantees is the only important subject of our extensive Commercial System on which no generally-received Text-book now exists. Every other head of Mercantile Law appears to have been made the subject of a separate Treatise by one or more writers. Thus, the Law of Bills of Exchange and Promissory Notes has been dealt with by Mr. Chitty, by Mr. Justice Byles, and by Mr. Justice Story. The Law of Carriers is the subject of several Treatises, both English and American. The Law of Shipping has not only been dealt with as a whole in more than one work, but its numerous and important sub-divisions—such as Bills of Lading, Charter-Parties, Insurance and General Average—have all been discussed in separate books and by different authors. The Law of Fire Insurance and of Life Insurance have each also been made the subject of a separate Text-book by Mr. Bunyon, and also by more than one American writer. The relationship of Principal and Agent, too, have likewise furnished a subject which has been discussed by learned authors, American as well as English; notably by the celebrated American jurist, Mr. Justice Story. Even the comparatively small subject of "Stoppage *in Transitu*" has received attention in a separate volume by Mr. Houston, devoted to its consideration.

But it is not only as a portion of our Mercantile Law that the subject of Guarantees claims attention from English lawyers, for guarantees are frequently given for the fidelity of persons holding public offices or places of trust; Government servants and those in the employment of public corporations being in particular very often called on to furnish such guarantees. Indeed, so common has the custom become, that, within the last few years, public companies have been established, some of which make it their exclusive business to give guarantees of the nature just mentioned, while others, and some of the older Insurance Offices, unite this business with a General Insurance business.

Its importance in this double character, both of a branch of Mercantile Law and also in connection with the holders of offices and places of trust, makes the subject of Guarantees one of great and daily practical interest. This alone would lead to the expectation that it would frequently furnish the subject for litigation; and, added to this, the Courts of Equity have dealt with it, as well as the Courts of Law, and have laid down certain peculiar doctrines with respect to it. Consequently, the number of reported cases upon the subject is very large. It is almost impossible to take up a volume of modern Law Reports without finding in it some decision upon the subject of Guarantees.

*   *   *   *   *   *

Under these circumstances it might have been expected that there must exist some received modern Text-book,—such, however, strangely enough, is not the case.

Many years ago, indeed, the Treatises of Mr. Fell and of Mr. Theobald appeared at nearly the same time, and probably then exhausted the subject; but the time which has elapsed since their publication has now rendered these works useless as practical Text-books.

These considerations will, it is hoped, furnish a sufficient explanation for the appearance of the present Volume. They lead the Author to think that there is room for a book on the subject, and have induced him to write the following pages.

*   *   *   *   *   *

For the Work as a whole the Author can only say that he has endeavoured to collect all the authorities on the subject treated of in the present Volume, and has spared neither time nor trouble.

The Author has great pleasure in acknowledging the able assistance rendered to him by his learned friend Mr. *George Lewis*, of the Western Circuit. The suggestions received by the author from Mr. *Lewis* have been invaluable, and have rendered the present Treatise much more accurate and serviceable than it otherwise would have been.

The Author desires also to mention that he has derived considerable assistance from a Treatise on "The Validity of Verbal Agreements," by a learned American jurist, Mr. *Throop*. In one part of his Treatise Mr. *Throop* endeavors, with infinite ingenuity, to arrange the American and English Cases on the Law of Guarantees according to principle. The Author has not, however, followed Mr. *Throop's* arrangement, but has adopted a simpler one more suited to a work which, like the present, deals only, or at least principally, with the *English Law* of Guarantees. He hopes, however, that it will be found that his attempt to refer each decision on the *English* Law of Guarantees to some principle has not been altogether unsuccessful.

The Author has, it is needless to add, consulted numerous works, both English and American.

*TABLE OF CONTENTS. [*xiii]

(1220)

[The paging refers to the [*] pages.]

Chapter V.

The Rights of the Surety.

Chapter VI.

The Discharge of the Surety.

(1221)

APPENDIX.

                        (1222)

(xv)

*TABLE OF CASES. [*xiii]

[The paging refers to the [*] pages.]

[The paging refers to the [*] pages.]

[The paging refers to the [*] pages.]

[The paging refers to the [*] pages.]

𝔄 𝔗reatise

ON

THE LAW OF GUARANTEES.

CHAPTER I.

OF THE FORMATION OF THE CONTRACT OF GUARANTEE.

A GUARANTEE is a collateral engagement to answer for the debt, default or miscarriage of another person. The person who gives the guarantee, is called the *surety* or *guarantor* (a); the person to whom it is given, is called the *creditor* or *guarantee*; and the person whose debt, default or miscarriage is the foundation of the guarantee, is called the *principal debtor*, or simply, *the principal.*

The contract of guarantee is of very ancient date, and appears, indeed, to be "coeval with the first contracts recorded in history" (b). It seems that originally the words warranty and guaranty (c) were the same; "the letter *g* of the Norman-French being convertible with the *w* of the German and English, as in the names *William or Guillaume. They are sometimes [*2] used indiscriminately (d); but, in general, warranty is

---

(a) In the recent case of *Imperial Bank* v. *London and St. Katherine's Dock Co.* (5 Ch. Div. at p. 500), *Jessel*, M. R., said :— "Whoever is liable to pay the debt of another, whether for value, as in the case of the broker who receives a commission for incurring liability, or gratuitously, as between himself and the person primarily liable is a surety ; and I can understand no definition of surety which will not include a person in that situation."

(b) See Story on the Law of Contracts, 5th ed., vol. ii., p. 319, note 1.

(c) Now spelt *guarantee* or *guarantie.*

(d) Not in England.

ranty and guarantee. applied to a contract as to the title, quality or quantity of a thing sold . . . ; and guaranty is held to be the contract by which one person is bound to another for the due fulfilment of a promise or engagement of a third party" (e). To constitute a guarantee, just as to the formation of any other contract, there are three essential requisites, namely, the mutual assent of two or more parties; that the parties be competent to contract; and that the contract, if not under seal, be supported by a valuable consideration. It will be as well to say a word or two upon each of these essential requisites, and, in doing this, to direct attention, as far as possible, to one particular kind of contract only, namely, the contract of guarantee, since it is with it that this work is immediately concerned.

Essential requisites of a guarantee.

First requisite. Mutual assent of parties. First, then, as to the mutual assent of the parties.

Every contract includes a concurrence of intention in two parties, one of whom promises something to the other, who, on his part, accepts such promise (f). Until, therefore, an acceptance be given (which must be an absolute and unqualified acceptance of the previous offer (g)), the promiser is not liable (h). In accordance [*3] dance *with this doctrine, it has been decided that a mere offer to guarantee is not binding until acceptance by the person to whom the offer is made (i). Till then,

Offer to guarantee not binding till acceptance.

(e) Parsons' Law of Contracts, 5th ed., vol. ii., p. 3.
(f) Pothier on the Law of Obligations (Evans' Edition), vol. i., p. 4; and see Ely (Marchioness). In re, 4 De G. J. & S. 638; Staines v. Wainwright, 6 Bing. N. C. 174; 8 Scott, 280.
(g) Appleby v. Johnson, L. R., 9 C. P. 158; and see Crossley v. Maycock, L. R., 18 Eq. 180; Smith v. Webster, 3 Ch. Div. 49.
(h) See generally on this subject, Head v. Diggon, 3 M. & Ry. 97; Adams v. Lindsell, 1 B. & Ald. 681; Cooke v. Oxley, 3 T. R. 653; Williams v. Carwardine, 4 B. & Ad. 621; Routledge v. Grant, 4 Bing. 653; 1 M. & Payne, 717; Denton v. Great Northern Ry. Co., 5 Ell. & Bl. 860; Thatcher v. England, 3 C. B. 254; Lancaster v. Walsh, 4 M. & W. 16; Lockhart v. Barnard, 14 M. & W. 674; Kennedy v. Lee, 3 Mer. 441, 454; Johnson v. King, 2 Bing 270; Holland v. Eyre, 2 Sim. & St. 194; The Sheffield Canal Co. v. The Sheffield and Rotherham Ry. Co., 3 Ry. & Canal Cases, 121 and 486; Hyde v. Wrench, 3 Beav. 334; Thomson v. James, 18 Dunlop, 1; Dunlop v. Higgins, 1 H. L. 381; Mactier v. Frith, 6 Wendell, 103, and judgment of Mr. Justice Marcey in that case; Payne v. Cave, 3 T. R. 148; Ramsgate Victoria Co. Limited v. Montefiore, L. R., 1 Exch. 109; Ex parte Bloxam, 33 L. J., Ch. 574, Ex parte Cookney, 28 L. J., Ch. 12; 3 De G. & J. 170; Ex parte Miles, 34 L. J., Ch. 123; Ex parte Beresford, 2 Mac. & G. 197; Hebb's case, L. R., 4 Eq. 9; Martin v. Mitchell, 2 Jac. & W. 413, 428; Countess of Dunmore v. Alexander, 9 Shaw & Dunlop, 190.
(i) M'Ivor v. Richardson, 1 M. & S. 557; Simmons v. Want, 2 Stark. 371; Gaunt v. Hill, 1 Stark. 10; Mozley v. Tinckler, 1 Cr., M. & R. 692; 5 Tyrr. 416; Newport v. Spirey, 7 L. T., N. S. 328.

it is *revocable* by the party making it (*k*). But when
an offer is sent by letter it cannot be withdrawn by
merely posting a subsequent letter which does not, in
the ordinary course of the post, arrive till after the first
letter has been received and answered (*l*). It is not, as **Acceptance may be express or implied.** a rule, necessary, however, that the acceptance should
be *express*; it may be *implied*. Thus, where an offer
of guarantee is in these terms, "I agree to be security **Examples of implied acceptance of offer to guarantee.** to you for T. C. for whatever, while in your employ,
you may trust him with, and, in case of default, to
make the same good," as soon as the person to whom
such a guarantee is given employs T. C. (but not
before) the guarantee attaches and becomes binding on
the party who gave it (*m*), without any formal acceptance.

In *Pope* v. *Andrews* (*n*) *Coleridge*, J., said, "If a person
offers a guarantee, and more still, if he signs a guarantee by which he makes himself liable, and that be sent
to the other party, such other party, if he means
*not to accept the guarantee, is bound expressly [*4]
to dissent within a reasonable time; and if he keeps
the guarantee an unreasonable time, he is bound to
accept it just the same as if he had assented to it by
words; and if he has ever accepted it either by *word or
by act*, he cannot afterwards retract."

In *Sorby* v. *Gordon* (*o*), the facts were as follow:—
The defendant, being desirous of having goods shipped
to R. & Co., his agents in India, on 9th July, 1868,
applied by letter to the plaintiffs, who were manufacturers of edge tools carrying on business at Sheffield,
asking the price of certain tools to be sent out to India
to the firm of Messrs. R. & Co. In reply, the plaintiffs
stated their list of prices, and that their terms were
cash settlement in England within a few weeks. On
the 11th of the same month the defendant wrote to them
as follows:—"I shall be very glad that you should
come to an arrangement with R. & Co., that they should
be your agents there, but that requires direct correspondence between you and them. I am quite willing
to guarantee the first shipment." The same day the

(*k*) *Offord* v. *Davies*, 12 C. B., N. S. 748 ; *Grant* v. *Campbell*, 6
Dow, H. L. C. 239 ; and see *Stevenson* v. *McLean*, 5 Q. B. D. 346.
(*l*) *Byrne* v. *Van Tienhoven*, 5 C. P. D. 344 ; 49 L. J., C. P. 316;
Stevenson v. *McLean*, *ubi sup.*
(*m*) Per *Parke* B., in *Kennaway* v. *Treleavan*, 5 M. & W. 498,
500, 501. See also *Offord* v. *Davies*, 12 C. B., N. S. 748.
(*n*) 9 C. & P. 564, 568.
(*o*) 30 L. T. R. 528.

plaintiffs enclosed a list of prices, and requested a confirmation of the order, which was accordingly sent by the defendant. The goods, amounting in value to 800*l.*, were thereupon shipped to R. & Co. in India. Other shipments followed. The sum of 300*l.* only having been paid by R. & Co. in respect of this first shipment, the plaintiffs, in July, 1871, wrote to the defendant, " We sincerely hope it may not be necessary to act upon your letter of the 11th July, 1868." In two letters which the defendant subsequently wrote to the plaintiffs he never disclaimed his liability, but, on the 26th September, 1871, he wrote, "As the event on which I expressed my willingness to guarantee never took place, it never became effective." Messrs. R. & Co. having stopped payment, and there being a sum of 530*l.* still [*5] *due upon the first shipment of goods, the plaintiffs sued defendant upon his letter of guarantee. It was held, that upon the facts there was an express offer of a guarantee and an intimation of acceptance.

Express acceptance necessary where offer contemplates it.

Sometimes, however, an offer to guarantee contemplates an *express* acceptance. When this is the case, the person to whom the offer is made cannot avail himself of it without showing an *express* acceptance of it. Thus in *Mozley* v. *Tinckler* (*p*), the defendant gave an alleged guarantee in the following form: " F. informs me that you are about publishing an arithmetic for him. I have no objection to being answerable as far as 50*l.*; *for my reference apply to B.*" This instrument was forwarded by B. to the plaintiffs, who never communicated their acceptance of it to the defendant. In an action against the latter, on the guarantee, it was held that the plaintiffs, not proving any notice of acceptance to the defendant, were not entitled to recover. In this case the court considered that the defendant only intended to be bound by the instrument, in case, upon inquiry, the plaintiff should be satisfied with regard to his solvency.

Minds of contracting parties must be ad idem as to subject of the contract.

A contract being the offspring of intention, it follows that the minds of the contracting parties must be *ad idem* as to the subject of the contract. Thus, if two persons enter into an apparent contract concerning a particular person or ship, and it turns out that each of them, misled by a similarity of name, had a different person or ship in his mind, no contract would exist between them (*q*). Again, if a person is induced to

(*p*) 1 Cr., M. & R. 692. See also *Martin* v. *Marshall*, 2 H. & C. 315; *Bank of Montreal* v. *Munster*, 11 Ir. C. L. R. 47, 58.
(*q*) L. R., 6 Q. B. 597.

buy certain oats from another, under the belief that they are *old* oats, the contract is binding though the oats are actually not old. But if the person had agreed to take the oats, not merely under the belief that they *were old*, but under the belief that the seller *contracted* *they were old, there would be no contract in such [*6] a case if this was brought to the mind of the seller by any means whatsoever (r). The reason of this somewhat subtle distinction is perfectly just. In the *former* case the minds of both parties would be *ad idem* as to the purchase of the oats in question, though the *motive* of the buyer in purchasing them might be in his belief that they were *old*. In the *latter* case the minds of the parties would not be *ad idem* as to the subject of the contract, for, whilst the buyer believed that the seller contracted to sell *old* oats, the seller, knowing this, intended to supply oats that were not old.

In Paley's Moral and Political Philosophy (s), it is stated that a promise is to be interpreted "in the sense in which the promiser apprehended at the time that the promisee received it." The English rule of law that the promiser is not bound "to fulfill a promise in a sense in which the promisee knew at the time the promiser did not intend it," is a corollary to this rule of morality (t). And, in considering the question, in what sense a promisee is entitled to enforce a promise, it matters not in what way the knowledge of the meaning in which the promiser made it is brought to the mind of the promisee, whether by express words, or by conduct, or previous dealings, or other circumstances (u). If by any means he knows that there was no real agreement between him and the promiser, he is not entitled to insist that the promise shall be fulfilled in a sense in which the mind of the promiser does not assent (x). Sometimes, owing to the way in which one *Party may be* of the contracting parties has conducted himself, he is *estopped by* precluded from showing that he intended something *conduct from* different from the other contracting party, and that, *denying concurrence of* *consequently there is not that necessary concur- [*7] *intention.* rence of intention essential to every contract. Thus, *Examples of* if, whatever a man's real intention may be, he so con- *this doctrine.* ducts himself that a reasonable man would believe that

(r) See *Smith* v. *Hughes*, L. R., 6 Q. B. 597, *passim*.
(s) Book iii., cap. v.
(t) L. R., C Q. B., 597, 610.
(u) *Ib.*
(x) *Ib.* See also observations of *Kindersley*, V.-C., in *Small* v. *Currie*, 2 Drew. 102, 114.

he was assenting to the terms proposed by the other party, and that the other party, upon that belief, enters into the contract with him, the man thus conducting himself would be equally bound as if he had intended to agree to the other party's terms (y). So where the defendant (by mistake) chose to sign a guarantee which gave full effect to the plaintiff's intentions, and thereby induced the plaintiff to supply goods to a third person on the faith of such guarantee, it was held that the defendant was liable on his guarantee, and that he had no equity to turn round on the plaintiff and say, "I meant what I have not stated, and although you have relied upon my statement, I will only be liable for what I meant" (z). So, too, where, in the case of a sale of goods by sample, the vendor (by mistake) exhibited a wrong sample, it was held that the vendor could not, on that accout, treat the contract as void (a). "But if in the last mentioned case, the purchaser, in the course of the negotiations preliminary to the contract, had discovered that the vendor was under a misapprehension as to the sample he was offering, the vendor would have been entitled to show that he had not intended to enter into the contract by which the purchaser sought to bind him" (b).

Second requisite of contract of guarantee. Competency of parties to contract.

Secondly, we come to another requisite of a contract, namely, the competency of the parties to contract.

We have already stated that every contract includes [*8] a *concurrence of intention in two parties. This, in fact, enters into the idea of every contract. Now intention is a *voluntary* mental operation, being produced by a joint exercise of the *will* and the *understanding* (c). Therefore the parties to a contract must be *mentally capable* of producing the necessary intention; for, unless both have this capacity, there can be no contract between them. In accordance with this view is the maxim of the *civil* law which declares that "*Furiosus nullum negotium gerere potest, quia non intelligit quod*

(y) Per *Blackburn, J.,* in *Smith* v. *Hughes,* L. R., 6 Q. B. 597, 607. See also *Freeman* v. *Cooke,* 2 Ex. 663 ; 18 L. J., Ex. 119.
(z) *Hymen* v. *Gover,* 25 L. T., N. S., Q. B. 903 ; and see *Rawstone* v. *Parr,* 3 Russ. 539.
(a) *Scott* v. *Littledale,* 8 E. & B. 815.
(b) Per *Hannen, J.,* in *Smith* v. *Hughes,* L. R., 6 Q. B. at p. 609.
(c) As to which of these two *powers* of the mind predominates in the formation of intention we are not called upon to discuss. "The faculties of *understanding* and *will,* are easily distinguished in thought but very rarely, if ever, disjoined in operation." See *Ried's Collected Writings, by Sir W. Hamilton,* 2nd ed., p. 537.

agit" (*d*). The mere existence, however, of a delusion in the mind of a person making a disposition or contract is not sufficient to avoid it, even though the delusion be connected with the subject-matter of such disposition or contract; it is a question for the jury whether the delusion affected the disposition or contract (*e*).

In England, in consequence of an old maxim of the common law, affirmed by Lord Coke, which declares that "a man shall not be allowed to stultify himself," insanity, it would seem, was never a good defence to an action of assumpsit, unless it also appeared that the plaintiff knew of it and took advantage of the circumstance to impose upon the defendant (*f*). Thus, in the case of *Brown* v. *Joddrell* (*g*), Lord *Tenterden* said, "I think that this defence cannot be allowed, and that no person can be suffered to stultify himself, and set up his own lunacy in his defence. If, indeed, it can *be shown that the defendant has been imposed [*9] upon by the plaintiff, in consequence of his mental imbecility, it might be otherwise, and such a defence might be admitted" (*h*). 'Where the contract was executed, in whole or in part, this affords an additional reason for not vacating it, on the ground of insanity (*i*). Whether, if a person supplies *necessaries* to a lunatic, *knowing* of the lunacy at the time, a contract on the part of the lunatic to pay for them can be implied, is a difficult point of law, which it seems has never yet been settled by authority (*j*). But where necessaries are supplied to a lunatic by a person, who has no reason to suppose him to be insane, an action will lie against the lunatic for the price (*k*). So, also, the law will raise an *implied* contract, and give a valid 'demand or debt

Contracts by insane persons.

Liability of a lunatic for necessaries.

(*d*) Inst. lib. 3, tit. 20, § 8; Dig. lib. 50, tit. 17, 1. 5, i. 40.
(*e*) *Jenkins* v. *Morris*, 14 Ch. Div. 674.
(*f*) *Lery* v. *Baker*, Mood. & M. 106 n.; *Beavan* v. *M'Donnell*, 9 Exch. 309; *Davis* v. *Kirkwall*, 8 C. & P. 679; *Moss* v. *Tribe*, 3 F. & F. 297; *Lovatt* v. *Tribe*, 3 F. &. F. 9; *Baker* v. *Cartwright*, 7 Jur., N. S. 1247; 30 L. J., C. P. 364; 10 C. B., N. S. 124.
(*g*) 3 C. & P. 30; M. &. M. 105.
(*h*) See *Beavan* v. *M'Donnell*, *supra*, as to proof of knowledge of defendant's incapacity. Also *Lovatt* v. *Tribe*, 3 F. &'F. 9.
(*i*) *Moulton* v. *Camroux*, 4 Exch. 17; *S. C.*, in court below, 2 Exch. 487.
(*j*) *Per curiam*, in *In re Weaver*, 21 Ch. Div. 615.
(*k*) *Bagster* v. *Portsmouth* (*Earl*), 7 D. & R. 614; 5 B. & C. 170; 2 C. & P. 178; *Read* v. *Legard*, 6 Exch. 637; 15 Jur. 494; 20 L. J., Exch. 309; *Stedman* v. *Hart*, 1 Kay, 607; 18 Jur. 744; 23 L. J., Ch. 908; and see the recent American case of *Fay* v. *Burditt*, 42 Amer. R. 142 (U. S.).

against the lunatic or his estate for moneys expended for the necessary protection of his person and estate (*l*).

Tendency of modern cases as to liability of lunatic for contracts.

In Chitty on Contracts (*m*), it is stated that modern cases have qualified the doctrine that a man of full age shall not be allowed to disable or stultify himself by pleading his own incapacity, and that "there is no doubt that, at this day, a man or his representatives may show that, when he made a promise, or sealed an instrument, he was so lunatic as not to know what he was about." And where, in an action on a guarantee(*n*), the defence was—(1) that the defendant was of unsound [*10] *mind when he executed the guarantee, and (2) that he had been induced by fraud to give the guarantee —the judge told the jury that if the defendant had a mind incapable of consenting to sign the guarantee, he could not sign, and finally left it to them to say whether the defendant was so unsound in mind as not to know what he was doing when he signed the instrument of guarantee sued on.

Courts of equity were always in the habit of giving relief where a person of weak intellect had entered into a contract, the nature of which justified the conclusion that the party had not exercised a deliberate judgment, but that he had been imposed upon, circumvented, or overcome by cunning or artifice, or undue influence (*o*). And the Chancery Division of the High Court of Justice has now power to set aside a contract in cases where the Court of Chancery formerly possessed jurisdiction to do so (*p*).

Contracts by persons in state of intoxication. How far binding.

Intoxication, if complete and not partial merely, will render an agreement entered into by a person in that state void (*q*). Thus, in *Pitt* v. *Smith* (*r*), where to an action for libel, in stating that the plaintiff had induced the defendant to execute an agreement in a state of intoxication, the general issue was pleaded, and evidence given under it to show that defendant was in a complete state of intoxication when he executed it, a nonsuit was directed by Lord *Ellenborough*, who said,

(*l*) *Williams* v. *Wentworth*, 5 Beav. 325. See also *Manby* v. *Scott*, 1 Sid. 112.
(*m*) 10th ed., p. 133.
(*n*) *Gray* v. *Warren*. See "Times," Thursday, April 24th, 1873.
(*o*) Story, Eq. Jur., 10th ed., par. 238.
(*p*) Supreme Court of Judicature Act, 1873, sect. 34, par. (3).
(*q*) *Gore* v. *Gibson*, 13 M. & W. 623; *Molton* v. *Camroux*, 4 Exch. 17, 19; *Butler* v. *Mulinhill*, 1 Bligh. 137; *Hawkins* v. *Bone*, 4 F. & F. 311.
(*r*) 3 Camp. 33.

"You have alleged that there was *an agreement* between the parties, and this allegation you must prove, as it is put in issue by the plea of *not guilty;* but there was no agreement between the parties if the defendant *was intoxicated in the manner supposed when [*11] he signed this paper. He had not *an agreeing mind."* It seems to have been held, formerly, that the intoxication of one of the contracting parties, to invalidate the contract, must have been known to the other party (*s*); and it seems that this may still be the law in a case of *partial* intoxication (*t*). Where, in a suit for specific performance of an agreement, the defence set up was incapacity at the time of executing it, on the ground of intoxication, it was held that the mere intoxication, *without fraud,* was not sufficient ground for getting rid of the agreement (*u*). And it is. to be observed, that, under any circumstances, the contract of a drunken man is voidable only, and not absolutely void, and therefore becomes binding if adopted by him after he is sober (*x*).

Contracts entered into by persons under a constraining force are voidable, on the ground of duress, and the courts will not allow a guarantee given under such circumstances to be taken advantage of (*y*). This is because persons entering into them, under these circumstances, are not in a state in which they can produce that necessary intention without which no contract can be formed. Thus, duress by imprisonment will avoid a contract. To constitute this, it seems, that either the imprisonment or the duress that is offered in prison must be tortious and unlawful (*z*). Duress by threat will also, sometimes, be sufficient to avoid a contract. No threat will, however, be sufficient to constitute such duress unless it amount to a threat of *personal* restraint or injury. Thus, menacing to [*12] commit a battery, or to burn the house (*a*), or spoil the goods of a person is not sufficient to invalidate a contract (*b*).

Duress a ground for avoiding contracts.

Guarantee obtained by, void.

(*s*) *Johnson* v. *Medlicote,* cited 3 P. Wms. 130 ; *Cooke* v. *Clayworth,* 18 Ves. 12.
(*t*) Byles on Bills, 13th ed., p. 64.
(*u*) *Shaw* v. *Thackray,* 17 Jur. 1045 ; 1 Sm. & G. 537 ; *Lightfoot* v. *Heron,* 3 Y. & C. 586.
(*x*) *Mathews* v. *Baxter,* L. R., 8 Exch. 132.
(*y*) Per *Kindersley,* V.-C., in *Small* v. *Currie,* 2 Drew. 102, 114; and see *Williams* v. *Bazley,* L. R., 1 H. L. 200 ; 35 L. J. Ch. 717.
(*z*) Bacon, Abr., Duress, A.
(*a*) But see Chitty on Contracts, 10th ed., pp. 188, 189.
(*b*) Bac. Abr.· A.

Duress of goods will not invalidate a contract. Again, duress of *goods* will not invalidate a contract (c). Thus, in *Skeate* v. *Beale* (d), Lord *Denman* said, " We consider the law to be clear and founded on good reason, that an agreement is not void because made under duress of goods. There is no distinction in this respect between a deed and an agreement not under seal; and with regard to the former, the law is laid down in 2 Inst. 483, and Sheppard's Touchstone, p. 61, and the distinction pointed out between duress of, or menace to, the person, and duress of goods. The former is a constraining force, which not only takes away *the free agency*, but may leave no room for appeal ·to·the law for a remedy: a man, therefore, is not bound by the agreement which he enters into under such circumstances; but the fear that goods may be taken or injured does not deprive any one of his free agency who possesses that ordinary degree of firmness which the law requires all to exert."

Upon whom duress must be exercised to avoid a contract. The duress that will avoid a contract must, as a rule, be exercised upon one of the contracting parties personally (e). Thus, duress to a third person, though a servant of the contracting party, will not avoid a master's contract, or *vice versâ* (f). However, duress to the son will, it seems, avoid the father's deed, and *vice versâ* (g). So, also, duress to the wife will avoid [*13] *the husband's contract (h). Under certain circumstances, duress on a person will avoid the contract of such person, though entered into for him *by an agent* (i).

By whom. Duress by a stranger, if at the instance of the party who will reap the benefit of it, is a good ground for invalidating a contract (k).

Contract obtained by ·duress void- A contract entered into under duress being merely voidable, if it be voluntarily acted upon by a party to it, with a knowledge of all the facts, he cannot

(c) *Atlee* v. *Backhouse*, 3 M. & W. 633, 650; *Astlee* v. *Reynolds*, 2 Str. 915; *Sumner* v. *Ferryman*, 11 Mod. 202; and see *Liverpool Marine Credit Co.* v. *Hunter*, L. R., 3 Ch. App. 487; 37 L. J., Ch. 386.
(d) 11 Ad. & Ell. 983, 990; 3 P. & D. 597; 4 Jur. 766.
(e) Bac. Abr., Duress, B., and Roll. Abr. 687.
(f) Ib.
(g) Ib. But see Story on Contracts, 4th ed., vol. i., p. 493, note (3).
(h) Bac. Abr., Duress, B., and Roll. Abr. 687.
(i) *Cumming* v. *Ince*, 11 A. & E. 112.
(k) Roll. Abr. 688.

avoid it when the result has turned out to his disadvantage (*l*).

Infants labour under a qualified incapacity to contract, which is founded upon the supposed absence in them of that mature intellectual power, without which no intention to contract can be formed. Infancy, by the Roman civil law, lasted, in the case of both males and females, until the age of seven was *completed* (*m*). During this period, minors laboured under an *almost* absolute incapacity to contract. After seven years, minors were said to possess *intellectus*, but not *judicium* (*n*). This latter power was, accordingly, in the case of minors *sui juris*, supplied by the tutor, and every contract entered into by a minor, *after* seven years of age, and under the age of puberty, was legally valid if made with the sanction of the tutor (*o*). If made without such consent, the infant might have the benefit of it if he pleased, though he could not be bound by it, *Unde in his causis ex quibus obligationes mutuæ nascuntur; ut in emptionibus, venditionibus, locationibus, conductionibus, mandatis, depositis; si tutoris auctoritas non interveniat, ipsi quidem qui cum his contrahunt obligantur; at invicem pupilli non obligantur (p).* At fourteen a male, and at twelve a *female, attained the age of [*14] puberty, and, if *sui juris*, could then act *in propriâ personâ* (*q*). However, though, as a rule, a person who had reached puberty (*minor pubes*) was not obliged, against his will, to remain under the control of another, yet, acting under the advice of his tutor, he almost always consented to the appointment of a *curator*, who, once appointed, held his office until the *minor pubes* [who was *sui juris*] attained majority, *i. e.*, twenty-five years, or until the emperor, by rescript, granted the *venia ætatis*, or dispensation of age, which could only be obtained by a *male* at twenty, and by a female at eighteen (*r*). The *curator*, unlike the *tutor*, did not supply any *mental deficiency* in the minor. He merely assisted him in the administration of his property (*s*).

able only, not void.

Contracts by infants.

(*l*) *Ormes* v. *Beadel*, 30 L. J., Ch. 1; 2 De G., F & J. 333.
(*m*) Mackeldeii Systema Juris Romani, § 126.
(*n*) See Institutes of Justinian (Sandars), 4th ed., p. 145.
(*o*) I. 1, 21 pr., Mackeldeii Systema Juris Romani, § 584.
(*p*) *Ib.*
(*q*) I. 1, 22 pr. ; I. 1, 23, 2 ; Mackeldeii Systema Juris Romani, § 126.
(*r*) I. 1, 23 pr. See also Institutes of Justinian (by Sandars), 4th ed., p. 150.
(*s*) Institutes of Justinian (by Sandars), 4th ed., p. 129.

Disability of infants to contract except for necessaries. Their contracts now incapable of ratification.

By the *English common* law, all persons under the age of twenty-one are infants, and, as such, they are altogether disabled from contracting, except in the case of necessaries and of acts in their nature beneficial to themselves (*t*). But formerly an infant might, on attaining his majority, have ratified previous contracts entered into by him (*u*). Now, however, it is provided by the Infants' Relief Act, 1874 (37 & 38 Vict. c. 62), [*15] *that all contracts entered into by infants, whether by specialty or by simple contract, except for necessaries, which were formerly voidable only, shall be void, and incapable of ratification.

What are necessaries.

As regards contracts for necessaries, the term necessaries is a relative one, and its meaning varies with the rank and fortune of the infant (*x*). It has recently been decided that articles of mere luxury cannot be necessaries suitable to the condition of any infant, but articles of utility, though luxurious and expensive, may be (*y*). Where an infant is sued for the price of goods supplied to him on credit, he may, for the purpose of showing that they were not necessaries, give evidence that, when the order was given, he was already sufficiently supplied with goods of a similar description, and it is immaterial whether the plaintiff did or did not know of the existing supply (*z*). Though a contract with an infant is voidable by him, yet it cannot be avoided by the opposite party (*a*).

Contracts by married women

By the *English common* law, a married woman could not, as a rule, bind either herself or her husband by any contract she might enter into. Two reasons were usually assigned for this incapacity—first, for her hus-

---

(*t*) *Burghart* v. *Angerstein*, 6 C. & P. 690; 1 M. & R. 458; *Meakin* v. *Morris*, 12 Q. B. D. 352.

(*u*) Lord Tenderden's Act (9 Geo. 4, c. 14) enacts by sect. 5. that no action shall be maintained whereby to charge any person, upon any promise made after full age, to pay any debt contracted during infancy, or upon any ratification, after full age, of any promise or simple contract made during infancy, unless such promise or ratification shall be made by some writing signed by the party to be charged therewith. This section is, *semble*, impliedly repealed by sect. 2 of the Infants Relief Act, 1874. See Chitty's Statutes, 4th ed., vol. iii. p. 547, note (*l*).

(*x*) *Peters* v. *Fleming*, 1 M. & W. 42; *Hands* v. *Slaney*, 8 T. R. 578; *Harris* v. *Fane*, 1 Scott, N. R. 287; 1 M. & G. 550; 4 Jur. 508; *Wharton* v. *Mackenzie*, 5 Q. C. 606; *Brayshaw* v. *Eaton*, 7 Scott, 183.

(*y*) *Ryder* v. *Wombwell*, L. R., 3 Exch. 90.

(*z*) *Barnes & Co.* v. *Toye*, 13 Q. B. D. 410.

(*a*) *Warwick* v. *Bruce*, 2 M. & S. 205; *Zouch* v. *Parsons*, 3 Burr. 1808.

band's safety, in depriving her of the power to injure <sub/>Their com-
him by any act without his concurrence or his assent, mon law in-
either expressed or implied; and secondly, for her own capacity to
security, in guarding against the husband's influence contract.
over her, by disabling her from disposing of her own
property, except by those methods and with the solem-
nities which the law itself prescribes (a). It is clear,
from the second of these reasons, that, as regards her
*own property, the reason a married woman could [*16]
not by the common law contract, was because, under ordinary circumstances, if she were to do so, her free will
would be so influenced by her husband that she would
really be incapable of producing the necessary intention
to contract; just as a person under *duress* is incapable
of doing so (b). This incapacity to contract under Changes
which married women laboured so long has been effected in
mitigated by modern statutes, commencing with the wife's power
Married Women's Property Act, 1870, and ending of making
with the Married Women's Property Act, 1882. In- the Married
deed, sect. 1 of the last-named statute practically Women's
removes all the old restraints of the common law upon Property
a married woman's capacity to contract, by providing Acts.
that she shall be capable of holding property, and of
contracting to the extent of her separate property, as a
feme sole (c); while sect. 12 of the same statute, in effect,
provides that every married woman, whether married
before or after the act, shall have in her own name,
against all persons whomsoever, including her husband,
the same civil remedies, and, with one exception, the
same redress by way of criminal proceedings, for the
protection and security of her own personal property as
if such property belonged to her as a *feme sole* (d).

The incapacities to contract, which have hitherto Incapacity to
been mentioned, rest on the want of power to produce contract on
the necessary intention to contract. There are, however, grounds of
others which rest on different principles, originating in public policy.
motives of *public policy*, and which perhaps it may be
as well to mention in this place. By the common law, Alien
all *alien enemies*, and all British subjects and subjects enemies.
of neutral nations domiciled in an enemy's territory, or
*engaged in the service of a hostile power, are [*17]

(a) Roper's Husband and Wife, 2nd ed., p. 2.
(b) As to duress, see *ante*, p. 11.
(c) This section is not retrospective. See *Connolan* v. *Leyland*,
27 Ch. Div. 632, *Turnbull* v. *Forman*, 15 Q. B. D. 234—C. A.
(d) For instance of a case in which guarantee was given by a
married woman, see *Morrell* v. *Cowan*, 7 Ch. Div. 151; 26 W. R.
90; 47 L. J., Ch. 173; 37 L. T. 586.

disabled from contracting with British subjects unless they have obtained a license to trade (e). But they may lawfully provide for the wants and necessities of Englishmen detained abroad, and may enforce contracts made for such purposes on the return of peace (f).

Alien friends. *Alien friends*, by the common law, labour under this partial incapacity to contract—namely, that they cannot lawfully enter or enforce any contracts connected with the acquisition and enjoyment of freehold estates (f). *Prisoners of war* seem, by the common law, to possess the same contracting power as *alien friends* (f).

Naturalization Act, 1870. The Naturalization Act, 1870 (g), has effected considerable alterations in the capacity of aliens as to property, it being enacted by sect. 2 of that act, that "real and personal property of every description may be taken, acquired, held and disposed of by an alien in the same manner in all respects as by a natural-born British subject." No distinction appears to be made by this act between alien friends and alien enemies, or between aliens residing in the country and those who do not. All aliens, therefore, would seem to enjoy the *express* power conferred by sect. 2, as to taking, acquiring and disposing of property, and the *implied* power conferred by that section, without which the express power would be almost useless,—namely, of entering into contracts for the taking, acquiring and disposing of real and personal property (h).

Incapacity to contract of felons and outlaws. Felons and outlaws are incapable of contracting (i). But the act abolishing forfeitures for treason and felony enables the crown to appoint administrators of convicts' property, in whom the convict's property shall [*18] *vest, and with absolute power to let, mortgage, sell, convey and transfer any part of such property (m).

Third requisite of contract of guarantee. The consideration. *Thirdly*, we now pass on to another requisite of a contract—the consideration.

Every contract not under seal must have a consideration to support it. This consideration is either expressed in words, or implied from the very nature of the contract. It is implied in the case of bills or notes, it being a presumption of law that every bill or note, whether expressed or not to be for value received, was

---

(e) Addison on Contracts, 8th ed., p. 151.
(f) Ib.
(g) 33 & 34 Vict. c. 14.
(h) See Chitty on Contracts, 10th ed., p. 179.
(i) See Addison on Contracts, 8th ed., pp. 151, 152 ; and see 33 & 34 Vict. c. 23, s. 8.
(m) 33 & 34 Vict. c. 23, ss. 9, 10, 12.

given for adequate consideration, which therefore need neither be alleged nor proved by the holder in suing on the instrument (n). However, want of consideration is a defence, in an action between the immediate parties. Contracts under seal or specialties not only are valid without any expressed consideration, but are valid without any consideration at all (o). The reason why a contract under seal is valid without consideration is, because an engagement of this description is of so solemn a character, that persons entering into it must be presumed to have previously determined upon what they were about to do (p).

Though, however, a contract under seal requires no consideration to support it, yet if it be found on an illegal consideration, this will render the contract void (q). It would *seem*, too, though this has never been actually decided, that the *total failure* of a consideration obviously intended to exist would afford a good defence to an action on instrument under seal (r).

*The contract of guarantee, like every other [*19] consideration contract, requires a consideration to support it, unless it be under seal (s). This was decided in the case of *Barrell* v. *Trussell* (t). There, it was contended at the bar, that a promise to answer the debt of another, if in writing, did not require any consideration to support it. The court, however, observed, that in all cases to make any promise valid, whether to pay the debt of another, or to do anything else, there must be a consideration for it, whether it be in writing or not in writing.

Guarantee not under seal requires a consideration.

No court of law has ever decided that there must be a consideration moving *directly* between the person giving and the person receiving a guarantee; it is enough if the person for whom the guarantee is given thereby receive a benefit or advantage; or if the party to whom

Nature of the consideration for a guarantee.

(n) Chitty on Bills of Exchange, 11th ed., p. 53.

(o) *Fallowes* v. *Taylor*, 7 T. R. 475 ; Chitty on Contracts, 10th ed., p. 5.

(p) *Morley* v. *Boothby*, 3 Bing. 106, 111 ; *Sharington* v. *Pledall*, Plowd. 308.

(q) *Fisher* v. *Bridges*, 3 Ell. & Bl. 642, 649 ; *Bunn* v. *Guy*, 4 East, 190, 200.

(r) See *Rose* v. *Poulton*, 2 B. & Ad. 822, 828.

(s) The consideration need not now be stated in writing. See *post*, p. 150.

(t) 4 Taunt. 117, 120. See also per *Abbott*, C. J., and *Bayley*, J., in *Saunders* v. *Wakefield*, 4 B. & Ald. 595, 600, 601 ; *Pillan* v. *Van Mierop and Hopkins*, 3 Burr. 1663 (where the whole subject of *consideration* is learnedly and fully discussed); *French* v. *French*, 2 M. Gr. 644 ; *Westhead* v. *Sproson*, 30 L. J., Ex. 265, 267 ; *Boyd* v. *Moyle*, 2 C. B. 644, 650.

it is given suffer a detriment or inconvenience, to form an inducement to the surety to render himself liable for the debt of the principal (u). Owing to the circumstances that, usually, persons by giving guarantees benefit third persons rather than themselves, it seems to have been assumed in some cases, that where the person giving a guarantee derived any *apparent benefit* from it, the whole character of the transaction was altered. These cases will be discussed hereafter, when we come to treat of the operation of the Statute of Frauds upon guarantees. In the case of *Ex parte Minet* (v), Lord *Eldon* is reported to have said, "that the undertaking of one man for the debt of another [*20] does not require a *consideration moving between them." Now, certainly, such a statement requires explanation. If it means that the consideration for a guarantee may consist of a *detriment* to the person to whom the guarantee is given, or, what is really the same thing, of a *benefit* conferred by the latter on the principal debtor, why then the statement in question is undoubtedly good law. If, however, Lord *Eldon* meant to say, that the existence of a debt between A. and B. is *of itself* a sufficient consideration for a guarantee of C., then, certainly, he laid down that which is not the law. Thus, it appears from numerous cases that a promise to pay a debt already incurred by a third person, without the intervention of the defendant, is not

Past or executed consideration insufficient. binding unless made on some *new* consideration (x); for a *past* or *executed* consideration, unless moved at the defendant's request, is not binding without some new consideration. However, an agreement by the creditor that he will forbear to sue the principal debtor

Forbearance a good consideration. for a past debt is a sufficient consideration for the guarantee of the surety. And where the guarantee is given in consideration of the plaintiff undertaking to forbear to sue for a certain period, or when the nature of the transaction shows that this was the intention of the parties, forbearance to sue before the expiration of

(u) Per *Best*, C. J., in *Morley* v. *Boothby*, 10 Moore, 395, 406. See also judgment of *Yates*, J., in *Pillan* v. *Van Mierop and Hopkins*, 3 Burr. 1663.

(v) 14 Ves. 189.

(x) *French* v. *French*, 2 M. & G. 644; 3 Scott, N. R. 121; *Wood* v. *Benson*, 2 Cr. & J. 94; 1 Roll. Abr. 27, pl. 49; *Payne* v. *Wilson*, 7 B. & C. 423, 426; *Lyon* v. *Lamb*, Fell on Guarantees, 2nd ed., 36—40; *Johnson* v. *Nicholls*, 1 C. B. 251; *Tomlinson* v. *Gell*, 6 Ad. & Ell. 564; *Thomas* v. *Williams*, 10 B. & C. 664; *Eastwood* v. *Kenyon*, 11 A. & E. 438; *Hunt* v. *Bate*, Dyer, 272a; *Broom* v. *Batchelor*, 1 C. B. 255.

the period agreed upon is a condition precedent to the plaintiff's right of action on the guarantee (*y*). It was formerly thought that forbearance to sue for an *indefi-* nite period was not such a consideration as could support a guarantee, unless, indeed, in those cases where a particular act had to be done which required some time to do it, and in which *the law *implied* a [21*] *reasonable* time (*z*). Thus forbearance *per paullulum tempus*, or for *some* time, was held bad (*a*); though forbearance *per magnum tempus* (*b*), or for a *reasonable* time (*c*), which seems certainly to be equally *indefinite*, was held good. These distinctions, however, no longer exist. Again, in *Ross* v. *Moss* (*d*), which it will be seen presently has been very much questioned, it was held, that the mere discontinuance of an action is not a sufficient consideration to support a promise, because the plaintiff may commence a *fresh* action the next day. On the other hand, where the defendant, in consideration of the plaintiff having, at the defendant's request, consented to suspend proceedings against A., promised to pay a certain sum on account of the debt "on the 1st day of April now next," it was held, that the consideration of the promise must be taken as a consent to suspend proceedings *at least until the 1st of April* (*e.*) In the case of *Harris* v. *Venabels* (*f*), the case of *Ross* v. *Moss* (*supra*) was questioned. In *Harris* v. *Venables*, the plaintiff having presented a petition for winding up a company, the defendant signed the following guarantee: "In consideration of your withdrawing the petition you have presented for winding up the company called John King & Co., Limited, we agree to pay you all the costs you have incurred of and in relation to such petition, and to indemnify you against all costs (if any) you may be liable to pay to the company, or to any other parties appearing for or in reference to the petition. We further agree to guarantee the payment to you, within *eighteen months from this date, by [*22] the company or the liquidator thereof, of the principal of your debt of 722*l*. It was held, that the consideration

Cases on this subject.

(*y*) *Roll* v. *Cozens*, 18 C. B. 673.
(*z*) *Semple* v. *Pink*, 1 Exch. 74; *Elkins* v. *Heart*, Fitzg. 202, *Payne* v. *Wilson*, 7 B. & C. 423.
(*a*) 1 Roll. Abr. 23, pl. 26; *Sackford's Case*, Cro. Eliz. 455.
(*b*) *Mapes* v. *Sidney*, Cro. Jac. 683.
(*c*) *Johnson* v. *Whitcheott*, 1 Roll. Abr. 24, pl. 33.
(*d*) Cro. Eliz. 569.
(*e*) *Payne* v. *Wilson*, 7 B. & C. 423.
(*f*) L. R., 7 Exch. 235; and see *Alhusen* v. *Prest*, 6 Exch. 720; 20 L. J., Ex. 404.

2

applied to both promises, that the consideration was
the withdrawal of the then pending petition and not
the forbearing for eighteen months to proceed with any
petition to wind up the company, and that such a consideration was sufficient to support the promise. Baron
Bramwell, in the course of his judgment, said, "First,
Mr. *Trevelyan* (*g*) says, 'withdraw' means 'not to present or persevere in a petition against the company for
the space of eighteen months,' and he says it must
mean this, because if it only meant that the plaintiff
would withdraw his petition for the moment, there
would be no consideration and no valid contract. For
this position he cites *Ross* v. *Moss*, which certainly goes
very far; but whether that case is good law, and would
be decided in the same way now, I will not say. If a
man expressly contracts that a particular petition being
withdrawn, he will pay a sum of money, that is a good
contract; it was his own folly not to provide against
another petition being filed. It is obvious that a real
benefit is gained by the withdrawal, because of the dis-
inclination to commence a new proceeding after so
much labour and expense have been wasted. I cannot
but doubt, therefore, whether *Ross* v. *Moss* is good law;
and I think that a promise made in consideration of
such an agreement would be good" (*h*). In this same
case of *Harris* v. *Venables*, in speaking of *Semple* v. *Pink*
(*i*) (in which the court seems to have thought that forbearance for an indefinite period is *bad*), *Cockburn*, C.
J., said, "But, supposing that the sole consideration
was the forbearing to press for immediate payment, I
should not be prepared to assent to the doctrine laid
down in *Semple* v. *Pink*;" and *Erle*, J., said, "I concur
[*23] with the *Lord Chief Justice with respect to the
case of *Semple* v. *Pink*. I do not assent to the doctrine
that a guarantee in consideration of an agreement to
give time is void, unless the time to be given is defined
in the contract." In the modern case of *Wynne* v.
Hughes (*k*), disapproval of the doctrine laid down in
Semple v. *Pink* was expressed by the court, and its
authority doubted.

Discontinu-
ance of an
action will

It may, perhaps, be laid down as a safe rule, that
discontinuance of an action or other proceeding is a
sufficient consideration to support a guarantee, not-

(*g*) The counsel for the plaintiff.
(*h*) See recent case of *Beer* v. *Foakes*, 11 Q. B. D. 221.
(*i*) 1 Exch. 74.
(*k*) 21 W. R. 628.

withstanding the risk which the promiser runs of com- afford con-
mencement of fresh proceedings immediately after the sideration for
discontinuance of the old proceedings; but that for- a guarantee.
bearance to sue for an *indefinite* period, where there is Also forbear-
no proceeding pending, is also a good consideration, ance for an
because it always means forbearance for a reasonable period.
time, and that what is a reasonable time must be left
to the jury (*l*). This construction of a forbearance for
an indefinite period is in accordance with decisions in
the analogous cases of guarantees, given in consideration
of past and future supply of goods; and where it seems
to have been held that the future supply must be *reasonable* to support the promise of the surety, where the
instrument is silent as to the *extent* of such a supply (*m*).
In *Oldershaw* v. *King* (*n*), where the guarantee was given
in consideration of forbearance to press for *immediate
payment*, the court expressed the opinion that this
amounted to an agreement to forbear for a reasonable
time, and that this, of itself, would be sufficient to support a guarantee. As, however, in that case, the contract disclosed a sufficient consideration, independently
of such forbearance, it became unnecessary for the
court actually to decide the point. In *Wynne* v.
Hughes (*o*) the facts were as follows:—"The [*24]
plaintiff's agent wrote to defendant, "I have this morning received the most peremptory instructions to settle
this account. Be good enough to arrange something
by to-morrow." The defendant, in reply, wrote, "I
undertake to pay 500*l.* on the account between my late
brother Mr. O. D. Hughes and your client on or before
this day three weeks." The plaintiff did not expressly
agree to forbear suing, but did in fact forbear for three
weeks. It was held that the correspondence, together
with the plaintiff's actual forbearance for three weeks
to sue, constituted a good and binding promise to pay
on the part of the defendant.

Where certain goods were seized by A. under a
warrant from the sheriff, in the belief that they were
goods of the debtor, and, upon the goods being claimed
by the debtor's brother, the plaintiff, at the request of
the defendant, disregarded the claim and sold the goods,
in consideration of his doing which the defendant pro-

(*l*) Per *Cockburn*, C. J., in *Oldershaw* v. *King*, 2 H. & N. 520.
(*m*) See *infra*.
(*n*) 2 H. & N. 520; and see observations of *Bramwell*, B., on
this case in *Wynne* v. *Hughes*, 21 W. R. 628, 629.
(*o*) 21 W. R. 628.

mised to indemnify him, the consideration was held to be sufficient (*p*).

Executory consideration for a guarantee.

A promise of guarantee is sufficiently supported by a *future* or *executory* consideration. Thus, an agreement by the plaintiff for the *future* supply of goods, or for a *future* advance, to a third person, is a sufficient consideration for the defendant's promise to be answerable for the payment to the plaintiff of *past* and *future* debts of such third person (*q*).

Examples.

Where, however, there is no agreement binding on the plaintiff to supply the goods, and no goods are in fact supplied, the guarantee fails for want of consideration (*r*).

Future advance or supply of goods.

Moreover, it seems that the supply must be *bonâ fide*, and to a reasonable [*25] *extent, and this question is for a jury to determine (*s*). Subject, however, to this condition, the amount to be supplied may be discretionary (*t*). Where it is evident that the future supply is to be on the same terms, and of a character similar to the past supply, the plaintiff will not be entitled to recover on the guarantee, unless it appear that this condition has been fulfilled (*u*).

Future employment of third persons.

Promises to be answerable for the behaviour of third persons in offices or employments are not invalid for want of consideration, merely because the promisee is not bound to employ such persons (*x*). These promises greatly resemble promises to be answerable for future supplies or advances made to third persons (*y*). In *both* cases the guarantees are not *mutually* binding *at first*, and are, therefore, revocable until the employment in the *one* case, and the supply or advance in the *other* (*z*). Thus, in *Offord* v. *Davies* (*a*) it was held, that a guarantee to secure moneys to be advanced to a third person on discount, to a certain extent, "for the space of twelve calendar months," is countermandable

---

(*p*) *Elliston* v. *Berryman*, 15 Q. B. N. S. 205.
(*q*) *White* v. *Woodward*, 5 C. B. 810; *Chapman* v. *Sutton*, 2 C. B. 634; *Boyd* v. *Moyle*, 2 C. B. 644; *Russell* v. *Moseley*, 3 B. & B. 211.
(*r*) *Westhead* v. *Sproson*, 6 H. & N. 728; *Boyd* v. *Moyle*, 2 C. B. 644—650.
(*s*) *Johnson* v. *Nicholls*, 1 C. B. 251; *White* v. *Woodward*, 5 C. B. 810, 818; *Broom* v. *Batchelor*, 1 H. & N. 255—264; *Wood* v. *Benson*, 2 C. & J. 94.
(*t*) *White* v. *Woodward*, *ubi supra*.
(*u*) *Johnson* v. *Nicholls*, *supra*.
(*x*) *Kennaway* v. *Treleaven*, 5 M. & W. 498; *Lysaght* v. *Walker*, 5 Bligh, N. S. 1; *Newbury* v. *Armstrong*, 6 Bing. 201.
(*y*) See *ante*, p. 24.
(*z*) See *post*, Chapter VI.
(*a*) 12 C. B., N. S. 748.

within that time, *before it has been in any way acted upon.* *Erle*, C. J., in his judgment in this case, says: "The promise, by itself, creates no obligation. It is, in effect, conditioned to be binding if the plaintiff acts upon it, either to the benefit of the defendants, or the detriment of himself. But until the condition has been *at least in part* fulfilled, the defendants have the power of revoking it (*b*). In the case of a simple guarantee for a proposed loan, the right of revocation *before the proposal has been acted upon, did not [*26] appear to be disputed. Then, are the rights of the parties affected, either by the promise being expressed to be for twelve months, or by the fact that some discounts had been made before that now in question and repaid? We think not. The promise to repay for twelve months creates no additional liability on the guarantor; but, on the contrary, fixes a limit in time beyond which his liability cannot extend. And, with respect to other discounts, which had been repaid, we consider each discount as a separate transaction, creating a liability on the defendant till it is repaid, and, after repayment, leaving the promise to have the same operation that it had before any discount was made and no more."

It has already been pointed out that a *past or executed* consideration is insufficient to support a promise of guarantee, but that an *executory* or *future* consideration is quite sufficient for the purpose. Now, it is very often by no means easy to determine whether, according to fair interpretation of the words of a guarantee, the promise of the surety is given for a past or an executed consideration, such as past advances to the original debtor, or for a future or executory consideration, such as future advances. Where the words of a guarantee are capable of expressing either a past or a concurrent consideration, the courts will adopt the latter construction, *ut res magis valeat quam pereat* (*c*). If, however, it should appear that the parties did not necessarily contemplate future advances, the guarantee will be void (*d*). Also, if the consideration for the promise is expressed to be past and future advances, whereas, as a *fact,* the consideration is *entirely* past or executed, and not moved *by a precedent request, it is certainly [*27]

Difficulty in some cases of determining whether consideration alleged is past or future

(*b*) As to revocation of guarantees, see *post*, Chapter VI.
(*c*) *Steel* v. *Hoe*, 14 Q. B. 431; *Edwards* v. *Jevon*, 8 C. & B. 436; *Broom* v. *Batchelor*, 1 H. & N. 255; *Goldshede* v. *Swan*, 1 Exch. 154; *Colbourn* v. *Dawson*, 10 C. B. 773.
(*d*) *Bell* v. *Walsh*, 9 C. B. 154.

invalid (e). It seems that if the expression of the parties is ambiguous, *parol* evidence is admissible to show that the parties meant not a past but a future supply of goods (f). In *Edwards* v. *Jevons* (g), the expression, in consideration "of your *giving* credit," was held to be equally applicable to future as to past advances. In *Haigh* v. *Brooks* (h), the words used were, in consideration "of your being in advance," and these were held not to necessarily imply a past advance. So it appears that the words, "having released" may be *prospective* (i), and the words "having resigned" were held equally to import either a *past* or a *concurrent* consideration (k). In *Coles* v. *Pack* (l), an agreement to become responsible for any sum of money "*for the time being*" due, was treated as including a liability for *future* indebtedness.

In *Broom* v. *Batchelor* (m), the guarantee was as follows : "In consideration of the credit given by B. to E., I hereby agree to guarantee the payment of all bills of exchange drawn by the said B. and accepted by E. Also, I hereby agree to guarantee the payment of any balance that may be due from the said E. to the said B. This guarantee to include all bills of exchange now running, as well as the balance of account at this day." It appeared that at the time of the giving of the guarantee there were bills running, and an account due from E. to B., and future dealings between the parties were contemplated. It was held, that the guarantee extended to future as well as to past advances.

In *Mockett* v. *Ames* (n), the plaintiffs supplied the defendant's son with some beer, and on their refusing to supply more without a guarantee, the son gave them [*28] *the following guarantee signed by the defendant: "I hereby undertake to pay you for all the beer supplied by you to the Star Brewery, 131, East Street, Walworth, on the completion of the purchase, which will take place in a few days." It was held, that the promise was *primâ facie* a promise to pay for goods to

---

(e) *Bell* v. *Walsh*, 9 C. B. 154.
(f) *Hoad* v. *Grace*, 7 H. & N. 494.
(g) 8 C. B. 436.
(h) 10 A. & E. 309.
(i) *Butcher* v. *Steuart*, 11 M. & W. 857.
(k) *Steele* v. *Hoe*, 14 Q. B. 431.
(l) L. R., 5 C. P. 65.
(m) 1 H. & N. 255.
(n) 23 L. T., N. S. 729.

be supplied ; and *semble*, that the promise also applied
to the goods already supplied.

The consideration for the promise of the guarantor
may be *concurrent* with such promise (o). It need not,
however, be *co-extensive* with it (p), for the courts refuse
to enforce a contract only where it is *nudum pactum,*
that is to say, where there is an *absence* of consideration,
not where the consideration is inadequate merely, for
the law has nothing to do with the prudence or impru-
dence of the bargain (q). Thus, the delivering up of a
worthless guarantee would be a good consideration for
the promise of the guarantor, for an inadequate security
may, from various motives which the courts will not
inquire into, be a very good consideration (r). A guarantee given for an *illegal* consideration cannot, it is
presumed, be enforced (s).

It was once thought that a *moral* obligation was in
all cases a good consideration for a promise. In *Lee* v.
Muggeridge (t), a feme covert, having an estate settled
to her separate use, gave a bond for repayment, by her
executors, of money advanced at her request on security
of that bond to her son-in-law. After her husband's
decease she wrote, promising that her executors should
*settle the bond. It was held, that the executors [*29]
were liable on this promise of the testatrix. It is conceived that this case is not now good law, for it has been
held that, except under circumstances presently to be
noticed, a mere moral consideration is not sufficient to
support a promise (u). In *Eastwood* v. *Kenyon* (x) the
facts were as follows : The plaintiff was executor
under the will of the father of the defendant's wife,
who had died intestate as to his real estate, leaving the
defendant's wife, an infant, his only child. The plaintiff had *voluntarily* expended his money for the improve-
ment of the real estate whilst the defendant's wife was

(Marginal notes: Considera-tion for gua-rantee may be concurrent. Insufficiency of moral con-sideration.)

(o) *Butcher* v. *Steuart*, 11 M. & W. 857 ; *Goldshede* v. *Swan*, 1 Exch. 154.
(p) *Johnson* v. *Nicholls*, 1 C. B. 251. See, however, *Thomas* v. *Williams*, 10 B. & C. 664.
(q) Per *Erle*, J. in *Johnson* v. *Nicholls*, 1 C. B. 251, 272. See also observations of *Cresswell*. J., at pp. 251 and 271 of 1 C. B., *Dutchman* v. *Tooth*, 7 Scott, 710 ; *Edwards* v. *Baugh*, 11 M. & W. 641.
(r) *Haigh* v. *Brooks*, 10 A. & E. 309.
(s) See the recent case of *Wood* v. *Barker*, L. R., 1 Eq. 139 ; and see *Coles* v. *Strick*, 15 Q. B. 2.
(t) 5 Taunt. 36.
(u) *Littlefield* v. *Shee*, 2 B. & Ad. 811, 812 ; *Wennall* v. *Adney*, 2 B. & A. 811.
(x) 11 A. & E. 438.

sole and a minor, and to reimburse himself borrowed money of one *Blackburn*, to whom he had given his promissory note. The defendant's wife, while sole, had received the benefit, and after she came of age assented to and promised to pay the note, and did pay a year's interest. After the marriage, the plaintiff's accounts were shown to the defendant, who assented to them, and it appeared that there was due to the plaintiff a sum equal to the amount of the note to *Blackburn*. The declaration, after alleging these facts, alleged that the defendant, in right of his wife, had received all the benefit, and in consideration of the premises promised to pay and discharge the amount of the note to *Black-burn*. It was held that, as the consideration disclosed by the declaration for the defendant's promise was a past benefit not conferred at the request of the defend-ant, the declaration was bad. Now here, no doubt, as well as in *Lee* v. *Muggeridge* (*supra*), there was a per-fect *moral* consideration for the promise.

Exceptions to rule that moral consid-eration in-sufficient.   Though, as a rule, a *moral* consideration will not, as already pointed out, support an express promise, yet there are certain cases, which we will now proceed to notice, which are exceptions to the general rule. These [*30] *exceptions are summed up in a learned note to the case of *Wennall* v. *Adney* (*y*) in the following words :—" That an express promise can only revive a precedent good consideration, which might have been enforced at law through the medium of an implied pro-mise, had it not been suspended by some positive rule of law; but can·give no original right of action, if the obligation on which it is founded never could have been enforced at law, though not barred by any legal maxim or statute provision" (*z*). Thus the contracts of in-fants, until the passing of the Infants' Relief Act, 1874, were *voidable* only, and were capable of ratification by express promise after age, while those of married women, which prior to recent legislation were *void*, could not be revived by ratification. So, again, it was held that a contract which, for want of written evi-dence required by statute, could not be sued upon might be revived by express promise, provided the statute did not render the contract *absolutely void* for want of written evidence (*a*). Again, where a person,

(*y*) 3 B. & P. 247, 249, 253.
(*z*) This note is cited with approval by Lord *Denman*, C. J., in *Eastwood* v. *Kenyon*, 11 A. & E. 438, 447.
(*a*) *Wilson* v. *Marshall*, 15 Ir. C. L. R., N. S. 466. ·

having entered into a written guarantee and become liable upon it, *verbally* promised to make good such liability, after the Statute of Limitations had barred the right of action on the guarantee, it was held, that the subsequent promise revived the right of action on the guarantee (b). Such a promise would not now have this effect unless it were in writing (c).

It will be seen, in a subsequent chapter (d), that a surety is discharged from his obligation if the creditor binds himself to give time to the principal debtor. However, just as a subsequent promise may revive a right of action on a guarantee, when such right has been barred by the Statute of Limitations, so also it *seems, that if a creditor having given time to [*31] the principal debtor makes a demand on the surety and receives a promise from him, that is sufficient to sustain the demand, not as the creation of a *new*, but as the revival of an *old*, debt (e).

Whatever may be the nature of the consideration for a guarantee it moves not from the principal debtor, but from the creditor. Consequently, even though the contract of guarantee be under seal, it does not extinguish the simple contract debt of the principal (f). For the surety does not discharge the obligation of the principal, but contracts another which is accessory to it. (g). *The consideration for a guarantee does not move from the principal debtor.*

No special form of words is necessary to the formation of a guarantee. But the parties must manifest their intention clearly. The *common law* did not even require the contract of guarantee to be *in writing*, but received *parol* evidence of it. The 4th section of the Statute of Frauds (h), however, enacts that no action *No special form of words necessary to formation of a guarantee. But the contract must be in writing as required by Statute of Frauds.*

(b) *Gibbons* v. *M'Casland*, 1 B. & A. 690.
(c) 9 Geo. 4, c. 14, s. 1.
(d) Chap. VI.
(e) Per Lord *Eldon* in *Mayhew* v. *Cricket*, 2 Swanst. 185, 192.
(f) *White* v. *Cuyler*, 6 T. R. 176, 177.
(g) Pothier on the Law of Obligations (Evans' Edition), vol. i., pp. 229, 230.
(h) 29 Car. 2, c. 3. The following are the exact words of the 4th section, which, it will be seen, applies to various transactions:—"And be it further enacted, that no action shall be brought whereby to charge any executor or administrator upon any special promise to answer damages out of his own estate, or whereby to charge the defendant upon any *special promise* to answer for the debt, default or miscarriages of another person; or to charge any person upon any agreement made upon consideration of marriage; or upon any contract *or sale of lands, tenements or hereditaments, or any interest in or concerning them; or upon any agreement that is not to be performed within the space of one year from the making thereof; unless the agreement upon which such action shall be brought, or some memorandum (Sic.)

shall be brought whereby to charge defendant upon any
special promise to answer for the debt; default, or miscarriage of another person, unless the agreement upon
[*32] *which such action shall be brought, or some
memorandum or note thereof, shall be in writing, and
signed by the party to be charged therewith, or some
other person thereunto by him lawfully authorized.
The effect of this enactment is not to render *verbal*
guarantees *void* (*i*), but to prevent their being *enforced*
by action (*j*), or other proceedings (*k*). And it would
seem that, whenever the Statute of Frauds requires
written evidence of a contract, such evidence must exist before action brought (*l*).

It would appear that where one of the parties to a
contract has *fraudulently* omitted to reduce it into
writing, he will not be allowed to cover his fraud by
setting up the Statute of Frauds as a defence (*m*).

Many years after the passing of the Statute of
Frauds, it was found that that portion of the 4th section which relates to guarantees was capable of being
evaded in certain cases, to which it was obviously necessary that it should apply, in order to prevent the per-
petration of those frauds and perjuries against which
this enactment is undoubtedly levelled. The case of
Pasley v. *Freeman* (*n*) inaugurated the evasion in
question. There an action founded in tort for deceit
was brought against the defendant for inducing the
plaintiff to supply with goods *on credit* a man known
to the defendant to have no means, and whom he false-
ly, fraudulently and deceitfully represented to the plaintiff to be a person safely to be trusted and given credit
[*33] to. It *was held that the action might be maintained. Now, here the foundation of the action was
the false *verbal* affirmation of the defendant, and there

Side notes:
Verbal guarantee no longer enforceable by action;

except where defendant by fraud prevents compliance with statute.

How this provision of Statute of Frauds formerly evaded.

Special promise treated as false re-

---

or note thereof shall be in writing and signed by the party to be
charged therewith, or some other person thereunto by him lawfully authorized."

(*i*) *Post.* p. 41 *et seq.*

(*j*) Also formerly by suit in equity, see per Lord *Eldon*, in
Cooth v. *Jackson*, 6 Ves. 72.

(*k*) *Laythoarp* v. *Bryant*, 2 Bing. N. C. 735, 747 ; *Crosby* v.
Wadsworth, 6 East, 602—611 ; *Leroux* v. *Brown*, 12 C. B. 823—825;
but see *Carrington* v. *Roots*, 2 M. & W. 248; *Reade* v. *Lamb*, 6
Exch. 130 ; 20 L. J., Ex. 161.

(*l*) *Bell* v. *Bament*, 9 M. & W. 36 ; *Longfellow* v. *Williams*, 2
Peake, 225 ; but see *Fricker* v. *Thomlinson*, 1 M. & G. 772, 773.

(*m*) *Lincoln* v. *Wright*, 4 D. & J. 16; *Davies* v. *Otty*, 35 Beav.
208 ; *Booth* v. *Turl*, L. R., 16 Eq. 182 ; *Haigh* v. *Kaye*, L. R., 7
Ch. 469.

(*n*) 3 T. R. 51.

can be no doubt that, if the action had not been shaped presentation upon *a tort*, but upon a contract, treating the *verbal* und action framed in affirmation as though it were a *special promise to* tort. answer for the debt, default or miscarriage of another person, the court would have held that the plaintiff was precluded from recovering by the 4th section of the Statute of Frauds.

In *Lyde* v. *Banard* (o), *Parke*, B., says, "Since the case of *Pasley* v. *Freeman* it is well known, from some reported cases, and from others which have not found their way into the books, that a practice had grown up of fixing a person with the debt of another, by parol evidence of a representation as to the solvency or trustworthiness of a third person, and proof that credit was given on the faith of that representation.   The practice did not extend to *all* cases within the Statute of Frauds. That statute applies to a guarantee, for good consideration, for a debt *already contracted*, as well as where credit was to be given; but the evil existed only in those cases in which credit was subsequently given, on the faith of the representation made.   In this respect the practice of bringing actions on such parol representations was an evasion of the Statute of Frauds."

It seems that, in these actions for false representations Action for as to character and credit, the plaintiff almost invariably false representation no succeeded.   This remarkable fact induced Lord *Ten-* sentation no longer main- *terden* to think that there was some latent injustice tainable un- which required a remedy, and he accordingly framed less represen- the 6th section of 9 Geo. 4, c. 14 (*p*) (Lord Tenterden's tation in writing. Act), which enacts, "That no action shall be brought Provision on *whereby to charge any person upon or by reason [*34] this subject of any representation or assurance made or given con- in 9 Geo. 4, cerning or relating to the character, conduct, credit, c. 14, s. 6. ability, trade or dealings of any other person, to the intent or purpose that such other person may obtain credit, money or goods upon (*q*), unless such representation or assurance be made in writing, signed by the party to be charged therewith." Since this enactment, therefore, whether the action be in *tort*, for false representation, or *in contract*, on a special promise to answer for another's default or miscarriage, the defendant is not chargeable

---

(o) 1 M. & W. 101.

(*p*) Such was the origin of this enactment, according to *Pollock*, C. B., in *Tatton* v. *Wade*, 18 C. B. 371—381.   See also observations of Lord ●●inger, C. B., and *Parke*, B., in *Lyde* v. *Barnard*, 1 M. & W. 101, 114. 117.

(*q*) Probably a mistake for "thereupon."   See observations of *Parke*, B., in *Lyde* v. *Barnard*, 1 M. & W. 101—115.

without *written evidence.* Where there are both *written* and *verbal* affirmations as to the character of another, the credit is thereby obtained, an action will lie against the party who made these affirmations, if the *written* representation be a *material* part of the inducement which moved the plaintiff to give the credit (*r*). No action will, however, lie for a false representation unless the party making it *knows* it to be untrue, and makes it with the intention of inducing the party to act upon it, and the latter does so act upon it and sustains damage in consequence (*s*). It is not, however, necessary that the defendant should benefit by the deceit (*t*).

Unsuccessful atfempt to evade this enactment.

In *Haslock* v. *Ferguson* (*u*), an attempt was made to evade the 6th section of Lord Tenterden's Act, which, however, happily proved unsuccessful. There, the action [*35] *was for money had and received, which form of action is usually adopted whenever the defendant has received money which belongs to the plaintiff *ex æquo et bono* (*x*). The plaintiff's case was that B., through a false *verbal* representation of his credit made by H., under defendant's sanction, had obtained goods from him, by the sale of which sums were raised by B., and handed over to the defendant in liquidation of certain debts due to him from B. These sums the plaintiff, therefore, sought to recover from the defendant. The plaintiff was, however, nonsuited, on the ground that, as there was no mode of fixing the defendant in this action, except through the medium of evidence as to representation of character, the statute 9 Geo. 4, c. 14, s. 6, applied. In short, in order to prove that the plaintiff was entitled, *ex æquo et bono,* to the money claimed, it was necessary to give in evidence the alleged false affirmation, and this could not be done, as it was not in writing. A rule for a new trial, which the plaintiff's counsel obtained in this case, was ultimately discharged.

What representations are within 9 Geo. 4, c. 14, s. 6.

With regard to the question what representations are within the statute, the following instances may be noticed:—A representation by the defendant that money

(*r*) *Wade* v. *Tatton,* 25 L. J., C. P. 240; see also *Tatton* v. *Wade,* 18 C. B. 371.

(*s*) *Behn* v. *Kemble,* 7 C. B., N. S. 260; see further, *Ashlin* v. *White,* Holt, 387; *Polhill* v. *Walter,* 3 B. & Ad. 114; and see 2 Sm. L. C., 6th ed., pp. 71, 88; notes to *Pasley* v. *Freeman,* 1 Sm. L. C., 6th ed., p. 165; *Chandelor* v. *Lopus,* and notes thereto; *Corbett* v. *Brown,* 8 Bing. 33.

(*t*) *Pasley* v. *Freeman,* 3 T. R. 51; see also *Foster* v. *Charles,* 4 M. & P. 61; 6 Bing. 396; 7 Bing. 105.

(*u*) 7 Ad. & E. 86.

(*x*) *Moses* v. *Macferlen,* 2 Burr. 1000, 1005.

might be safely lent to A. B., *because* the title deeds to
an estate which A. B. had just bought were in the defendant's possession, and that nothing could be done
without the knowledge of the defendant, and that the
plaintiff would be safe in making the loan, is a representation as to the ability of A. B., within 9 Geo. 4, c.
14, s. 6. This was decided in *Swann* v. *Phillips* (*y*).
Lord *Denman*, C. J., in his judgment, said, "That if
the words spoken by the defendant amounted only to an
assertion that the defendant, being in possession of the
*title deeds, would know what A. B. was doing, [*36]
the statute did not apply. If they meant that A. B.
might be trusted, then they constituted a representation
as to his credit and ability." *Littledale*, J., in his judgment in the same case, said: "The representation is entire; no one part can be separated from the rest. In the
ordinary course of things, if a man states another to be
a man of ability, he is asked why he says so; he may
answer, 'Because he has had a legacy left to him,' by
way of enforcing his representation as to the ability.
Here the substance of the conversation is similar; the
defendant says, 'You may trust him, and my reason
for saying so is, that I know the estate which he has
bought, and have his title deeds.' That is one entire
representation concerning his credit."

An action cannot, it seems, be maintained against a
trustee for a false representation, by *parol*, of the in-
cumbrances effected on the trust fund by the *cestui que
trust*, such a representation being within the statute
(*z*). In *Turnley* v. *Macgregor* (*a*), a similar point was
raised, though not decided. There the representation
complained of was, that a certain claim which a third
person alleged he had upon the Government would be
sure to be paid. Where, as in this case, the representation is as to the condition or value of a particular
part of a man's property, whether it relate to or concern "his character, conduct, credit, ability, trade or
dealings," must depend upon the facts of each particular case (*b*).

A representation made by the defendant as to the
credit and circumstances of a firm, of which he is a
*member, is a representation as to the credit of [*37]

(*y*) 8 Ad. & E. 457, 460, 461; see also *Turnley* v. *Macgregor*, 6
M. & G. 46; S. C., 6 Scott, N. R. 906.
(*z*) Per Lord *Abinger*, C. B., and *Gurney*, B., diss. *Parke*, B.,
and *Alderson*, B. ; *Lyde* v. *Barnard*, 1 M. & W. 101; 1 Gale, 388.
(*a*) 6 Scott, N. R. 906; *S. C.*, 6 M. & G. 46.
(*b*) See, on this subject, *Lyde* v. *Barnard*, 1 M. & W. 101.

"another person," within the meaning of the statute 9
Geo. 4, c. 14, s. 6 (c).

To whom the representation must be made.

A question sometimes arises as to the person to whom
the representation must be made, in order to render the
defendant liable. Upon this point it has been decided
that, in order to enable a person injured by a false representation to sue for damages, it is not necessary that
the representation should be made to the plaintiff
directly; it is sufficient if the representation be made to
a third person to be communicated to the plaintiff, or
to be communicated to a class of persons of whom the
plaintiff is one, or even if it is made to the public generally, with a view to its being acted on, and the plaintiff as one of the public acts on it and suffers damage
thereby (d).

By whom it must be signed.

As to the signature of the representation in respect
of which the action is brought, it is to be observed that
the 6th section of 9 Geo. 4, c. 14, requires that the
written representation shall be signed by the party to
be charged. Consequently, the signature of an agent
is not, it seems, sufficient, because, whenever the legislature intends that the party to be charged shall be
bound by the signature of his agent, there is an express
enactment to that effect, and in other cases the signature
must be the signature of the actual party to be charged
(e). Even where the party to be charged can sign in no
[*38] *other way but by its agent, this rule was, in
Swift v. Jewsbury (P. O.) and Goddard (f), held to apply. There the facts were as follows : The plaintiff
sued W. and G. jointly for a false representation with
respect to the solvency of R. The defendant W. was
sued as the public officer of a banking company formed
under 7 Geo. 4, c. 46, and the defendant G. was the
manager of one of their branches. The plaintiff was
the customer of the S. Bank, and requested the manager
of that bank to inquire for him as to R.'s credit. The
manager wrote a letter addressed to "The Manager " of
the defendant's banking company, requesting informa-

(c) *Devaux* v. *Steinkeller*, 8 Scott, 202.

(d) Per *Quain*, J., in *Swift* v. *Winterbotham*, L. R., 8 Q. B. 244,
253. This case was reversed, on another point, by the Exchequer
Chamber.

(e) *Williams* v. *Mason*, 21 W. R. 386 ; 28 L. T. 232; *Clark* v.
Alexander, 8 Scott, N. R. 147 ; *Hyde* v. *Johnson*, 3 Scott, 289 ; 2
Bing. N. C. 776 ; which are decisions on the *first* section of 9 Geo.
4, c. 14, which section is *in pari materiâ* with section *six* of the
same statute. See also observations of *Quain*, J., in *Swift* v.
Winterbotham, L. R., 8 Q. B. 244.

(f) L. R., 8 Q. B. 244 *S. C.*, L. R., 9 Q. B. 301; 22 W. R. 319.

tion whether R. was responsible to the extent of 50,-
000l. The defendant G. wrote a letter, which he signed
as manager, giving a favourable reply as to R.'s responsibility. The plaintiff, acting upon the faith of this
letter, supplied R. with goods, for which he was never
paid, in consequence of R.'s insolvency. The statement
made by G. was false to his knowledge. The defendant's banking company had no knowledge, otherwise
than through G., that such a letter had been written,
and gave G. no express authority to write the letter,
but the writing of such letter was an act done within
the scope of the general authority conferred on G. as
manager. It was held, on appeal, first, that G. was
liable personally for the false representation ; secondly,
that by 9 Geo. 4. c. 14, s. 6, a false representation as to
the credit of another person is not actionable unless it
is signed by the person making it, and not by an agent
merely, and that, therefore, if G. was to be considered
an agent, the banking company was not liable (g); thirdly
*(overruling the decision of the Court below), [*30]
that the signature of G. to the letter could not be considered the signature of the banking company itself ;
and, fourthly, that the letter was the representation of
G., and not of the banking company.

(g) It is right to mention, however, that, while expressing this
opinion, Lord *Coleridge*, C. J., stated that if the banking company had actually *profited* by the act of their manager, it might
not be open to them to repudiate the liability accruing to them
by his act. See also *Barwick* v. *English Joint Stock Bank*, L. R. 2
Ex. 259 ; 36 L. J., Ex. 147 ; 16 L. T. 461 ; 15 W. R. 877; *Mackay*
v. *Commercial Bank of New Brunswick*, L. R., 5 P. C. 412 ; *Swire*
v. *Francis*, L. R., 3 App. Cas. 106.

[*40]   *CHAPTER II.

THE OPERATION OF THE STATUTE OF FRAUDS ON
PROMISES TO GUARANTEE.

The second clause of 4th section Stat. Frauds relates to guarantees. THE 4th section of the Statute of Frauds (a) has, it is almost needless to say, a very extensive and important bearing upon the subject of guarantees. The part of the section which deals with this subject is the second clause. That clause is, in substance (and omitting words not relating to the present subject), in the following terms: "No action shall be brought whereby to charge the defendant upon any special promise to answer for the debt, default or miscarriage of another person, unless the agreement or some memorandum or note thereof shall be in writing and signed by the party to be charged therewith, or some other person thereunto by him lawfully authorized."

Division of present chapter. . The second clause of the 4th section of the Statute of Frauds is carefully and accurately drawn, and important decisions have taken place upon every word of it. It is, therefore, proposed in this Chapter to consider it word by word, and to discuss (A) the *operation* of the statute in cases which it affects, as that operation is pointed out by the words "no action shall be brought"; (B) to what kind of *promises* the section applies, as ascertained by the phrase "any special promise"; (C) the *kind of liability*, promises to answer for which fall within the section, as being intended by the words "the debt, default or miscarriage of another."

(A) The *operation* of sect. 4 Stat. Frauds on cases within it. (A) The *operation* of the statute upon cases to which it applies is, and doubtless its framers intended that it should be, governed by the words "no action shall be [*41] *brought." These words should, therefore, be noted. It has been held that they do not make verbal contracts, which are required by the enactment to be in writing, absolutely void; they merely prevent their being entirely by action in default of a memorandum in writing. But, as pointed out in *Leroux* v. *Brown* (b), to say that no action shall be brought upon a contract is, for most purposes, equivalent to saying that it shall

Verbal guarantees are not void, but are not enforceable by action.

(a) 29 Car. 2, c. 3.
(b) 12 C. B. 801; 22 L. J., C. P. 1.

(1266)

be void (b). There are, however, cases in which verbal guarantees may be taken advantage of. Thus, it seems that superior courts of justice, by virtue of that jurisdiction which they possess over their own officers, will sometimes enforce a *verbal* guarantee against a person who has given it in his official capacity. This was decided in the case of *Re Greaves* (c). There an action having commenced in the Common Pleas, and judgment obtained, *Greaves*, an attorney of the Court of *King's Bench* (but not an attorney of the Court of *Common Pleas*), who was attorney for the defendant, proposed to compromise the action, and agreed verbally to give his two promissory notes for the debt and costs, payable at six and nine months, in consideration of the plaintiff staying proceedings. This was accepted by the plaintiff. But *Greaves* afterwards declined to give the notes. Thereupon a rule was obtained in the *King's Bench*, calling upon *Greaves* to pay the debt and costs. The court, in making this rule absolute, said, " Even supposing the undertaking to be void by the Statute of Frauds, the court might exercise a *summary jurisdiction* over one of its officers, an attorney of the court. The undertaking was given by the party in his character of attorney, and · in that character the court may compel him to perform it. An attorney is conusant of the law, and, if he give an undertaking which he must know to *be void, he shall not be allowed to take [*42] advantage of his own wrong, and say that the undertaking cannot be enforced." Again, it appears that an agreement, required by the 4th section to be in writing, may be proved by *parol evidence* in order to support a defence (d). So a verbal guarantee is so far good, that if money be paid under it, it cannot be recovered (e). Again, when an action is brought on a bill of exchange, it may be proved by parol évidence that one of the parties is a surety (f). Thus, if the buyer of goods accepts a bill drawn upon him for the price by a surety, who afterwards indorses it to a seller, the surety cannot refuse to pay the amount upon default of the

[marginal notes: Verbal guarantee enforceable against an officer of superior court. May be given in evidence in support of a defence. Money paid under verbal guarantee cannot be recovered. It may be proved by parol evidence that]

(b) And see per *Bowen*, L. J., in *In re Rownson, Field* v. *White*, 29 Ch. Div. at p. 364.
(c) 1 Cr. & J. 374, n.; and see *Evans* v. *Duncombe*, 1 C. & J. 372.
(d) *Lavery* v. *Turley*, 30 L. J., Ex. 49; see also *Macrory* v. *Scott*, 20 L. J., Ex. 90.
(e) *Shaw* v. *Woodcock*. 7 B. & C. 73.
(f) *Garret* v. *Jull*, 1 S. N. P., 11th ed. 407; *Hall* v. *Wilcox*, 1 M. & Rob. 58; *Pooley* v. *Harradine*, 7 El. & Bl. 431; *Greenough* v. *M'Clelland*, 2 Ell. & Ell. 424; 30 L. J., Q. B. 15.

one of the parties to a bill is a surety.

principal debtor, because the agreement under which the bill was signed was not in writing (g). The law merchant implies a contract of suretyship between the drawer and indorsee, and between the indorser and subsequent holders of a bill of exchange; and the Bills of Exchange Act, 1882 (45 & 46 Vict. c. 61), contains provisions on the subject which are declaratory of the common law (h). The indorsing of a bill of exchange does not, however, create a contract of suretyship between the indorser and the prior parties to the bill (i).

An executor cannot by retainer obtain benefit of verbal guarantee given to him by his testator.

It might be considered that where a person, to whom a verbal guarantee has been given, becomes executor, under the surety's will, he ought to possess, by retainer, the right of enforcing such guarantee, since he can in this way pay himself the amount due, without [*43] *bringing an action to recover it. It has, however, been decided, in a very recent case, that an executor or administrator has no right of retainer in respect of a debt which, for want of written evidence, cannot be enforced by the 4th section of the Statute of Frauds (k). The ground of this decision would appear to be that, as an executor or administrator would commit a devastavit who paid a debt to a creditor who is prevented from enforcing it by the 4th section of the Statute of Frauds, for the same reason, the right of retainer does not extend to such a debt (l). Another consequence of the determination that the 4th section of the Statute of Frauds applies not to the validity of the contract, but only to the procedure, is that an action will not lie in the courts of this country to enforce an oral agreement made in France (and valid there), which, if made in England, could not, by reason of the 4th section of the Statute of Frauds, have been sued upon (m). This is in accordance with the rule applicable to foreign contracts, namely, that so much of the law as affects the rights and merit of the contract, all that relates " ad litis decisionem," is adopted from the

(g) Wilkinson v. Unwin, 7 Q. B. D. 636, 638.
(h) Bills of Exchange Act, 1882, s. 55, sub-s. (2); and see Castrique v. Buttigieg, 10 Moo. P. C. 94, 108; Steel v. M'Kinlay, L. R., 5 App. Cas. 754, 769.
(i) Wilkinson v. Unwin, ubi supra.
(k) In re Rownson, Field v. White, 29 Ch. Div. 358—C. A.; and see Wildes v. Dudlow, L. R., 19 Eq. 198.
(l) In re Rownson, Field v. White, ubi supra, per Fry, L. J.; other reasons are, however, given for this decision by Cotton, L. J., and Bowen, L. J.
(m) Leroux v. Brown, 12 C. B. 801.

foreign country; so much of the law as affects the *remedy* only, all that relates "*ad litis ordinationem*," is taken from the *lex fori* of that country where the action is brought (*n*).

Another question, which may arise upon the meaning of the words, "no action shall be brought," is this : it sometimes happens that a promise is, as to *part* of the thing promised, within the Statute of Frauds, but as to the *remainder*, is not within the statute. The point then arises, whether an action can be maintained upon the *part not* within the statute. The words of [*44] the section do not, it will be noted, make the whole promise void, but simply say, "no action shall be brought." The rule applicable to such cases appears to be this : if the parts are *severable*, an action will lie on the part *outside* the statute; but, if the parts are *inseparable*, then no such action lies. In the case of *Chater* v. *Becket* (*n*), the plaintiff and defendant were both creditors of one Harrison, who had become insolvent, and with whom all the creditors, but the plaintiff, were anxious to come into a composition. The plaintiff, however, declined to accept the composition unless certain expenses he had been put to were paid him, as well as the proposed composition. The defendant, accordingly, verbally promised to pay him what he asked, and subsequently paid the amount of the composition, but refused to pay the expenses ; whereupon the plaintiff paid the expenses incurred by him, and brought this action against the defendant to recover them. The plaintiff declared upon the special agreement, and for money paid to the defendant's use. Two points were made : first, whether the special agreement was void by the Statute of Frauds? and, secondly, supposing it to be so, whether the plaintiff could not recover the costs paid to the attorney as for money paid to the defendant's use? Lord *Kenyon*, in delivering his opinion, said : "The promise, therefore, was certainly void in part by the statute; and the agreement being entire, the plaintiff cannot now separate it and recover on one part of the agreement, the other being void; and, if that agreement be void, there is an end of the case; for where there is an express promise, another promise cannot be implied." *Grose*, J., in the same case, said: "It seems admitted that part of this promise is void by

Promise may be partly within the 4th section and partly outside of it.

No right of action on part outside statute where not separable from other part.

(*n*) Per *Tindal*, C. J., in *Huber* v. *Steiner*, 2 Scott, 304—326.
(*n*) 7 T. R. 201. See observations on this case in *Wood* v. *Benson*, 2 C. J. 94.

the statute; but it was one indivisible contract, and the plaintiff cannot recover on any part."

[*45] *The same point was decided in *Thomas* v. *Williams* (*o*). There the verbal promise of the defendant was to pay rent *actually due* to the plaintiff from A., and also rent to *become* due, in consideration that the plaintiff would not distrain A's goods. It was held, by the court, that as the promise to pay rent, to *become* due, was void by the Statute of Frauds, the entire promise was therefore void. So, also, in the old case of *Lexington* v. *Clarke* (*p*), it appeared that the plaintiff allowed the widow of A. B. to retain possession of certain premises which the plaintiff had demised to A. B., on receiving from her a promise to pay arrears of rent, due from A. B. at the time of his death, and also 260*l*. more. It was argued at the bar, that, inasmuch as the promise to pay rent in arrear was alone affected by the 4th section of the Statute of Frauds, the promise might stand good as to the 260*l*. "But, by the opinion of all the court, judgment was given for the defendant; for the promise, as to one part being void, it cannot stand good for the other; for it is an entire agreement, and the action is brought for both the sums, and indeed could not be otherwise without variance from the promise."

Where the promise is separable action maintainable on part outside the statute. — Where, however, from the nature of the case, it is possible to separate that part of the promise which is within the statute from that which is not, the plaintiff can recover upon the latter portion. This was decided in the case of *Wood* v. *Benson* (*q*). There the guarantee was in the following words: "I, the undersigned, do hereby engage to pay the directors of the Manchester Gas Works, or their collector, for all the gas which may be consumed in the Minor Theatre, and by the lamps outside the theatre, during the time it is occupied by my brother-in-law, Mr. Neville; and I do also engage to pay for all arrears which may now be due." An action on *assumpsit* was brought up on his guarantee, [*46] *and there was also a count for gas and goods sold and delivered. The defendant pleaded the general issue. It was objected, at the trial at Nisi Prius, that there was no consideration apparent on the face of the instrument for the promise to pay the arrears, and that the agreement being consequently void as to part under the Statute of Frauds, was also void as to the whole.

(*o*) 10 B. & C. 664.
(*p*) 2 Ventr. 223.
(*q*) 2 C. & J. 94.

The jury were directed by the judge to find for the plain·
tiff, with leave to the defendant to enter a non-suit. A
rule having been subsequently obtained and argued, Lord
Lyndhurst, C. B., in delivering judgment, said: "The case
of *Thomas* v. *Williams* may, as it appears to me, be supported. Part of the contract in that case was void by the
Statute of Frauds. The declaration stated the entire contract, including that part of it which was void, and therefore the contract, as stated in the declaration, was not
proved. The same observation applies to *Lexington* v.
Clarke and *Chater* v. *Becket*, and I have no disposition
to complain of those decisions, because in none of those
cases does there appear to have been any count upon
which the plaintiff could recover. But the question in
the present case is widely different. The contract
resolves itself into two parts. One is, 'I engage to
pay for all the gas which may be consumed,' &c.: that
is a distinct agreement. The other part is, 'And I do
also engage to pay all arrears,' &c. Now, this latter
part cannot be sustained, for if it be a distinct engagement, there is no consideration to support it expressed
on the instrument (r). The question then is, if I
undertake to pay for goods which may be supplied,
though there is no promise to supply the goods, whether,
when the goods are supplied, a right of action does not
accrue to recover the amount. It is quite clear that it
does. And though the latter part of the engagement
cannot be sustained under the first part of the engagement, *the plaintiff is entitled to recover for the [*47]
gas subsequently supplied, and therefore the verdict
must stand for 15l. 4s. 6d." *Bayley*, B., in his judgment in this case, says: "In each of the cases referred
to for the purpose of showing that the contract, if void
in part was void *in toto*, there was a failure of proof.
The declaration in each of those cases (s) stated the
entire promise, as well that part which was void as that
which was good. I think, therefore, that these cases are
to be supported on the principle of the failure of proof
of the contract stated in the declaration, but that they
do not establish that, if you can separate the good
part from the bad you may not enforce such part of
the contract as is good. I am, therefore, of opinion

(r) This is now no longer necessary ; see 10 & 20 Vict. c. 97,
s. 3.

(s) I. e., *Chater* v. *Becket*, 7 T. R. 201 ; *Lexington* v. *Clarke*, 2
Vent. 223 ; *Thomas* v. *Williams*, 10 B. & C. 664.

that the verdict must stand for the amount of the gas subsequently supplied."

(B) The *kind* **of promises to which the 4th section of Statute of Frauds applies.**

(B) The section of the Statute of Frauds which is now under consideration, next proceeds to point out the *kind of promises* to which it is intended to apply. For it was not intended that the statute should apply to *all* possible cases in which a person is liable to answer, as on a contract, for the debt, default or miscarriage of another, and it does not so apply. The kind of promises to which it is applicable are ascertained by the words "any special promise."

Whether indemnities within the statute.

Thus, for instance, the question has been raised whether an indemnity is a promise which falls within the statute. Upon this question, however, it appears that no general rule can be laid down. It was, indeed, stated, as a general proposition, in *Thomas* v. *Cooke* (t), that a promise to *indemnify* does not fall within the words or the policy of the Statute of Frauds. That proposition was, however, denied by the full Court of Queen's Bench in *Green* v. *Cresswell* (u). This last-[*48] *named case, which we shall discuss in detail later on, was, however, disapproved of, though not reversed, by the Court of Exchequer Chamber, in *Cripps* v. *Hartnoll* (x), and by *Malins*, V.-C., in *Wildes* v. *Dudlow* (y), in which case it was held that where one person induces another to enter into an engagement, by a promise to indemnify him against liability, that is not an agreement which the Statute of Frauds requires to be in writing. So far, therefore, as concerns *express* promises to indemnify, perhaps the best solution of the difficulty is that suggested in Smith's Mercantile Law (z), namely, "that a promise to indemnify may or may not be within the statute, according to circumstances"

Implied indemnities are outside the statute.

(a). There are, however, many cases in which the law *implies* indemnities in obedience to principles of justice (b). And, so far as regards implied indemnities, it may

---

(t) 8 B. & C. 728.
(u) 10 Ad. & E. 453.
(x) 4 B. & S. 414. See also the cases of *Reader* v. *Kingham*, 13 C. B., N. S. 344 ; *Batson* v. *King*, 4 H. & N. 739 ; *Fitzgerald* v. *Dressler*, 7 C. B., N. S. 374, 385, 386, where the case of *Green* v. *Cresswell* is observed upon.
(y) L. R., 19 Eq. 198.
(z) Note (k), 7th ed., p. 462.
(a) For instances of indemnities within the Statute of Frauds, see *Adams* v. *Dansey*, 4 M. & P. 245 ; 6 Bing. 506 ; *Green* v. *Cresswell*, 10 A. & E. 453 ; *Cresswell* v. *Wood*, 10 A. & E. 460 ; *Winsworth* v. *Mills*, 2 Esp. 484 ; *Mallet* v. *Bateman*, L. R., 1 C. P. 163.
(b) See *Edmunds* v. *Wallingford*, 14 Q. B. D. 811 ; *Dugdale* v. *Lovering*, L. R., 10 C. P. 196 ; 44 L. J., C. P. 197 ; 32 L. T. R.

safely be stated that they are clearly excluded from the operation of the 4th section of the Statute of Frauds. This results from the adoption of the phrase "*special promise*," which is evidently opposed to the phrase "*express* promise" (c). Of these this work does not profess to treat.

It has also been made the subject of discussion whether or not a promise to *give* a guarantee (as distinguished from a promise to *procure* one) (d) is a special *promise which falls within the statute. It is, [*49] however, obvious that a promise to give a guarantee at a future time entirely falls within the mischief which the enactment was intended to guard against, and, indeed, that if the statute could be evaded by making such a promise it would be useless. Accordingly it has been held, that a promise to *give* a guarantee must be in writing. This was decided in *Mallet* v. *Bateman* (e). *Pollock*, C. B., in delivering the judgment of the Court of Exchequer Chamber in this case, said : " My brother *Blackburn* has, in the course of the argument, stated that which appears to me to dispose of this case, viz., that a contract to give a guarantee is required to be in writing as much as a guarantee itself. If we were to hold that a contract of guarantee must be in writing, but that a contract to give a guarantee need not, we should, I think, be committing the same mistake as our predecessors did with reference to the Statute of Uses. The object of that statute was that the possession should go along with the use ; but a construction was early adopted whereby the possession should go to A. in trust for B., and so the effect of the statute was simply to add a few words to the conveyance. Whether the decisions of the Courts of Equity as to uses and trusts were beneficial or not I do not stop to inquire, but undoubtedly the whole doctrine arose out of a desire to frustrate the intention of the Statute of Uses. I trust we shall not commit a similar mistake in construing the statute now under consideration."

(C) Having pointed out the *operation* which it is intended to have, and the *kind of promises* to which it is

Side notes: Promise to give a guarantee is within the statute.

(C) The kind of liability to

155; *Benson* v. *Duncan*, 3 Ex. 644 ; *Walker* v. *Bartlett*, 18 C. B. 845.

(c) Throop on the Validity of Verbal Agreements, p. 166.

(d) See *Bushell* v. *Beavan*, 1 Bing. N. C. 103, and *post*, p. 77, as to promises to *procure* a guarantee to be signed by a third person.

(e) L. R., 1 C. P. 163; *S. C.* (in court below), 16 C. B., N. S. 530.

which 4th section of Statute of Frauds applies.

Differences of liability indicated by words "debt, default, or miscarriage."

Meaning of the words "debt, default or miscarriage" discussed.

intended to apply, the section under discussion next proceeds to define the *kind of liability*, promises in respect [*50] *of which are intended to be affected. This it does in the words "the debt, default or miscarriage of another." These words, it will be at once seen, are most comprehensive. And they have been made the subject of a good deal of learned discussion. To commence with the words "debt, default or miscarriage": it would seem that these three words, "debt, default or miscarriage" point to three distinct kinds of guarantee, namely, (1) guarantees for the payment of a "*debt*" already contracted by another person; (2) guarantees against the "*default*" of another person, *i. e.*, for the payment of debts to be contracted by another person, or against loss that may occur from another's future breaches of duty; and (3) guarantees against the "*miscarriage*" of another person, *i. e.*, against loss that may occur from another's *past* or *future* breaches of duty.

The words "debt, default or miscarriage" have frequently been commented upon, and it has been doubted whether the word "miscarriage" is not superfluous. Certainly the word "default" is large enough to include promises to be answerable for *future* breaches of contract, as well as promises to be answerable for *future* breaches of *duty*. And, on the other hand, it appears that the word "miscarriage" can clearly only apply to breaches of *duty*, and cannot apply to breaches of contract. But it is submitted that, unlike the word "default," the word "miscarriage" includes *past* breaches of duty as well as *future* breaches, and that, therefore, it is not a superfluous word at all.

Mr. Throop, in his able work on the Validity of Verbal Agreements (*f*), says that, but for the word "default" occurring in the 4th section of the Statute of Frauds, the words "debt" and "miscarriage" would, perhaps, have been confined to *past* transactions, being peculiarly applicable to such. Now, it is submitted [*51] that, *though the word "debt" is certainly peculiarly applicable to past transactions, the word "miscarriage" is not, and that it clearly includes both *past* and *future* breaches of duty. If this view be correct, then it would seem that the word "default" must have been used by the framers of the 4th section in a restricted sense, namely, as applying merely to future *debts*, and not to future breaches of *duty*, though our courts have certainly treated it as equally applicable to both.

(*f*) Page 192.

(1274)

If, however, the legislature had omitted to employ the word "miscarriage," the 4th section of the Statute of Frauds might well have been confined to promises to be answerable for *past* and *future* breaches of *contract*, on the ground that the word "default" was meant merely to supplement the word "debt," and must be so confined in its meaning, though capable of a larger construction. In fact, the word "debt" would have been the *key-word* in the clause, and would have served as an indicator of the sense in which the word "default" was used by the legislature.

Notwithstanding the employment of the word "miscarriage" in the 4th section of the Statute of Frauds, it seems, at one time, to have been thought that this enactment did not effect promises to be responsible for the future wrongful acts or torts of third persons. Thus, in *Birkmyr* v. *Darnell* (g), it seems to have been considered that, if the alleged principal debtor had not been chargeable in contract, but had only been liable to an action of tort, the promise of the defendant to be answerable for him would not have been within the statute. Thus, *Powell*, J., says (h): "The objection that was made was, that if *English* did not re-deliver the horse, he was not chargeable in an action upon the promise, but in *trover* or detinue, which are founded upon the *tort*, and are for *a matter subsequent [*52] to the agreement. But I answered that *English* may be charged on the bailment in detinue on the original bailment, and a detinue is the adequate remedy ; and upon the delivery *English* is liable in detinue, and consequently this promise by the defendant is collateral, and is within the reason and the very words of the statute." Any doubt that may have been caused by these observations of Justice *Powell*, or by the decision in *Read* v. *Nash* (i), was certainly entirely removed by the case of *Kirkham* v. *Marter* (k). There A. had wrongfully, and without the license of B., ridden his horse, and thereby caused its death. It was held, that a promise by a third person to pay the damage thereby sustained, in consideration that B. would not bring any action against A., was a collateral promise within the Statute of Frauds, and must be in writing. "This case," said *Holroyd*, J., in his judgment, "is certainly

---

(g) 2 Lord Raym., p. 1085. where it is called *Buckmyr* v. *Darnell*.
(h) In the other reports of this case the judgment of *Powell*, J., is not given.
(i) 1 Wills. 305.
(k) 2 B. & Ald. 613, 616, 617.

within the mischief contemplated by the legislature, and it appears to me to be within the plain, intelligent import of the words of the act of parliament." So *Abbott*, C. J., in the same case, said: "The wrongful riding of the horse of another without his leave and license, and thereby causing its death, is clearly an act for which the party is responsible in damages, and therefore, in my judgment, falls within the meaning of the word 'miscarriage'" (*l*).

The meaning of the words "debt, default or miscarriage" was also discussed in the following cases :—In the case last cited, of *Kirkham* v. *Marter* (*m*), *Abbott*, C. J., says: "Now the word 'miscarriage' has not the same meaning as the word 'debt' or 'default'; it seems to me to comprehend that species of wrongful act, for the consequences of which the law would make the [*53] *party civilly responsible. The wrongful riding the horse of another without his leave and license, and thereby causing its death, is clearly an act for which the party is responsible in damages, and therefore, in my judgment, falls within the meaning of the word 'miscarriage.'" In the same case *Holroyd*, J., said: "I think the term *miscarriage* is more properly applicable to a ground of action founded upon a tort than to one founded upon a contract; for, in the latter case, the ground of action is, that the party has not performed what he agreed to perform, not that he has misconducted himself in some manner for which by law he is liable. And I think that both the words *miscarriage* and *default* apply to a promise to answer for another with respect to the non-performance of a duty, though not founded upon a contract."

In *Mountstephen* v. *Lakeman* (*n*), *Willes*, J., said: "Again, if there was a contract with reference to a liability, not existing at the time, by reason of the debt not being due at the time, that would come under the word *default*, and there would be no difficulty about that."

On the other hand, it should be mentioned that, in *Eastwood* v. *Kenyon* (*o*), Lord *Ellenborough* seemed to think there was no distinction in meaning between the words "default" and "miscarriage."

(*l*) See also Throop on the validity of Verbal Agreements, pp. 193, 194.

(*m*). 2 B. & A. 613, 616, 617. See this case *supra*.

(*n*) L. R., 7 Q. B. 197, 202 ; *S. C.*, L. R., 5 Q. B. 613 ; *S. C.*, 7 H. L. 17.

(*o*) 2 East, 325.

These observations and authorities will probably throw sufficient light upon the meaning of the words "debt, default or miscarriage." It remains to notice the words "of another." Like the other words of the statute, they are of much importance, and a large body of law has turned upon their meaning. Their operation has, however, now been ascertained by a long current of authority, which has indisputably established that they restrict the 4th section of the Statute of Frauds to *cases where, either at the time the [*54] promise is made, there is some person actually liable, *in the first instance*, to the promisee, and who remains so liable, notwithstanding such promise, *or*, where, at the time such promise is made, the future *primary* liability of a third person to the promisee is contemplated, as the very foundation of the promise. The same idea is often expressed by the words, "the promise must be *collateral*" (*p*).

It is, however, necessary to observe, that there are many cases where the promise is, undoubtedly, in a certain sense, collateral, and yet to which the 4th section of the Statute of Frauds has no application. These will sufficiently appear while we are discussing the rules for determining what contracts are within the meaning of the second clause of the 4th section of the Statute of Frauds. It is often very difficult, with the aid of the broad principles just alluded to, to assert whether a contract falls within the second clause of section 4 of the Statute of Frauds. In order to bring a promise within the terms of this enactment, it must fall within certain principles. These principles may be reduced to five separate rules. These rules are as follows :— *{Rules for determining what promises are within Statute of Frauds, sect. 4.}*

I. At the time the promise is made there must be some person actually liable, in the first instance, to the promisee for the debt, default or miscarriage guaranteed against, or, at all events, the creation of such liability, at some future time, must be contemplated as the foundation of the contract. *{Rule I. Liability of third party for debt, &c. guaranteed must exist or be contemplated.}*

II. The promise must be made to the creditor, *i. e.*, to the person to whom another is already or is thereafter to become liable. *{Rule II. Promise must be made to the creditor.}*

(*p*) The term *collateral* does not, however, occur in the 4th section of the Statute of Frauds, and, moreover, it involves the question, "What is a *collateral promise ?*" which is quite as difficult to answer as the question, "What is a promise to answer for the debt, default or miscarriage of another person within the 4th section of the Statute of Frauds ?"

Rule III.
Absence of
liability on
part of surety
other than on
his guaran-
tee.
Rule IV.
Fulfilment of
third party's
obligation
the main ob-
ject of prom-
ise.
Rule V.
Transaction
must not
amount to a
sale by cred-
itor to surety.
RULE I.
———
Liability of
third party
for debt, &c.
guaranteed
must exist
or be con-
templated.
This rule
laid down in
Birkmyr v.
Darnell.

[*55] **III.** There must be an absence of any liability on the part of the promiser (the surety), except such as arises from his express promise.

IV. The *main* or *immediate* object of the agreement must be the payment of a debt or the fulfilment of a duty by a third person.

V. The agreement between the promiser and the creditor, to whom the promise is made, must not amount to a sale by the latter to the former, either of the security for a debt or of the debt itself.

It is proposed to treat of these rules in the order above given.

RULE I.—*At the time the promise is made there must be some person actually liable, in the first instance, to the promisee for the debt, default or miscarriage guaranteed against, or, at all events, the creation of such liability, at some future time, must be contemplated as the foundation of the contract* (q).

The present or future primary liability of another person to the person to whom the promise is made is the very basis or foundation of the contract of guarantee. This proposition is, in effect, laid down by the [*56] judges *in the celebrated case of *Birkmyr* v. *Darnell* (r), where it was held, that a promise is not within the Statute of Frauds, 4th section, unless the creditor have a right of action against the principal debtor. The facts of this well known case [which was argued fully, and upon which all the judges were consulted] are simple enough, as will be seen from the following report taken from 1 Salkeld, p. 27: "Declaration—That in consideration the plaintiff would deliver his gelding

(q) It has been suggested by Judge *Stonor*, in his very able judgment in *The Crystal Palace Gas Co.* v. *Smith* (De Colyar's County Court Cases, p. 38), that a guarantee is not within sect. 4 of the Statute of Frauds unless the liability of some third person be actually *contemplated* by the contracting parties, even though, as a matter of fact, such liability may *exist*. While admitting that this is a reasonable view (as the nature of every contract depends upon the intention of the contracting parties), and that, moreover, it is countenanced by certain *obiter dicta* of the judges in *Mountstephen* v. *Lakeman* (L. R., 7 Q. B. 197; S. C., 7 H. L. 17), it has been thought best not to alter the original wording of this rule, because in some of the reported cases (see *post*, p. 5 *et seq.*) the Statute of Frauds has been held to apply when the liability of a third person *existed* in *fact*, without considering whether or not the parties had *contemplated* such liability as the foundation of their contract.

(r) 6 Mod. 248; 2 Lord Raym. 1085; 1 Salk. 27. See observations on this case by Lord *Hardwicke* in *Tomlinson* v. *Gill*, Amb. 330.

to A., the defendant promised that A. should re-deliver RULE I.
Ante, p. *55.
him safe, and evidence was given that the defendant
undertook that A. should re-deliver him safe; and this
was held a collateral undertaking for another, for where
the undertaker comes in aid only to procure a credit to
the party, in that case there is a remedy against both,
and both are answerable according to their distinct engagement; but where the whole credit is given to the
undertaker; so that the other party is but as his servant,
and there is no remedy against him, this is not a collateral
undertaking.   But it is otherwise in the principal case,
for the plaintiff may maintain detinue upon the bailment against the original hirer, as well as *assumpsit*
upon the promise against this defendant. *Et pur cur.:*
If two come to a shop and one buys, and the other, to
gain him credit, promises the seller, *If he does not pay
you, I will*, this is a collateral undertaking, and void
without writing by the Statute of Frauds. But if he
says, *Let him have the goods; I will be your paymaster*,
or, *I will see you paid*, this is an undertaking as for
himself, and he shall be intended to be the very buyer,
and the other to act but as his servant."

In the second volume of Lord Raymond's Reports,
p. 1087, the following report of the judgment of *Holt*,
C. J., in *Birkmyr* v. *Darnell*, is given: "The last day
of the term the Chief Justice delivered the opinion of
*the court. He said that the question had been [*57]
proposed at the meeting of judges, and that there had
been great variety of opinions between them, because
the horse was lent wholly upon the credit of the defendant, but that the judges of this court were all of
opinion that the case was within the statute. The objection that was made was, that if *English* did not re-
deliver the horse he was not chargeable in an action
upon the promise, but in *trover* or detinue, which are
founded upon the *tort* are for a matter subsequent to
the agreement (*s*). But I answered, that *English* may
be charged on the bailment in detinue on the original
delivery, and a detinue is the adequate remedy, and
upon the delivery *English* is liable in detinue; and consequently this promise by the defendant is collateral
and is within the reason and the very·words of the
statute, and is as much so as if, where a man was indebted, J. S., in consideration that the debtee would
forbear the man, should promise to pay him the debt,
such a promise is void unless it be in writing. Sup-

(*s*) See remarks on this part of the judgment, *ante*, p. 51.

RULE I.
Ante, p. *55.

pose a man comes with another to a shop to buy, and the shopkeeper should say, 'I will not sell him the goods unless you shall undertake he shall pay me for them,' such a promise is within the statute; otherwise if a man had been to pay for the goods originally. So, here, detinue lies against *English*, the principal; and the plaintiff having this remedy against *English*, the principal, cannot have an action against the defendant, the undertaker, unless there had been a note in writing."

In the note to *Birkmyr* v. *Darnell* (*t*), if is stated that, " from all the authorities it appears, conformably to the doctrine in this case, that if the person for whose use the goods, &c., are furnished is liable at all any other person's promise is void, except in writing" (*u*).

Observations of *Willes*, J., in *Mountstephen* v. *Lakeman*

[*58] * On this proposition Mr. Justice *Willes* made the following remarks in the important case of *Mountstephen* v. *Lakeman* (*x*): "The leading case upon the application of the Statute of Frauds has generally been considered to be *Birkmyr* v. *Darnell*, and in the note to Mr. Evans' edition of Salkeld's Reports it is stated, that ' from all the authorities it appears, conformably to the doctrine in this case, that if the person for whose use the goods are furnished is liable at all any other person's promise is void, except in writing.' I think that they may very well be modified,—or if his liability is made the foundation of a contract between the plaintiff and the defendant and that liability fails, the promise is void,—so as to include the case which I put to Mr. *Charles* (*y*) of persons wrongfully supposing that a third person was liable and entering into a contract on that supposition. If, in such a case, it turned out that the third person was not liable at all the contract would fail, because there would be a failure of that which the parties intentionally made the foundation of the contract. The *lex contractûs* itself would make an end of the claim, and not the application of the Statute of Frauds, whether the contract was in writing or not, and whether signed or not. The law of contract gives you as foundation that a person was taken to be liable, and that a suretyship was a suretyship in respect of that liability. Take away the foundation of the principal contract, the contract of surety-

(*t*) 1 Salk. 27, Evans' edition.
(*u*) See also Comyns' Digest, Action on Assumpsit (F. 3), 5th ed. Vol. I., p. 319, note (*f*).
(*x*) L. R., 7 Q. B. 197 ; *S. C.*, L. R., 5 Q. B. 613 ; 7 H. L. 17.
(*y*) The counsel for the plaintiff.

RULE I.
Ante, p. *55.

ship would fail. Again, if there was a contract with reference to a liability not existing at the time, by reason of the debt not being due at the time, but being payable *in futuro,* that would come under the word 'default,' and there would be no difficulty about that. So, if there was a contract, 'if A. B. will employ you to do work, I promise to become surety for him that he shall pay you;' in that case the promise *would [*59] clearly come within the statute, because, although there was no liability existing at the time when the promise was made, there was a liability contemplated as the foundation for the promise of the defendant. It was a contract of suretyship in respect of a liability to be created; but if the liability were not created, there again the *lex contractûs* would prevail. There would be the condition precedent to the arising of any liability as surety, that there should be a principal debtor established. In all these cases, no doubt, one agrees thoroughly with what was laid down in the Court of Queen's Bench, because you have the case of principal debt contemplated by the parties and suretyship founded in respect of that principal debt. *But to bring the case within that rule you must first of all show that the parties did intend that there should be a principal debtor"* (z).

In accordance with the principles which have thus been laid down, it is now a well-established rule, that, where *a liability on the part of a third person exists or is contemplated,* the promise falls within the statute; but that *where no liability on the part of a third person exists or is contemplated,* the promise does *not* fall within the statute.

There are numerous reported cases in which it has been held that a liability did exist on the part of a third person, and that, therefore, the rule first enunciated caused the statute to apply.

Thus, for instance, in *Coleman* v. *Eyles* (a), one Allen, the landlord of certain premises, in respect of which rent was due, gave a warrant to a man named Gray, to distrain upon the tenant. The defendant was a creditor of *Allen,* and he paid the broker who valued the goods. He also put the plaintiff on the premises to keep possession of the goods and promised to pay him his charges, and also to repay him certain sums to be *advanced to one *Emmett,* who was also in [*60]

Examples of Rule I. discussed.

Cases where liability of third person existed. *Coleman* v. *Eyles.*

(z) See also the judgment of Lord Selborne in the same case at p. 24 of 7 H. L.
(a) 2 Stark. 62.

RULE I.
Ante, p. *55.

possession of the goods distrained. An action was brought against the defendant for payment of these sums, and it was contended that he was liable to pay them. But Lord *Ellenborough* was of opinion, that, since there was a principal, namely, the landlord, who was responsible for the necessary expenses of the distress, the case was within the Statute of Frauds, and that the debt was to be considered as the debt of another; and, consequently, that the defendant could not be liable without a note in writing.

Tomlinson v. *Gell.*

The decision in *Tomlinson* v. *Gell* (b) turned upon the same principle. There A. had commenced a Chancery suit against B. T. acted as A.'s attorney in the suit, and 30l. had become due to him for his costs in the suit, when he and B. agreed, with the consent of A., that the suit should be discontinued, and that B. should pay T. the costs which were due. B., in consideration of this promise, and that A. had consented to discontinue and plaintiff (T.) to accept his costs from B., promised plaintiff (T.) to pay him such costs. It was held, that such promise was a promise to pay the debt of another within the 4th section of the Statute of Frauds. Now, in this case A. remained liable to his attorney, T., notwithstanding the promise of B. The transaction was neither more nor less than the defendant undertaking to pay the bill of costs which the plaintiff in Chancery owed the plaintiff in this suit.

Brunton v. *Dallas.*

So also, in *Brunton* v. *Dallas* (c), it was held, that a promise to pay a debt to be transferred from promiser's account to that of a third party, his agent, is a valid guarantee, and that parol evidence was admissible to identify the debt. The report of this case is exceedingly brief. It appeared that B., acting as agent for the defendant, ordered goods for him from the plaintiff. It [*61] *was subsequently agreed that these goods should be supplied to B., and that the order, which had been entered by plaintiff to the defendant, should be accordingly entered in the plaintiff's books to B. instead. In consideration of this arrangement the plaintiff required a security, and the defendant wrote to him in these terms, "with regard to the transferring of B.'s order, it shall be paid." Now, such a promise would clearly come within the 4th section of the Statute of Frauds, because it would only amount to a promise to pay for the goods supplied to B., if B. did not himself pay for them.

(b) 4 Ad. & E. 564.
(c) 1 F. & F. 450.

The case of *Chater* v. *Becket* (d), if it was rightly decided, also belongs to the class of cases now under review. In that case, in consideration that the plaintiff would *stay all proceedings* against one *Harris*, and would accept certain bills of exchange, drawn or accepted by the defendant, for a certain part, namely, 10s. 3d., the defendant undertook and promised to give the plaintiff such bills for the same, and to pay all the expenses which the plaintiff had been put to, in and about a certain intended commission of bankruptcy. It was held, that the promise of the defendant to pay 10s. in the pound of *Harris's* debts was within the Statute of Frauds. Now, with reference to this case, it is proper to remark that the question, whether *Harris* remained liable notwithstanding the promise of the defendant, does not seem to have been brought before the court, and altogether the decision in this case is far from satisfactory. But it is presumed, that if this case decides that though *Harris*, the principal debtor, was released from liability by the promise of the defendant, such promise was within the 4th section of the Statute of Frauds, it is no longer law.

<small>RULE I.
Ante, p. *55.
Chater v. *Becket*.</small>

Another example of the operation of the rule, that if *a third person is liable the statute applies, is [*62] afforded by the case of *Re Willis* (e). In that case A. & Co. bought certain wools of B. & Co., to be paid for by the buyer's acceptance at eight months. Before the sale was completed, B. & Co., requiring some security, in consideration of 1l. per cent., obtained the following instrument from C., signed by him : "Gentlemen, in consideration of 1l. per cent., I hereby guarantee the due and correct payment of half the amount of 186 bales of wool, sold to Messrs. A. & Co., as per contract," &c. It was held, that the instrument was a guarantee.

<small>*Re Willis.*</small>

Where a person promises that the creditors of a third person shall be paid the amount of a composition in lieu of their original debts, the application of the 4th section of the Statute of Frauds to such a promise depends upon whether or not the third person remains liable to the creditors notwithstanding such promise. If the third person continues liable then the promise is within the statute, otherwise it is not within it.

<small>Promises that third person shall pay agreed composition to his creditors, when within statute.</small>

In *Emmet* v. *Dewhurst* (f), where W. D., by indenture, agreed to guarantee a certain composition to all the creditors of J. D., who should before a fixed day

<small>*Emmet* v. *Dewhurst.*</small>

(d) 7 T. R. 201. *Vide ante*, p. 44.
(e) 4 Exch. 530.
(f) 3 Mac. & G. 587.

RULE I.
Ante, p. *55.
execute a *release* of their debts, it was held, that this was an agreement required by the 4th section of the Statute of Frauds to be in writing, and that its terms could not, therefore, be varied by parol. Now, in this case it appears that J. D. continued liable for the amount of the composition, notwithstanding the promise of W. D., for each creditor, on executing the deed of release, received, in pursuance of the agreement, the *joint* notes of J. D. and W. D., for the proportionate part of the debt due to the creditor. Vice-Chancellor *Knight-Bruce*, in his judgment in this case, says : "It is a special promise to answer for the debt of another person. It is not a promise, upon good consideration, to take the *debt exclusively* upon [*63] himself. It professes in terms to be a case of guarantee. The composition notes were to be the joint notes of J. D., the principal debtor, and of the defendant W. D., as his guaranty or surety. The agreement is clearly within the 4th section of the Statute of Frauds, and must be in writing. Any alteration of the agreement must also be in writing."

Anstey v. Marden.

In *Anstey* v. *Marden* (*g*), A. being insolvent, a verbal agreement was entered into between several of his creditors and B., whereby B. agreed to pay the creditors 10s. in the pound in satisfaction of their debts, which they agreed to accept, and to assign their debts to B. It was held, that this agreement was not within the 4th section of the Statute of Frauds. Now, there can be no doubt that this decision is perfectly correct, for the effect of the transaction in question was to substitute B. as debtor in lieu of A. Consequently, the promise of B. was an original promise. It was, in short, a contract to purchase the debts of the several creditors, instead of being a contract to answer for the debts owing by A. As *Mansfield*, C. J., said, "The creditors agreed to accept 10s. in the pound from B. in *full satisfaction* of their debts, and undertook to assign their debts to him" (*h*).

Cases in which there being no principal debtor statute held not to apply.

On the other hand, there are very many cases in which effect has been given to the other branch of this part of the rule, and it has been held, that, it appearing, under the circumstances, that there was no third person liable—in other words, that there was no principal debtor—the Statute of Frauds had no application whatever. Thus, for example, in the case of *Tomlinson* v.

(*g*) 1 N. R. 124.
(*h*) See also *post*, where another reason is given for excluding this case from the operation of the Statute of Frauds.

Gill (*i*), it was held, that a promise by A., that, if the
widow of the intestate would permit him to be joined
with her in the letters of administration, he would
make good any deficiency of assets to pay debts, was
not within *the 4th section of the Statute of [*64]
Frauds. Now, it is submitted, that, under no circumstances, could such a promise be within the 4th section
of the Statute of Frauds. It clearly cannot be maintained for a moment that A.'s widow, to whom the promise in question was made, was a *creditor*, and this circumstance of itself, as will presently be seen (*k*), is
sufficient to exempt the promise from the operation of
the statute. But, it may perhaps be said, that A.'s
widow occupied the position of *principal debtor*. Now,
even assuming this to be the case, the Statute of Frauds
would have no application, since it does not operate
upon promises made to principal debtors (*l*). It is,
however, submitted, that, inasmuch as at the time the
promise was made, A.'s widow had not taken out letters
of administration, she was not even a *principal debtor*.
For though an executor may act before probate, "with
respect to an administrator, the general rule is, that a
party entitled to administration can do nothing as administrator before letters of administration are granted
to him, inasmuch as he derives his authority, not, like
an executor from the will, but entirely from the appointment of the court" (*m*). If, therefore, A.'s widow
did not, in fact, occupy the position of principal debtor,
another reason why the promise in question is not
within the Statute of Frauds is, because the promise of
the defendant is not to answer for the debt of another,
but to answer for the sufficiency of the assets of an intestate, or, in other words, it is a promise to answer for
the debts of a *deceased person*.

It is right, however, to mention that the Lord Chancellor *Hardwicke*, in excluding this case from the operation of the Statute of Frauds, grounded his decision
on the alleged distinction "between a promise to pay
the *original debt, and on the footing of the [*65]
original contract, and where it is on a new consideration" (*n*)

RULE I.
Ante, p. *55.

Tomlinson v.
Gill.

(*i*) Amb. 330.
(*k*) See *post*, "Rule II.," p. 110.
(*l*) See *post*, p. 110.
(*m*) Williams' Law of Executors, Vol. I., 6th ed., p. 389;
Wankford v. *Wankford*, 1 Salk. 301, by *Powys*, J.
(*n*) See this distinction commented upon, *post* pp. 118, 119,
120.

RULE I.
Ante, p. *55.*

Lexington v.
Clarke.

In *Lexington* v. *Clarke* (o), the promise was somewhat similar to that in *Tomlinson* v. *Gilt.* In consideration of the plaintiff allowing the widow of A. B. to retain possession of certain premises which the plaintiff had demised to A. B., the widow of A. B. (who was also his executrix) promised to pay to the plaintiff the arrears of rent due to the plaintiff from A. B. at the time of his death, and also 260*l.* more. It was held, that the promise to pay the arrears of rent due from A. B., deceased, was within the 4th section. For the reasons above stated it is submitted that this decision is erroneous. Under the following circumstances, too, it was on the same principle held, that no note in writing was required. An action was brought against a sheriff for taking the plaintiff's goods on a *fi. fa.* against a third person. The sheriff failed on the trial, and the execution creditor then employed an attorney to apply for a new trial, and (on obtaining a rule for a new trial) to act as attorney on the second trial. It was held, that the attorney could recover his bill against the execution creditor, although there was no memorandum in writing. *For the execution creditor is a person primarily liable to him.* But if the attorney had in the first instance been employed *by the sheriff*, it would be otherwise (p).

Houlditch v.
Milne.

The case of *Houlditch* v. *Milne* (q) appears to be regarded by some text writers as being another example of the principle now under consideration. There the plaintiff had a lien on certain carriages belonging to A., for the cost of repairs which he had done to them. The plaintiff parted with such lien and gave up the carriages, on the defendant's promising to pay what [*66] *was due for such repairs from the person in whose name the bill for such repairs had been made out. After the promise of the defendant, the plaintiff appears to have made out the bill in the name of the defendant. It was held, that the 4th section of the Statute of Frauds did not apply. This case, which we shall have occasion to notice at greater length in another part of this book, is very badly reported. It is only cited in this place, because in 1 Wms. Saund. 233, it is stated, that the reason the statute did not apply was, because credit was given to the defendant and not to the owner of the carriages, who was not therefore liable to the plaintiff at all. There was, in fact, no principal debtor.

_____

(o) 2 Ventr. 223.
(p) *Noel* v. *Hart*, 8 C. & P. 230.
(q) 3 Esp. 86. See also *Castling* v. *Aubert*, 2 East, 325.

The case of *Walker* v. *Hill* (r) may be cited as another instance of the rule that there must be a principal debtor. In that case, one *Hulls*, who was agent for the plaintiffs, being desirous of retiring, the defendant applied for the agency. *Hulls* was indebted to the plaintiffs, and, on the other hand, claimed a commission for introducing customers. It was agreed that the plaintiffs should allow *Hulls* 52*l.* on that account, and that the defendant, on taking the agency, should allow the plaintiffs to retain six months' salary, which amounted to 52*l.* In an action by the plaintiffs for money received by the defendant as such agent, to which the defendant pleaded a set-off for six months' salary, it was held, that this was not an undertaking to answer for the debt of another within the 4th section of the Statute of Frauds. The ground on which it was insisted that the Statute of Frauds applied was thus stated by the defendant's counsel (s):—He said, "The agreement is one which is required by the Statute of Frauds to be in writing. The plaintiffs say, 'If you will enter our service, and allow us to retain twenty-six weeks' salary, we will give *Hulls* 52*l.*, whereby so much will be wiped off the debt due from him to us.' [*67] The defendant, by assenting to that, undertakes to answer for so much of the debt of *Hulls*. It is an agreement to give the value of service for a certain time, to be applied in reduction of a debt due from a *third person* to the plaintiffs." *Pollock*, C. B., in giving judgment in this case, said: "If a person agrees that whatever shall hereafter become due to him shall be disposed of in a particular way, such an agreement need not be in writing. Stripped of immaterial details and placed upon a broad ground, the transaction seems simply to have amounted to a purchase by the defendant of the agency for the plaintiff at a certain price, the plaintiff being guided in fixing the price by a wish to make good the loss he had sustained by his former agent. In this view of the case the *old* agent had really nothing to do with *the contract* (as such), and there was therefore no principal debtor."

There is another class of cases which is sometimes considered referable to the principle that the statute only applies where there is a principal debtor. These are cases in which a person makes a promise to a landlord, in consideration of his desisting from distraining

RULE I.
Ante, p. *55.

Walker v
Hill.

Promises to
pay rent in
arrear if landlord will not
distrain.

(r) 5 H. & N. 419.
(s) Mr. Hopwood.

RULE I
Ante, p. *55.

Edwards v.
Kelly.

Williams v.
Leper.

Thomas v.
Williams.

for rent in arrear. In such cases the promise need not be in writing. Thus, in the case of *Edwards* v. *Kelly* (*t*), *after* goods had been *actually distrained* for rent, the plaintiff consented to give them up to one of the defendants, upon all the defendants giving a joint undertaking to pay to the plaintiff all such rent as should appear to be due from the tenant. It was held that this agreement was not within the Statute of Frauds. *Bayley*, J., in his judgment in this case, said, that after the plaintiff had distrained, he held in his own hands the remedy for recovering the rent, *and the tenant was at that time no longer indebted;* for so long [*68] as the *landlord held the goods under distress, the debt due from the tenant was *suspended.* One reason (*u*), therefore, for this decision was that there was no principal debtor.

The earlier case of *Williams* v. *Leper* (*x*) is very similar to *Edwards* v. *Kelly.* The circumstances, indeed, are exactly similar, except that in *Williams* v. *Leper,* when the promise of the defendant was made, the goods had *not* been actually distrained. It was held that the 4th section of the Statute of Frauds did not apply. The following judgment was delivered by the majority of the judges who decided this case:—"This is not a promise to pay the debt of another; the goods were debtor, and the defendant was in the nature of a bailiff for the landlord, and, if the defendant had sold the goods and received money for them, an action for money had and received for the plaintiff's use would have laid." Mr. Justice *Aston,* however, thought that if the goods had not sold for so much money as the plaintiff's rent, he would be liable for no more than they sold for.

Lord *Tenterden,* C. J., in *Thomas* v. *Williams* (*y*), said: "In *Williams* v. *Leper* there was no actual distress, but there was a power of immediate distress, and an intention to enforce it; and I think the judges must be understood to have considered that power *as equivalent to an actual distress.* It is not necessary now to decide whether it was rightly so considered."

(*t*) 6 M. & S. 204.
(*u*) *Vide post*, pp. 118, 146, for another reason.
(*x*) 2 Wils. 308 ; 3 Burr, 1886. This case is also cited under Rule III., at p. 123, where it will be seen that there is another reason why the 4th section of the Statute of Frauds does not apply to it. See also p. 70.
(*y*) 10 B. & C. 664, 670. See also remarks of *Bayley,* J., in *Edwards* v. *Kelly, supra.*

In *Bampton* v. *Paulin* (z), too, where *Williams* v. *Le-*   RULE I.
per is followed, the promise was made *before* the goods   *Ante*, p. *55.
had been distrained. It would seem, therefore, that,
whether the *promise is made *before* or *after* [*69]
the distress, the statute does not apply, because, at
the time the promise is made, there is no principal
debtor other, indeed, than the *goods* themselves.

·*Love's Case* (a), it is presumed, rests upon the same   *Love's Case.*
principle as the cases just cited. There the sheriff had
taken goods in execution upon a *fi. fa.*, and a promise
to the officer, by a third party, to pay him the debt, in
consideration that he would restore them, was held to
be an original promise not within the 4th section of the
Statute of Frauds.

A further example of the rule, that the Statute of   Promise to
Frauds does not apply unless there be a principal   pay a debt
debtor, is furnished by a line of cases which decide that   out of fund
a promise made to a third person's creditors to pay the   belonging to
debt of that third person *out of the proceeds of a sale of*   debtor is not
that third person's goods need not be in writing, and is   statute.
not within the 4th section of the Statute of Frauds.
Such a promise is not a promise to answer for the debt
of another person, but a promise to answer for the sufficiency of a certain fund, or for the due application of
such fund, as the case may be. In such a case, you
undertake or promise, *not* for *another*, but for *yourself.*
You undertake, not that *another* shall pay out of the
proceeds of the sale, but that you yourself will do so.
Consequently, there is no one liable, or to become liable,
in the first instance, to do that which you promise or
undertake to do, and, thereupon, the operation of the
4th section of the Statute of Frauds is excluded by the
rule now under consideration. If it is a promise to
answer only for the *application* of a certain fund to the
payment of the debt due to the promisee from the third
person, it seems that the party making such a promise
is not liable for a greater sum than the goods may
realize *by the sale (b). In *Williams* v. *Leper* [*70]
(c), where the promise of the defendant was to pay rent
due to the plaintiff from a third party out of the produce of the sale of that third party's goods; in *Edwards*
v. *Kelly* (d), where the promise was almost the same

(z) 4 Bing. 264.
(a) Salk. 23. This case is also cited, *post*, p. 115, under Rule
II., and at p. 144, under Rule V.
(b) *Stephens* v. *Pell*, 2 C. & M. 710 ; but see *Williams* v. *Leper*,
2 Wils. 308.
(c) *Ubi supra.*
(d) 6 M. & S. 204, 208, *ante*, p. 67.

RULE I.
Ante, p. *55.

as in *Williams* v. *Leper* (*e*) ; in *Bampton* v. *Paulin* (*f*), where the promise was "to pay rent out of the proceeds of sale"; and' in *Stephens* v. *Pell* (*g*), where the promise was to pay the sum due for rent "out of the produce of the effects," the Statute of Frauds, sect. 4, was held to have no application.

Promise to pay another's debt out of debtor's money when received by promiser, whether within statute.

There is also a class of cases, greatly resembling those just cited, which proceed on the same principal, and therefore further exemplify the present rule. These are cases in which, in consideration of goods supplied on credit to a third person, the defendant has promised to pay for such goods out of certain moneys about to be received by him (the defendant) for such third person. Now, in these cases, the promise is really nothing more nor less than a promise to pay the *third party's debt with the third party's money*, for, when the promise is made, it is known whether the money to be received will be sufficient in amount to cover the debt. The person giving such a promise or undertaking does not therefore undertake any responsibility whatever, and certainly does not stand in need of the protection afforded by the Statute of Frauds. His engagement, like that of a person who undertakes to pay another's debt out of the produce of the sale of such other's goods, is not that the principal debtor shall pay, or, in default, that he himself will do so, but that he himself will pay out of moneys coming to him for such other person. In such [*71] *cases there is, in fact, *no third person answerable, in the first instance, for the debt or default guaranteed against,* for it is the promiser who undertakes that *he himself* will apply, in a certain way, a third party's fund over which he (the promiser) has or is to have control. He does not undertake that *another* shall do this. In such cases, therefore, the event on which the liability of the promiser is to depend is, not the default of another, but the receipt by the promiser of a certain sum of money. The promiser's undertaking to pay out of a certain fund creates a privity of contract between himself and the third person's creditor, and enables the latter to maintain against the former an action for money had and received, and, where the appropriation in question is made with the debtor's consent, renders such appropriation irrevocable as far as the debtor is concerned.

(*c*) *Supra.*
(*f*) 4 Bing. 264.
(*g*) 2 C. & M. 710.

For the above reasons, it is submitted that the Statute of Frauds has no application to a promise to pay another's debt out of such other's funds when they are received by the promiser in consideration of goods to be supplied to such other person on credit. However, on an examination of the authorities, it will be found that in the *two* cases in which this view was adopted, the goods were supplied on the *sole credit* of the promiser, and, therefore, for this reason alone, the statute could not apply, whilst, in the one case in which this view was *not* adopted, *credit* was given to a third party. Thus, in *Andrews* v. *Smith* (*h*), one *Hill* was employed to do certain work, and the defendant was appointed surveyor over him, and to receive moneys due to *Hill* for such work. The defendant promised the plaintiff, in consideration that he would deliver to *Hill* materials, as he might require to enable him to do the work in question, that he (defendant) would pay him for them out of such moneys received by him (the defendant) as should become due to *Hill* for the work, if *Hill* would give *him an order for that purpose. The prom- [*72] ise of the defendant was held to be original, and therefore not within the Statute of Frauds. Now, in this case, it appeared that there was nothing on the face of the declaration to imply a contract by the plaintiff with *Hill*, i. e., there was no principal debtor. Lord *Abinger*, C. B., however, while admitting that this was an answer to the objection raised by the defendant, went on to say: "But further, if the defendant contracted, not to pay *Hill's* debt out of his own funds, but only faithfully to apply *Hill's* funds for that purpose when they should come to his hands, that contract would not be within the operation of the statute." *Parke*, B., too, said: "There is nothing on the face of the declaration to imply a contract by the plaintiff with *Hill*. If that be so, it is clear the defendant's contract was an original, not a collateral one, and so not within the statute. But, even if that were otherwise, this is nothing more than a prospective assignment of funds which were to come to the defendant's hands for *Hill*, and an attornment, as it were, by the defendant to that assignment; and the authorities show that in such case the contract is not within the statute. On this ground, also, the plaintiff is entitled to the judgment of the court." In *Dixon* v. *Hatfield* (*i*), W. undertook to complete the carpenter's

RULE I.
Ante, p. *55.

Cases on this subject somewhat conflicting.

Andrews v. *Smith.*

Dixon v. *Hatfield.*

(*h*) 2 Cr., M. & R. 627.
(*i*) 2 Bing. 439 ; 10 Moore, 24.

RULE I.
Ante, p. *55.

Morley v.
Boothby.

Promises in
consideration
of stay or

work in the defendant's house, and find all materials.
W. being delayed for want of credit or funds to procure timber, it was supplied by M. on the defendant's
signing the following undertaking: "I agree to pay M.
for timber to house in A. C. *out of the money* that I have
to pay W. provided W.'s work is completed." It was
held, that this was not a guarantee to pay if W. should
fail, but a direct undertaking to pay when the work
should be completed. Now here, again, it does not
appear that there was any contract between M. and W.,
[*73] *and Mr. Justice *Park*, in his judgment, seemed
to think that, had this been the case, the defendant's
promise would have amounted to a guarantee. On the
other hand, Mr. Justice *Gaselee* seemed to think that,
even if credit had been given by M. to W., the defendant would have been liable, as he undertook to pay for
the timber on the completion of the work.

In the case of *Morley* v. *Boothby* (k), the defendants
promised the plaintiffs that if they would deliver to A.
B. certain goods, &c., to the value of 174l. 13s. 5d., required for the building of St Philip's Church, to be
paid for by bill of exchange, to be drawn by the plaintiffs on A. B., the said bills should be paid, at maturity,
out of money to be received from St. Philip's Church.
It seems to have been admitted that the promise was
within the Statute of Frauds, and the only question for
the decision of the court was, whether a certain agreement was a sufficient memorandum in writing to satisfy
the 4th section of the Statute of Frauds, and the court
held that it was not, on the ground that no consideration appeared on the face of the agreement. Now, in
this case, as pointed out by Lord *Abinger*, C. B., in
Andrews v. *Smith*, *supra*, there could be no doubt that
A. B. was indebted to the plaintiffs:—in other words,
that there was a third person who was primarily liable
to pay the debt. The question, however, whether the
defendant had assumed a liability to see that such third
person paid, or had merely undertaken to apply the
funds coming from St. Philip's Church to the payment of the debt, was not (as has been observed) argued at all. The decision of the court does not, therefore, touch the principle of the decisions which we
have just been considering.

In the following cases, it is submitted, it will also be
found that the promise or undertaking of the defendant
[*74] *was for himself, and not for another, and that

(k) ⬤ Bing. 107.
(1292)

there was no one liable, in the first instance, to the plaintiff, within the meaning of Rule I. They are all instances in which the defendant's promise was made in consideration of proceedings against a third party being stayed or withdrawn, and in which, therefore, at first sight, the statute might appear to apply. Thus, in *Jarmain* v. *Algar* (*l*), the defendant promised to sign a bail bond for a defendant in a civil action, in consideration of the plaintiff forbearing to arrest such defendant on a suit already sued out. But it was held, that this promise was not within the 4th section of the Statute of Frauds. For, as will not have escaped the reader's notice, the undertaking was that defendant *himself* would sign the bail bond, not that *another* should do so.

So, also, it had been previously decided, in the case of *Read* v. *Nash* (*m*), that a promise by C. to A. to pay him 50*l.* and costs if he would withdraw the record, in an action of assault brought by A. against B. need not be in writing, as it is not a promise within the Statute of Frauds. *Lee*, C. J., in his judgment in this case, says: "The single question is, whether this promise, which is confessed by the demurrer not to have been in writing, is within the Statute of Frauds and Perjuries, that is to say, whether it be a promise for the debt, default or miscarriage of another person? And we are all of opinion that it is not, but that it is an original promise, sufficient to found an *assumpsit* upon against *Nash*, and is a lien upon *Nash*, and upon him only. *Johnson* was not a debtor; the cause was not tried; he did not appear to be guilty of any default or miscarriage; there might have been a verdict for him if the cause had been tried, for anything we can tell ; he never was liable to the particular debt, damages or costs. The true difference is between an *original* *promise and a *collateral* promise; the *first* is [*75] out of the statute, the *latter* is not, when it is to pay the debt of another which was already contracted."

In *Chater* v. *Becket* (*n*), Lord *Kenyon*, C. J., referred to the case of *Read* v. *Nash. supra*, and seemed to approve of it.

In 1 Wms. Saund. p. 231, however, it is stated that *Read* v. *Nash* is in effect overruled by *Kirkham* v. *Marter* (*o*). The facts of *Kirkham* v. *Marter* are as fol-

RULE I.
Ante, p. *55.

withdrawal of proceedings against third party.

Jarmain v. *Algar*.

Read v. *Nash*.

Chater v. *Becket*.

Kirkham v. *Marter*.

(*l*) 2 C. & P. 249.
(*m*) 1 Wils. 305.
(*n*) 7 T. R. 201.
(*o*) 2 B. & A. 613.

RULE I.   lows :—A. had ridden the plaintiff's horse without his
Ante, p. *55.   leave, and thereby caused his death, and the defendant
——————   (the father of A.) promised to pay the plaintiff the
damage he had sustained, in consideration of the plaintiff forbearing to sue A. : it was held, that the defendant's promise was void, not being in writing ; but *Abbott*, C. J., in delivering his judgment, expressly recognized *Read* v. *Nash*, distinguishing *Kirkham* v. *Marter*
from it. He says : "The case of *Read* v. *Nash* is very
distinguishable from this ; the promise there was to
pay a sum of money as an inducement to withdraw a
record in an action of assault brought against a third
person. It did not appear that the defendant in that
action had even committed the assault, or that he had
ever been liable in damages ; and the case was expressly decided on the ground that it was an original and
not a collateral promise. Here the son had rendered
himself liable by his wrongful act, and the promise
was expressly made in consideration of the plaintiff's
forbearing to sue the son."

It is submitted that the distinction between the two
cases is perfectly clear. In *Read* v. *Nash* the promise
simply was, "forbear to proceed with the action you
have commenced against A. and I will pay you 50l."
In *Kirkham* v. *Marter* it was, "do not make A. pay for
his default, and I will do so myself."

Fish v. Hut-   [*76] *The older case of *Fish* v. *Hutchinson* is much
chinson.   the same in effect as *Kirkham* v. *Marter*. In *Fish* v.
Hutchinson (p) the plaintiff declared that, whereas one
A. was indebted to him in a certain sum of money, and
he had commenced an action for the same, the defendant, in consideration that the plaintiff would stay his
action, promised to pay the money due to him by A. Demurrer and joinder. *Et per totam curiam* : "This case
is very clearly within the statute ; for here is the debt
of another party still subsisting, and a promise to pay
it. It is not like the case of *Read* v. *Nash*. In that
case there was no debt in another, it being an action
of battery ; and it could not be known, before trial,
whether the plaintiff would recover any damages or
not. But, in the present case, there is the debt of another still subsisting, and a promise to pay it." It is
quite possible to distinguish *Read* v. *Nash* from *Fish*
v. *Hutchinson*. For in *Read* v. *Nash* the promise of
the defendant was to pay 50l. and costs. On the other
hand, in *Kirkham* v. *Marter* and *Fish* v. *Hutchinson*,

_____

(p) 2 Wils. 94.

the defendants promised not to pay the plaintiff a fixed sum of money, but something that a third person was liable to pay. In the following case of *Bird* v. *Gammon* (q), it will be seen that *Read* v. *Nash* was followed. In *Bird* v. *Gammon* the facts were as follows:—The plaintiff having issued execution against *Lloyd* for debt, *Lloyd*, with the assent of the plaintiff, conveyed all his property to the defendant, who thereupon undertook to pay the plaintiff the debt due from *Lloyd*, plaintiff withdrawing the execution. It was held, on the authority of *Read* v. *Nash*, *supra*, that the defendant's undertaking was not within the 4th section of the Statute of Frauds. *Tindal*, C. J., thus described the transaction: "It appears, then, that the plaintiff, with the consent of *Lloyd* and the defendant, had relinquished his execution against *Lloyd*, to look to *the defendant; that the defendant admitted his [*77] liability when the account was presented; and that the jury found such to have been the agreement between the parties. No objection, therefore, can be raised on the Statute of Frauds, for this is not an agreement to pay the debt of a third person; but an agreement that if the plaintiff would forego his claim on *Lloyd*, the defendant would pay the amount of his debt on his own account. The case, therefore, falls within the principle of *Read* v. *Nash* (r). . . . It is objected that the plaintiff, if he fails in this action, may still sue *Lloyd* or issue execution; but if he were to do so, *Lloyd* might show on plea or *audita querela* that on good consideration the plaintiff gave up his remedy against *Lloyd*, and took the defendant's liability instead; which, though not properly accord and satisfaction, would be a complete defence on the general issue. *Good* v. *Cheeseman* (s), and the cases there cited."

In the case of *Bushell* v. *Beavan* (t) we have an instance of a promise, which, at first sight, would appear to obviously fall within the Statute of Frauds. For the promise was "to *procure* the signature to a third person to a guarantee"(u). And this would seem to be, in effect, an undertaking that the third person shall do a certain thing, namely, sign the guarantee. Here, again, no person "*other* than the defendant himself was ever

RULE I.
Ante, p. *55.

Bird v. *Gammon.*

Promise to procure the signature of a third person to a guarantee not within statute.
Bushell v. *Beavan.*

(q) 3 Bing. N. C. 8, 83.
(r) 1 Wils. 305.
(s) 2 B. & Adol. 328.
(t) 1 Bing. N. C. 103.
(u) As to promises to *give* a guarantee, see *Mallet* v. *Bateman*, L. R., 1 C. P. 163, *ante*, pp 48—49.

RULE I.
Ante, p. *55. liable *on the promise sued upon.*" The facts were as follows:—The plaintiffs, owners of a ship hired on charter-party by *H. Semphill*, refused to let her sail till certain disputes about the freight between them and *H. Semphill* were settled, by *H. Semphill* giving security; whereupon the defendant, in consideration that the plaintiffs would let *H. Semphill's* ship sail, without giving security, undertook to get *P. Macqueen* to sign a [*78] guarantee and *deliver it to the plaintiffs in a week. The guarantee, which it was promised that *P. Macqueen* should sign, ran as follows: "Whereas *H. Semphill* has hired your ship for six months from the. 12th July, 1830, and such longer time as his intended voyage may require, and has paid or secured the freight for six months from the 20th August, 1830, and is about to leave England, I guarantee the payment of freight which shall accrue for any portion of the voyage after the said six months." And the court held, that this guarantee was within the Statute of Frauds. Nevertheless, the court also held—and it is submitted rightly held—that the defendant's promise to procure *Macqueen's* signature to this document *did not* fall within the statute. *Tindal*, C. J., in the course of his judgment, said: "The promise on which the first count is framed is an immediate undertaking by the defendant to get a copy of a guaranty which is written above it, duly signed by Mr. *Potter Macqueen*, and within a week afterwards delivered to the plaintiff's agent. The immediate consideration for that promise was the removal by the plaintiff of a stop which they had put upon the vessel, then lying in St. Katharine's Docks, and the permitting her to sail on the voyage before the security was signed. Under these circumstances the contract appears to us not to be a contract to answer for the debt, default or miscarriage of any other person, but a new and immediate contract between the defendant and the plaintiffs. If Mr. *Macqueen* had signed the guaranty, that guaranty would, indeed, have been within the Statute of Frauds; for his is an express guaranty to be answerable for the freight due under the charter-party, if *Semphill* did not pay it. But no person could be answerable on the promise to procure his signature but the defendant. *Semphill* had never engaged to get the guaranty of *Macqueen*, nor had *Macqueen* engaged to give it. There was, therefore, no default of any one [*79] for which the defendant made *himself liable; but he did so simply on his own immediate contract. For, as to any default of *Semphill* in paying the freight,

the action, on the undertaking of the defendant, could **RULE I.**
not be dependent on that event; for it would have been *Ante*, p. *55.
maintainable if the guarantee were not signed at any time
after the day on which the defendant engaged it should
be given, that is, long before the time when the freight
became payable." The ground of the decision, as stated
in the judgment of the court, may be briefly stated to
be, that, from *the very nature of the case*, it was impossible
that any one could be liable to the plaintiff *simulta-
neously* with the defendant. For, as soon as the lia·
bility of the third person (*Macqueen*) *commenced*, by
his signing the guarantee, the liability of the defendant
ceased, and, until the third person signed the guarantee,
obviously, there could be no one liable but the defendant.

Again, in the old case of *Elkins* v. *Heart* (*x*), just as **Promise that**
in *Bushell* v. *Beavan*, the promise was *seemingly* to **a third person**
answer for another within the Statute of Frauds. There **shall not**
the plaintiff having sued J. G., the defendant's son-in- **kingdom**
law, for money due from him to the plaintiff for diet **without pay-**
and lodging, the defendant, in consideration that the **ing his debt**
plaintiff would forbear to sue the said J. G. for the said **not within**
sum, promised that the said J. G. should not leave the **statute.**
kingdom without paying the same. The court inclined ***Elkins* v.**
to the opinion that this case was not within the 4th sec- ***Heart*.**
tion of the Statute of Frauds. Now, in this case, it will
be observed that the terms of the engagement of the
defendant simply were that J. G. should not leave the
kingdom without paying his debt. But it does not
appear that J. G., by leaving the kingdom, incurred
any liability to the plaintiff. Consequently there was
no principal debtor or defaulter within the meaning
of Rule I. The event on which the liability of the
*defendant was to attach, namely, J. G. leaving [*80]
the country without paying his debt, would not make
J. G. liable to the plaintiff. Just as, on the other hand,
the failure of J. G. to pay his debt (provided he did not
leave the country) would not render the defendant liable
to J. G. The decision may, in a word, be put upon the
ground that the defendant's promise was that J. G.
should not leave the kingdom; but J. G. made no such
promise, and therefore no one but the defendant himself
was ever liable upon the promise in question.

The following cases, again, form another class in **Promises to**
which the Statute of Frauds has no application, because **indemnify**
there is no other person liable but the defendant him- **third person**
self. It frequently happens that one person is induced, **against costs**

(*x*) Fitzg. 202.
(1297)

RULE I.
Ante, p. *55.

of litigation
undertaken
at promiser's
request.

at the request of another, to defend or commence some legal proceeding in consideration of a promise, by the person making such request, to indemnify him against the costs of the suit. In these cases it is submitted that the 4th section of the Statute of Frauds has no application. The foundation of a promise to answer for the debt, default or miscarriage of another is the present or future liability of a third person in the first instance to the promisee. Take away this liability, and not the Statute of Frauds, but the *lex contractûs*, puts an end to the contract (*y*), which cannot survive the loss of its *essential* ingredient, the liability of a third person. Now, in the present class of cases, it will be observed, on examination, that the foundation of the contract is not, as in the case of a guarantee, the present or future liability of a third person to the promisee. True, such a liability *may* arise, but *whether it arises or not* the promiser is equally liable, whereas in the case of a guarantee, as already pointed out, if it does not arise, the contract is at an end for loss of one of its *essential* ingredients. [*81] *To make this still clearer. If a person at your request defends or commences an action, and you engage to indemnify him, you are liable on your engagement whether he is successful or whether he prove unsuccessful. But it is *only in the former event* that a third person is liable in the first instance, for, unless you succeed, your adversary has not to pay you either costs or damages. In the latter event the promisee has to pay at least his own costs, and these are covered by your indemnity, which exists, though the liability of a third person has *not* arisen, because such a liability is an *accidental*, and not, as in the case of a guarantee, an *essential* ingredient of such a contract. Accordingly, in consonance with these principles, in the case of *Bullock* v. *Lloyd* (*z*), it was held that the promise of an indorser of a dishonoured bill of exchange to indemnify a subsequent indorsee against costs, if he would bring an action against the acceptor, would certainly not require to be in writing. The only case which seems to militate against this view is *Winckworth* v. *Mills* (*a*), where it was decided, that a promise by the indorser of an unpaid note to indemnify the holder if he would proceed to enforce payment against the other parties on the note, must be in writing, or it would be void under the

---

(*y*) Per *Willes*, J., in *Mountstephen* v. *Lakeman*, L. R., 7 Q. B. 197; 7 H. L. 17.
(*z*) 2 C. & P. 119.
(*a*) 2 Esp. 484.

Statute of Frauds. Much importance cannot, however, be attached to this latter case, which was decided at Nisi Prius many years ago, and which is at variance with modern authorities, though it has never been expressly overruled. Besides, Lord *Kenyon* offered to save the point, but the plaintiff's counsel declined. Moreover, the case of *Howes* v. *Martin* (b) is an authority to the same effect as *Bullock* v. *Lloyd.* In *Howes* v. *Martin* plaintiff had accepted a bill for 20*l.* for the accommodation and on account of the defendant. This bill was not taken up by the *defendant [*82] when due, and the defendant accordingly prevailed upon the holder of the bill to accept 16*l.* in part and the plaintiff's acceptance for six guineas (being the balance due on the bill, including the interest then due) for the remainder. This bill for six guineas not being paid when due, the holder of the bill brought an action on it against the plaintiff as the acceptor. On the action being brought, plaintiff acquainted the defendant with the circumstance, and he desired the plaintiff to defend the action. In consequence of this representation plaintiff did accordingly defend, when the holder of the bill obtained a verdict for the amount of the bill, which, with costs, amounted to 32*l.* To recover this sum the plaintiff brought an action of assumpsit for money laid out and expended to the use of the defendant, declaring on the common counts. At the trial it was objected that, under the Statute of Frauds, this action was not maintainable, inasmuch as there was no note in writing, and the object of the action was to recover from the defendant a sum of money which was the debt and costs in an action against the plaintiff herself on her own acceptance, and which, therefore, was to be deemed her own debt. In support of this view a case of *Hitchcock* v. *Hicks* was cited, which was said to have been decided before Lord *Kenyon.* This case does not, however, appear to be reported anywhere. Lord *Kenyon* overruled the objection in the present instance, and held that the case was not within the Statute of Frauds. He said that it appeared that the plaintiff never had any consideration whatever for her acceptances, which were given merely on the defendant's account and for his use; that the defence to the action on the note was on his account, and from whence he could have derived a benefit; that as he, therefore, was *personally interested*, and directed the

RULE I.
Ante, p. *55.

Howes v. *Martin.*

(b) 1 Esp. 162.

RULE I.
Ante, p. *55.

defence to be made by which he might have been
benefited, the money must be considered to have been
[*83] *laid out by the plaintiff on his account and to
his use, and that the plaintiff, therefore, was entitled to
recover it from him.

Adams v.
Dansey.

To the same effect, also, is the case of *Adams* v.
Dansey (c). There the plaintiff, an occupier of land, at
the request of the defendant, and upon a promise of indemnity, resisted a suit of the vicar for tithes. It was
held, that the defendant's promise was not a promise
required by the Statute of Frauds to be in writing. Now,
the ground of this decision is, that the promise was not
an undertaking for the debt, default or miscarriage of
another, but for a liability to which the plaintiff
himself was to be exposed at the request of the defendant. This case, therefore, so far resembles the case of
Eastwood v. *Kenyon* (d), (which will be cited hereafter
to show that the promise is not within the statute unless
made to the creditor,) that it is a promise made to the
debtor and not to the creditor. But it differs from that
case in this, that here the promise was not, as in *Eastwood* v. *Kenyon*, to pay the promisee's debt to the
creditor of the promisee, but to pay the promisee himself the expenses which he might incur at the promiser's
request. It is, therefore, submitted that the true reason
for excepting such a promise from the operation of the
4th section of the Statute of Frauds is because it
amounts to a promise to pay the promiser's *own* debt.

Promises to
be jointly
liable with
another not
within
statute.

There is another class of cases governed by the rule
that the Statute of Frauds does not apply unless
there is a principal debtor. It sometimes happens that
a transaction has the appearance of being a contract
between debtor, surety and creditor, but it is not so in
reality. If it should appear, by evidence, that such was
not the nature of the transaction, and that the alleged
principal debtor and surety are, in fact, nothing more
[*84] *than *joint* debtors, the operation of the 4th section of the Statute of Frauds will be excluded.

Batson v.
King.

Thus, in *Batson* v. *King* (e), it was held that a promise
made by the defendant, that, if the plaintiff would draw
a bill, to be accepted by one *Dalton* and *indorsed by the
defendant*, he (plaintiff) should not be called upon, need
not be in writing, under the 4th section of the Statute
of Frauds. *Martin*, B., delivered the following judgment:—" As between the holder of the bill of exchange

(c) 6 Bing. 506; 4 M. & P. 245.
(d) 11 A. & E. 438.
(e) 4 H. & N. 739.

and the parties whose names were on it, *Dalton*, as acceptor, was primarily liable; and the drawer and indorser stood in the relation of sureties for him. *But as between the parties, it may always be proved what is the real nature of the transaction.* As between themselves, *Dalton* and the defendant were the real principals. The plaintiff, having paid the bill, had a right to sue the defendant for money paid to his use. The Statute of Frauds has no application to the case; and the question in *Green* v. *Cresswell* does not arise here. It might have been otherwise if *Dalton* had been entirely separate from the defendant and the plaintiff had become responsible for *Dalton*, upon the defendant's promise to indemnify him. *Dalton* and the defendant, being both principals, the only answer which the defendant had was by a plea in abatement for the non-joinder of *Dalton*." The effect of this decision really is, that, where the actual transaction, though *apparently* resembling a guarantee, *really* is not one, the court will treat it as being outside the 4th section of the Statute of Frauds. So, it appears, that if a man says to another, "If you will, at my request, put your name to a bill of exchange, I will save you harmless," this is not within the statute (*f*). "It is not a responsibility for the debt of another. It amounts to a contract by one, that if the other will put himself in a certain situa-*tion, the first will indemnify him against the [*85] consequences " (*g*).

The rule that the 4th section of the Statute of Frauds only applies where, at the time the promise is given, the present or future legal liability of some third person is contemplated by both the promiser and the promisee, is further illustrated by cases in which the third person referred to is under disability. For a promise to answer for the debt, default or miscarriage of a person incompetent to contract, or not answerable for his wrongful acts, need not be in writing. Thus, in the case of *Harris* v. *Huntbach* (*h*), the plaintiff declared, first, for money lent and advanced by the plaintiff at the defendant's request; and, secondly, for money laid out and expended by the plaintiff at the defendant's request. The question upon the case reserved at the trial was, whether the evidence supported the declaration. A note of the defendant was produced in evidence by

RULE I.
Ante, p. *55.

Promises to be answerable for persons under disability.

Infants.

(*f*) Per *Pollock*, C. B., *dictum* in *Batson* v. *King*, 4 H. & N. 739.

(*g*) *Ib.*
(*h*) 1 Burr. 373.

RULE I.
Ante, p. *55.
the plaintiff, in the following words :—"3rd December, 1751. Then received of Mr. *Harris* the sum of 1*l.* on the *behalf of my grandson*, which I promise to be *accountable for*, on demand. Witness my hand. *S. Huntbach.*" It appeared that the grandson, on whose behalf the note was given, was an *infant.* Mr. Justice *Foster*, in giving his opinion, said : " The *infant* was not *liable*, and, therefore, it *could not* be a *collateral* undertaking. It was an *original* undertaking of the defendant to pay the money." So, also, from the old case of *Duncombe* v. *Tickridge* (*i*), decided in 24 Car. 2, it appears that an undertaking by a stranger to pay for "diet, lodging and apparel of an infant," is an original promise, which extinguishes the liability of an infant. Much importance cannot, however, be attached to this case, for it is apprehended that an undertaking to pay for necessaries supplied to an infant, made on [*86] proper *consideration, would amount to a *collat eral* promise, within the 4th section of the Statute of Frauds, since the infant would himself be liable for necessaries (*j*).

Promise to be answerable for a married woman.

Whether a promise by a person other than the husband to answer for the debt, default or miscarriage of a *married woman* was an original or a collateral promise, appears never to have been decided in England (*k*). However, there are two cases which throw some light on this question. The first is *White* v. *Cuyler* (*l*).

White v. *Cuyler.*

There the defendant's wife, without any authority from the defendant, her husband, by articles of agreement, *under seal*, between herself and a Mr. *Low*, of the one part, and the plaintiff of the other part, agreed to take the plaintiff with her to *Barbadoes*, as a waiting-maid, and also agreed, amongst other things, to pay the plaintiff's passage home to England, in case she (the defendant's wife) should dismiss the plaintiff from her service. The defendant's wife having dismissed the plaintiff, but not having paid the plaintiff's passage home to England, the plaintiff brought an action of assumpsit against the defendant. In moving for a rule to enter a nonsuit (the verdict having passed for the plaintiff), it was, *inter alia*, contended at the bar that the action was wrongly conceived, if either the defen-

(*i*) Aleyn, 94.
(*j*) As to what are necessaries, see *ante*, p. 15.
(*k*) See, however, American cases of *Kimball* v. *Newall*, 7 Hill, 116; *Miller* v. *Long*, 4 Pennsylv, 350; *Conncrat* v. *Goldsmith*, 6 Geng. 14.
(*l*) 1 Esp. N. P. C. 200 ; *S. C.*, 6 T. R. 176.

dant or *Low* could be sued on the covenant contained in the above-named articles of agreement under seal. Lord *Kenyon*, in discharging this rule to enter a nonsuit, said, "And, with regard to *Low*, the contract of a guarantee or surety under seal does not, by operation of law, extinguish the debt of the principal" (*m*). *In this case, therefore, Lord *Kenyon* seems to [*87] have been disposed to treat *Low* as a surety, under the articles of agreement, though the principal debtor under such instrument was clearly (if any one) the married woman. Perhaps, however, it would not be incorrect to say that, in this case, the husband must be treated as the principal debtor, though his liability did not certainly arise under the articles of agreement (*n*). Indeed, until recently (*o*), whenever the wife had express or implied authority to enter into contracts, the *husband alone* was liable. It would seem, therefore, that (subject to the provisions of the Married Women's Property Acts (*p*)), whenever a person promises to answer for a married woman's *breach of contract*, in a case where she is expressly or impliedly authorized by her husband to enter into such a contract, the husband is the principal debtor, and the promiser is the surety. Where she has no such authority, either the promiser is *solely* liable, or else is not liable at all, according to the circumstances of the case.

The next case throwing light on the present question is *Darnell* v. *Tratt* (*q*). There, a married woman took her son to school, but no evidence was given of what passed at that time. Afterwards, a bill was delivered to the boy's uncle, who said it was quite right to deliver the bill to him, for that he was answerable. It was *held*, that the Statute of Frauds, section 4, did not apply, and that it was proper to leave it to the jury to say, under those circumstances, whether the *original* *credit was not given to the uncle. In this case, [*88]

Darnell v. *Tratt*.

(*m*) The defendant could certainly not have been sued on the articles of agreement, because he never authorized his wife to execute them at all, and supposing that he had done so, by writing *not under seal*, that would have been an insufficient authority to her to execute a deed. Moreover, supposing she had been authorized *by deed* to execute the said articles they would not have bound her husband, as she signed her own name instead of his.

(*n*) See last note.

(*o*) See now Married Women's Property Acts, *ante*, p. 16.

(*p*) *Ante*, p. 16. The Married Women's Property Act, 1882, does not seem to have affected the liability of the husband for contracts made by his wife as his agent, or by his authority. Macqueen's Husband and Wife, 3rd ed., 98.

(*q*) 2 C. & P. 82.

RULE I.
Ante, p. *55.

therefore, though the alleged principal debtor was a married woman, it was thought proper to treat this case as one presenting no extraordinary features, and make the nature of the uncle's liability depend on the answer of the jury to the question, *To whom was credit given* (r)? If, however, in this case the jury had found as a fact that credit was given to the *married woman*, in the first instance, the court would probably have held that the transaction was within the Statute of Frauds, on the ground that the wife was acting as the implied agent of her husband (s). In a case decided long before recent legislation enabling a married woman to contract as a *feme sole*, to the extent of her separate property, it was held that an undertaking by a husband to pay a loan made to his wife, at his request, was not a collateral undertaking (t).

Promises which extinguish principal debtor's liability not within the statute.

As a further corollary from the principle that a promise is not within the Statute of Frauds unless there be a third person who is primarily liable, it follows, as a general rule, that wherever the promise of the defendant has the effect of *extinguishing* or *releasing* the liability of the third person, it amounts to an *original* promise, and is therefore not within the 4th section of the Statute of Frauds In such cases there is, in fact, no principal debtor. Thus, as, under the old law, the discharge of a debtor taken under a *ca. sa.* destroyed the debt, it was held that a promise to *pay* the debt for which a person was thus taken was not within section 4 of the Statute of Frauds. For instance, in *Goodman v. Chase* (u), the plaintiff had taken A. B. under a *ca. sa.*

Goodman v. *Chase*.

[*89] *The defendant promised to pay A. B.'s debt in consideration of the plaintiff discharging him from custody. It was held that, as by the discharge of A. B. from custody, with the *consent* of the plaintiff, the debt itself was extinguished ; the promise made in consideration of that discharge was an original promise. .Lord *Ellenborough*, C. J., said : "By the discharge of *Chase* with the plaintiff's consent, the debt as between those persons was satisfied. . . . . Then, if so, the promise by the defendant here is not a collateral, but an original, promise, for which the consideration is the discharge of the debt as between the plaintiff and *Chase*. That be-

---

(r) In the case of *Maggs* v. *Ames*, too, cited *post* p. 90, the fact of the principal debtor being a married woman does not appear to have been noticed, though coverture was pleaded in order to show a want of consideration.
(s) See *ante*, p. 87.
(t) *Stevenson* v. *Hardie*, 2 W. Bl. 872 ; and see *post*, p. 129.
(u) 1 B. & A. 297.

RULE I.
Ante, p, *55.

ing so, it becomes wholly unnecessary to consider the
question arising out of the construction of the 4th section of the statute."

In *Butcher* v. *Steuart* (x), where the promise was also in
consideration of the discharge from custody of a third person arrested under a *ca. sa.*, *Goodman* v. *Chase* was followed

Butcher v.
Steuart.

So, again, in *Lane* v. *Burghart* (y), plaintiffs, having
taken one *Bacon* in execution for a debt, discharged
him upon the following undertaking of the defendant :
"In consideration of your discharging *Bacon* out of
custody, I undertake that he shall pay the debt due to
you by four half-yearly instalments," &c. The defendant subsequently became bankrupt and obtained his
certificate. Lord *Denman*, C. J., said : "*Bacon* was at
this time in custody under a *ca. sa.* for the debt in
question ; and, as that was entirely discharged by the
execution, and he could no longer be sued for it, or
make default in respect of it, it was argued, on the
authority of *Goodman* v. *Chase* (z), that this undertaking
was an original one, on the part of the bankrupt, to pay
the amount of the sum that had been due from *Bacon*,
and though in form it was an undertaking that *Bacon*
*should pay, yet, at most, it was an undertaking [*90]
by the defendant to pay by the hand of *Bacon*. On
consideration we agree that this is correct ; the unpaid
instalments might, therefore, have been estimated and
proved under the commission. It follows that his certificate is a bar to the action."

Lane v. *Burg-
hart.*

In *Maggs* v. *Ames* (a), the first count of the declaration stated that *Ann Prickett*, a married woman, was
indebted to the *Howells* before they became bankrupts,
and was arrested at their suit ; that, thereupon, in consideration that the *Howells* (before their bankruptcy)
would procure the discharge of *Ann Prickett*, and take
her bill of exchange for the amount of the debt, the
defendant undertook to pay the amount of the bill of
exchange, in case it should be dishonoured by *Ann
Prickett*. The *second count* was upon an undertaking
to pay the debt for which *Ann Prickett* was arrested, in
consideration of the *Howells* procuring her discharge.
It was held, that the undertaking stated in the first
count was within the Statute of Frauds, but that that
stated in the second count was not. It will be observed, that the reason the undertaking stated in the

Maggs v.
Ames.

(x) 11 M. & W. 857.
(y) 1 Q. B. 933.
(z) 1 B. & Ald. 297.
(a) 4 Bing. 470 ; 1 M. & P. 294. See *ante*, note (r), p. 88.

RULE I.
Ante, p. *55.

Where there
is a complete
novation the
statute does
not apply.

Anstey v.
Marden.

Transfer to
creditor of
debt due to
debtor from
third person
not within
statute.

second count could not be within the 4th section of the
Statute of Frauds is, because the consideration for it
was the discharge from arrest of the principal debtor,
and her consequent release from all liability.

On the same principle, where there is a complete
novation, that is to say, an arrangement, by which it is
provided that an old debt shall be discharged, and an
entirely new agreement and liability entered into, the
Statute of Frauds does not apply. Thus, in *Ex parte
Lane* (b), it was decided that if A. be a creditor of B.,
and B. and C. purpose to enter into, or have entered
into partnership, and say to A., " We wish this debt to
be a debt from us both, and we will pay it," and A.
[*91] *accedes to that, although there is no writing, the
agreement is valid and effectual, and is not in any way
affected by the Statute of Frauds. The effect of such
an agreement is to *extinguish* the first debt, and, for a
valuable consideration, to substitute the second debt.

So, again, in *Anstey* v. *Marden* (c), A. being insolvent,
a verbal agreement was entered into between several of
his creditors and B., whereby B. agreed to pay the creditors 10s. in the pound in satisfaction of their debts,
which they agreed to accept, and to assign their debts
to B. It was held that this agreement was not within
the Statute of Frauds, not being a collateral promise to
pay the debt of another, but an original promise to
purchase the debts.

Where A. sold goods to B., who, being unable to pay
for them, made a transfer thereof to C., who promised
A. to pay for them, it was held that this constituted a
new sale to C., and not a mere promise by C. to pay
the debt due from B. (d).

There is another class of cases turning upon the same
principle. These cases, which are of frequent occurrence, are cases in which a person to whom another is
indebted assigns or transfers the debt owing to him to
a person to whom he is himself indebted (e).

(b) 1 De Gex, 300.
(c) 1 N. R. 124. See this case *post*, pp. 143, 144. In the case
of *Emmet* v. *Dewhurst*, 3 Mac. & G. 587, which is very similar to
Anstey v. *Marden*, it did not appear that the liability of the principal debtor was extinguished, and the Statute of Frauds was
held to apply.
(d) *Browning* v. *Stallard*, 5 Taunt. 450.
(e) See *Israel* v. *Douglas*, 1 H. Bl. 239; *Tatlock* v. *Harris*, 3 T.
R. 174; *Hodgson* v. *Anderson*, 5 D. & R. 735; *S. C.*, 3 B. & C.
842; *Wilson* v. *Coupland*, 5 B. & A. 228; *Cuxon* v. *Chadley*, 3 B. &
C. 591; *Wharton* v. *Walker*, 6 D. & R. 288; 4 B. & C. 163; *Fairlie*
v. *Denton*, 2 M. & R. 353, and note (c), 355; *S. C.*, 8 B. & C. 395;
Roe v. *Haugh*, 3 Salk. 14.

Thus, suppose A. is debtor to B., and C. is debtor to A. for the same or a larger amount, and that the three agree that C. shall be B.'s debtor instead of A., and that *C. promises to pay B., in such a case B. may [*92] maintain an action against C. (*f*). "These cases are exceptions to the rule of law that a chose in action cannot be assigned. It is a necessary ingredient to this exception that the original debt from A. to B. should be extinguished, for B. cannot sue C. if he retains the right to sue A. (*g*). To such cases, therefore, the 4th section of the Statute of Frauds can have no application, since it is essential to the *validity* of the transaction that the transferor's liability be *extinguished*. In such a case, the substituted debtor, in fact, pays *his own debt* with *his own money*, to a substituted creditor, *i. e.*, the transferee (*h*). Thus, in *Lacy* v. *M'Neile* (*i*), one *Goodfellow*, indebted to the plaintiffs for goods sold, upon being released from his liability, assigned to them a debt due to him from the defendants. Notice of the assignment was given to a partner in the defendant's firm. who, *by parol*, promised, in the name of such firm, to pay the debt to the plaintiffs out of the partnership funds. It was held, in an action by the plaintiffs against the defendants for money had and received, that the promise was not within the Statute of Frauds. *Abbott*, C. J., in the course of the argument, said: "The defendant's debt to *Goodfellow* was assigned to the plaintiffs, and *Goodfellow* discharged from all liability to them; then, surely, the old debt by him was extinguished, and a new one by the defendants created."

Wilson v. *Coupland* (*k*) is another instance of this kind. There the plaintiffs were creditors, and the defendants debtors of T. & Co., and, by consent of all parties, *an arrangement was made that the de- [*93] fendants should pay to the plaintiffs the debt due from them to T. & Co. *The Statute of Frauds does not seem to have been alluded to in the case*, and it was held, that, as the demand of T. & Co. on the defendants was for money had and received, the plaintiffs were entitled to recover on a count for money had and received

*Rule I. Ante, p. *55.*

Lacy v. M'Neile.

Wilson v. Coupland.

(*f*) *Wilson* v. *Coupland*, 5 B. & A. 228; *Fairlie* v. *Denton*, 2 M. & R. 353, and note (*c*), 355; *S. C.*, 8 B. & C. 395.
(*g*) 1 Wms. Saund. p. 226, and the following cases there cited, viz., *Cuxon* v. *Chadley*, 3 B. & C. 591; *Wharton* v. *Walker*, 6 D. & R. 288; *S. C.*, 4 B. & C. 163. (See also *Parker* v. *Wise*, 6 N. & S. 239; *Liversieg* v. *Broadbent*, 4 H. & N. 603.)
(*h*) See also *post*, p. 125.
(*i*) 4 D. & R. 7, 9.
(*k*) 5 B. & Ald. 228.

RULE I.
Ante, p. *55.

Parkins v.
Moravia.

Hodgson v.
Anderson.

Browning v.
Stallard.

against the defendants (*l*). Now, in this case, the debt transferred actually *existed.*

In the case of *Parkins* v. *Moravia* (*m*), on the other hand, the transfer was not of an *existing* debt, but of a *contingent* one. There the defendant, in consideration that the plaintiffs would discount a bill of exchange for a person named *Benjamin, undertook* to pay the plaintiffs such sum of money as should be due from him to *Benjamin* for work done within a specified time. It was contended that the case was within the Statute of Frauds. *Abbot,* C. J., said, "It is an assignment of a thing not *in esse. Wilson* v. *Coupland* is not like this case." He also said, in answer to plaintiff's counsel, "it is to go to reduce the bill, and, therefore, it is to answer for the debt of another." It appears, from the report of this case, that another question was also raised as to the amount of stamp duty required, and a verdict was taken for the plaintiff, subject to the two points of law, in order that the opinion of the court above might be had on them, or a motion to enter a nonsuit. This motion never appears to have been made, and no further report of this case appears anywhere. Much importance cannot, therefore, be attached to it. Indeed, between this case and *Wilson* v. *Coupland* there seems to be no rational distinction (*n*).

Again, in *Hodgson* v. *Anderson* (*o*), where the [*94] *defendant, who owed A. B., a debtor of the plaintiff, a sum of money, at A. B.'s request promised the plaintiff to pay him what he (the defendant) owed A. B., such promise was held not to be within the 4th section of the Statute of Frauds, for A. B.'s debt was extinguished by the defendant's promise. The case of *Browning* v. *Stallard* (*p*) involves the same principle. There A. sold goods to B., who, being unable to pay for them, transferred them to C., who promised A. to pay for them. It was held, that the promise was not within the 4th section of the Statute of Frauds, as B. was discharged from all liability.

The cases which have now been cited abundantly illustrate the proposition that, to bring a case within the Statute of Frauds, there must be *a liability, present* or *future,* existing on the part of some person, other

---

(*l*) Otherwise he would, under the old rules of pleading, have had to declare specially. See *Wharton* v. *Walker,* 4 B. & C. 163.
(*m*) 1 C. & P. 376.
(*n*) Smith's Merc. Law, 9th ed., p. 463, n. (*o*).
(*o*) 5 D. & R. 735; *S. C.,* 3 B. & C. 842.
(*p*) 5 Taunt. 450.

than the promiser. It will not have been forgotten, RULE I.
however, that the rule we have laid down states, in the *Ante*, p. *55.
alternative, that there must *either* be some other person
actually liable in the first instance, *or* that the creation
of such liability at a future time must be contemplated.
Hitherto we have only considered the absolute necessity
which the rule creates, that there should be some actual
liability by a third person. It now becomes necessary
to discuss the question suggested by the terms of Rule
1, and to consider when, in point of time, a liability
may take its origin, and yet be such as to bring a case
within the Statute of Frauds.

Now, formerly, it was necessary that, *at the time* of Formerly, if
the making of the promise, some one should be *actually* promise made
liable, in the first instance, to the promisee, and a con- by surety be-
tract did not fall within sect. 4, if, at the time of the *fore* creation
of third
making of the promise, the creation of such liability at party's liabil-
some future period was only contemplated and not ity, statute
actually in existence. If, therefore, the promise were did not
made before creation of liability on the part of [*95] apply.
a third party for a debt, default or miscarriage, it was
deemed an original undertaking, and, therefore, not
within the Statute of Frauds. This enactment was
held to apply only to the promises made *after* the debt,
default or miscarriage of a third party.

This distinction, which now no longer exists, was first *Mowbray* v.
taken in the case of *Mowbray* v. *Cunningham* (q). There *Cunningham.*
goods were delivered to A., at the request of B., who
said *he would see them paid for.* Lord *Mansfield* held,
that, as the promise was *before* delivery of the goods, it
was not within the Statute of Frauds, because at the
time the promise was made there was no debt at all.
In *Jones* v. *Cooper* (r), Lord *Mansfield*, though at first
inclined to follow the case just cited, ultimately decided,
on the facts of the case before him, that there was a collateral promise within the Statute of Frauds. It is
right to mention, however, that there could be no doubt
that the promise, in *Jones* v. *Cooper*, was within the
statute, for it was in these words: "I will pay you if
Smith does not." But, in *Mowbray* v. *Cunningham*,
the words were: "If you supply goods to A. I will see
you paid," and the latter expression is clearly open to
a double construction.

(q) Sittings after Hil. T. 1773, at Guildhall, cited by *Buller*,
J., in *Matson* v. *Wharam*, 2 T. R. 80, and by Lord *Mansfield* in
Jones v. *Cooper*, Cowp. 227.

(r) Cowp. 227.

RULE L.
Ante. p. *55.

Peckham v.
Faria.

The next case which throws light upon the subject under discussion is *Peckham* v. *Faria* (*s*), where *Jones* v. *Cooper* was commented on. The facts are briefly as follows : The defendant, and one *Sylva*, came to the plaintiff's warehouse and agreed on a parcel of goods for *Sylva*, and the plaintiff asked if the defendant would answer for him ; the defendant said that he would guarantee the payment. *Sylva* came, on another occasion, by himself, and ordered other goods, when the [*96] *plaintiff sent to the defendant and asked him whether he would engage for *Sylva*. The defendant said, "You may not only ship that parcel, but one, two, or three thousand pounds more, *and I will pay you if he does not.*" This promise was made *before* the delivery of the goods to *Sylva*. The goods were *subsequently* delivered to *Sylva*. In giving judgment, Lord *Mansfield* said : "Before the case of *Jones* v. *Cooper*, I thought there was a solid distinction between an undertaking after credit given, and an original undertaking to pay ; and that, in the latter case, the surety, being the object of the confidence, was not within the statute, but, in *Jones* v. *Cooper*, the court was of opinion that, wherever a man is to be called upon only in the second instance, he is within the statute ; otherwise, where he is to be called upon in the first instance. Here, by the words of the promise, *Sylva* was to be called on first, the defendant undertaking to pay if *Sylva* did not pay.

Abrogation
of distinction
drawn in
Mowbray v.
Cunningham.

The case is not distinguishable from *Jones* v. *Cooper*, and the words of the statute are very strong." The distinction that was drawn in *Mowbray* v. *Cunningham* was finally abrogated in *Matson* v. *Wharam* (*t*). There the defendant asked the plaintiff whether he was willing to serve one R. C. with groceries ; and, upon the plaintiff answering that he did not know him, the defendant replied, "If you do not know *him* you know *me*, and I will see you paid." On the faith of this promise goods were sent to R. C.'s order, and R. C. was debited for the amount in the plaintiff's books. R. C. making default by not paying for the goods, the plaintiff sued the defendant, and a verdict was given for the plaintiff, subject to the opinion of the court upon the case as stated. On the argument, *Jones* v. *Cooper* and *Mowbray* v. *Cunningham* were cited by the plaintiff's counsel to show that there was a recognized distinction between [*97] *a promise for the payment of goods for another person *before* delivery and *after*. The court, however,

---

(*s*) 3 Dougl. 13.   (*t*) 2 T. R. 80.

RULE I.
Ante, p. * 55.

was clearly of opinion that that distinction had been overruled, though it may be observed that, in the judgment, no cases to this effect were cited (u). It will be noticed, however, from the judgment of *Buller*, J., that he regrets that the authorities do not *allow him* to decide in accordance with *Mowbray* v. *Cunningham.* He says, " If this were a new question, the leaning of my mind would be the other way ; for, Lord *Mansfield's* reasoning, in the case of *Mowbray* v. *Cunningham,* struck me very forcibly. But the authorities are not now to be shaken ; and the general line now taken is, that if the person for whose use the goods are furnished be liable at all, any other promise by a third person to pay that debt must be in writing, otherwise it is void by the Statute of Frauds, 29 Car. 2, c. 3, s. 4."

In many cases, and particularly where, as in *Birkmyr* v. *Darnell* (x), the promise *precedes* the liability of the third person, it often becomes extremely difficult to determine whether it is intended by the parties, that the third person should be primarily liable. In these cases the nature of the contract depends on the answer given by the jury to the question, " *To whom was credit given ?*" The well-known case of *Mountstephen* v. *Lakeman* (y), part of the judgment in which has been previously cited (z), furnishes an apt illustration of what has just been stated. It is proposed, therefore, to give a somewhat lengthy report of this case. The following facts were proved at the trial, which took place before *Kelly,* C. B., at the Devon Summer Assizes, 1870 :— The *plaintiff had been employed to construct a main [*98] sewer by a local board of health, of which the defendant was the chairman. Notice having been given by the board to the owners of certain houses, to connect their house drains with the main sewer within twenty-one days, the surveyor of the said board, before the expiration of that period, proposed to the plaintiff that he should construct the connections between the house drains and the main sewer. This the plaintiff said he was willing to do if the board would see him paid; and the plaintiff, accordingly, commenced the construction of the connections before the expiration of the twenty-one days. The plaintiff stated in evidence, that the

Where promise precedes third party's liability sometimes difficult to determine to whom credit given.

Mountstephen v. *Lakeman.*

(u) But see *Peckham* v. *Faria, ante,* and *Parsons* v. *Walter,* cited in note (c), 3 Dougl. 14.
(x) 1 Salk. 27 ; 2 Ld. Raym. 1085.
(y) L. R., 7 Q. B. 107 ; *S. C.,* L. R., 5 Q. B. 613 ; *S. C.,* 7 H. L. 17.
(z) *Ante,* p. 58.

RULE I.
Ante, p. *55.

day on which the construction of the connections was commenced, and an hour previous to the commencement, he was leaving with his carts and men, when the surveyor of the board stopped him and requested him not to go away, as there was more work to be done. The plaintiff asked who was to be responsible for the payment, and the surveyor answered that the defendant was waiting to see the plaintiff about it. The plaintiff then had an interview with the defendant, at which the following conversation took place. The defendant said, "What objection have you to making the connections?" The plaintiff said, "I have none, if *you* or the *board* will order the work or become responsible for the payment." The defendant replied, "Go on, *Mountstephen*, and do the work, and I will see you paid." The plaintiff, accordingly, did the work under the superintendence of the surveyor of the board; and on 5th December, 1860, sent in the account to the board, debiting them with the amount. The board refused payment, alleging that they had never, themselves, agreed with the plaintiff, or authorized any officer of the board to agree with him for the performance of the work in question. The plaintiff, for the first time, on the 20th November, 1869, applied to the defendant for payment [*99] of the work, and (the *defendant having refused to pay him) commenced the action.

The first count of the declaration alleged that, in consideration the plaintiff would do certain work for the board at the request of the defendant, as and assuming to be agent of the board, the defendant promised the plaintiff that he was authorized by the board to make such request. That the plaintiff did the work, but that the defendant turned out not to be authorized, and the plaintiff was unable to make the board pay. There was a second count, alleging the defendant's promise to be, that he would procure a contract from the board, whereby they should be bound to pay for the work. The third count was the common money count for work, labour, &c.

At the trial a further count was added, alleging the defendant's promise to be, that in consideration that the plaintiff would do the work for the board, the defendant promised to pay for the work, if the board should at any time refuse to pay.

The pleas were as follows :—To the money counts: Never indebted. And, to the other counts—

1. That the defendant did not promise as alleged.
2. That the plaintiff did not do the work at the de-

(1312)

RULE I.
Ante, p. *55.

fendant's request, as alleged. At the close of the plaintiff's case, the defendant claimed a nonsuit, on the ground that there was no evidence of any liability on the part of the defendant.

The judge declined to nonsuit, stating his opinion that there was evidence to support a count in the form above given, and which he gave the plaintiff leave to add. The defendant's case was then entered into, and the defendant denied that any conversation of the kind deposed to by the plaintiff had ever taken place. The judge left it to the jury to say whether the conversation did take place, and the jury returned a verdict for the plaintiff for the amount claimed. Leave was *re- [*100] served to the defendant to move to enter a nonsuit, if it should appear that either upon the original declaration, or upon the declaration as amended, there was no evidence which ought to have been left to the jury. The defendant obtained a rule to enter a nonsuit accordingly, on the ground that there was no evidence of original liability on the part of the defendant to the plaintiff for the work to be done ; or, for a new trial, on the ground that the verdict was against the evidence. The Court of Queen's Bench afterwards made the rule absolute to enter a nonsuit, on the ground that the defendant's promise was an undertaking to be answerable for the debt of another, within sect. 4 of the Statute of Frauds, and not being in writing was void. The Court of Exchequer Chamber, however, reversed the judgment of the Queen's Bench, on the ground that there was evidence on which the jury might have found that the defendant agreed to be primarily liable. It will be observed that, in this case, the real question was, what did the plaintiff and the defendant understand to be the effect of the conversation which passed between them? Did the defendant mean to make himself liable to the plaintiff whether the board became so or not, or did he mean to make himself liable only in the event of the board becoming liable, and then only in the *second* instance, and in which of these senses did the plaintiff understand the promise, or, in other words, *To whom did he give credit ?* *Willes*, J., in his judgment in the Exchequer Chamber, thus defines the nature of the contract entered into between the parties in this case: "It is," he says, "a bargain, therefore, by the defendant to pay for the work, though it was known that there was no person liable at the time, and whether a third person should become liable in future or not, that is, whether or not there was or might be a third

(1313)

RULE I.   person who could be *liable* for a debt, or *guilty* of a
Ante, p. *55. default or miscarriage in the matter. And it is only
[*101] *in respect of such a third person that the Statute
of Frauds applies." In the same judgment we also find
the following passage:—"In this case, seeing that the
parties knew that the board was not liable, and that
the plaintiff would not go on unless he had the board
or the defendant liable, and did not care to have the
defendant liable if the board was liable, the facts seem
to exclude, and the jury might well find that they excluded, the notion of the defendant becoming surety
for a liability, either past, present or future, upon the
part of the board; and they might look upon the defendant's contract as a contract to pay, whether the
board have been, are, or shall be liable or not. Do
that work now, and you shall be paid for that work.
So that is a case of principal liability." There are
also many other cases to be found in the reports, in
which, just as in *Mountstephen* v. *Lakeman*, it has been
held that the evidence showed a state of facts, from
which it might be inferred, that the liability of the
defendant was an original and primary liability. Thus,
Smith v. *Rud-* in *Smith* v. *Rudhall* (*a*), the defendant employed a
hall.   builder to erect some houses, and gave a guarantee for
a supply of materials to the builder to a certain amount.
Afterwards, the defendant gave an *order* for a future
supply to a certain amount: more materials were, ac
cordingly, supplied on the order of the builder, and,
at the trial, it was proved that the defendant himself
was constantly on the premises. Under these circumstances, it was held that it was for the jury to say
whether the defendant had so acted as to lead the
plaintiff to believe that the latter supply was to be on
his credit.

Edge v. *Frost.* A somewhat similar case is that of *Edge* v. *Frost* (*b*).
There the defendant undertook in writing that, if the
plaintiff would put up a certain gas apparatus in a
[*102] *theatre for one *John Brunton,* he (the defendant) would see the plaintiff paid for the said gas
apparatus. It appeared, however, at the trial, that the
defendant had himself given orders about the work
before and *after* the guarantee was given. *Abbot, C. J.,*
left it to the jury to determine whether the defendant,
though he had no interest in the theatre at the period
in question, was not one of the persons who had origi-

(*a*) 3 F. & F. 143.
(*b*) 4 D. & R. 243.

nally given orders for the gas apparatus, for, if he was, a verdict might be recovered upon his own personal liability, without regard to the guarantee (c).

So in *Scholes and another v. Hampson and Merriott* *Scholes v.* (d), the defendant *Hampson* having asked the plaintiffs *Hampson.* to sell him a quantity of goods upon credit, and the plaintiffs having refused to let him have them, unless some one would be *answerable for the payment*, he afterwards brought with him the other defendant, who was a near relation of his, but not at all connected with him in business, all of which facts were well known to the plaintiffs. The defendant *Merriott* then requested the plaintiffs to let *Hampson* have what cotton he might want; and *agreed verbally, that the credit should be given to them jointly, and the invoices made out in their joint names.* Several parcels of cotton were accordingly delivered by the plaintiffs to *Hampson*, who from time to time made payments for the same. But, becoming insolvent, this action was brought against him and *Merriott* for the balance. *Hampson* had let judgment go by default, and the question was as to the liability of *Merriott.* It was objected, on his behalf, that upon these facts *Merriott* could not be considered a partner, but was only surety for *Hampson's* payments, and that, *therefore, his undertaking was for the debt of [*103] another, and void by the Statute of Frauds as not being in writing. And it was contended that the permitting such parol promises to avail would be virtually to repeal the statute. But *Chambre*, J., overruled the objection, not thinking this to be a case within the statute, and the case was never afterwards questioned.

The same principles were acted upon in *Simpson* v. *Simpson v.* *Penton* (e). There the plaintiff introduced the defendant *Penton.* to one *Overston*, an upholsterer, and in his presence asked *Overston* if he had any objection to supply the defendant with some furniture, and that if he would, he (the plaintiff) "would be answerable." The upholsterer, having asked the plaintiff how long credit he wanted, plaintiff replied, "he would see it paid at the end of six months." *Overston* having agreed to give this credit, the plaintiff gave him the order, and the goods were accordingly supplied. At the end of six months the

---

(c) In this case the jury found their verdict for the plaintiff for the sum demanded, on the common counts for work and labour, and materials found, on the ground, that the defendant was one of the persons who originally gave the order for the work.
(d) Cited in Fell on Guarantees, 2nd ed., p. 27.
(e) 2 C. & M. 430. See also *Dixon v. Hatfield*, 2 Bing. 439.

RULE I.
Ante, p. *55.

defendant, not having paid the amount, the upholsterer applied to the plaintiff for payment, and he paid the money. The entry in *Overston's* book was, "Mr. Penton (*f*) per Mr. *Simpson*" (*g*). It was held, that this was an original and not a collateral undertaking, on the ground that credit was clearly given entirely to the defendant, and that the jury were warranted in so finding. In this case, *Bayley*, B., said: "I think that the expressions 'I'll be answerable,' and 'I'll see you paid,' are equivocal expressions. And then we ought to look to the circumstances to see what the contract between the parties was. I do not say that without authority; for [*104] there was a case (*h*) which I believe will *be found in the 2nd Volume of Douglas (*i*), in which the Court of King's Bench said, that a contract might be collateral or not, according to circumstances, and that it depends on the circumstances whether it is collateral or not. It was the case of *Oldham* v. *Allen*, and was decided in Michaelmas Term, in the 24th of Geo. 3: there the defendant had sent for a farrier to attend some horses, and said to the farrier, 'I will see you paid.' The plaintiffs knew the parties, who were owners of some of the horses, and made them debtors, but debited the defendant for the others, whose owners he did not know; the court held, that the promise was original, in respect of those owners, whose names he did not know; but, in respect of the others whom he did know, that it was collateral. In that case there was a construction on the very same words, making the promise either original or collateral, according to the circumstances. Here it is quite clear that the goods were furnished for *Penton's* benefit; but it does not appear that he said one word by which he pledged himself, so as to give *Overston* a right to call upon him. *Simpson* was asked what time he wanted to pay. He says, 'I'll see it paid in six months.' . It was left to the jury to say whether he was the original debtor, and they found that he was. I think the jury were warranted in that finding. My opinion is founded substantially on the facts of the case, and not on the equivocal expressions, as I consider the words capable of being explained by other circumstances. I am satisfied that, though *Overston* was willing to see if

(*f*) *I. e.*, the defendant in the above case.
(*g*) *I. e.*, the plaintiff in the above case.
(*h*) See, however, *Gordon* v. *Martin, post*, p. 105, which is perhaps the earliest authority on this point.
(*i*) *Semble*, not reported anywhere.

Penton would pay, he never had a legal claim upon him but upon *Simpson* only " (*k*).

RULE I.
Ante, p. *55.

*Perhaps, however, one of the earliest author- [*105] ities for the principles just laid down is the case of *Gordon* v. *Martin* (*l*). There the promise was as follows: "If L. S. shall go through the purchase (the defendant's brother having been then in the treaty, with the said L. S. for the sale of an estate), my brother will.give you a handsome gratuity for the trouble and pains you shall be at in transacting the affair, which I promise and assure you, shall not be less than 300*l.* My meaning is, you shall be paid when the conveyances shall be executed." The whole court held, that though the promise was that the defendant's brother shall pay the gratuity, yet it bound the defendant as much as if he had promised for himself; for the work and labour was at his request and upon his credit. And Mr. Justice *Lee* said, that there was a difference between a conditional and an absolute undertaking, as if A. promise to pay B. such a sum if C. does not, there A. is but a security for C. But if A. promise that C. will pay such a sum, A. is the principal debtor; for the act done was on his credit, and no way upon C. The Statute of Frauds was not, it seems, directly referred to in this case.

Gordon v.
Martin.

On the other hand, there are several cases in which the attempt to render the defendant liable, as on a primary and original agreement, has failed. And the courts have held, that, *upon the facts of the case*, the liability was clearly only collateral, and there was no evidence from which a primary liability could possibly be inferred. A leading instance of this kind is the case of *Keate* v. *Temple* (*m*). There the defendant, a first *lieutenant in the Navy, serving on board her [*106] Majesty's ship *Boyne*, requested the plaintiff, a tailor and slopseller, to supply the crew of the *Boyne* with clothing, at the same time making use of the following words:—"*I will see you paid at the pay-table: are you satisfied?*" the plaintiff answered, "*Perfectly so.*" It

Cases in which facts rebut existence of primary liability and promiser is a mere surety.

Keate v. Temple.

(*k*) In the following cases the words " I'll see you paid," or words almost identical with these, were made use of by the promiser. See *Birkmyr* v. *Darnell*, Salk. 27; 2 Lord Raym. 1085; *Matson* v. *Wharam*, 2 T. R. 80; *Bateman* v. *Phillips*, 15 East, 472; *Mountstephen* v. *Lakeman*, 7 H. L. 17; L. R., 7 Q. B. 197; S. C., 5 Q. B. 613; *Clancy* v. *Piggott*, 4 Nev. & Mann. 496; *Watkins* v. *Perkins*, 1 Lord Raym. 224; *Mowbray* v. *Cunningham*, cited by *Buller*, J., 2 T. R. 80; *Simpson* v. *Penton*, 2 C. & M. 430; *Keate* v. *Temple*, B. & Pull. 158. See also observations of *Holt*, J., in *Austen* v. *Baker*, 12 Mod. 250.

(*l*) Fitzg. 302.

(*m*) *Ubi supra.*

appeared in the evidence that the clothes were delivered on the quarter deck of the *Boyne ;* that slops were usually sold on the main deck; that the defendant produced samples to ascertain whether his directions had been followed; that some of the men, who said they did not want clothes at all, were compelled by the defendant to take them; while others, who did not want a complete suit, were compelled against their will to take what they did not want. It also appeared that some time after the delivery the *Boyne* was burnt, and the crew dispersed into different ships. The plaintiff then expressed some apprehensions for himself and was told by the defendant, "Captain *Grey* (captain of the *Boyne*) and I will see you paid: you need not make yourself uneasy."

Lawrence, J., who tried the action (which was *assumpsit* for the goods sold and delivered, work and labour and common money counts), left it to the jury to say, if they were satisfied on the evidence that the goods in question were advanced on the credit of the defendant as immediately responsible, in which case the plaintiff would be entitled to a verdict; or if they believed that, at the time the goods were furnished, the plaintiff relied on being able, through the assistance of the defendant, to get his money from the crew, then they ought to find for the defendant. The jury found a verdict for the plaintiff. A rule *nisi* was then obtained for a new trial, on the ground that the defendant's undertaking was within the Statute of Frauds, section 4. This rule was made absolute, but only on the ground that the verdict was against the weight of the evidence. The court considered that, upon the facts, the weight of the evidence [*107] *went to show that credit was originally given to the crew, and not to the defendant, whose very position tended to negative the supposition that he had made himself answerable, *in the first instance,* for so large a sum as the amount of the plaintiff's claim.

Rains v. *Story.* A similar conclusion was arrived at in the case of *Rains* v. *Story* (*n*). There A. applied to B. for goods; B. asked for a reference; A. referred him to C. C., on being applied to, inquired the amount of the order, and on what terms the goods were to be furnished, and, on being told, said, "You may send them, and *I'll take care that they are paid for at the time.*" He was afterwards written to, to accept a bill for the amount, to which he replied, that he was not in the habit of ac-

---

(*n*) 3 C. & P. 130.

cepting bills, *but that the money would be paid when*   Rule I.
due. After this, B., the seller, wrote to C. about the   *Ante*, p. *55.
goods, and spoke of them in his letter as goods which
C. had "*guaranteed,*" and the attorney of B.'s assignees
(when B. had become bankrupt) wrote to A. for the
money, and threatened process; but this letter was a
circular, written in pursuance of a list made out for
him by B., and without any knowledge of the circumstances under which the debt was contracted. It was
held, that on this evidence C. was not primarily liable,
but only as a guarantor of the debt of A.

To a like effect is the case of *Anderson* v. *Hayman*   *Anderson* v.
Hayman.
(*o*). There, the plaintiff's traveller, at the request of
the defendant, wrote to the plaintiff, requesting him to
supply the defendant's son with goods, stating that the
defendant would be answerable for the payment of the
money due for the goods, as far as 800*l.* or 1,000*l.* went
The defendant's son was debited in the plaintiff's books,
and, being applied to for payment, wrote to say that he
had expected a twelvemonth's credit, and added : "I
shall, *at this rate, make you remittance for the [*108]
different parcels as they come due." The son failed,
and the defendant was accordingly sued for the value
of the goods. The declaration contained seven counts,
which were as follows :—The first was on an agreement
by the defendant to pay, &c., in consideration that the
plaintiff would sell the goods to his son; the second
was on a *quantum meruit;* the third was for goods sold
and delivered to the son at the request of the defendant; the fourth was on a *quantum meruit;* the fifth was
for money paid to the use of the defendant; the sixth
was for goods sold and delivered to the son on a promise by the defendant to see the plaintiff paid, to the
amount of 800*l.*; the seventh was the same promise on
a *quantum meruit.* The defendant *pleaded* the general
issue. *Heath,* J., who tried the cause, directed the jury
whether the plaintiff gave credit to the defendant *alone,*
or to him, *together with his son,* telling them that, in
the former case, they would find a verdict for the plaintiff; in the latter, for the defendant, being of opinion
that, if any credit was given to the son, the promise of
the defendant, not being in writing, was void by the
Statute of Frauds. A verdict was found for the defendant. A rule was obtained to show cause why this
verdict should not be set aside, and a new trial granted.
Ultimately this rule was discharged, as the court was

(*o*) 1 H. Bl. 120; see also *Croft* v. *Smallwood,* 1 Esp. 121.

RULE I.
Ante, p. *55.

Entry in plaintiff's books sometimes indicates to whom credit was given.

Austen v. *Baker.*

clearly of opinion that this promise, not being in writing, was void by the Statute of Frauds, as it appeared from the evidence that credit was given to the defendant's son as well as to the defendant.

The manner in which the transaction is entered in the plaintiff's books often has a great effect in determining to whom credit was originally given, and so in determining whether defendant's liability is original or not

Thus, in *Austen* v. *Baker* (p), which was decided about [*109] *the year 1790, we read that, *assumpsit* having been brought against *Baker,* upon a promise supposed to be made by him to pay for goods delivered by the plaintiff to A., *Holt,* C. J., took this difference : "If B. desire A. to deliver goods to C., and promise to see him paid, there *assumpsit* lies against B., though, in that case, he·said at *Guildhall,* he always required the tradesman to produce his books, to see whom credit was given to. But if, after goods delivered to C. by A., B. says to A., ' *You shall be paid for the goods,*' it will be hard to saddle him with the debt."

Stow v. *Scott.*

So, also, in the more modern case of *Stow* v. *Scott* (q), it was held that, when a tradesman makes out an account for goods in the name of a particular person, it must be taken that they were furnished on the credit of such person, unless it be shown by *unequivocal* evidence, that the credit was, in fact, given to another.

Sometimes, though credit entirely given to promiser, Statute of Frauds applies.

Moreover, the question, "To whom was credit given?" is not an infallible test by which to discover, in all cases, whether or not the promise falls within the 4th section of the Statute of Frauds. For sometimes it happens that credit is entirely given to the promiser, and yet the promise is within the 4th section of the Statute of Frauds. This is the case whenever the promise *has not the effect of discharging the original debtor.* Thus, in *Barber* v. *Fox* (r), where A. promised an attorney that, if he would *continue* to act for B. in certain legal proceedings, he would pay him whatever was to be paid, it was held that the 4th section of the Statute of Frauds applied. Lord *Ellenborough,* in giving judgment, said: "This was the inchoate business and debt of another, and if the defendant had promised in writing, he would have made himself liable; without a promise in writing, he is not liable."

Barber v. *Fox.*

(*p*) 12 Mod. 250.
(*q*) 6 C. & P. 241.
(*r*) 1 Stark. 270.

*RULE II.—*The promise must be made to the* [*110]   RULE II.
creditor, i. e., to the person to whom another is already,
or is thereafter, to become liable.*   The promise
    It is now quite clear that a promise to answer for the must be
debt, default or miscarriage of another person, to come creditor.
within the 4th section of the Statute of Frauds, must
be made to the person to whom another is already, or
is thereafter, to become liable (s). This was first decided in *Eastwood* v. *Kenyon* (t). There, the plaintiff *Eastwood* v.
was liable to a Mr. *Blackburn* on a promissory note, and *Kenyon.*
the defendant, for a valid consideration, promised the
plaintiff to pay and discharge the note to *Blackburn.*
It was held that, as the promise was made to the debtor,
and not to the creditor, the statute did not apply. Lord
Denman, C. J., in the course of his judgment in this
case, said: "If the promise had been made to *Blackburn,*
doubtless the statute would have applied; it would
then have been strictly a promise to answer for the debt
of another; and the argument on the part of the defendant is, that it is not less the debt of another, because the promise is made to that other, viz., the debtor,
and not to the creditor, the statute not having in terms
stated to whom the promise contemplated by it is to be
made. *But, upon consideration, we are of opinion that
the statute applies only to promises made to the person
to whom another is answerable* (u).
    So, also, in the case of *Reader* v. *Kingham* (x), it *Reader* v.
appeared that one *Malins* had recovered a judgment in *Kingham.*
the county court against one *Hitchcock* for 34l., debt
and costs. A warrant had been obtained for the com-
mittal of *Hitchcock* to gaol for thirty days, and placed
in the hands of the plaintiff, *Reader,* who was bailiff of
*the county court. Though the debt and cost [*111]
exceeded 34l., the bailiff appears to have been instructed
by *Malins* to accept 17l. in satisfaction. The bailiff
being about to arrest *Hitchcock, Kingham* verbally
promised the bailiff (plaintiff) that, if he would abstain
from executing the warrant, he would, on the following
Saturday, either pay the 17l. or surrender *Hitchcock.*
The money not having been paid, and *Hitchcock* not
having been surrendered, the bailiff brought an action
to recover the 17l. On the argument, it was conceded

(s) Per *Parke,* B., in *Hargreaves* v. *Parsons,* 13 M. & W. 561.
(t) 11 A. & E. 438, 3 P. & D. 276, 4 Jur. 1081.
(u) *Gregory* v. *Williams,* 3 Meriv. 582, is also an instance of a
promise made to a debtor to pay his debt to a third party, though
it was decided on other grounds.
(x) 13 C. B., N. S. 344.

RULE II.
Ante, p. *110.

Wildes v.
Dudlow.

that the arrest and imprisonment of *Hitchcock*, under the warrant, would not have operated to discharge the debt; but it was held, that, inasmuch as the debt was due to *Malins* from *Hitchcock*, and as the promise was made to *Reader* (the bailiff), that the Statute of Frauds did not apply to the case, and that, therefore, the defendant was liable on his promise to the plaintiff, though it was not in writing. The decision in *Reader* v. *Kingham* was followed in the recent case of *Wildes* v. *Dudlow* (*y*). There A. at the request of, and on a verbal offer by B. to indemnify him against loss, joined with C. in a joint and several promissory note which he was afterwards compelled to pay. It was held, that the offer to indemnify A. was not an agreement within the statute, and therefore need not be in writing, and that A., having afterwards become the executor of B., was entitled to retain the amount paid by him on the note as a debt due to him from B.'s estate. Another instance of the same doctrine is afforded by the case of *Hargreaves* v. *Parsons* (*z*). In that case the defendant and one *Parker* agreed for the sale by *Parker* to the defendant of the "put or call" of fifty foreign railway shares at a certain price per share premium at any time on or before the 18th February, 1844. Before that day the defendant agreed to re-sell the option to the [*112] *plaintiff and to guarantee the performance of the agreement by *Parker*. On the 16th February the plaintiff "called" the shares, but it was at the same time *verbally* agreed between him and the defendant and *Parker* that they should be delivered by *Parker* to the plaintiff not on the 18th February, but on the 2nd March, at Paris. It was held, that this was not an agreement by the defendant to be answerable for the default of *Parker*. *Parke*, B., in his judgment, says: "*The statute applies only to promises made to the persons to whom another is already or is to become answerable.* It must be a promise to be answerable for a debt of or a default in some duty by that other person *towards a promisee.* This was decided, and no doubt rightly, by the Court of Queen's Bench, in *Eastwood* v. *Kenyon* (*a*) and in *Thomas* v. *Cook* (*b*). In this case, *Parker* had not contracted with the *plaintiff*, nor was it intended that he should; there was no privity between them; the non-performance of *Parker's* con-

(*y*) L. R., 19 Eq. 198.
(*z*) 13 M. & W. 561.
(*a*) 11 A. & E. 438.
(*b*) 8 B. & C. 728.

tract with the *defendant* would be no default towards RULE II.
the plaintiff, and, consequently, the undertaking by the *Ante*, p. *110.
defendant was no promise to answer for the default or
miscarriage of *Parker* in any debt or duty towards the
plaintiff. It was an original promise that a certain
thing should be done by a third person."

The case of *Thomas* v. *Cook* (c) proceeded upon the *Thomas v*
same principle. There it had become necessary for *Cook.*
Cook (who was a debtor of one *Morris*) to find sureties.
He applied to the plaintiff to join him in a bond and
bill of exchange, and undertook to save him harmless.
It was *held*, that the promise of the defendant was not
within the 4th section of the Statute of Frauds. *Bayley*, J., in his judgment, says: "Here the bond was
given to *Morris* as the creditor, but the promise in question was not made to him. A promise to him would
have been to answer for the default of the debtor."
Parke, J., said, "If the plaintiff, at the request [*113]
of the defendant, had paid money to a third person, a
promise to repay it need not have been in writing, and
this case is, in substance, the same."

The cases of *Green* v. *Cresswell* (d) and *Cripps* v.
Hartnoll (e), when read together, also will exemplify
the rule laid down by Baron *Parke* in *Hargreaves* v.
Parsons (*ante*), that a promise to be within the 2nd
clause of the 4th section of the Statute of Frauds,
"must be a promise to be answerable for a debt of or
a default in some duty by that other towards the
promisee."

In *Green* v. *Cresswell* (f) the plaintiff became bail for *Green v.*
another person in a *civil* case, at the request of the de- *Cresswell.*
fendant, in consideration of the defendant promising
to indemnify the plaintiff against the consequences. It
was held, that no action lay on the defendant's promise, as it was not in writing. In *Cripps* ⊕ *Hartnoll* (g),
on the contrary, where the plaintiff, at the request of
the defendant, entered into a recognizance of bail for

(c) *Supra.*
(d) 11 A. & E. 453. It is stated, in Chitty on Contracts, 9th
ed., p. 484, note (q), that the case of *Jarmain* v. *Algar*, (2 C. & P.
249), conflicts with *Green* v. *Cresswell.* But, it is submitted, that
is not the case ; for, whilst in the *latter* case the bail bond was *actually signed*, in the *former* case the bail bond was *never executed*
by the defendant, who was, therefore, never *actually bail* for the
third person. The case of *Jarmain* v. *Algar* has already been
commented on, *ante*, p. 74.
(e) (In Cam. Scac.), 4 B. & S. 414, reversing the decision of
the Q. B., in 2 B. & S. 677.
(f) See note (d), *supra.*
(g) 4 B. & S. 414.

RULE II. the appearance of a third person to answer a *criminal*
Ante, p. *110 charge, and the defendant, in consideration thereof,
———   promised to indemnify the plaintiff against all liability
and from all costs, damages and expenses in respect of
the same; it was *held*, that the defendant's promise
was not within the 4th section of the Statute of Frauds.
The distinction between these two cases is well pointed
out by *Williams*, J., in his judgment in the case last
cited : "I ought," he says, "to remark, that I do not
[*114] deem it at *all necessary for us to say whether
the case of *Green* v. *Cresswell* is good law or not, but I
think there is a distinction between the recognizance of
bail in a *civil* suit and the recognizance given for the
appearance of a defendant in a *criminal* proceeding.
whether, in a case where the plaintiff becomes bail for
a stranger in a *civil* suit, there is a duty, as between
the defendant in the action and the surety, that he will
render or pay the debt, so as to reconcile the case of *Green*
v. *Cresswell* with the doctrine that the statute applies
only to promises made to a person for whom another is
answerable, I think that, where bail is given in a *crim
inal* suit, there is certainly no debt or duty which can
be considered as due to the surety from the party on
whose behalf the recognizance is given. The statute,
therefore, cannot be held to apply to such a case with
out overruling the doctrine to which I have alluded,
which was not disputed in argument before us, and is
established by the cases of *Eastwood* v. *Kenyon* and
Hargreaves v. *Parsons*. In *Thomas* v. *Cook* it may be
observed, that, although *Bayley*, J., puts the case upon
the ground that the 4th section of the Statute of Frauds
does not apply to a promise to indemnify, *Parke*, J., afterwards Lord *Wensleydale*, who was the only other
judge in that case, certainly does not put it at all upon
that ground."

It remains to notice that there are also one or two
cases which, although not decided upon this ground,
may be supported upon the principle that a promise to
answer for another's debt, default or miscarriage, is not
within sect. 4 of the Statute of Frauds, unless it be
Castling v. made to the creditor himself. The case of *Castling* v.
Aubert.   *Aubert* (h) is an instance of this kind. There the
plaintiff, being a broker, had, as such, a lien upon certain policies of insurance for acceptances he had given
for A. The defendant, who was also a broker, being
[*115] *employed by A. to conduct his insurance busi
ness, was anxious to procure the polices in order to col-

———

(h) 2 East, 325.

lect, for his principal, the moneys due thereon, and, ac-   RULE II.
cordingly, induced the plaintiff to part with his lien on   *Ante*, p. *110.
the said policies by *verbally* promising to provide for
the plaintiff's acceptances at maturity.   It was held,
that the defendant's promise was not within the 4th
section of the Statute of Frauds.   Now, here, it will be
observed, that, as first pointed out by Mr. *Throop*, in
his work on the Validity of Verbal Agreements (*i*), the
promise of the defendant was made to one who, as acceptor, was a principal debtor, and this reason is, of
itself, sufficient to exclude the case from the operation
of the statute.   It is proper to observe, however, that
the case is put upon other grounds in the judgment,
which rests the decision upon the principle that the
transaction was to be considered as a purchase by the
defendant of the plaintiff's interest in the policies—a
promise by the defendant to pay what the plaintiff
would be liable to pay, if the plaintiff would furnish
him with the means of doing so—and that it, therefore,
fell within the decisions which have before been considered (*k*).

A similar case is *Love's Case* (*l*), where the sheriff had   *Love's case.*
taken goods in execution upon a *fi. fa.*, and a promise
to the officer, by a third party, to pay him the debt, in
consideration that he would restore them, was held to
be an original promise not within the statute.   This
case, like *Castling* v. *Aubert*, just cited, may be supported upon the ground that the promise was not made
to a person to whom another was already liable, and,
therefore, fell within *Eastwood* v. *Kenyon* (*m*) and *Hargreaves* v. *Parsons* (*n*) ; although it may also be placed
upon the ground that, after the seizure, the goods, and
not the execution debtor, were liable for the debt, and
that the *decision consequently fell within the [*116]
principle of a class of cases which have before been
discussed (*o*).

RULE III.— *There must be an absence of all liability*   RULE III.
on the part of the promiser (the surety), except such as
arises from his express promise.   Promiser's
The decision of the Court of Common Pleas in *Fitz-*   liability
must arise

(*i*) See p. 389.
(*k*) See *ante*, p. 70.
(*l*) 1 Salk. 23.
(*m*) 11 A. & E. 438.
(*n*) 13 M. & W. 561.
(*o*) See *ante*, p. 67.

92

THE LAW OF GUARANTEES.

RULE III.
Ante, p. *116.

from his express promise only.

Fitzgerald v. *Dressler.*

gerald v. *Dressler* (p) expressly recognizes the existence of a general rule to the effect here set out. Before that decision there had been (as we shall presently see) numerous cases, the decisions in which are in truth to be referred to the existence of the rule; but the rule itself never seems to have been before propounded in terms. *Fitzgerald* v. *Dressler* was as follows : A. sold goods to B., through a broker, which goods B. afterwards sold to C. through the same broker. C. was under terms to pay B. for the goods, before the time fixed for payment from B. to A. In order to induce A. to hand over the goods before the day fixed for payment of the goods by B., C. promised A. that B. should pay on the day named. A. accordingly parted with his vendor's lien. It was held, that C.'s promise was not within the 4th section, because at the time of C.'s promise the goods were the property of C., subject to A.'s lien for the price. *Cockburn,* C. J., in delivering judgment, said : "We are all agreed that the case is not within the Statute of Frauds. The law upon this subject is, I think, correctly stated in the notes to *Forth* v. *Stanton,* 1 Wms. Saund. 211, e, where the learned editor thus sums up the result of the authorities : 'There is considerable difficulty in the subject, occasioned, perhaps, by unguarded expressions in the reports of the different cases ; but the fair result seems to be, that the question whether any particular case comes within this [*117] clause of the statute (s. 4) or not depends, *not on the consideration for the promise, but on the fact of the original party remaining liable, coupled with the absence of any liability on the part of the defendant or his property, except such as arises from his express promise.' I quite concur in that view of the doctrine, provided the proposition is considered as embracing the qualification at the conclusion of the passage; for though I agree that the consideration alone is not the test, but that the party taking upon himself the obligation upon which the action is brought, makes himself responsible for the debt or default of another, still it must be taken with the qualification stated in the note above cited, viz., an absence of prior liability, on the part of the defendant or his property ; it being, as I think, truly stated there, as the result of the authorities, that if there be something more than a mere undertaking to pay the debt of another, as where the property in consideration of the giving up of which the party

(p) 7 C. B., N. S. 374.
(1326)

enters into the undertaking is in point of fact his own, RULE III. or is property in which he has some interest, the case *Ante,* p. * 116. is not within the provision of the statute, which was intended to apply to the case of an undertaking to answer for the debt, default or miscarriage of another, where the person making the promise has no interest in the property which is the subject of the undertaking. I therefore agree with my learned brothers that this case is not within the Statute of Frauds."

The rule, in the terms in which it is thus set forth, is, it is submitted, the true rule, and one which will on examination be found to support a large number of cases which without it seem difficult to understand, and some of which, in the absence of the explanation afforded by it, appear to conflict with each other. But it is only right to observe that, in many cases which it is submitted are really illustrations of the present rule (*q*), *and in some others also (*r*), the reason given [*118] for their exception from the operation of the Statute of Frauds is, because there was a new consideration arising between the plaintiff and defendant, or, as it is sometimes put, because the consideration was an advantage to the defendant rather than to a third party. Now, it is submitted, that though these cases are rightly decided, yet that the test suggested by them for ascertaining whether a case falls within that portion of the Statute of Frauds relating to guarantees or not, is by no means satisfactory. For, if you adopt as a test the question, "Is there a new consideration arising between the creditor and the promiser?" or the question, "Is the consideration an advantage to the defendant rather than to a third party?" you give rise to great misconception. It either leads to the supposition that a promise to be answerable for the debt, default or miscarriage of another person, requires no consideration at all to support it; or to the equally erroneous supposition, that the consideration for such a promise *must* be an advantage to the promiser. Besides, either of the above-mentioned tests concentrates the attention upon the *consideration* for the promise, instead of upon the *promise* itself; and whatever formerly may have been the rule, it is quite clear now that, to determine whether or not a case falls within the 2nd clause of the 4th

Margin notes:
Many cases referable to this rule (III.), *semble,* decided on wrong grounds.

The nature of the *promise* determines whether statute applies.

(*q*) See *Houlditch* v. *Milne,* 3 Esp. 86; *Walker* v. *Taylor,* 6 C. & P. 652; *Williams* v. *Leper,* 2 Wils. 308; *Thomas* v. *Williams,* 10 B. & C. 664.
(*r*) See *Edwards* v. *Kelly,* 6 M. & S. 204; *Tomlinson* v. *Gill,* Amb. 330.

RULE III.
Ante, p. *116.

section of the Statute of Frauds, the question to be asked is, "What is *the promise?* not what is the *consideration* for such promise?" (s)

The only case in which the consideration can affect the terms of the promise is, where the consideration is the *extinguishment* of the liability of the original party.

Cases in which a lien or other such security given up in consideration of defendant's promise.

It will be best to consider under different heads the various cases which it is submitted really fall within the rule now under consideration, but in which another and [*119] *different reason for their being outside the Statute of Frauds was given by the judges who decided them. The first class of cases of this kind are those in which a lien or some similar security has been given up in consideration of the defendant's promise. A good instance of this sort is afforded by the case of *Walker* v. *Taylor* (t).

Walker v. *Taylor.*

There one of the partners of a firm of distillers having died, his widow deposited with the undertaker of her husband's funeral the beer and spirit licences of the house, as security for the payment of his bill. Being in want of these licences the surviving partner promised the undertaker that, if he would give them up, he would pay his bill for the funeral. It was held, that the undertaker, having given up the licences to the surviving partner, might recover his bill against him, although the widow was his original employer, and although he had made out his account charging the administrator as his debtor. On its being suggested that the above promise of the surviving partner to the undertaker was to pay the debt of another, *Tindal*, C. J., said, "You mean under the Statute of Frauds. But it is a new contract, under a new state of circumstances. It is not 'I will pay if the debtor cannot;' but it is, 'In consideration of that which is an advantage to me, I will pay you this money.' There is a whole class of cases in which the matter is excepted from the statute on account of the consideration arising immediately between the parties. It is a new contract; it has nothing whatever to do with the Statute of Frauds at all" (u). In this case it is to be noticed that the defendant, being part owner of the property which formed the subject of the lien, was liable independently of his promise.

(s) See also observations on this subject in 1 Wms. Saund. (last ed.), note to *Forth* v. *Stanton*.
(t) 6 C. & P. 652.
(u) See Chitty on Contracts, 8th ed., p. 478, for observation on this case, which, however, is not repeated in the subsequent editions.

The cases of *Gull* v. *Lindsay* (x), *Clancy* v. *Piggott* (y), **RULE III.**
*seem at first sight to conflict with *Walker* v. [*120] *Ante*, p. *116.
Taylor (*supra*), and with the case of *Houlditch* v. *Milne*
(which has been cited at a previous page (z)). It is,
however, submitted that these cases are easily reconcil-
able when viewed by the light of the explanation which
Rule III. affords. In *Gull* v. *Lindsay*, the plaintiff (an   *Gull* v.
agent) was employed to procure charterers for a ship,   *Lindsay.*
on the terms of paying himself out of the freight which
he was to receive for that purpose. Before the freight
was earned the ship changed owners, and the new owners
being anxious to obtain possession of the ship, the defendants, who were the brokers of the new owners, promised plaintiff that if he would abandon his right of receiving the freight, they, the defendants, would pay him
his said commission. It was held, that this was an
agreement to answer for the debt of another within the
Statute of Frauds. *Pollock*, C. B., in giving the judgment of the court making the rule absolute to set aside
a verdict which had been entered for the plaintiff, and
to enter a nonsuit or verdict for the defendant (*inter
alia*), said: "We think that the defendants' counsel
were right in saying that this contract was a contract
made to pay the debt of another within the Statute of
Frauds. It was not a case of transfer of liability, as
if A. had agreed to accept C., a debtor of B., as his debtor,
in lieu of him. It is plain that, although the defendants
agreed to pay the plaintiff, *yet the debt to him still remained due from the owners by whom he was retained.*
It was, therefore, necessary that the consideration should
appear in writing, signed by the defendants; and the consideration we have already stated is a very different one
from that declared on."

In *Clancy* v. *Piggott* (a), the declaration in assumpsit   *Clancy* v.
stated, that A. owed the plaintiff 5*l.*, and that the   *Piggott.*
plaintiff had a lien on goods of A.; that the defendant,
*in consideration that the plaintiff would aban- |*121]
don such lien and restore such goods to A., promised to
see him paid the said 5*l.* within three months. Averment, that plaintiff abandoned his lien. The plea alleged that this was a promise within the Statue of
Frauds, and that there was no agreement in writing
stating the consideration. It was held, that the promise was clearly within the meaning of the Statute of

---

(x) 4 Exch. 45.
(y) 4 Nev. & Mann. 496.
(z) See *ante*, p. 65, where the case is discussed under Rule I.
(a) 4 Nev. & Mann. 496.

RULE III.
Ante, p. *116.

Frauds. Now, it is submitted, that the two cases just cited do not in reality, and when explained by Rule III., at all conflict with the authorities previously mentioned. For in the two cases just cited the persons making the promises were not the owners of the property which formed the subject of the lien, and were not under any liability whatever independently of the promise; whereas, in the other cases, the promises were made by persons who, being sole or part owners of the property subject to the lien, were under some liability independently of such promises, *i. e.*, were liable on the part of their property. To the latter and not to the former cases, therefore, the rule given in Wms. Saunders, which we have already mentioned, and which is adopted in *Fitzgerald* v. *Dressler*, as we have shown above, applies (*b*).

Thomas v.
Cook.

A further example of a case, which it is submitted is in reality founded on the rule now under discussion, is that of *Thomas* v. *Cook* (*c*). In that case it was decided that, under the state of facts there before the court, a promise to indemnify a person, if he would become surety for another, was not within the 4th section of the Statute of Frauds. *Thomas* v. *Cook* (*d*), according to *Bayley*, J., was decided on the ground that a promise to indemnify does not fall within either the [*122] words or *the policy of the Statute of Frauds (*e*); and according to *Parke*, J., on the ground that the promise in question was nothing more than an original one. There was, however, another reason for holding, in the particular case of *Thomas* v. *Cook*, that the Statute of Frauds did not apply. In *Thomas* v. *Cook*, the defendant (who gave the promise of indemnity) was surety *jointly* with the plaintiff (the promisee) for the person for whom the plaintiff became surety, at the defendant's request. Consequently, independently of his express promise, the defendant was liable to indemnify the plaintiff to a certain extent, owing to the operation of the doctrine of contribution amongst sureties, which we shall treat of later on (*f*). For this reason, therefore, the case, it is submitted, falls within the rule recognized in *Fitzgerald* v. *Dressler* (*g*).

(*b*) The case of *Castling* v. *Aubert*, 2 East, 325, very much resembles the cases just discussed. This case has been already fully noticed, *ante*, pp. 114 *et seq.*
(*c*) 8 B. & C. 728.
(*d*) *Ibid.*
(*e*) See this observation commented on, *ante*, pp. 47 *et seq.*
(*f*) *Vide post*, Chap. V.
(*g*) 7 C. B., N. S. 374, *ante*, p. 116.

Another class of cases which in reality also falls within the rule we are now applying, but which has been supposed to rest on other grounds, remains to be considered. These are cases in which, in consideration of the defendant's promise, a right to distrain another's goods is given up. Now, in all the cases of this kind which are about to be cited, it will be noticed that the person giving the promise, if not *actual owner* of the goods about to be distrained, had at least *an interest* in them, so as to bring the promises within the rule laid down in *Fitzgerald* v. *Dressler* (*supra*). At the same time the reader must be again reminded, that to such cases the remark, which has in substance been before made, applies with peculiar force, namely, that though the decisions themselves are correct, the conflicting reasons given for them by the judges are unsatisfactory in the extreme; and that in none of them is *that* reason for *the decision given which it is [*123] submitted is the true reason, namely, that the party promising was *owner* or at least *interested in* the goods distrained. A leading case of this class is that of *Williams* v. *Leper* (*h*). There a tenant of a messuage belonging to the plaintiff was in arrear for rent and was also insolvent. He accordingly made a bill of sale to the defendant (*Leper*) of all his goods in the messuage, in trust to be sold for the use of his creditors. The defendant advertised these goods for sale in the messuage, and on the morning fixed for the auction the plaintiff, as landlord, came to distrain the goods. *Leper*, on being informed of the plaintiff's intention to distrain promised the plaintiff to pay him the rent in arrear if he would desist from distraining. It was held, that the promise of the defendant was not within the 4th section of the Statute of Frauds. A sufficient reason for this decision is, because the defendant had under the bill of sale *an interest in the property liable to distress*. A similar case to *Williams* v. *Leper* is that of *Bampton* v. *Paulin* (*i*). There it appeared that the defendant, an auctioneer, was employed by A. and B. to sell goods on certain premises for which rent was in arrear. The landlord applied to the defendant, the auctioneer, for the payment of such arrears of rent, saying that it was better to apply so than to distrain. The defendant, after inquiring the amount, said, "You shall be paid; my clerk shall bring

Side notes:
RULE III.
Ante, p. *116.

Cases in which, in consideration of defendant's promise, right to distrain goods of third party given up.

Williams v. *Leper*.

Bampton v. *Paulin*.

(*h*) 2 Wils. 308; 3 Burr. 1886. See also pp. 68, 70, where this case is cited under Rule I.
(*i*) 4 Bing. 264.

7   (1331)

RULE III. you the money." It was held that this case was not
Ante, p. *116. distinguishable from *Williams* v. *Leper*, and that an action lay on the defendant's promise without a note in
writing. Now, in this case, as in *Williams* v. *Leper*,
the only true and intelligible ground for the decision
is, that the party making the promise, though not the
actual owner, yet had an interest in the goods about to
be distrained.

Thomas v.   [*124] *To a similar effect is the case of *Thomas* v.
Williams.   *Williams* (k). There the plaintiff's tenant was in arrear for rent, and the defendant, an auctioneer, was employed by such tenant to sell his goods. The plaintiff,
on the day fixed for the sale, went on the premises to
distrain for an unpaid balance of rent due the preceding Lady-day. The defendant promised the plaintiff,
that if he would not distrain, he would pay him, not
only the rent in arrear, but also rent that would accrue
due on the following Michaelmas. It was held that,
though the promise, so far as regarded the payment of
rent in arrear, was not within the 4th section of the
statute, yet that that portion of it which related to rent
to become due was within the statute; and that therefore,
in the absence of written evidence of the promise, the
whole was void. This decision is quite in harmony
with the other cases above cited, and is in remarkable
accordance with the rule in *Fitzgerald* v. *Dressler;* for
clearly, though as regarded the rent in arrear, property
in which defendant had an interest was liable to distress,
this was not the case as regarded the rent to become
due, for which therefore neither the defendant, independently of his promise, nor property in which he had an
interest, was liable.

Lord *Tenterden*, C. J., in delivering the judgment of
the court in this case, said the plaintiff could not have
distrained for rent not yet due. "The defendant, by
paying all that was due to Lady-day, might have proceeded to sell the goods. If that sum were paid or
secured, the plaintiff sustained no loss or detriment by
the sale of the goods. So that the promise to pay the
accruing rent exceeded the consideration, and cannot be
sustained on the ground on which the cases referred
to are to be sustained, but is nothing more than a promise
to pay money that would become due from a third
[*125] *person, and is within the words of the statute,
and the mischief intended to be remedied thereby. And, as
to so much, therefore, the promise is void by the statute."

_____

(k) 10 B. & C. 664.
(1332)

Another class of cases, which, it is submitted, are RULE III. referable to the rule now under consideration (Rule *Ante*, p.'*116. III.), are promises to answer for your *own* debt. It is Promises to settled that such promises are not within the Statute of answer for Frauds, which is confined in its application to promises promiser's to answer "for the debt, default or miscarriage" of *other* own debt. persons. In these cases, you are liable independently of your promise.

The case of *Ardern* v. *Rowney* (*l*) is an instance of *Ardern* v. this class of cases. In *Ardern* v. *Rowney* these were the *Rowney.* facts. One *Alder*, (who afterwards became a bankrupt) applied to the plaintiff to discount a cheque for 100*l*., drawn by *Alder* upon *Rowney*, the defendant. Before the plaintiff would give cash for it he sent his clerk to the defendant, who asked the defendant if the draft was a good one. The defendant answered that it would be honoured, as he was in *Alder's* debt 200*l*. The plaintiff's clerk then observed that the cheque was post dated, and could not, therefore, be recovered. The defendant said, that that did not signify, and that it should be paid. The plaintiff advanced the money, which was never repaid. The plaintiff having accordingly brought assumpsit against the defendant on the cheque for 100*l*., money had and received, with the other common money counts, it was objected that the plaintiff could not recover on the count on the cheque, as it was *admitted* to be void; and as to the second, the defendant's counsel said it was clear, that if this was a mere promise of the defendant, by which he promised the plaintiff that if the plaintiff would advance 100*l*. on his cheque to *Alder* he would pay it, it would be decidedly void within the Statute of Frauds, as being a promise to pay the debt *of another without a note in writing*, so that it [*126] could not be money had and received. Lord *Ellenborough*, C. J., said that if this had been an agreement to pay the amount of any money which the plaintiff might advance to *Alder*, and no specific sum of money had been mentioned which was to be advanced, the case would have been within the Statute of Frauds. He held, however, that this was an appropriation of 100*l*., part of the money which the defendant said he owed to *Alder*, amounting to 200*l*., and that the plaintiff might recover. It was then suggested by the defendant's counsel that plaintiff could not recover beyond the money actually due by *Rowney* to *Alder*, and, on

---

(*l*) 5 Esp. 254.

RULE III. his showing that 80*l.* only was due, Lord *Ellenborough*
Ante, p. *116.* directed the verdict to be entered for that amount.

Hodgson v.   Again, in *Hodgson* v. *Anderson* (m), A. was indebted
Anderson. to B., while C., who resided abroad, was indebted to A.
A. proposed to assign to B. the debt owing from C. to
him, which B. agreed to accept. A. wrote to C.'s agents
in this country, "As soon as you have funds belonging
to C., pay, on my account, to B. 201*l.* 10s., and I will
credit C., *having received his order to that effect.*" C.'s
agents *verbally* promised B. to pay him as soon as they
should have funds of C. in hand. A., afterwards,
ordered C. to pay to another creditor the debt owing
from C. to A., and C. gave an undertaking to pay that
creditor, with a memorandum, stating that as it was
alleged that a payment had been made by some person
to A., on account of C., it was declared that should C.
prove such payment to have been made, the amount
should be deducted. C. refused to pay the debt to this
latter creditor, on the ground that his agents were liable
to pay it to B., and C.'s agents, in fact, afterwards paid
it to B. It was held (*inter alia*), that C.'s promise to
pay B. was not a promise to pay the debt of a third
[*127] *person, and therefore was not within the
Statute of Frauds. *Bayley, J.*, in his judgment in this
case, says, "I think the case is not within the Statute
of Frauds, because it was a promise by the defendant
to pay his own debt with his own money, only paying
it to the banking company instead of to the plaintiff.
It was not a promise to pay with his own money the
debt of the plaintiff, a third person. A written promise,
therefore, was not necessary, in order to impose upon
the defendant an obligation to pay the banking company, because there was no agreement to pay money
which the party, by law, was not obliged to pay; there
was a full and adequate consideration for the payment."

Stephens v.   Another case, of this same class, is *Stephens* v. *Squire*(n),
Squire. in which the facts were as follows :—An action was
brought against *Squire*, an attorney, and two others,
for appearing for the plaintiff without a warrant. The
cause was carried down to be tried at the assizes, and
the defendant (*Squire*) promised that, in consideration
that the plaintiff would not prosecute the action, he
would pay 10*l.* and costs of suit. On this promise
another action was subsequently brought against *Squire.*
The question was, whether the 4th section of the Statute
of Frauds required this promise to be in writing. The

(m) 5 D. & R. 735; *S. C.*, 3 B. & C. 842.
(n) 5 Mod. 205.

court was of opinion that this could not be said to be a RULE III.
promise for another person, but for his *own* debt, and *Ante*, p. *116.
that it was, therefore, not within the statute. Now, in
this case it will be observed that *Squire*, the defendant,
was, independently of his express promise, partially
liable, at all events, to the plaintiff. This case, therefore, could not be affected by the Statute of Frauds.
Mr. Fell, in his work on Guarantees (o), gives as a
reason for taking this case out of the statute, that the
defendant, who made the promise on which the action
was brought, was *interested* in the original transaction.
*An apt illustration of the principle now under [*128]
consideration is also furnished by the case of *Orrell* v. *Orrell* v.
Coppock (p), in which the following were the facts:— *Coppock.*
A testator appointed his son, *Alfred Orrell*, and three
other persons, trustees and executors of his will. *Alfred
Orrell* disclaimed and renounced probate, and afterwards
purchased a portion of the testator's property. One of
the trustees, named *Winterbotham*, who proved the
will, was transported, and Mrs. *Brooks*, a daughter of
the testator, expressed dissatisfaction at the way in
which the trustees had acted, and claimed 5,000l. from
Alfred Orrell. *Alfred Orrell* denied all knowledge or
participation in the matters in dispute, but, for the sake
of peace, instructed his solicitor, Mr. *Coppock*, to make
some pecuniary offer. Mr. *Coppock* ultimately *wrote* on
behalf of *Alfred Orrell* to the claimants, agreeing to
pay 3,000l. in satisfaction of the alleged losses Mr. and
Mrs. *Brooks* had sustained from the acts of the trustees.
It was held that, as against *Alfred Orrell*, this letter
was not within the Statute of Frauds as an agreement
to answer for the debt, default or miscarriage of another,
and that it was not invalid for want of consideration.
The reason for this decision is ably given by *Kindersley*,
V.-C., in his judgment in the case. He says: "Now it
is clear, according to this arrangement, that it was not
a case in which Mr. *Alfred Orrell* was saying, 'A. B.
and C. D. may be liable to you, and I will undertake
that if they do not pay this debt I will.' It is no such
case. It cannot be said to be an agreement for any
debt, default or miscarriage of another, within the
meaning of the Statute of Frauds; that statute does
not apply to the case where a party giving the guarantee *is himself liable to the demand* which he is purport
ing to guarantee, it must be *exclusively* the debt, default or miscarriage of the other to bring it within the

(o) 2nd ed., pp. 18, 19.
(p) 26 L. J., Ch. 269.

RULE III.   [*129] statute; and therefore it *appears to me that,
Ante, p. *116. in this case, when Mr. *Alfred Orrell* was incurring this
obligation it was not merely to satisfy the debt of
another, but the debt which, it was insisted, rightly or
wrongly, that he was liable for; and it is clear, from
the arrangement, that none of the losses, except that of
Winterbotham, were individual, but that all were liable
for those losses, and therefore *Alfred Orrell* was not
only to be himself discharged, but all the others."

Promise by   A promise that the promiser's agent shall, on a cer-
principal   tain event, pay money, or that, on his failure to do so,
that if his   the promiser will, is not one to which the Statute of
agent does   Frauds applies, as such promise is merely expressive of
not pay he   an already-existing liability on the part of the promiser
will, not   (*q*). So, again, it was held, in a case decided long be-
within   fore the Married Women's Property Acts, that a promise
statute.   to pay money lent to the wife of the promiser at his
Application   request is not a collateral undertaking, as there is such
of statute to   a privity and union between them that a loan to the
a promise by   wife must be treated as a loan to the husband (*r*). On
husband to   the other hand, a promise by the wife to pay her hus-
pay wife's   band's debt out of her separate estate is strictly collat-
debt, or by   eral, and must be in writing (*s*). It is submitted that
wife to pay   any guarantee given since the Married Women's Prop-
husband's   erty Act, 1882, by a husband to secure repayment of
debt.   money lent to a wife, who is possessed of separate
Guarantee by   estate, is within the Statute of Frauds, and is not en-
husband for   forceable against him unless it be in writing.
his wife,
semble now
within
statute.

RULE IV.   RULE IV.—*The main, or immediate, object of the
                agreement between the parties must be to secure the pay-*
Main object   [*130] *ment of a debt, or the fulfilment of a duty, by
of the pro-   a third person.*
mise must be
to secure   It cannot but be a matter of regret that the judges
fulfilment of   should ever have laid down the above rule, as one test
third party's   for ascertaining whether the second clause of the 4th
obligation.   section of the Statute of Frauds applies to a particular
Difficulty of   agreement. Its application must obviously be attended
applying this   with much difficulty. It is also to be regretted that,
rule.   this rule once established, it should not *always* have
been adhered to, and that in many cases in which one
would suppose it to apply it is not even noticed in the

(*q*) *Masters* v. *Marriott*, 3 Levinz, 363.
(*r*) *Stevenson* v. *Hardie*, 2 W. Black. 872 ; and see *ante*, p. 88.
(*s*) *Wilcocks* v. *Hannington*, 5 Ir. Ch. Rep. 38 ; and see *Robin-*
son v. *Gee*, 1 Ves. sen. 251 ; *Huntingdon* v. *Huntingdon*, 2 Bro. P.
C. 1.

decisions (*t*). The first case in which the rule in question appears to have been laid down is *Castling* v. *Aubert* (*u.*) There the plaintiff, a broker, having a lien on certain policies of insurance, effected for his principal (one *Grayson*), for whom he had given his acceptances, the defendant promised that he would provide for such acceptances as they became due, upon the plaintiff's giving up to him such policies, in order that he might collect for the principal the money due thereon from the underwriters. This was accordingly done, and the money was afterwards received by the defendant. It was held that this was not a promise within the 4th section of the Statute of Frauds. Lord *Ellenborough*, C. J., in his judgment, says: "I am clearly of opinion that this is neither an undertaking for the debt, default or miscarriage of another person within the statute. It could not be for the *debt*, but rather for the *credit*, of another; for when the promise was made, no debt was incurred from *Grayson* to the plaintiff; therefore, if at all within the statute, it must be for the default or miscarriage of . another. But see what the case is. The plaintiff, who was *Grayson's* broker, had policies of *insurance in his hands [*131] belonging to his principal, which were securities on which he had a lien for the balance of his account, and on the faith of these he agreed to accept bills for the accommodation of his principal. One of these bills became due, and actions were brought against the plaintiff as acceptor, and against *Grayson* as drawer; and it was desirable that the policies should be given up by the plaintiff to the defendant in order to enable the money for the losses incurred to be received from the underwriters, the defendant undertaking, upon condition the policies were made over to him, to settle the acceptances due, and lodge money in a banker's hands for the satisfaction of the remainder as they became due. The defendant then procured from the plaintiff the securities upon the faith of this engagement, *in entering into which he had not the · discharge of Grayson principally in his contemplation, but the discharge of himself*. That was his moving consideration, though the discharge of *Grayson* would eventually follow. It is rather, therefore, *a purchase* of the securities which the plaintiff held in his hands. This is quite against the mischief provided against by the statute, which was

RULE IV.
Ante, p. *129.

Castling v. *Aubert.*

(*t*) See many of the cases cited, *ante*, as illustrations of Rule I. This rule is adopted, with seeming approval, in Selwyn's Nisi Prius, Vol. II., 13th ed., p. 777.

(*u*) 2 East. 325; cited also *ante*, pp. 114—115, 121.

RULE IV.
Ante, p. *129.

Elkins v
Heart.

Macrory v.
Scott.

that persons should not by their own unvouched under-taking, without writing, charge themselves for the debt, default or miscarriage of another. In the case of a bill of exchange for which several persons are liable, if it be agreed to be taken up and paid by one, eventually others may be discharged; and the same objection might be made there; but the moving consideration is the discharge of the party himself, and not of the rest, though that also ensues. Upon the whole, there-fore, I agree with the decision in *Williams* v. *Leper* to the full extent of it. I agree with those of the judges who thought the case not within the Statute of Frauds at all." A similar view was put forward by the court [*132] in *the case of *Elkins* v. *Hart* (x), which we have had occasion to cite before, though upon another point (y). In that case the payment of the third party's debt was not the *main* object of the agreement between the parties, as will be seen on examination of the facts, which were as follows. The plaintiff having sued J. G., the defendant's son-in-law, for money due from him to the plaintiff for diet and lodging, the defendant promised, in consideration that the plaintiff would for-bear to sue the said J. G. for the said sum, that the said J. G. should not leave the kingdom without pay-ing the same. The court inclined to the opinion that this case was not within the 4th section of the Statute of Frauds. Now here, clearly, the *main direct* object of the agreement between the parties was to prevent the third party leaving England. The *indirect* object was the payment of such third party's debt. Of course, on such third party leaving England, the measure of the damages against the defendant would be the debt due from such third party. This circumstance would not, however, alter the nature of the transaction and bring it within the 4th section of the Statute of Frauds, if it were not so for other reasons. Another authority, in which the rule under consideration appears to have been recognized, is that of *Macrory* v. *Scott* (z). In that case it appeared that a certain judgment was given to the plaintiff by the defendant as security for advances which the plaintiff had made to the firm of *Scott Brothers* at the defendant's request. Afterwards, in considera-tion that the plaintiff would discharge *Scott Brothers* from all their existing liabilities, and would pay to the *Ulster Banking Company* 800*l.*, and would also advance

(x) Fitz. 202.
(y) See *ante*, p. 79, under Rule I.
(z) 5 Exch. 907.

to *Scott Brothers* 200l., it was agreed by the defendant
that the said judgment against him should remain as a
security for the 1,000l. This agreement *being [*133]
evidenced by a memorandum or note in writing, sufficient to satisfy the Statute of Frauds, it was unnecessary
for the court to decide on the above mentioned facts,
whether the case was within the statute. *Parke, B.*, however, in his judgment in the case, says: " First, it is said
that there ought to be a note or memorandum in writing, because this is a promise to be answerable for the
debt or default of another, within the Statute of Frauds.
But I do not think this case is within that statute.
· *It is not directly a promise to pay the debt of another,*
but an agreement stating that property already pledged
for one debt shall remain pledged for another. Although the ultimate effect is that the debt may be paid,
*yet the immediate object is merely to appropriate the
fund in a different manner.* It therefore falls within
the principle of the decision in *Castling* v. *Aubert*"(*a*).
And again, Baron *Martin*, in his judgment in the same
case, says: "The substance of the arrangement was, that
the defendant, who had been a party to a former judgment, should permit the judgment to remain as a security for 1,000l., which was to be advanced and given
by the plaintiff to the *Ulster Banking Company*, on the
terms of his *discharging Scott*. The transaction is, in
effect, this:—' I, the defendant, will consent to the judgment against me remaining as a security if you, the
plaintiff, will wipe off all existing demands against
Scott & Co., and advance 800l. to the *Ulster Bank* and
200l. to *Scott & Co.*' To my mind this is clearly not a
case within the Statute of Frauds. It is not an undertaking to answer for the debt, default or miscarriage of
another; but an agreement that a certain existing obligation shall continue. The cases, all of which will be
found in the note to *Forth* v. *Stanton*, establish that,
for the purpose of bringing a contract within the Statute
of Frauds, it must be an *engagement for the [*134]
debt, default or miscarriage of another, which this is
not. So that, even if it had been a parol contract, it
would have been perfectly good, as the Statute of Frauds
does not apply."

The case of *Jarmain* v. *Algar* (*b*), which has been
before cited (*c*), may, perhaps, also be considered as

RULE IV.
Ante. p. *129.
——

Jarmain v.
Algar.

(*a*) 2 East. 325.
(*b*) 2 C. & P. 249.
(*c*) *Ante*, pp. 74, 113.

RULE IV.
Ante, p. *129.

In *Jarmain* v. *Algar* it was held, that a promise by a party to execute a bail bond on a writ to be sued out against A. B., in consideration of the plaintiff forbearing to arrest A. B., on a writ already sued out, is not a promise to answer for the debt, &c., of another within the 4th section of the Statute of Frauds. The reason for this *nisi prius* decision does not appear from the report of the case in 2 Carrington & Payne. It is submitted, however, that the reason may very probably have been because the *immediate* or *main* object of the transaction was not the payment of a third party's debt, though this might be indirectly attained.

Promise by a del credere agent not within statute.

The most remarkable instance in which the rule now under consideration (Rule IV.) applies, and, consequently, excludes the operation of the 4th section of the Statute of Frauds, is, undoubtedly, the case of a *del credere* (d) agent. A *del credere* agent is, as is well known, an agent who, for a higher commission, guarantees the solvency of the purchasers of the goods of his employers,—in other words, is answerable for the debts of third persons. Now, a *del credere* agent is not answerable *in the first instance* (e), though this was once thought to be the case (f). He is really nothing [*135] more *than a surety. The nature of his liability is thus defined by Lord *Ellenborough,* C. J., in delivering the judgment of the Court of King's Bench in *Morris* v. *Cleasby* (g):—"In correct language," he remarks, "a commission *del credere* is the premium or price given by the principal to the factor for a guarantee. . . . But, whatever term is used, the obligation of the factor is the same; it arises on the guarantee. The guarantor is to answer for the solvency of the vendee, and to pay the money if the vendee does not; on the failure of the vendee, he is to stand in his place and make his default good." Many ingenious suggestions have been made by learned text writers for the purpose of justifying the exclusion from the operation of the 4th section of the Statute of Frauds of the undertaking of a *del credere* agent. We will notice some of these sug-

Morris v. Cleasby.

Reasons assigned in

(d) "The phrase *del credere* is borrowed from the Italian language, in which its signification is exactly equivalent to our word guaranty or warranty." See Story on Agency, 7th ed., pp. 30, 31.

(e) See Smith's Mercantile Law, 9th ed., p. 115, and the cases there cited.

(f) See 4 M. & S. 574.

(g) 4 M. & S. 566, 574.

gestions before discussing the reason assigned by our
English courts for the exclusion in question. Mr.
Throop, in his work on the Validity of Verbal Agreements (*h*), says: "It may be doubted whether the
statute would apply, irrespective of these suggestions,
for it is by no means clear that the transaction would
satisfy the language of this clause. It does not appear
to be a promise to answer for the debt or default of *any
particular person;* for there was no debt in existence
at the time the contract is made; not in the sense of
Lord *Mansfield's* proposition in *Mowbray* v. *Cunningham* (*i*), which he subsequently abandoned, but in the
sense that there is no debtor or person proposing to become a debtor, to whom the term 'another person' can
apply. Indeed, no reason is perceived why a distinct
class should not be added to those already recognized,
where the promise is without the statute, because those
words are not satisfied ; comprising not only *del credere*
contracts, but all promises where the person for whose
debt or default *the promiser undertakes to [*136]
answer is not designated at the time of the contract.
If A. undertakes to procure competent mechanics to
build a house for B., and that it shall be completed by
them in a certain time, and according to certain speci-
fications (it being perfectly understood that A. is not
to do any of the work himself), in one sense A. undertakes for their default or miscarriages ; but, probably,
no one would doubt that the contract was not within
this clause of the statute. That the reason is because
the persons for whom A. undertakes are not then *in esse*,
for the purpose of the contract, will be apparent from
the fact that, if they had been designated at the time,
and the undertaking was that they should perform,
probably no one would doubt that it was within the
statute. So in the case of a factor's contract with his
principal : if the buyer was named, doubtless the statute
would apply to a *del credere* contract ; and so if an
ordinary factor, having already made a sale for his
principal, should guarantee the payment of the price
by the purchaser for a new consideration, passing between him and his principal."

Again, another reason is suggested in the 6th American edition of Smith's Leading Cases (*k*). It is there
stated(*l*), that the true explanation of the cases which

RULE IV.
Ante, p. *129.

America for
this decision.

Mr. Throop's
comments on
this case.

(*h*) Page 660.
(*i*) Cited *ante*, pp. 74, 113.
(*k*) Vol. I. p. 489.
(*l*) This reference is taken from Throop on the Validity of Verbal Agreements, note (*c*), p. 658.

RULE IV.
Ante, p. *129.

hold that the statute does not apply to sales on a *del credere* commission, may perhaps be found in the doctrine that any promise to pay the debt of another upon a consideration, no matter how disproportionate, moving to the promiser, is not within the statute ; but that the point cannot be considered as decided. However, he afterwards adds (*m*) : "One of the reasons given for this conclusion is, that, as agents are liable for good faith and due diligence in the transaction of the business confided to their care, a stipulation by which this [*137] *liability is defined, or even extended, cannot be regarded as a promise for the default of another in the exclusive sense contemplated by the statute. But it would also appear that a guaranty or insurance of a debt, for a percentage or commission, would be valid aside from this ground ; on the general principle that a party who promises to pay the debt of another for value received, makes the debt his own, and cannot rely on the statute as a defence to an action, brought to compel the engagement into which he has entered."

American case of *Wolff* v. *Koppel*.

A complete summary of the various views upon the subject is also to be found in the judgment of the court delivered by *Cowen*, J., in the American case of *Wolff* v. *Koppel* (*n*). The judgment is in itself a very instructive one, and the reasoning it contains was afterwards adopted by the English courts in the case of *Couturier* v. *Hastie* (*o*). It will be well, therefore, to give it at length.

Judgment of Justice *Cowen* in *Wolff* v. *Koppel*.

In this case of *Wolff* v. *Koppel* (*n*), Justice *Cowen* spoke as follows :—"It is objected that the contract of a factor, binding him in the terms implied by a *del credere* commission, is within the Statute of Frauds, and should, therefore, be in writing. Such is the opinion expressed by Theobald (*p*), and in Chitty on Contracts (*q*). The question was also mooted in *Gall* v. *Comber* (*r*), but not decided, as seems to be implied in the careless manner in which the case is quoted by Chitty (*s*). All the authority presented by the argument grows out of the nature of the contract, as held by the King's Bench in *Morris* v. *Cleasby* (*t*). That case certainly defines the liability of the factor some-

(*m*) Page 494.
(*n*) 5 Hill, New York Rep. 458.
(*o*) 8 Exch. 40 ; *S. C.*, 9 Exch. 102 ; *S. C.*, 5 H. L. 673.
(*p*) Principal and Surety, 64, 65.
(*q*) Page 209, 10th American edition of 1842.
(*r*) 1 B. Moor. 279.
(*s*) 8 Taunt. 558, *S. C.*
(*t*) 4 M. & S. 566, 574, 575.

what differently from what several previous cases seem
to have done.   The effect of acting under the commission *is said to be, that the factor becomes a [*138]
guarantor of the debts which are created ; that is to
say, they are debts due to the merchant, and the factor's engagement is secondary and collateral, depending
on the fault of the debtors, who must first be sought
out and called upon by the merchant (x).   On this we
have the opinion of learned writers, that if the agreement *del credere* be made without writing, the case
comes within the statute.   On the other hand, approved writers assert that this is not so (y).   It is true
these latter go on the more stringent obligation supposed by Lord *Mansfield;* that of a principal debtor
on the part of the factor, the accessorial obligation
lying rather on the purchaser.   This view of the matter was no longer correct, after the cases I have mentioned were decided.   The consequence sought to be
derived, however, by writers is merely speculative, and
the contrary has lately been directly held by the Supreme Court of Massachusetts, in *Swan* v. *Nesmith* (z).
It is said, this was without the court being aware of
Morris v. *Cleasby.*   Be that as it may, they seem to
have been fully aware of the rule laid down in that
case, and to have recognized it as correct.   They considered the obligation as a guaranty.   But a guaranty,
though by parol, is not always within the statute.   Perhaps, after all, it may not be strictly correct to call the
contract of the factor a guaranty, in the ordinary sense
of that word.   The implied promise of the factor is
merely that he will sell to persons in good credit at the
time ; and, in order to charge him, negligence must be
shown.   He takes an additional commission, however,
and adds to his obligation that he will make no sales
except to persons absolutely solvent ; in legal effect,
*that he will be liable for the loss which his [*139]
conduct may bring upon the plaintiff, without the *onus*
of proving negligence.   The merchant holds the goods,
and will not part with them to the factor without this
extraordinary stipulation, and a commission is paid to
him for entering into it.   What is this, after all, but
another form of selling the goods?   Its consequences

RULE IV,
Ante, p. *129.

(x) See also *Horaby* v. *Lacy,* 6 Man. & Selw. 166, 171, 172;
Peele v. *Northcote,* 7 Taunt. 478, 484 ; 1 B. Moor. 178 ; *S. C., Lev-
rick* v. *Meigs,* 1 Cowen, 645, 664.
(y) 1 Beawes, 46, 6th Lond. ed. ; 3 Chit. Commercial Law,
220, 221.
(z) 7 Pick. 220.

RULE IV. are the same in substance. Instead of paying cash, the
Ante, p. *129. factor prefers to contract a debt or duty which obliges
him to see the money paid. This debt or duty is his
own, and arises from an adequate consideration. It is
contingent, depending on the event of his failing to
secure it through another—some future vendee, to
whom the merchant is first to resort. Upon nonpayment
by the vendee, the debt falls absolutely on the factor.
As remarked by *Parker*, C. J., in *Swan* v. *Nesmith*, the
form of the action does not seem to be material in such
a case, that is to say, whether the merchant sue for
goods sold, or, on the special agreement. The latter
is perhaps the settled form; but still the action is, in
effect, to recover the factor's own debt. In the later
case of *Johnson* v. *Gilbert* (a), the defendant, in consideration of money paid for him by the plaintiff,
assigned a chattel note and guaranteed its payment.
In such a case the declaration must be on a guaranty to
pay the debt of another : but this is so in form merely.
We held that the contract was to pay the defendant's
own debt; that it was not a contract to pay as the
surety of another. All such contracts, and many
others, are, in form, to pay the debt of another, and
so, literally, within the statute, but without its intent.
A promise by A. to B., that the former will pay a debt
due from the latter, is not within the meaning, though
it is within the words (b). So are a numerous class of
[*140] cases *where the promise is made in consideration of the creditor relinquishing some lien, fund or
security (c). The merchant gives up his goods to be
sold, and pays a premium. Is not this, in truth, as
much and more than many of those cases require which
go on the relinquishment of a security? Suppose a factor agrees, by parol, to sell for cash, but gives a credit.
His promise is, virtually, that he will pay the amount
of the debt he thus makes. Yet, who would say his
promise is within the statute? The amount of the argument for the defendant would seem to be, that an
agent for making sales, or, indeed, a collecting agent,
cannot, by parol, undertake for extraordinary diligence,
because he may thus have the debt of another thrown
upon him. But the answer is, that all such contracts
have an immediate respect to his own duty or obliga-

(a) 4 Hill, 178.
(b) *Conkey* v. *Hopkins*, 17 John. 113; *Eastwood* v. *Kenyon*, 11
A. & E. 438.
(c) Theobald's Principal and Surety, 45, and the cases there
cited.

tion. The debt of another comes incidentally, as a measure of damages."

RULE IV.
Ante, p. #129.

Coming to the reasons which have been given by English judges and text writers, in Selwyn's *Nisi Prius* (*d*), we find the following words :—

Reasons assigned by English

"On the same principle as that on which the class of cases, commencing with *Williams* v. *Leper* (*e*), may be explained, as before suggested, viz., that the principal object of the transaction is to be regarded ; it has been held, that a retainer, of an agent to dispose of goods, under a *del credere* commission, need not be accepted in writing by the agent."

judges and text writers for holding that promise of *del credere* agent not within statute.

The case of *Couturier* v. *Hastie* (*f*) was the first in which it was ever actually held in *England*, that the contract of a factor, acting under the terms of a *del *credere* commission, is not within the Statute [*141.] of Frauds. And the reason given by the Court of Exchequer, in their judgment, in this case, is because the *main* object of the agreement between such an agent and his principal is, not the payment of the debt of another, but the taking greater care by the agent in finding purchasers for the goods of his principal. Baron *Parke*, who delivered the judgment of the court, said : "The other and only remaining point is, whether the defendants are responsible, by reason of their charging a *del credere* commission, though they have not guaranteed by writing signed by themselves. We think they are. Doubtless, if they had for a percentage guaranteed the debt owing, or performance of the contract by the vendee, being totally unconnected with the sale, they would not be liable, without a note in writing, signed by them ; but, being the agents to negotiate the sale, the commission is paid, in respect of that employment ; a higher reward is paid in consideration of their taking greater care in sales to their customers, and precluding all question whether the loss arose from negligence or not, and also for assuming a greater share of responsibility than ordinary agents, namely, responsibility for the solvency and performance of their contracts by their vendees. This is the *main object* of the reward being given to them ; and, though it may terminate in a liability to pay the debt of another, that is not the *immediate object* for which the consideration is

Couturier v. *Hastie*.

(*d*) 13th ed., Vol. II., p. 776.
(*e*) 3 Burr. 1886 ; *S. C.*, 2 Wils. 308.
(*f*) 8 Exch. 40, 55, reversed on appeal to Exch. (see *Hastie* v. *Couturier*, 9 Exch. 102), but affirmed in the H. L. (see *Couturier* v. *Hastie*, 5 H. L. 673.)

RULE IV.
Ante, p. *129.

given; and the case resembles, in this respect, those of *Williams* v. *Leper* (*g*) and *Castling* v. *Aubert* (*h*). We entirely adopt the reasoning of an American judge (Mr. Justice *Cowen*) in a very able judgment, on this point, in *Wolff* v. *Koppel*" (*i*).

Wickham v.
Wickham.

[*142.] *And, sub:equently, in the case of *Wickham* v. *Wickham* (*k*), *Wood*, V. C., made the following observations on *Couturier* v. *Hastie* :—" If the engagement entered into by the firm of *John . Finch & Sons* was a contract for a *del credere* agency, then, on the other hand, I concur with what was urged on the part of the plaintiffs, that the case of *Couturier* v. *Hastie* seems to establish that it would not operate as a guarantee, and would not be a promise to answer for the debt of another within the 4th section of the Statute of Frauds. When I look at the whole of that case and consider the reasons given by the judges in delivering their judgments, though given very cautiously and guardedly, I cannot but conclude that they consider that an agent entering into a contract in the nature of a *del credere* agency, entered in effect into a new substantial agreement with the person whose agency he undertook ; that the agreement so entered into by him was not a simple guarantee, but a distinct and positive undertaking on his part on which he would become primarily liable ; otherwise I cannot see how the learned judges could arrive at the conclusion that the undertaking was not within the Statute of Frauds. Certainly the opinion of the American judge, which one of the learned judges referred to with approbation in delivering judgment in *Couturier* v. *Hastie*, goes to the full extent which I have described."

RULE V.
——
The agreement between promiser and creditor must not amount to a sale by latter to former of debt or security for debt.

RULE V. *The agreement between the promiser and the creditor, to whom the promise is made, must not amount to a sale by the latter to the former of a security for a debt, or of the debt itself.*

It sometimes happens that a promise to pay the debt of another is made in consideration of the delivery up of a security for such debt, or of the assignment of the debt itself. When this is the case, and the transaction [*143] *really amounts to nothing more than a sale or transfer of a security or of a debt itself, the 4th section

(*g*) 3 Burr. 1886 ; 2 Wils. 308.
(*h*) 2 East, 325.
(*i*) This case is reported in 5 Hill, New York Rep. 458, and see note (*c*) to *Couturier* v. *Hastie*, p. 56 of 8 Exch.
(*k*) 2 K. & J. 478, 486, 487.

of the Statute of Frauds would appear to have no appli- RULE V.
cation. It seems that, for the existence of this rule, there *Ante*, p. *142
are only *two direct* authorities, namely, *Castling* v. *Aubert*
(*l*), and *Anstey* v. *Marden* (*m*). Several other cases are,
however, *said* to have been decided on this ground (*n*).
In the following cases, which are cited as illustrations
of the present rule, it will be noticed, *firstly*, that in
some only of the cases the agreement had the effect of
extinguishing the liability of the original debtor ; and,
secondly, that sometimes the price of the sale was the
actual debt of a third person, sometimes a portion only
of such debt.

In *Castling* v. *Aubert* (*o*), the plaintiff, an agent, had *Castling* v.
a lien on certain policies of insurance effected for his *Aubert.*
principal, for whom he had given his acceptances. The
defendant induced the agent to waive his lien and give
up to him (the defendant) the policies, by promising to
provide for the acceptances as they became due. The
court held this promise not to be within the 4th section
of the Statute of Frauds, and Lord *Ellenborough*, C.
J., in giving judgment, said: "It is rather, therefore,
a *purchase* of the securities which the plaintiff held in
his hands. This is quite beside the mischief provided
against by the statute." And *Lawrence*, J., in the
same case said: "This is to be considered as a *purchase*
by the defendant of the plaintiff's interest in the policies. It is not a bare promise to the creditor to pay the
debt of another due to him, but a promise by the defendant to pay what the plaintiff would be liable to pay
*if the plaintiff would furnish him with the [*144]
means of doing so."

In *Love's case* (*p*) the defendant, a stranger, verbally *Love's case.*
promised to pay a third party's debt, in consideration
of the sheriff's officer restoring goods which he had
taken in execution on a *fi. fa.* It was held, that the
transaction amounted to no more than a *sale* of the
goods taken in execution. The Statute of Frauds does
not, however, appear to have been taken notice of in
this decision.

In *Anstey* v. *Marden* (*q*), A. being insolvent, a verbal *Anstey* v.
Marden.

(*l*) 2 East. 325.
(*m*) 1 N. R. 86. See also observations of *Cockburn*, C. J., in
Fitzgerald v. *Dressler*, 7 C. B., N. S. 374.
(*n*) See Throop on the Validity of Verbal Agreements, p. 573,
note (*f*); p. 576, note (*j*); p. 579, note (*m*); p. 615, note (*d*); p.
638, note (*y*).
(*o*) 2 East. 325.
(*p*) Salk. 28.
(*q*) 1 N. R. 124.

RULE V.
Ante, p. *142.

Houlditch v.
Milne.

agreement was entered into between several of his creditors and B., whereby B. agreed to pay the creditors 10s. in the pound in satisfaction of their debts, which they agreed to accept, *and to assign their debts to B.* It was held that this agreement was not within the Statute of Frauds, not being a collateral promise to answer for the debt of another, but an original contract to *purchase* the debt. In this case *Mansfield*, C. J., seems to rest his decision partly on the circumstance that the promise of B. was to pay only 10s. in the pound, and not the *whole* debt due from A. It is submitted, however, that if A. was liable in the first instance for the 10s., this circumstance could make no material difference in the character of the transaction in question (r). Another case which seems to be also an example of the rule under consideration, is that of *Houlditch* v. *Milne* (s). In that case, which has been before cited on another point, the action was in assump-[*145] sit for the repair of a *carriage. The following facts seem to have been proved at the trial. The defendant sent certain carriages, the property of one Mr. *Copey*, to be repaired. The defendant applied to the plaintiff to have the carriage sent on board ship, whereupon the plaintiff asked who was he to look to for payment of the repairs. The defendant answered that he had sent them, and that he would pay for them. In consequence of this statement the carriages were sent on board ship, and the bill made out and delivered to the defendant. The defendant declared that the bill was very high, but promised to settle it in a few days. As he did not do so the plaintiff's attorney called on the defendant, when the defendant said he was told the bill was a most exorbitant one, and a fit subject to refer. The defendant, however, also said that he had the money to pay it, but did not say whether the money was *his own* or Mr. *Copey's.* Lord *Eldon*, in giving judgment, said : "He was not disposed to nonsuit the plaintiff. In general cases, to make a person liable for goods delivered to another, there must be either an original undertaking by him, so that the credit was

---

(r) It appears, however, as already explained, that the agreement in question, discharged A. from all liability, and, therefore, for this reason *alone*, the statute could not apply, see *ante*, p. 91. In *Chater* v. *Becket*, 7 T. R. 201 (cited *ante*, p. 61), the original debtor remained liable; and though the facts were somewhat similar to those in *Anstey* v. *Marden*, yet the transaction could not have been sustained on the ground of a *purchase* or *sale* of a debt.

(s) 3 Esp. 86, cited *ante*, p. 63.

given solely to him; or there must be a note in writing.
There might, however, be cases where this rule did not apply. If a person got goods into his possession on which the landlord had a right to distrain for rent, and he promised to pay the rent, though it was clearly the debt of another, yet a note in writing was not necessary —it appeared to apply precisely to the present case. The plaintiffs had, to a certain extent, a lien upon the carriages *which they parted with on the defendant's promise to pay:* that, he thought, took the case out of the statute, and made the defendant liable for the amount of the bill." Now it is submitted that this case might have been, and probably was, decided on similar grounds to those on which the decisions in *Castling* v. *Aubert* and *Love's case* appear *to rest [*146] (*t*). Another case, which is also an instance of the rule now under consideration, is that of *Barrell* v. *Trussell* (*u*), in which the following were the facts:—

J. A. made a good bill of sale of goods to the plaintiff, to secure a debt of 122*l*. 19*s*. due from him to the plaintiff. The plaintiff being about to sell the goods in satisfaction of the debt, the defendant undertook to pay the plaintiff the 122*l*. 19*s*. if he would forbear to sell. *Mansfield*, C. J., held this not to be a transaction within the Statute of Frauds. He said, "What is this but the case of a man who having the absolute uncontrolled power of selling goods refrains upon the request of another ?"

From the report of this case, it appears that the plaintiff, by virtue of the bill of sale, was absolute owner of the goods in question. Consequently the defendant's promise was nothing more than an original one to *buy* the said goods, fixing the price at the amount of a third person's debt, which, under the circumstances, was a fair and convenient measure of the price.

The cases of *Williams* v. *Leper* (*y*), *Edwards* v. *Kelly* (*z*), and *Bampton* v. *Paulin* (*a*), where, in consideration of the delivery up of goods actually taken, or about to be taken, in distress for rent due from a third person, the defendant promised to pay such rent, would seem to be nothing more than purchases, and *might*, therefore, have been exempted from the operation of

(*t*) See, however, *ante*, p. 63, where it is shown that there was, apparently, another ground for this decision.
(*u*) 4 Taunt. 117.
(*y*) 3 Burr. 1886 ; *S. C.*, 2 Wils. 308.
(*z*) 6 M. & S. 204.
(*a*) 4 Bing. 264.

RULE V.
Ante, p. *142.

Thomas v.
Williams.

Clancy v.
Piggott.

the Statute of Frauds on that ground; and possibly some of them *were* exempted partly on that ground; though, as already pointed out, there were certainly [*147] other more prominent *reasons for holding the statute to be inapplicable to those cases.

The case of *Thomas* v. *Williams* (b) indeed, where the defendant promised to pay rent *due* and to *become* due from a third person, in consideration of the plaintiff forbearing to distrain certain goods for the rent then due, is certainly, as pointed out by Mr. Throop, in his work on the Validity of Verbal Agreements (c), at war with the theory, that where the goods are given up to the promiser the transaction amounts to a purchase, and is, therefore, not within the 4th section of the Statute of Frauds. For, in *Thomas* v. *Williams*, the statute was held to apply, *because* the promise was not merely in consideration of rent *then due*, but also in consideration of rent to *become* due. But, as Mr. Throop rightly observes, if this was indeed a purchase, it would be immaterial what price the defendant agreed to pay. Moreover, from the case of *Clancy* v. *Piggott* (d), *it would seem* that in no case can the transaction be treated in the light of a purchase, where the goods liable to distress are, on the defendant's promise to pay what is due from the third party, given up to such third party, and not to the principal debtor.

(b) 10 B. & C. 664.
(c) Page 576, note (j).
(d) 4 Nev. & Mann. 496. See Throop on the Validity of Verbal Agreements, note (m), p. 579.

(117)

*CHAPTER III.　　　　[*148]

WHAT IS A SUFFICIENT MEMORANDUM IN WRITING
TO SATISFY THE REQUIREMENTS OF THE FOURTH
SECTION OF THE STATUTE OF FRAUDS.

WE have already stated that the 4th section of the Statute of Frauds (a) requires the contract of guar- antee to be evidenced by writing, for it provides that the *agreement* upon which the action shall be brought, *or some memorandum or note thereof, must be in writ- ing and signed by the party to be charged therewith, or some other person thereunto by him lawfully authorized.* It will be observed that the statute requires that "*the agreement*" be in writing. In the celebrated case of *Wain* v. *Warlters* (b) the guarantee sued upon was written in the following words :—

Statute of Frauds (sect. 4) requires the agreement to be in writing.

"Messrs. *Wain & Co.*:

"I will engage to pay you, by half-past four this day, fifty-six pounds and expenses on bill, that amount on *Hall.*

"*John Warlters.*

"2, *Cornhill*, April 30, 1803."

This memorandum was held insufficient to satisfy the Statute of Frauds, because only *part* of the agreement appeared in writing, namely, *the promise*, but the 4th section requires "the agreement" to be in writing, and not any *specified part* of it. And it appears, that an agreement is not perfect, unless in the body of it, or by necessary inference, it contains the names of the two *contracting parties, the subject-matter of the [*149] contract, the consideration, and the promise (c).

What the term agree- ment in- cludes.

If the legislature had intended that the *promise* only should appear in writing, they would doubtless have employed such language as they have used in the 17th section of the Statute of Frauds, which, instead of pro- viding that "*the agreement*" shall be in writing, re- quires only "that some note or memorandum in writing

Respective requirements of 4th and 17th sects. of Statute of Frauds as to written evi- dence con- trasted.

(a) 29 Car. 2, c. 3.
(b) 5 East, 10.
(c) Per *Tindal*, C. J., in *Laythoarp* v. *Bryant*, 2 Bing. N. C. 742.
See also Sheppard's Touchstone, p. 85.

(1351)

of the said bargain be made and signed by the parties to be charged by such contract, or their agents thereunto lawfully authorized." In *Egerton* v. *Mathews* (d), it was contended, that there was no substantial difference in language between the 4th and 17th sections of the Statute of Frauds. The court, however, took a different view, and *Lawrence*, J., in giving judgment, said: "The case of *Wain* v. *Warlters* proceeded on this, that, in order to charge one man with the debt of another, the *agreement* must be in writing; which word *agreement* we considered as properly including the *consideration* moving to, as well as the *promise* by, the party to be so charged; and that the statute meant to require that the whole agreement, including both, should be in writing."

Rule established by *Wain* v. *Warlters* and *Saunders* v. *Wakefield* as to sufficiency of memorandum to satisfy sect. 4.

For a long time the case of *Wain* v. *Warlters* was regarded as of doubtful authority (e), and two of the judges (*Lawrence*, J., and *Le Blanc*, J.) who decided the case only gave a hesitating assent to the decision. The case was, however, at last confirmed in *Saunders* v. *Wakefield* (f), and was never afterwards doubted (g). The rule that the consideration, as well as the promise, must appear on the face of a guarantee, which was thus [*150] laid *down, proved a grievance to the mercantile community (h), and was at last rescinded by the 3rd section of the Mercantile Law Amendment Act (i).

This rule abrogated by 19 & 20 Vict. c. 97, s. 3. Promise of surety need only be in writing, not consideration for it.

That section enacts, that "No special promise to be made by any person after the passing of this act to be answerable for the debt, default or miscarriage of another person, being in writing and signed by the party to be charged therewith, or some other person by him thereunto lawfully authorized, shall be deemed invalid to support an action, suit or other proceeding to charge the person by whom such promise shall have been made by reason only that the consideration for such promise does not appear in writing, or by necessary inference from a written instrument."

This enactment not retrospective.

This enactment is not retrospective in its operation

(d) 6 East, 307.
(e) See *Ex parte Minet*, 14 Ves. 189; *Ex parte Gardom*, 15 Ves. 286; *Phillips* v. *Bateman*, 16 East, 356; *Goodman* v. *Chase*, 1 B. & A. 300; 1 Wms. Saund. (last ed.), p. 226; 1 Sm. L. C., 8th ed., p. 330; Fell on Guarantees, 2nd ed., Appendix IV., p. 262.
(f) 4 B. & Ald., 505.
(g) 1 Sm. L. C., 6th ed., p. 278, and *ib.*, 8th ed., p. 330 and cases there cited.
(h) 1 Wms. Saund. (last ed.), p. 227.
(i) 19 & 20 Vict. c. 97.

(k), and it only dispenses with any *written statement* of the consideration, the *existence* of a consideration being quite as necessary as it was before (l). Nor must it be supposed that, in the case of guarantees not under seal, a consideration is *presumed* to exist until the contrary is shown (m), for such a presumption is applicable only to bills of exchange and promissory notes (n). Accordingly, in suing upon a guarantee, the consideration for it must be stated, whereas it is never necessary for a plaintiff to aver a consideration for any engagement on a bill or note (o). Since the passing of the Mercantile Law Amendment Act, section 3, though parol evidence may be given to show the consideration for a guarantee, it cannot be admitted to *explain* the promise, which, by *the Statute of Frauds, sec [*151] tion 4, must still be complete in writing (p). The above enactment does not, says *Byles*, J. (q), make a *promise* good which was not good before. Formerly, the consideration expressed *in writing* might be looked at, not only to support, but to explain, the promise. But the *parol* consideration cannot be looked at to explain the promise (r). If an instrument of guarantee states a *bad* consideration, it would not be helped by the Mercantile Law Amendment Act (s). Moreover, where the parties choose to state in writing the consideration for the promise, they are, it is presumed, bound by such statement, and cannot vary it by parol evidence (t). But if the language of the guarantee is sufficiently ambiguous, parol evidence is admissible to show that the alleged consideration is sufficient in law

Marginal notes:
Existence of a consideration still necessary, though it need not be specified in writing.

The written promise cannot be explained by parol evidence.

If had consideration set forth in memorandum parties cannot vary it by parol evidence.

(k) Taylor on Evidence, 5th ed., Vol. II., p. 895, and see *ib.*, 8th ed., p. 831, where the wording of the enactment is commented upon.

(l) 1 Sm. L. C., 8th ed., p. 330, and see *Glover* v. *Halkett*, 2 H. & N. 487.

(m) Fell on Guarantees, 2nd ed., pp. 5 and 6.

(n) *Rann* v. *Hughes*. 7 T. R. 350, note (a) ; 4 Brown Parl. Cas.; Chitty on Bills of Exchange, 10th ed., p. 47.

(o) *Popplewell* v. *Wilson*, 1 Stra. 264, and see Byles on Bills, 10th ed., pp. 118 and 119.

(p) *Holmes* v. *Mitchell*, 7 C. B., N. S. 361.

(q) *Ib.* p. 367.

(r) Per *Byles*, J., and *Williams*, J., in *Holmes* v. *Mitchell, supra,* pp. 367, 370.

. (s) Per *Bramwell*, B., in *Wood* v. *Priestner*, L. R., 2 Ex. 66.

(t) See 1 Sm. L. C., 6th ed., p. 279, and see Taylor on Evidence, 8th ed., Vol. II., p. 881 ; *Oldershaw* v. *King*, 2 H. & N. 399 ; *S. C., ib.* (Cam. Scacc.), p. 517. As to admissibility of evidence to add to consideration expressed in agreement, see *Re The Barnstaple Second Annuity Society and others*, 50 L. T. R. 424.

(*u*). And, as is stated in a subsequent chapter (*x*), in the construction of guarantees the rule that the construction must be given, *ut res magis valeat*, is applicable. This was decided in the case of *Broom* v. *Batchelor* (*y*). And in determining whether the *promise* to answer for another's debt, default or miscarriage does appear in writing, regard must be had, not only to those cases in which the courts had to decide whether the statement of the *promise* was sufficient, but also to those analogous cases (occurring before 19 & 20 Vict. c. 97, s. 3), in which the question to be decided was [*152] *whether the statement of the *consideration* was sufficient. Consequently, although it is no longer necessary now that the consideration should appear on the face of the guarantee, the decisions on this point may usefully be referred to. The following are some of the most important of such cases.

Previous decisions as to whether statement of consideration sufficient a guide to whether statement of promise now sufficient.

Lyon v. *Lamb.*

In *Lyon* v. *Lamb* (*z*) *Lyon* had been induced by *Lamb* to give credit to one *Anderton* for divers quantities of raw cotton under what was alleged to be an implied guarantee of *Lamb*. The circumstances were these. The invoices for the goods supplied had been regularly sent by *Lyon* to *Lamb*, and accepted by him, and were in the following form :—" Mr. *John Anderton* guaranteed by *J. Lamb*, bought of *J. Lyon*," &c. *Lamb* had been induced to endeavor to gain credit for *Anderton*, from *Anderton's* sending his manufactured goods to him to sell upon commission. Upon *Anderton's* ceasing to do this, *Lamb* sent back the next invoice, and gave *Lyon* the following note in writing :—

" *Mr. John Lyon.*

" You will receive back your invoice of nine bags left on Wednesday, as Mr. *Anderton* does not now send me his goods to sell. I guarantee all he has bought from you before Tuesday, but I will guarantee no further."

(Signed, &c.)

It was admitted, both in the argument and in the judgment, that if credit had been given to *Anderton* at the request and upon the verbal guarantee of *Lamb*, that would have been a good consideration for the subsequent promise in writing, and it was further admitted,

---

(*u*) *Hoad* v. *Grace*, 31 L. J., N. S., Exch. 78 ; *Goldshede* v. *Swan*, 1 Ex. 154 ; *Bainbridge* v. *Wade*, 16 Q. B. 89 ; *Edwards* v. *Jevons*, 8 C. B. 436 ; *Haigh* v. *Brooks*, 10 Ad. & E. 309 ; *Colbourn* v. *Dawson*, 10 C. B. 765.
(*x*) See *post*, Chap. IV., p. 180.
(*y*) 1 H. & N. 255.
(*z*) Fell on Guarantees, 2nd ed., App., No. III.

that the invoices might be used to explain the memorandum ; however, it was held that such consideration did not sufficiently appear on the face of the memorandum and invoices. Again, in *Stapp* v. *Lill* (a), the *Stapp* v. *Lill*. *memorandum was as follows:—"I guarantee the [*153] payment of any goods which Mr. *John Stapp* shall deliver to Mr. *Nicholls*, of *Brick Lane*." It was held, that though, by the agreement, the plaintiff was not obliged to deliver goods, there appeared a sufficient consideration for the defendant's promise to be answerable if any should be delivered. The court said that this case differed from *Wain* v. *Warlters* (b), as the agreement contained the thing to be done by the plaintiff, which was the foundation of the defendant's promise. Very similar to this case is that of *Ex parte* *Ex parte* *Gardom* (c), which came before the Lord Chancellor *Gardom.* *Eldon*, upon petition for the admission of the proof of a debt upon the following guarantees, given to the petitioner by the bankrupts :—

"We agree and engage to guarantee for what twist T. T. may purchase from you from &c. to &c."
         (Signed, &c.).

After the expiration of the date there mentioned, the following note of guarantee was given :—

"Whatever cotton twist you may dispose of to T. T., we agree and engage to guarantee the same." (Dated and signed.)

It was objected to these guarantees, that they did not state any consideration, as between the petitioners and the bankrupts. Lord *Eldon* expressed some difficulty in distinguishing this from the case of *Wain* v. *Warlters* (b), but added, "My opinion is that this is an agreement, within the meaning of the statute, to pay for the debt of another," and ordered the proof to be admitted.

In *Stead* v. *Liddard* (d), it was held, in an action on *Stead* v. a guarantee, that the reference, by the indorsement, to *Liddard.* the terms of the agreement, as forming part of one transaction, was a sufficient memorandum of the consideration within the statute.

*In *James* v. *Williams* (f), a letter was [*154] *James* v. written and sent by the defendant to the plaintiff, in *Williams.*

(a) 9 East, 348 (there cited as *Stadt* v. *Lill*), and 1 Camp. N. P. R. 242.
(b) 5 East, 10.
(c) 15 Ves. 286.
(d) 8 Moore, 2.
(f) 5 B. & Ald. 109.

the following words : "As you have a claim on my
brother for 5l. 17s. for boots and shoes, I hereby undertake to pay you the amount within six weeks from
this day." It was held that the consideration, viz.,
forbearance for six weeks to the principal debtor, could
not necessarily or fairly be drawn from the above letter,
and that therefore it did not satisfy the Statute of
Frauds.

*Newbury v.
Armstrong.*

In *Newbury* v. *Armstrong* (g), the guarantee was in
these words : "I agree to be security to you for J. C.,
late in the employ of J. P., for whatever you may in-
trust him with, while in your employ, to the amount of
50l." It was held, that the consideration, viz., that the
plaintiff should employ J. C., sufficiently appeared.

*Jarvis v.
Wilkins.*

In *Jarvis* v. *Wilkins* (h), the guarantee was in the
following words :—

"Septr. 11th, 1839. I undertake to pay to Mr.
Robert Jarvis the sum of 6l. 4s. for a suit of order by
Daniel Page.

"*S. W. Wilkins.*"

It was held, that the consideration, which was, that
if the plaintiff would sell to *Page* clothes, he (the defendant) would pay for them, could be collected by
necessary inference from the above instrument.

*Caballero v.
Slater.*

In *Caballero* v. *Slater* (i), the declaration set out an
agreement between *Mary Ann Caballero* (the plaintiff),
of the first part, and *David Thompson*, of the second
part, signed by the said *David Thompson*, and also by
the defendant *Slater*, whereby *Caballero* agreed to let
the premises to *Thompson*, at a certain rent, payable
quarterly, and which agreement concluded as follows:—

"And Mr. *Michael Thring Slater* does also agree and
undertake to see the rent paid quarterly by the said
David Thompson."

[*155]   *It was held, on demurrer to this declaration,
that a sufficient consideration for the defendant's promise appeared by necessary implication from the instrument set out.

*Hawes v.
Armstrong.*

In *Hawes* v. *Armstrong* (k), it was held, that, to

(g) 6 Bing. 201.
(h) 7 M. & W. 410.
(i) 14 C. B. 300.
(k) 1 Scott, 661. See also *Shortrede* v. *Cheek*, 1 Ad. & E. 57;
Lysaght v. *Walker*, 5 Bligh. N. S. 1; *Emmett* v. *Kearns*, 5 Bing.,
N. C. 559 ; *Kennaway* v. *Treleavan*, 5 M. & W. 498; *Haigh* v.
Brooks, 10 Ad. & E. 309; *Bentham* v. *Cooper*, 5 M. & W. 621;
James v. *Williams*, 5 B. & Ad. 1009; *Powers* v. *Fowler*, 4 E. & B.
511, 516.

constitute a valid agreement to answer for the debt or default of a third person, it was not necessary that the consideration should appear in *express terms:* it was sufficient if the memorandum were so framed that a person of ordinary capacity must infer, from the perusal of it, that such, and no other, was the consideration upon which the undertaking was given. In that case the guarantee was as follows:—

"*Messrs Hawes*—Gentlemen, Inclosed I forward you the bills drawn per *J. T. Armstrong* upon and accepted by *Leonard Dell*, which, I doubt not, will meet due honor; but, in default thereof, I will see the same paid. I remain, &c., *B. J. Armstrong, Hatton Wall*, 13th May, 1829" The consideration, stated in the declaration, was "that the plaintiffs, at the request of the defendant, would give time for the payment of the debt of 260*l.*, then due from *J. T. Armstrong* and *Dell*, and would take, accept and receive, by way of security for the payment of the same, the several bills of exchange set out in the declaration, and would forbear and give time to the said *J. T. Armstrong* and *Dell* for payment of the said debt or sum of 260*l.*, until the said bills should respectively become due and payable." But it was held, that the consideration did not sufficiently appear in the memorandum, and also that no consideration could be *implied* from such a memorandum.

*In *Jenkins* v. *Reynolds* (*l*), the court held [*156] that the words "to the amount of 100*l.* be pleased to consider me as security on *Mr. James Cowie & Co.'s* account," did not sufficiently indicate the consideration. *Jenkins v. Reynolds.*

In *Russell* v. *Moseley* (*m*), the following instrument was held sufficiently to disclose a consideration:—"I hereby guarantee the present account of H. M., and what she may contract from this day to 30th September next." *Russell v. Moseley.*

Where the instrument was so ambiguously worded that the consideration appeared to be made up of two considerations, *one of which was sufficient*, and the other was not, it was held that the instrument was invalid (*n*). *Where* the consideration, expressed in the instrument of guarantee, was that the plaintiff would withdraw "the promissory note," parol evidence was admitted to show what promissory note was meant; for here the parol

(*l*) 3 Brod. & B. 14.
(*m*) 3 Brod. & B. 211.
(*n*) *Raikes* v. *Todd*, 8 A. & E. 846; *Cole* v. *Dyer*, 9 L. J.; Ex. 109; but see *Bainbridge* v. *Wade*, 16 Q. B. 89; *Steele* v. *Hoe*, 19 L. J., N. S. (Q. B.) 89.

evidence was only required to identify the subject-matter of a written instrument, and this is always admitted (o).

Edwards v. Jevons. In *Edwards* v. *Jevons* (p), the memorandum to satisfy the statute was in the following words: "In consideration of Messrs. E. R. & Co. giving credit to Mr. D. J., I hereby engage to be responsible to and to pay any sum not exceeding 120l. due to Messrs. E. R. & Co. by D. J." The court admitted extrinsic circumstances in evidence, to show that the words "giving credit" were intended to apply to a particular credit agreed upon, and that the guarantee therefore disclosed a good consideration, and was not bad for uncertainty.

Goldshede v. Swan. In *Goldshede* v. *Swan* (q), parol evidence was admitted [*157] *to explain the meaning of the words "you having this day advanced" which appeared in a guarantee, and which may mean, either in consideration that you *have* this day advanced, or in consideration that you *shall* have this day advanced.

Bainbridge v. Wade. In *Bainbridge* v. *Wade* (r), the court upheld an instrument of guarantee, which, *explained by the circumstances stated in the declaration*, showed a good consideration for the promise of the defendant (s).

The object of the Statute of Frauds is to reduce contracts to a certainty, in order to avoid perjury, on the one hand, and fraud on the other. Consequently, where an agreement has been reduced to such a certainty, and the substance of the statute has been complied with, in the material part, that is sufficient (t).

Names of the contracting parties must appear in writing to satisfy statute. It is necessary, in order to satisfy the Statute of Frauds, that the names of the parties to the contract of guarantee should appear in writing (u). And it seems that the names of the parties to a contract, within the Statute of Frauds, must appear, *as such*, on the face of

(o) *Shortrede* v. *Cheek*, 1 A. & E. 57. See also *Bateman* v. *Phillips*, 15 East, 272.

(p) 8 C. B. 436; 14 Jur. 131; 19 L. J., C. P. 50.

(q) 1 Exch. 154.

(r) 16 Q. B. 89.

(s) In the following cases, also, the question to be determined was, whether the *consideration* sufficiently appeared on the face of the instrument of guarantee. *Price* v. *Richardson*, 15 M. & W. 539 ; *Emmett* v. *Kearns*, 5 Bing., N. C. 559 ; *Boehm* v. *Campbell*, 3 Moo. 15 ; *Peate* v. *Dicken*, 1 C. M. & R. 422 ; *Pace* v. *Marsh*, 1 Bing. 216 ; *Tanner* v. *Moore*, 9 Q. B. 1 ; *Bushnell* v. *Beavan*, 1 Bing. N. C. 103 ; *Saunders* v. *Wakefield*, 4 B. & Ald. 595 ; *Wain* v. *Warlters*, 5 East, 10.

(t) Per Lord Chancellor *Hardwick*, in *Welford* v. *Beazely*, 3 Atk. 503.

(u) *Williams* v. *Lake*, 29 L. J., Q. B. 1. See also *Williams* v. *Byrnes*, 2 N. R. 47; and *Champion* v. *Plummer*, 1 N. R. 252.

the contract, and not merely as descriptive of the subject-matter of the contract (x). In order to satisfy the Statute of Frauds, it is not, however, necessary that *the memorandum should be addressed to the [*158] other contracting party (y). Thus, where a guarantee was addressed to the *attorney for the plaintiff*, by the defendant, it was held that the plaintiff was entitled to the benefit of it (z.) *But the written memorandum need not be addressed to a contracting party.*

Moreover, it has been held that a guarantee, not addressed to anybody, will enure for the benefit of those to whom, or for whose use, it was delivered (a). It has also been held, that a guarantee addressed to one partner will enure for the benefit of all, if there be evidence that this was intended (b). *Effect of a guarantee not addressed to any one.*

With regard to the signature to a guarantee, it is to be observed, that such signature may be either by the "party to be charged" or by his agent. The "party to be charged" *only* need sign (c). And, on this principle, a written proposal containing the terms of a proposed contract, signed by the defendant, and *verbally* assented to by the plaintiff, is a sufficient agreement to satisfy the 4th section of the Statute of Frauds (d). So, a guarantee signed by the defendant and acted upon by the plaintiff, without any express verbal or written acceptance of it, is sufficient (e). *The signature of the memorandum.*

When the signature to a guarantee is not by the principals themselves but by an agent, it is not necessary that any particular formalities should be complied with in the appointment of such agent. Thus, the agent's authority need not be in writing (f). It appears, however, that such agent cannot delegate his au- [*159] *Signature by an agent. His authority to sign need not be in writing.*

(x) *Vandenbergh* v. *Spooner*, L. R., 1 Ex. 316; 35 L. J., Ex. 201; but see 2 Sm. L. C., 8th ed., pp. 268, 270, where this case appears to be questioned. And see *Newell* v. *Radford*, 3 C. P. 52; *Sarl* v. *Bourdillon*, 1 C. B. , N. S. 188.

(y) *Gibson* v. *Holland*, L. R., 1 C. P. 1.

(z) *Bateman* v. *Phillips*, 15 East, 272. See also *Longfellow* v. *Williams*, 2 Peake, 225.

(a) *Walton* v. *Dodson*, 3 C. & P. 162; but see *Williams* v. *Lake*, 29 L J., Q. B. 1.

(b) *Garrett* v. *Handley*, 4 B. & C. 664; and *Walton* v. *Dodson*, *supra.*

(c) See Taylor on Evidence, 8th ed. Vol. II. p. 879; *Laythoarp* v. *Bryant*, 2 Bing. N. C. 735, 743; 8 Scott, 238.

(d) *Smith* v. *Neal*, 2 C. B., N. S. 67.

(e) *Liverpool Borough Banking Co.* v. *Eccles*, 4 H. & N. 139; 28 L. J., Ex. 122.

(f) *Emmerson* v. *Heelis*, 2 Taunt. 38; *Coles* v. *Trecothick*, 9 Ves. 234, 250; *Mortlock* v. *Buller*, 10 Ves. 292, 311. See also *Stansfield* v. *Johnson*, 1 Esp. 101; *Rucker* v. *Camayer*, cited in Fell on Guarantees, 2nd ed., p. 87; *Cleman* v. *Cooke*, 1 Sch. & Lef. 22.

He cannot delegate his authority. Ratification of agent's signature by principal.

thority to another, though, if he do so, it would seem that the principal may ratify the act (g). A subsequent recognition of the act of an agent, signing an agreement required by the Statute of Frauds to be in writing, would seem to be sufficient to charge the principal. (h). And it is not necessary that a person signing a guarantee should expressly sign *as agent*. For the Statute of Frauds does not, it seems, exclude parol evidence, that a written contract was made by a person as

When agent signs his own name and that of his principals, must be taken to have signed as a contracting party. Agent need not sign the name of his principal.

agent only for another (i). And where a person, acting under a power of attorney from a firm, signed at the foot of a guarantee their name and his own name also, it was held that evidence of his having intended to sign in his own right, as well as on behalf of the firm, did not contradict the document, and was admissible, and that he must be taken to have signed as a contracting party (k). It is not necessary that a person signing an instrument should sign the name of his principal. In such cases, however, the agent cannot defeat an action on the instrument by proving that he signed only as agent for another, for this would, by *discharging* the agent, violate the rule of law, that parol evidence is not admissible to *contradict* a written instrument (l). A person may, however, now allege (as he could formerly also have done by equitable defence) that though he signed the instrument sued upon in his own name, and without adding that he was agent for another, yet it was agreed between himself and the principal, at the time of the [*160] *execution of the instrument, that he was not to be liable as principal (m). Moreover, though parol evidence is not admissible, *on behalf* of a person who has signed an instrument *as principal*, to show that he is *an agent* merely, yet, it is admissible on behalf of a plaintiff suing the undisclosed principal, for the purpose of *charging* the latter, for this evidence is *consistent* with the instrument (n). But the authority of the agent may be countermanded at any time before a memorandum of the contract is written and signed by him pursuant to the Statute of Frauds (o).

(g) *Blore* v. *Sutton*, 3 Mer. 236.
(h) *Gobell* v. *Archer*, 2 Ad. & E. 500, 507 ; and *Maclean* v. *Dunn*, 4 Bing. 722 ; *Fitzmaurice* v. *Bayley*, 6 E. &. B. 868.
(i) *Wilson* v. *Hart*, 7 Taunt. 295.
(k) *Young* v. *Schuler*, 11 Q. B. D. 651 ; 49 L. T. 456.
(l) *Higgins* v. *Senior*, 8 A. & E. 834 ; and see 2 Sm. L. C., 6th ed., notes to *Thompson* v. *Davenport*.
(m) *Wake* v. *Harrop*, 6 H. & N. 768 ; and in error, 1 H. & C. 202.
(n) *Wilson* v. *Hart*, 7 Taunt. 295 ; and remarks on this case at p. 407 of 2 Sm. L. C., 8th ed.
(o) *Farmer* v. *Robinson*, cited in a note, 2 Camp. p. 339.

It is, however, necessary that the agent should have Agent must *some* authority to bind the defendant. On the one hand, have some if he have not, the principal is not bound at all. Thus, authority to a memorandum, written by the plaintiff's clerk, in the sign guaran- presence of the defendant, that "the latter had called tee. to say, that he would be responsible for goods delivered to Mr. H.," is not a sufficient undertaking within the Statute of Frauds (p). But, in *Watkins* v. *Vince* (q), it was held by Lord *Ellenborough*, at *Nisi Prius*, that the son of the defendant, aged sixteen years, who was proved to have signed for his father in three or four instances, and to have accepted bills for him, was a sufficient agent to sign a memorandum of guarantee. While, thus, on the one hand, a principal is not bound by a signature made by a person who has no authority to sign, on the other hand, liability may personally attach to a person so signing. For upon the other hand, a person signing a contract as agent for another, without any authority to so, exposes himself to legal liability, varying according to circumstances of *each* particular case. If there was no principal existing at the *time [*161] who *could* be bound, and the contract would be wholly inoperative, unless binding on the person who signed it, the agent signing it is personally liable upon it (r). If, however, there was a person existing at the time who could (but did not) authorize the agent to sign, and who *could be bound*, the agent will be liable to an action for thus misrepresenting his authority (s); unless, indeed, he had once had an authority, the determination of which could not be known to him (t).. An agent *ignorantly* or *wilfully* misrepresenting his authority, is, it seems, also liable in an action upon his implied promise that he really possessed the authority which he pretended to have (u).

The question, whether a person has authority to bind What class of another, is thus of great importance, both as regards agents possess the liability of the alleged principal, and also with re- implied au- ference to the liability of the person thus signing on give guaran- another's behalf. It will, therefore, be well to consider tee—

(p) *Dixon* v. *Broomfield*, 2 Chit. 205.
(q) 2 Stark. 368.
(r) *Kelner* v. *Baxter*, L. R., 2 C. P. 174.
(s) *Thomas* v. *Edwards*, 2 M. & W. 215; *Lewis* v. *Nicholson*, 18 Q. B. 503. See also Sm. Merc. Law. 9th ed., p. 161.
(t) *Smout* v. *Ilbery*, 10 M. & W. 1.
(u) *Collen* v. *Wright*, 7 E. & B. 301; *Simons* v. *Patchett*, 7 E. & B. 568; *In re National Coffee Palace Co.*, *Ex parte* v. *Panmure*, 24 Ch. D. 367, C. A. (where the measure of damages is discussed); 2 Sm. L. C., 8th ed., p. 377, notes to *Thompson* v. *Davenport*.

it in detail, and with regard to the various classes of
agents which exist.

Brokers.
A *broker*, instructed by one person to buy and by another to sell goods, is equally the agent of both parties (x). If, therefore, such broker, doubting the credit of the purchaser, were to take the guarantee of another, reduce a sufficient memorandum thereof into writing, and sign it, it is *conceived* that he would be a sufficient agent for that purpose (y).

Auctioneers.
Nor does it appear ever to have been decided whether [*162] *an *auctioneer*, instructed to sell some land, and receiving a guarantee for the price, instead of a deposit from the purchaser, could act as agent of the person giving the guarantee and affix such person's name to it.(z).

A party to the contract.
One of the *contracting parties* cannot, it seems, act as authorized agent for the other contracting party and bind him by his signature, for the agent contemplated by the Statute of Frauds must be a *third* person (a).

Partners. Right of one partner to bind rest by a guarantee depends on nature of business or previous course of dealing. Hope v. Cust.
It is very difficult to lay down any rules in regard to the power of one *partner* to bind the rest by executing a guarantee in the name of the partnership firm, as the nature of a partner's power or authority to bind his copartners varies in each case. It depends on the nature of the business carried on by the firm, or on the previous course of dealing. Perhaps, the only general rule on this subject that can be laid down, with any degree of safety, is that given by Lord *Mansfield* in *Hope* v. *Cust* (b), viz., "that the act of every single partner in a transaction relating to the partnership binds all the others. If one give a letter of credit or guarantee in the name of all the partners it binds all."

Ex parte Nolte.
In *Ex parte Nolte* (c), the view taken by Lord *Mansfield* in *Hope* v. *Cust* was upheld by Lord Chancellor *Eldon*, who decided that a partner may give a guar-

(x) Benjamin's Sale of Personal Property, 3rd ed., pp. 236—237; and see *Thompson* v. *Gardiner*, 1 C. P. D. 777.
(y) Fell's Law of Mercantile Guarantees, 2nd ed., p. 89.
(z) Fell's Law of Mercantile Guarantees, 2nd ed., p. 94.
(a) *Farebrother* v. *Simmons*, 5 B. & Ald. 333; *Wright* v. *Dannah*, 2 Camp. 203; *Sharman* v. *Brandt*, 40 L. J., N. S. 312; S. C., L. R., 6 Q. B., 720 (which are decisions on the 17th sect. of the Statute of Frauds, but are equally applicable to the 4th sect.). See, however, *Bird* v. *Boulter*, 4 B. & Ad. 443, 447, and see observations in Blackburn on Contract of Sale, p. 76.
(b) Sittings at Guildhall after Michaelmas Term, 1774. This case is cited by *Lawrence* in *Shirreff* v. *Wilkes and others*, 1 East, at p. 53.
(c) 2 Glyn & J. 295; and see *In re West of England Bank, Ex parte Booker*, 14 Ch. Div. 317.

antee where the obligation has reference to business
connected with the partnership, and where the guarantee is notified to the firm, and they do not dissent
from it.

Upon the general question as to the power of one
*partner to bind the firm by giving a guar- [*163]
antee, the case of *Sandilands* v. *Marsh* (d), is worthy *Sandilands v.*
of careful consideration. There, one *Creed*, a member *Marsh.*
of a firm of navy agents, in consideration of the plaintiff employing the firm as his agents to lay out 4,000l.
in the purchase of an annuity, and of a commission of
5l. per cent. to be paid to such agents, guaranteed the
punctual half-yearly payment of the annuity to the
plaintiff. An action having been brought on this guarantee, the question arose whether *Marsh*, who was the
partner of *Creed*, who gave the guarantee in the name
of the firm, was bound by it. At the trial the learned
judge left it to the jury to say, whether, under the circumstances of the case, *Marsh* was cognizant of the
transaction as to the purchase of the annuity, though
he might be ignorant as to the facts of the guarantee
itself, telling them that, in that case, he thought the
defendant was liable. The jury found this fact in the
affirmative, and the plaintiff obtained a verdict. Leave
to move was given, and a rule *nisi* obtained. In discharging this rule, *Abbott*, C. J., said: "Two material
questions have been made; the first (e) of which, and
the most important and extensive in its consequences
is, whether this defendant shall be held to be bound
by the guarantee given without his knowledge by his
partner *Creed*, and if the verdict of the jury, finding
him to be so bound be not sustainable, it will be very
dangerous hereafter to deal with a partnership; for the
business in each department of a firm is generally
transacted by one partner only. It has, undoubtedly,
been held that, in a matter wholly unconnected with
the partnership, one partner cannot bind the others.
But the true construction of the rule is this, that the
act and assurance of one partner, made with reference
to business transacted by the firm, will bind all the
*partners. In this case, the proper business of [*164]
Marsh and *Creed* was to receive the money due from
the navy board to their customers, and their dividends
in the public funds. . . . It was no part of their
ordinary business to guarantee annuities or to lay out

(d) 2 B. & Ald. 673.
(e) The second question has no bearing on the subject now under discussion.

the monies of their customers in the purchase of them. Under these circumstances the original proposal was made by *Creed*, in answer to which the joint power of attorney was transmitted to *Marsh* and *Creed*, under which the stock was afterwards sold. Now that sale must have appeared in the partnership books, and if that fact were doubtful, it is proved by the balance stated in the accounts transmitted by the partnership: that sale, therefore, and the fact that the proceeds had been laid out in the purchase of an annuity, either were actually known, or ought to have been known by *Marsh*. Now, if that whole transaction were known to him, the guarantee, which is connected with it, becomes, in point of law, an assurance made by one partner with reference to business transacted by both; and, according to the rule previously stated, it will bind both. To illustrate this position, a case may be put where two persons, in partnership for the sale of horses, should agree between themselves never to warrant any horse: yet, though this be their course of business, there is no doubt that if, upon the sale of a horse, the property of the partnership, one of them should give a warranty, the other would be thereby bound." In the same case, *Bayley*, J., in his judgment, says: "It is true that one partner cannot bind another out of the regular course of dealing by the firm. But where the assurance has reference to business transacted by the partnership, *although out of the regular course*, it is still within the scope of his authority, and will bind the firm."

In *Ex parte Gardom* (f), *Gardom* being applied to by *Thomas Tapp*, of *Manchester*, to sell him cotton twist, [*165] *desired a reference. Accordingly, *Goodwin*, of the house of *Hargreave & Goodwin*, verbally informed *Gardom* that their house would guarantee what twist *Gardom* might sell to *Tapp*, up to the 1st of January, 1808, as *Tapp* was manufacturing goods for them. In due course the following engagement was drawn up in writing to be signed by *Hargreave* and *Goodwin*: "We agree and engage to guarantee for what twist *Thomas Tapp* may purchase from you from the 28th ult. to the first of January, 1808. *Hargreave & Goodwin*." That paper was signed by *Goodwin* only. A renewal of the guarantee afterwards took place, in similar terms. Sales took place under both guarantees. A commission of bankruptcy issued against *Tapp;* and another against

(f) 15 Ves. 286.
(1364)

Hargreave & Goodwin. Under that commission *Gardom* offered to prove the residue of his demand upon *Tapp,* but proof was rejected upon three grounds, one of which was, *that the signature* of *Goodwin* alone could not bind the partnership. This ground, however, was ultimately given up, whereupon Lord Chancellor *Eldon* said: "The objection, that the partnership was not bound by the signature of one partner, is properly given up."

It appears that, in the case of ordinary merchants, one partner has no incidental authority to bind another in the name of the firm, by a guarantee given out of the course of ordinary business. This was decided in *Duncan* v. *Lowndes* (g). There a guarantee was given for the due payment of a bill of exchange to the plaintiff for 670l. 15s., accepted by *Dickinson & Co.,* for the price of goods which the plaintiff had sold them. It appeared that the guarantee was signed by the defendant *Lowndes,* who was one of the partners, in the name of the partnership firm. Lord *Ellenborough* held, that it was necessary to prove that *Lowndes* had authority from his co-partner to execute the guarantee *in the name of the partnership firm, as it was [*166] not usual for merchants, in the common course of business, to give collateral engagements of the sort in question. "It is not incidental to the general power of a partner to bind his co-partners by such an instrument." It was also held, that proof of a subsequent recognition of the guarantee by the partner who did not actually sign it, as well as prior command or proof of a previous course of dealing in which such guarantees were given, and to which all the partners were privy, would be sufficient evidence of an authority to execute the guarantee in the name of the partnership firm.

One member of an ordinary mercantile firm has no implied power to bind the rest.

Duncan v. Lowndes.

So, in *Crawford* v. *Stirling* (h), *Crawford & Co.,* the plaintiffs, were manufacturers and merchants at *Glasgow,* in *Scotland;* but *Andrew Mitchell,* one of the partners, resided in *London,* and conducted the business of the house there. One *Kirkpatrick,* who lived in *Liverpool,* having occasion for goods in the course of his trade, in which the defendant dealt, procured the guarantee of *Mitchell* to the defendant, on account of the house of the plaintiffs, for which the house received an allowance of 2½ per cent. There was evidence of adoption of the guarantee by the firm of *Crawford & Co.* It was held, that this guarantee bound the entire firm. Lord *Ellenborough* said: "A guarantee given by one

Crawford v. Stirling.

(g) 3 Camp. 477.
(h) 4 Esp. 207.

partner in the partnership's name, unless it was in the
regular line of business, could not bind the other partners; but if they afterwards adopted it, and acted on
it, it should bind them."

In *Brettell* v. *Williams* (*i*), the defendants, who were
in partnership as railway contractors, contracted with a
railway company to do certain works. U. & R. made a
sub-contract with the defendants to do part of the work,
and, for that purpose requiring coals to make bricks,
one of the defendants, without the knowledge or assent
[*167] *of his co-partners, signed in the name of the
firm, and delivered to the plaintiffs a guarantee, not
addressed to any person, for payment of coals to be
supplied to U. & R. It was *held*, that the guarantee did not bind the firm of railway contractors, there
being no evidence that it was necessary for carrying
into effect the partnership contract, or that the other
partners had adopted it. Baron *Parke*, in his judgment in the case, ably reviews the authorities on the
subject we are dealing with. He says: "That one of
two partners engaged in business as merchants had not,
by reason of that connection alone, power to bind the
other by a guarantee, apparently unconnected with the
partnership trade, was decided by Lord *Ellenborough*,
in the case of *Duncan* v. *Lowndes* (*k*); and the Court
of Queen's Bench gave a similar decision in that of
Hasleham v. *Young* (*l*), where the defendants were in
partnership as attornies. No proof was given in either
of these cases of the previous course of dealing or
practice of the partners, which, it is admitted in both
cases, might be sufficient to prove a mutual authority;
nor was any evidence given of the usage of similar
partnerships to give such guarantees; nor was there
any of a recognition and adoption by the other partners
which would have the same effect. The case of *Sandilands* v. *Marsh* (*m*) proceeded on the latter ground.
In the present case, no evidence was given to show the
usage of the defendants in this particular business, or
of others in a similar business; nor was there any evidence of the sanction by the other defendants of the
act of their co-partner; for a witness, who was called
to prove the latter fact, would not, on cross-examina-
tion, swear that he was authorized by them to write a
letter, which, if proved to have been so written, would

(*i*) 4 Exch. 628.
(*k*) 3 Camp. 477.
(*l*) 5 Q. B. 836.
(*m*) 2 B. & Ald. 673, *ante*, p. 163.

have been sufficient. Simply as railway contractors they could not have any such power. The only *ques- [*168] tion then is, whether they had it in this particular case, in consequence of its being a *reasonable* mode of carrying into effect an acknowledged partnership contract. One partner does communicate to the other, simply by the creation of that relation, and as incident thereto, all the authority necessary to carry on their partnership in its ordinary course (n), and all such authority as is usually exercised by partners in the same sort of trade, but no more. To allow one partner to bind another by contracts out of the apparent scope of the partnership dealings, because they were reasonable acts towards effecting the partnership purposes, would be attended with great danger. Could one of the defendants in this case have bound the others by a contract to lease or buy lands, or a coal mine, though it might be a reasonable mode of effecting a legitimate object of the partnership business? Our opinion is, that one partner cannot bind the others in such a case, simply by virtue of the partnership relation. In the case of *Ex parte Gardom* (o), this point was not fully discussed, but given up by Sir S. *Romilly*, who had two other objections to the guarantee, on which he could rely, and on one of which he succeeded. Besides, we are not sufficiently informed by the report whether there might not have been some peculiar circumstances in the case which caused the abandonment of that point. We do not think that is an authority sufficient to establish the doctrine now contended for."

Similar doctrines are applied in the case of other business, such as attorneys. Thus, in *Hasleham* v. *Young* (p), one of two attornies in partnership, in order to procure the release of a client from custody, gave an undertaking in the name of the firm, to pay the debt and costs on a day named, and it was held that the firm *was not liable. It did not appear that the [*169] guarantee was any advantage to the firm, there was no evidence that the guarantee was given in pursuance of the ordinary practice of the parties, and, as *Patteson*, J., said, "Certainly such a transaction is not in the usual course of the business of attorneys."

In *Payne* v. *Ives* (q) *Abbott*, C. J., left it to the jury to say whether a guarantee had been given with the

Hasleham v. *Young.*

Payne v. *Ives.*

(n) See *Hawtaine* v. *Bourne*, 7 M. & W. 595.
(o) 16 Ves. 286. See *ante*, pp. 164—165.
(p) 5 Q. B. 836.
(q) 3 D. & R. 664.

134   THE LAW OF GUARANTEES.

privity and consent of all the partners. There *Mann*,
of the firm of *Ives, Sargon & Mann*, gave a guarantee
in his own handwriting, and signed by him only, on the
part of the firm, to Messrs. *Payne & Co.*, whereby
Messrs. *Ives, Sargon & Mann* undertook to indorse any
bill or bills which one *John Stubbs* might give to Messrs.
Payne & Co., in part payment of an order for certain
goods then being executed for him.

Power of one partner to bind the rest by guarantee under seal. *Harrison* v. *Jackson*.
As regards the power of one or more in a partnership
to bind the whole firm by a guarantee *under seal*, there
can be no doubt that the rule laid down by Lord *Kenyon*, C. J., in *Harrison* v. *Jackson* (r), would apply to
such a case, namely, that a "general partnership agreement, though under seal, does not authorize the partners to execute deeds for each other, unless a *particular power* be given for that purpose."

Effect of subsequent acknowledgment by firm of signature of guarantee under seal by member of firm.
It seems, moreover, that the subsequent acknowledgment of the partner or partners, who did not execute
the deed, that it was executed with their authority, is
not sufficient to make the instrument binding upon
them (s). "However, though one partner has no *implied* authority generally to bind his co-partner by deed,
yet, if one partner execute a deed on behalf of the
firm, in the presence and with the consent of his co-
[*170] partners, *that will bind the firm; *in such case
the sealing and delivery by one is deemed to be the act
of all* " (t).

Semble guarantee only binds existing members of firm, not subsequent members.
It seems that a guarantee given by a partnership firm
does not bind persons who subsequently become members of the firm (u).

Liability of a company on guarantee given by directors.
As regards the liability of a *company*, on a guarantee
given by its *directors*, it appears that the company is
not bound, in the absence of proof, that the directors
had power to give it (x). The directors of a company
may, however, become sureties for it, and they then
possess the rights and incur the responsibilities attach-

(r) 7 T. R. 207; and see Lindley on Partnership, 4th ed., p. 278.

(s) Collyer on Partnership, 2nd ed., p. 309 ; *Steiglitz* v. *Eggington*, Holt, N. P. C. 141; *Brutton* v. *Burton*, 1 Chit. 707; but see *Harvey* v. *Kay*, 9 B. & C. 356.

(t) Collyer on Partnership, 2nd ed. pp. 309. 310; *Ball* v. *Dunsterville*, 4 T. R. 313 ; *Burn* v. *Burn*, 3 Ves. 573; *Smith* v. *Winter*, 4 M. & W. 454.

(u) Fell's Law of Mercantile Guarantees, 2nd ed., pp. 120, 121.

(x) *In re Era Life Assurance Society*, 1 W. N. 309. See also *Ridley* v. *Plymouth Grinding Co.*, 2 Ex. 711; *Kirk* v. *Bell*, 16 Q. B. 29a.

(1368)

, ing to the ordinary contract of suretyship (y). And where directors guarantee the performance by a company of a contract which is *ultra vires*, and cannot therefore be enforced against the company, the directors are nevertheless liable under their guarantee. (z). Where directors are sureties for an unlimited company which is being wound up, they cannot set off payments made by them, after the winding-up order, in discharge of their suretyship liability, against calls made before the filing of the petition and enforced by a subsequent order but not yet paid (a).

As regards the *position* of the signature of the party to be charged to a written memorandum required by the Statute of Frauds, it appears that, provided the *name be inserted in an instrument in such a [*171] manner as to have the effect of *authenticating* it, the requisition of the act with respect to signature is complied with, and it does not matter *in what part* of the instrument the name is found (b). A mere casual introduction of the name would not, however, amount to a sufficient signature (c). The position of the signature to memorandum of guarantee.

Where the party to be charged has not signed the instrument in the *usual* place, the question is always open to the jury, whether the party, not having signed it regularly at the foot, meant to be bound by it as it stood, or whether it was left so unsigned because he refused to complete it (d). Where it is obvious that the parties did not intend that the agreement should be perfect till their names were added at the foot, the Statute of Frauds will not be satisfied (e).

As regards the *kind* of signature, we may observe that a mark by a marksman is a sufficient signature of an agreement in writing within the Statute of Frauds (f). There must, however, be a signing, *i. e.*, an actual signa- The *kind* of signature to memorandum of guarantee.

(y) *Gray* v. *Seckham*, L. R., 7 Ch. App. 680; and see *In re Booth-Browning* v. *Baldwin*, 27 W. R. 644; *Deans* v. *Walls*, 29 L. T. R. 599; *MacDonald* v. *Whitfield*, 8 App. Cas. 733.
(z) *Yorkshire Railway Wagon Co.* v. *Maclure*, 19 Ch. Div. 478; *Chambers* v. *Manchester & Milford Railway Co.*, 5 B. & S. 588, 612.
(a) *In re Norwich Equitable Fire Assurance Co., Brasnet's case*, 33 W. R. 1010.
(b) *Ogilvie* v. *Foljambe*, 3 Mer. 53; *Caton* v. *Caton*, L. R., 2 H. L. 127. See also *Lobb* v. *Stanley*, 5 Q. B. 574; *Simmonds* v. *Humble*, 13 C. B., N. S. 258; *Propert* v. *Parker*, 1 Russ. & My. 625.
(c) See *Stokes* v. *Moore*, 1 Cox, 219.
(d) Per Lord *Abinger*, C. B., in *Johnson* v. *Dodgson*, 2 M. & W. 653, 659. See also *Knight* v. *Crockford*, 1 Esp. 190, 193, and *Saunderson* v. *Jackson*, 2 B. & P. 238, 239.
(e) *Hubert* v. *Treherne*, 3 M. & G. 743.
(f) *Selby* v. *Selby*, 3 Mer. 2. See also *Hubert* v. *Moreau*, 12 Moore, 216, 219; *Baker* v. *Dening*, 8 A. & E. 94.

ture of the name, or something intended by the writer to be equivalent to a signature; for it is not enough that the party may be *identified;* the statute requires him to sign (g). It seems that a signature by *initials* is sufficient (h), if the initials be intended as a signature [*172] *by the party who writes them (i). However, the *christian* name may be set out at length, denoted by initials, or left out altogether (k). A printed signature would seem to be sufficient. Certainly this is the case where there is subsequent recognition, or where part of the instrument is in the handwriting of the party(l). It seems to be doubtful, having regard to decided cases, whether a signature by a person mentioned in the memorandum as a contracting party, though he profess to sign as a witness, is sufficient (m). But it would seem that where the signature is not that of the agent of the party to be charged, *quà* agent, but only in the capacity of witness to the writing, it will not suffice (n). The mere altering of a draft is not a sufficient signature, because the party clearly did not intend to be bound thereby (o). Where, however, a parol agreement in writing was entered into, and a draft of it was prepared, and, by indorsement on this draft, the defendant admitted the agreement, but excused himself from performing it, it was held that the 4th section of the Statute of Frauds was satisfied (p).

A guarantee drawn up in the plural number, and concluding as, "Witness our hands," but signed by one surety only, is binding upon the surety who signed it(q).

Margin notes: Initials sufficient. Printed signature sufficient. Signature by a witness. Signature by indorsement of draft. Guarantee drawn up in plural num-

---

(g) Ibid.
(h) *Chichester* v. *Cobb*, 14 L. T., N. S. 433, Q. B.; *Gobrie* v. *Woodley*, 17 Ir. C. L. R. 221; *Jacob* v. *Kirk*, 2 Moo. & R. 221; *Sweet* v. *Lee*, 3 M. & G. 452; *Parker* v. *Smith*, 1 Coll. 608; *Hubert* v. *Moreau*, 2 C. & P. 528; and see Benjamin on Sales, 3rd ed., pp. 220, 221. See also *In re Goods of Blewitt*, 5 P. D. 116.
(i) Per Lord Westbury, in *Caton* v. *Caton*, 2 H. L. 127, 143.
(k) *Lobb* v. *Stanley*, 5 Q. B. 574, 581, 582. See 2 Sm. L. C. 6th ed., p. 233.
(l) *Schneider* v. *Norris*, 2 M. & S. 286. See also *Saunderson* v. *Jackson*, 2 B. & P, 238. And see Benjamin on Sales, 3rd ed., p. 223 *et seq.*
(m) *Welford* v. *Bazeley*, 1 Ves. sen. 6; *Coles* v. *Trecothick*, 9 Ves. 234, 250; *Blore* v. *Sutton*, 3 Mer. 237; *Gosbell* v. *Archer*, 2 Ad. & E. 500.
(n) Benjamin on Sales, 3rd ed., p. 236.
(o) *Hawkins* v. *Holmes*, 1 P. W. 770.
(p) *Shippey* v. *Denison*, 5 Esp. 190. See also *Backworth* v. *Young*, 26 L. J., Ch. 153; *Jackson* v. *Lowe*, 1 Bing. 9; *Warner* v. *Willington*, 25 L. J., Ch. 662; *Bailey* v. *Sweeting*, 30 L. J., C. P. 150; *Gibson* v. *Holland*, L. R., 1 C. P. 1.
(q) *Norton* v. *Powell*, 4 M. & G. 42.

*A letter beginning, "We hereby guarantee," [*173] ber and signed with the name of a firm, and by each of the signed by partners, though it would only have been a joint guar- one person antee if signed in the name of the firm alone, or only by each of the partners, has been held to be a separate guarantee by each partner as well as a guarantee by the firm (r).

It has recently been decided that the signature of the Signature of party to be charged to instructions for a telegraphic instructions message, accepting the plaintiff's written offer, is a suf- for tele- ficient signature under the Statute of Frauds (s). graphic message.

It is not necessary that the note in writing, to be Memoran- binding under the statute, should be contemporary with dum in writ- the agreement. It is sufficient if it had been made at ing need not any time, and adopted by the party afterward, and be contem- then anything under the hand of the party, expressing porary with that he had entered into the agreement, will satisfy the agreement. statute, which was only intended to protect persons from having parol agreements imposed on them (t). But, as But when the held by Fry, J., in a very recent case, the memorandum memoran- or note of agreement required by the 4th section must dum is made be a memorandum of an agreement complete at the a complete time the memorandum is made (u). agreement in existence.

To satisfy the Statute of Frauds, it is not necessary existence. that the agreement of the parties should be contained Agreement in one written instrument. It may be contained in need not be several different papers, which, taken together, form the one written agreement between the parties (x). But these different instrument. *papers must be, in themselves, and on the face [*174] of them, connected, either in express words or by con- taining those which are capable of an interpretation

---

(r) Ex parte Harding, In re Smith, 12 Ch. Div. 557 ; 41 L. T. 3'8 ; 28 W. R. 158.

(s) Godwin v. Francis, L. R., 5 C. P. 295 ; M'Blain v. Cross, 25 L. T., N. S. 804.

(t) Per Lord Ellenborough, in Shippey v. Denison (ubi supra), p. 193. See also Tawney v. Crowther, 3 Bro. C. C. 161 ; Bradford v. Roulston, 8 Ir. C. L. R., N. S. 468.

(u) Munday v. Asprey, 13 Ch. Div. 855.

(x) Stead v. Liddard, 8 Moo. 2 ; Redhead v. Cater, 1 Stark. 14 ; Sandilands v. Marsh, 2 B. & Ald. 680 ; Buxton v. Rust, L. R., 1 Ex. 1 ; Hemming v. Perry, 2 M. & P. 375 ; Hare v. Richards, 5 M. & P. 235 ; Brettell v. Williams, 4 Exch. 623 ; Macrory v. Scott, 5 Exch. 907 ; Colbourn v. Dawson, 10 C. B. 765 ; Coe v. Duffield, 7 Moo. 252. See also Jackson v. Lowe, 7 Moo. 219 ; Dobell v. Hut- chinson, 3 A. & E. 355 ; Hammersley v. Baron de Biel, 12 Cl. & F. 45 ; De Bert v. Thompson, 3 Beav. 471 ; Ridgway v. Wharton, 6 H. L. 238 ; 27 L. J., Ch. 46 ; Ogilvie v. Foljambe, 3 Mer. 53 ; Horsey v. Graham, L. R., 5 C. P. 9 ; Jones v. Williams, 7 M. & W. 493 ; Nene Valley Drainage Commissioners v. Dunkley, 4 Ch. Div. 1 ; Baumann v. James, L. R., 3 Ch. App. 508.

which, in its sense, connects the different instruments.
Parol evidence is not admissible for the purpose of con-
necting them (y).

In *Bluck* v. *Gompertz* (z), the defendant gave to the
plaintiff a guarantee, signed by the defendant. Subsequently, it was discovered that there was a mistake in
the instrument of guarantee. This mistake was accordingly rectified by an indorsement written across the
guarantee itself by the defendant, but signed by the
plaintiff only. It was held that the instrument was a
valid memorandum of the contract declared on, within
the Statute of Frauds, since the indorsement, having
been made for the purpose of correcting the mistake,
and being written by the defendant on the same piece
of paper as the original undertaking, must be considered
as authenticated by the original signature of the defendant.

If signed paper refer to unsigned paper, statute satisfied.	It is also sufficient if a signed paper refer to another paper which is not signed, and which contains the terms of the agreement between the parties (a).
Rule where contract has to be collected from correspondence.	Where a court has to find a contract in a correspondence and not in one particular note or memorandum formally signed, the *whole* of that which has passed between the parties must be taken into consideration, [*175] *even though the first two letters of the correspondence seem of themselves to constitute a complete and binding contract (b).
The stamping of a guarantee. It cannot be given in evidence without a stamp.	It may be as well to say a few words here as to the *stamping* of an instrument of guarantee (c). The instrument of guarantee cannot be given in evidence unless it is properly stamped (d). This is the case even where the instrument does not state on its face the consideration for the promise (e). In *Glover* v. *Hackett* (f), H., being tenant to E., G. signed the following document:—"August 2nd. According to Mr. H.'s request, the land at B., under Mr. E., I will be bound for

---

(y) 1 Sm. L. C., 8th ed., pp. 336, 337. See *Wilkinson* v. *Evans*,
L. R., 1 C. P. 407.
(z) 7 Exch. 862.
(a) *Tawney* v. *Crowther*, 3 Bro. Ch. Cas. 161 ; *Allen* v. *Bennet*, 3
Taunt. 169 ; *Saunderson* v. *Jackson*, 2 B. & P. 238 ; *Stead* v. *Liddard*, 1 Bing. 196 ; *De Bert* v. *Thompson*, 3 Beav. 471 ; *Coldham*
v. *Showler*, 3 C. B., N. S. 312.
(b) *Hussey* v. *Horne Payne*, L. R., 4 App. Cas. 311 ; and see
May v. *Thomson*, 20 Ch. D. 705.
(c) The Stamp Act, 1870 (33 & 34 Vict. c. 97), governs this
subject.
(d) 33 & 34 Vict. c. 97, s. 17.
(e) *Whitfield* v. *Moojen*, 1 F. & F. 290.
(f) 29 L. J., Ex. 416.

till next Ladyday; rent 48l., (Signed) J. G." The document being tendered in evidence, in an action by G. against H. for money paid to the landlord, it was held that it required an agreement stamp. However, a guarantee in writing *for the payment of goods* thereafter to be purchased by a third person to a certain amount is within the exception of the Stamp Act, 1870, "a contract for or *relating to the sale* of goods," and need not be stamped (g). In *Haigh* v. *Brooks* (h), the promise was alleged in the declaration as having been given in consideration of the giving up of a guarantee. Plea, that it was not given up. It was held that this guarantee could be given in evidence without being stamped. Where the defendant wrote on the back of a letter of the plaintiff an undertaking to be answerable for the debt of another, and which indorsed undertaking made reference to the *terms of the agree- [*176] ment on the other side, it was held, in an action on the guarantee, that only one stamp was required on this paper (i). A guarantee for the due performance of a charterparty does not require to be stamped as "a charterparty or agreement for the charter of any ship, or any memorandum, letter or other writing between the captain or owner of any ship and any other person for or relating to the freight or conveyance of goods, &c., on board such ship, &c.." within 5 & 6 Vict. c. 79, s. 2, and Schedule (k).

Guarantee for payment of goods requires no stamp.

It is sufficient if the Statute of Frauds has once been satisfied by a memorandum in writing. Thus, before 9 Geo. 4, c. 14, a *verbal* promise was sufficient to revive a liability on a *written* guarantee which was barred by the Statute of Limitations (l).

Sufficient if Statute of Frauds once satisfied by memorandum in writing.

It was decided in *Longfellow* v. *Williams* (m), that although a promise on a consideration not to sue out execution on a judgment against another be at its commencement by parol, if it be afterwards acknowledged in writing to a third party, it is not within the Statute of Frauds, sect. 4.

(g) *Warrington* v. *Furbor*, 8 East, 242. See also *Curry* v. *Edensor*, 3 T. R. 524; *Watkins* v. *Vince*, 2 Stark. 36⁓; *Waddington* v. *Bristow*, 2 B. & P. 452; *Martin* v. *Wright*. 6 Q. B. 917; *Sadler* v. *Johnson*, 16 M. & W. 775; *Chatfield* v. *Cox*, 18 Q. B. 321.
(h) 11 Ad. & Ell. 309.
(i) *Stead* v. *Liddard*, 1 Bing. 196.
(k) *Rein* v. *Lane and others*, L. R., 2 Q. B. 144.
(l) *Gibbons* v. *M'Casland*, 1 B. & Ald. 690.
(m) 2 Peake, N. P. R. 225.

[*177]   *CHAPTER IV.

THE LIABILITY OF THE SURETY.

Extent and
nature of
surety's lia-
bility to be
ascertained
from guaran-
tee itself.

IN order to ascertain the extent and nature of a surety's liability, the instrument under which his liability
arises must be looked at. It is therefore proposed, in
the first place, briefly to call attention to the general
rules which exist as to the *construction of guarantees.*

The construc-
tion of con-
tracts of
guarantee.

In the construction of all contracts, it is a general
rule that all words are to be taken most strictly against
the grantor or contractor. An idea seems formerly to
have prevailed, and, indeed, in some cases it was actually
laid down, that the contract of guarantee must in this
respect be construed differently from other contracts.

To be con-
strued
strongly
against pro-
miser.

Thus, in *Nicholson* v. *Paget* (a), *Bayley*, B., said :
" Now this is a contract of guarantee, which is a contract of a peculiar description; for it is not a contract
which a party is entering into for the payment of his
own debt, or on his own behalf, but it is a contract
which he is entering into for a third person, and we
think that it is *the duty* of the party who takes such a
security to see that it is couched in such words as that
the party so giving it may distinctly understand to
what extent he is binding himself." Now, this opinion
of *Bayley*, B., is directly opposed to the ordinary rule
of construction, which is embodied in the maxim, *Verba
fortiús accipiuntur contrá proferentem.* And it seems
clear that the rule of construction which the learned
judge thus laid down in *Nicholson* v. *Paget* can no
longer be considered as accurate. Thus, in *Mayer* v.
[*178] *Isaac* (b), *Alderson*, B., *disapproved of the
ruling of *Bayley*, B., and said he preferred the rule laid
down in *Mason* v. *Pritchard* (c), where it is said that
the ordinary rule of construction is applicable to the
contract of guarantee, and that, like all other contracts,
it must be construed *strongly against the party executing it* (d). So also in the modern case of *Wood* v.
Priestner (e) the court declined to adopt the opinion

(a) 1 C. & M. 68; *S. C.*, 3 Tyr. 164. See also *Evans* v. *Whyte*,
5 Bing. 485.
(b) 6 M. & W. 605.
(c) 12 East, 227.
(d) See also *Hargreave* v. *Smee*, 6 Bing. 249.
(e) L. R., 2 Ex. 66.

of *Bayley*, B., in *Nicholson* v. *Paget.* (*f*); and Baron *Martin* said, he thought that the contract of guarantee should be read in the same way as any other contract. The result of the authorities, therefore, seems to be, that in the construction of guarantees it is a general rule that a guarantee is, like any contract, to be construed most strongly against the person giving it.

Though, however (as just pointed out), a guarantee is to be construed most strongly against the party giving it, yet there is a second general rule which must never be lost sight of, and which may in some instances restrain the operation of the first. This is the rule that a surety is not to be charged beyond the precise terms of his engagement (*g*). Dealing with it as a mercantile contract, the Court does not apply to a guarantee mere technical rules, but construes it so as to give effect to what may fairly be inferred to have been the real intention and understanding of the parties as expressed in the writing; for, to bind a person by a contract of guarantee, the language used must express clearly an intention to take on himself the liability of a surety (*h*). If the writing falls short of that, or if the expressions *used be doubtful or ambiguous [*179] (provided they cannot be explained) no contract of guarantee arises (*i*).

Surety not to be charged beyond precise terms of his engagement.

Where a party becomes surety to another, but the instrument by which he becomes surety in terms creates only a joint liability, then, in the absence of any proof to the contrary, the intention of the parties must be taken to be that the surety is only so to the extent limited by the instrument. He does not intend to become, and does not become, surety out and out and under all circumstances, but he only undertakes a joint liability with others (*k*).

A third general rule is, that in the construction of guarantees, as indeed in the construction of all contracts, their natural or literal meaning must be given

Natural meaning to be given to words of guarantee.

(*f*) 1 C. & M. 68; 3 Tyr. 164.
(*g*) *Wright* v. *Russell*, 2 W. Bl. 934 ; *Tanner* v. *Woolmer*, 8 Ex. 492; 22 L. J., Ex. 259; *Pearsall* v. *Summersett*, 4 Taunt. 593; *Chalmers* v. *Victors*, 16 W. R. 1046; *Walker* v. *Hardman*, 11 C. & F. 258; 11 Bligh, 299; *Carr* v. *Wallachian Petroleum Co., Limited*, L. R., 2 C. P. 468; *Meek* v. *Wallis*, 27 L. T. R. 650.
(*h*) *Per Fitzgerald*, J., in *Bank of Montreal* v. *Munster Bank*, 11 Ir. C. L. R., at p. 55.
(*i*) *Ibid.*
(*k*) Per *Kindersley*, V.-C., in *Other* v. *Iveson*, 3 Drew. 182 ; and see *York City and Banking Co.* v. *Bainbridge*, 43 L. T. R. 732.

to the words employed (*l*), unless such natural or literal meaning would lead to an absurdity (*m*). And where there are no words of doubtful trade meaning, and the extrinsic facts are not in controversy, the question whether the words used amount to a contract of guarantee are not for the jury, but are for the determination of the Court alone (*n*).

Whole contract must be considered. It is likewise a general rule that *the whole instrument* must be considered in construing a guarantee. Thus, when the guarantee is by bond, the *extent* of the *condition* of such bond may be *restrained* by the *recitals*, as will be seen in a subsequent part of this chapter (*o*).

Whether the condition of the bond is actually restrained by the recitals, is often a very difficult question to determine (*p*).

Construction should give effect to contract if possible. [*180] *It is a further general rule that the construction shall be favourable, so as to support and give effect to the instrument, if possible (*q*):

In construing a guarantee, as in the construction of every contract (whether under seal or not), the court will, if possible, give effect to it, it being a maxim of our law that *Benignæ faciendæ sunt Interpretationes propter simplicitatem Laicorum ut res magis valeat quam pereat; et verba intentioni, non e contra, debent inservire* (*r*). In the case of *Wood* v. *Priestner* (*s*), which was an action upon a guarantee, Baron Bramwell said, that there was a *presumption* against the defendant giving an invalid document or the plaintiff receiving it.

Parol evidence not admissible to contradict In addition to these general rules of construction, it will be well also to call attention in this place to a principle of law, which, though not itself a rule of construction, frequently has an important bearing when

---

(*l*) *Allnutt* v. *Ashenden*, 5 M. & G. 397; *Haigh* v. *Brooks*, 10 A. & E. 309; *S. C.*, in error, *ib.*, p. 323.
(*m*) *Chalmers* v. *Victors*, 16 W. R. 1046.
(*n*) *Bank of Montreal* v. *Munster Bank*, 11 Ir. C. L. R. 47.
(*o*) See *post*; and see *Glyn* v. *Hertel*, 8 Taunt. 208; *Pearsall* v. *Summersett*, 4 Taunt. 593. But see *Bank of British North America* v. *Cuvillier*, 4 L. T. 159.
(*p*) See *Parker* v. *Wise*, 6 M. & S. 239; *Gordon* v. *Rae*, 8 E. & B. 1605; *Evans* v. *Earle*, 10 Exch. 1; and see note (*d*), 3 Dougl. 326.
(*q*) *Broom* v. *Batchelor*, 1 H. & N. 255; *Steele* v. *Hoe*, 14 Q. B. 431; *Oldershaw* v. *King*, 2 H. & N. 517; *Heffield* v. *Meadows*, L. R., 4 C. P. 595; *Ford* v. *Beech*, 11 Q. B. 852; *Pugh* v. *Stringfield*, 4 C. B., N. S., 364; *Dally* v. *Poolly*, 6 Q. B. 494.
(*r*) Co. Litt. 36 a.
(*s*) L. R., 2 Exch. 66.

questions arise as to the meaning of a written in- written docu-
strument. This is the doctrine that parol evidence is ment, but
not admissible to *contradict* a written document, and only to *ex-*
consequently, that where there is no ambiguity in the *plain* it.
words used, parol evidence to fix a meaning upon them
is not admissible at all. Parol evidence is, however, Surrounding
admissible to *explain* a written instrument when am- circumstan-
biguities occur in it (*t*). "The surrounding circum- ces may be
stances" are frequently looked at where the contract given in evi-
requires explanation: *e. g.*, to ascertain the subject- dence in
matter of the *contract (*u*). Thus, in a recent [*181] explanation.
case, where the wife of a retail trader who was possessed of separate estate, in order to obtain credit for
her husband from a wholesale merchant with whom he
dealt, gave the following guarantee: "I do hereby
guarantee to you the sum of 500*l*. This guarantee is
to continue in force for the period of six years and no
longer," it was held that in the construction of this
document the Court was entitled to look at the surrounding circumstances, that is to say, to consider,
first, who the parties were; secondly, in what position
they were; and, thirdly, what the subject-matter of the
agreement was. Upon full consideration of these circumstances the Court came to the conclusion that the
guarantee was limited to the goods actually supplied to
the husband after it was given (*x*).

Having thus briefly treated of the construction of the The liability
contract of guarantee, let us now proceed to consider— of the surety.
First. The nature of the surety's liability. *Secondly.* Division of
When the liability of the surety arises. *Thirdly.* How the subject.
such liability may be enforced. *Fourthly.* What is the
extent of such liability?

First, the nature of the surety's liability. *First*, the
It appears from the very definition of a guarantee, nature of the
that the person *giving* it is not answerable till the de- surety's lia-
fault of another person (*y*). bility.

The liability of the former (the surety) is, therefore, Difference
between the

(*t*) *Edwards* v. *Jerons*, 8 C. & P. 436; *Hoad* v. *Grace*, 7 H. &
N. 494; 31 L. J., Exch. 98; *Goldshede* v. *Swan*, 1 Exch. 154;
Bainbridge v. *Wade*, 16 Q. B. 89; *Garrett* v. *Handley*, 4 B. & C.
664.

(*u*) *Heffield* v. *Meadows*, L. R., 4 C. P. 595; *Chalmers* v. *Victors*,
16 W. R. 1046; *Spark* v. *Heslop*, 1 El. & El. 563, 570; *Coles* v.
Pack, L. R., 5 C. P. 65, 70, 71; *Leathley* v. *Spyer*, L. R., 5 C. P.
595; *Laurie* v. *Scholefield*, L. R., 4 C. P. 622.

(*x*) *Morrell* v. *Cowan*, 7 Ch. Div. 151; 26 W. R. 90; 47 L. J.,
Ch. 173; 37 L. T. 586.

(*y*) Fell on Guarantees, 2nd ed., p. 1; and *Mallet* v. *Bateman*,
L. R., 1 C. P. 163.

liability of the surety and that of the principal debtor.

No privity of contract between surety and principal debtor.

Consequences of this.

termed *secondary*, whilst that of the latter (the principal debtor) is termed *primary*.

Between the surety and the principal debtor there is no privity of contract, for the surety contracts with the creditor. Consequently, in the absence of special [*182] agreement, *a judgment or an award against a principal debtor is not binding on the surety, and is not evidence against him in an action in which he is sued by the creditor, for it is *res inter alios acta* (b). Moreover, the debtor's admission of liability does not dispense with proof thereof in an action against the surety brought by the creditor (c). However, the entry by a deceased collector of taxes of monies received by him made in a book which he kept for his own *private* convenience was in one case held to be good evidence as against his surety, though the persons from whom the money was received were alive and might have been called as witnesses (d). In a recent American case it was held that the surety for good behaviour in an office is not estopped from contesting the correctness of the principal debtor's voluntary official reports as to the amount of money in his hands at the commencement of the term for which the bond was given (e). But official books and reports which the official is bound to furnish as one of the duties incidental to his office, would seem to be presumptive evidence against him and his sureties (f). Where a Guarantee Society became surety for an official liquidator and entered into a bond which provided that the certificate of the chief clerk on taking the accounts of the liquidation should be conclusive evidence against the surety as to the amount due from the liquidator, it was held that even after such certificate had been given the Court had power to allow the accounts to be re-opened at the surety's request, upon certain terms, as it was proved that the liquida- [*183] tor's accounts had (but in accordance *with the usual practice) been carried in and vouched without notice to the surety (g).

(b) *Ex parte Young, In re Kitchin*, 17 Ch. Div. 668 ; 50 L. J., Ch. 824 ; 45 L. T. 90. See also American cases of *Douglass* v. *Howland*, 24 Wendell, 35 ; *Graves* v. *Bulkley*, 37 Amer. R. 249 (U. S.).

(c) *Evans* v. *Beattie*, 5 Esp. 26.

(d) *Middleton* v. *Melton*, 5 B. & C. 317.

(e) *Van Sickel* v. *County of Buffalo*, 42 Amer. R. 753 (U. S.).

(f) *Town of Union* v. *Bermes*, 43 Amer. R. 369 (U. S.) ; *Borne County* v. *Jones*, 37 Amer. R. 229 (U. S.).

(g) *In re Birmingham Brewing, Malting and Distillery Co.*, Limited, 31 W. R. 414 ; 52 L. J., Ch. 358 ; 48 L. T. 632.

It was formerly a rule of pleading, that if he who was party or privy in estate or interest, or he who justified in right of him who was party or privy, pleaded a deed, he must make profert of it to the court (*h*). But in the case of *Bain* v. *Cooper* (*i*), it was held, that a *surety* might plead a release to his *principal* without making profert of the deed. *Parke*, B., in his judgment, said, "The general rule with respect to profert is correctly stated in *Dangerfield* v. *Thomas* (*k*), viz., that a party is not required to make profert of an instrument, to the possession of which he is not entitled. The only exceptions to that rule are, where the party pleading acts as tenant of another, or where there is a privity of interest between them, as in the case of a release to a reversioner, of which the tenant for life may avail himself. So, also, in the cases of heir and executor, he may plead a release to the ancestor or testator whom they respectively represent; so, also, with respect to several tortfeasors, *for, in all these cases, there is a privity between the parties which constitutes an identity of person; but there is no privity between the surety and principal, for the surety contracts with the creditor. They do not constitute one person in law, and are not jointly liable to the plaintiff.*"

Except under certain circumstances, to be explained hereafter, the surety is not liable. on his guarantee, where the principal debt cannot be legally enforced. This is in accordance with the *lex contractus*, which prevents contracts from becoming operative, *unless and until* all conditions precedent are fulfilled, and, as is obvious, the existence of a principal debtor is [*184] a condition precedent to the operation of the contract of guarantee (*l*). Thus, it is stated in *Pothier on Contracts* (*m*), that, "As the obligation of sureties is according to our definition an obligation accessary to that of a principal debtor, it follows that it is of the essence of the obligation that there should be a valid obligation of a principal debtor; consequently, if the principal is not obliged, neither is the surety, as there can be no accessary without a principal obligation according to the rule of law, *cum causa principalis non consisti, nec*

As a general rule surety not liable if principal debt not legally enforceable.

(*h*) *Dr. Leyfield's Case*. 10 Co. 88 ; *profert* has been rendered unnecessary by the C. L. P. Act, 1852 (15 & 16 Vict. c. 76), s. 55.

(*i*) 1 D. P. C. 11, 14.
(*k*) 9 Ad. & E. 292.
(*l*) *Mountstephen* v. *Lakeman*, L. R., 5 Q. B. 613 ; L. R., 7 Q. B. 196, 202 ; 7 H. L. 17.
(*m*) Evans' ed., vol. i., p. 229.

10 (1379)

œa quidem quæ sequuntur, locum habent. L. 178, ff. de Reg. Jur." (*n*). However, where directors guarantee the performance of a contract by their company which does not bind the latter, as being *ultra vires*, the directors' suretyship liability is enforceable (*o*).

Surety's liability may continue even after that of the principal debtor has ceased.

Again, the liability of a surety may continue even after that of the principal debtor has ceased. Thus, in the case of a surety to the assignor of a lease for the due payment of rent and fulfilment of covenants by the assignee, if, on the bankruptcy of the latter, the trustee in bankruptcy (or now the official receiver) disclaim all interest in the lease, such disclaimer, though it may operate to relieve the bankrupt assignee from liability, does not extinguish the liability of the surety, which continues during the remainder of the term assigned (*p*). And it is provided by "The Bankruptcy Act, 1883," that an order discharging a bankrupt "shall not release any person who, at the date of the receiving order, was a partner of a co-trustee with the bankrupt, or was *jointly bound or had made any [*185] joint contract with him, or any person who was *surety or in the nature of a surety for him*" (*q*).

Secondly, When does the liability of the surety arise?

Secondly, when does the surety's liability arise? Principal debtor must have made default.

It is, in all cases, essential, before the surety can be called upon to fulfil his engagements, that the principal debtor shall have made default. Thus, if the alleged default were owing to the creditor's misconduct, the surety will not be held liable (*r*). Again, if the principal debtor has not made default at all, the surety is not liable. This appears from the case of *Walker* v. *British Guarantee Association* (*s*), where the following were the facts:—The treasurer of a benefit building society, within statutes 6 & 7 Will. 4, c. 32, and 10 Geo. 4, c. 56, covenanted with the society's trustees that he would faithfully discharge the duties of treasurer, duly obey the directions of the trustees in relation to such duties, and punctually account to the trustees for all and every sum and sums of money, bills, notes, securities, goods and chattels, which he, in his office of treasurer, should receive on the society's account. The

---

(*n*) See *Lewis* v. *Jones*, 4 B. & C. 506, 513.
(*o*) *Yorkshire Railway Wagon Co.* v. *Maclure*, 19 Ch. D. 478.
(*p*) *Harding* v. *Preece*, 9 Q. B. D. 281 ; 47 L. T. 100 ; 51 L. J., Q. B. 215 ; 31 W. R. 42 ; see also *Ex parte Walton*, 17 Ch. Div. 746, 755 ; *East and West India Dock Co.* v. *Hill*, 22 Ch. Div. 14.
(*q*) 46 & 47 Vict. c. 52, s. 30, par. 4.
(*r*) *Halliwell* v. *Counsell*, 38 L. T. 176.
(*s*) 18 Q. B. 277 ; *Lloyds* v. *Harper*, 16 Ch. Div. 290 ; 50 L. J., Ch. 140 ; 29 W. R. 452 ; 43 L. T. 481 ; *King* v. *Cole*, 15 Q. B. 628.

defendants, as his sureties, guaranteed to the building
society the due observance of this covenant. It appeared that the treasurer was bound by the rules of the
society to pay over, in a given time, the *same* moneys
which he received. It was held, that such an obligation was only that of a bailee, that he did not violate
such obligation, if, after receiving moneys, and before
he had an opportunity of paying them over, he was
robbed of them by irresistible violence and without
fault of his own, and that, to an action against the
*sureties of the treasurer by the trustees of the [*186]
society, complaining that the treasurer had not paid the
said moneys, a plea by the sureties of robbery committed upon their principal, in excuse of his non-payment,
was an answer to the action.

Once the principal has actually committed a *default,*
for which the surety is responsible, *as a general rule a
cause of action immediately arises against the surety.*
And, consequently, as a general rule, and in the absence
of any express or implied stipulation to the contrary,
the creditor need not, *before* suing the surety, sue the
principal debtor (*s*), even though such principal debtor
be quite solvent (*t*). If, indeed, the guarantee contain
an express stipulation that the surety shall not be liable
to the creditor, except on the failure of the "utmost
efforts and legal proceedings" of the creditor to obtain
payment or compensation from the principal debtor, the
creditor, before he can recover, must show that this
stipulation has been complied with (*u*). But where
the guarantee contained a proviso, that, before the
surety was to be called upon, the creditor must have
availed himself to the utmost of any *bonâ fide* securities
which he held of the principal debtor, and it was proved
that the plaintiff had neglected to adopt means to enforce *payment of a bill by a party *who was shown* [*187]

*After default
made, credi-
tor may sue
surety before
suing prin-
cipal debtor.*

*Aliter, where
guarantee
contain
express stipu-
lation to the
contrary.*

(*s*) *Ranelagh* v. *Hayes,* 1 Vern. 189; *Wright* v. *Simpson,* 6 Ves.
jun. 714, 733. See *post,* Chap. V. as to the *right* of the surety to
compel the creditor to sue the principal debtor *before* having recourse to the surety. The provision in Magna Carta (c. 8) that
"neither shall the pledges of the debtor be distrained as long as
the principal debtor is sufficient for the payment of the debt,"
applies only to pledges and nuncupators who, by express words,
are not responsible unless their principals become insolvent, and
so are conditional debtors only. *Attorney-General* v. *Resby,* Hardres, p. 377; *Attorney-General* v. *Atkinson,* 1 Y. & J. 212; and see
also *The Queen* v. *Fay,* 4 Ir. L. R. 606.
(*t*) See Hardres's Reports in the Exchequer, p. 377; and see
Smith v. *Freyler,* 47 Amer. R. 358 (U. S.).
(*u*) *Holl* v. *Hadley,* 2 A. & E. 758.

to be totally insolvent, it was held that the surety was not discharged (x).

Creditor may sue surety before resorting to securities for debt received from debtor.

It is quite clear, therefore, that, *in the absence* of express stipulation to that effect, a creditor who holds sureties from the principal debtor for his debt need not first resort to them before suing the surety (y). This doctrine of the English law, that a right of action accrues to the creditor as against the surety *immediately* upon any default of the principal debtor, is a peculiar one, and does not, generally speaking, prevail in other systems of jurisprudence.

Roman law gave sureties right to compel creditors to sue principal debtor first.

The *Roman law* (z) gave to sureties the power to compel the creditor to sue the principal debtor, before having recourse to the sureties, unless, indeed, he could show that such a proceeding would be useless by reason of the debtor's insolvency or absence, or unless the surety expressly renounced this power of compelling the creditor to sue (a).

This right exists in most countries.

This provision of the Roman law seems to have been adopted in most of those countries whose municipal law is based upon the Roman civil law. Chancellor *Kent* (b) has well remarked, that "a rule of such general adoption shows that there is nothing in it inconsistent with the relative rights and duties of principal and surety, and that it accords with a common sense of justice and the natural equity of mankind."

In absence of express contract, principal debtor need not be requested by creditor to pay before surety is sued.

Besides the rule that it is unnecessary for the creditor, before having recourse to the surety, to sue the debtor, there are also many other important rules which follow as the consequences of the English law, that a right of action accrues to the creditor immediately upon [*188] a *default by the principal debtor. Thus, except where by the terms of the contract the debtor is not chargeable without it, he need not even be requested to pay (c).

The case of *The Belfast Banking Company* v. *Stanley* (d), is an important decision, delivered in Ireland, proceeding upon this principal. There a promissory note was given by A. and B. jointly. The note having

---

(x) *Musket* v. *Rogers*, 8 Scott, 51.
(y) *Ranelagh* v. *Hayes*, 1 Vern. 189 ; *Wilks* v. *Heeley*, 1 C. & M. 249.
(z) Nov. 4, c. 1.
(a) Mackeldeii, Systema Juris Romani, § 438.
(b) In *Hayes* v. *Ward*, 4 Johns. Ch. Cas. 123.
(c) *Rede* v. *Farr*, 6 M. & S. 121 ; *Lilly* v. *Hewett*, 11 Price, 494; *Holbrow* v. *Wilkins*, 1 B. & C. 10 ; *Warrington* v. *Furbar*, 8 East, 242 ; *Walton* v. *Mascall*, 13 M. & W. 452.
(d) 15 W. R. 689 ; I. R. 1 Com. Law, Q. B. 693.

become long overdue, the payee sued upon it. One of
the defendants, B., upon this, pleaded that he joined
in the note as surety for A., of which the plaintiff was
aware, and that he was discharged from such suretyship
by the plaintiff having delayed, for an unreasonable
time, to demand payment from A. (the other maker),
to wit, for ten years. It was held that this plea did
not disclose any defence, and was consequently bad.
So, again, in the absence of express stipulation to that
effect (e). the creditor is entitled to sue the surety
without previously demanding payment of him (f) ; just
as a debt due can, in ordinary cases, be sued for without a previous demand. However, it sometimes happens that, under the circumstances of the case, a right
of action against the surety does not arise till some
demand has been made on him ; and in some cases it is
necessary for the creditor to call upon the surety to
fulfil his engagement, though he be not *expressly* bound
to do so. Thus, where a person binds himself, by
guarantee, to indorse any bills which may be given in
part payment of a debt, to be contracted by a third
person, the rule of law is, that a demand upon the
surety to fulfil his engagement must be made, and
within a reasonable and convenient *time (g). [*189]
As the surety can be sued without any previous demand
being made upon him, it is, as a rule, not even necessary that the creditor should previously inform him of
the default or neglect to pay of the principal debtor,
unless the surety has *expressly* stipulated for notice (h);
though an omission to give the surety this information
might affect the question of costs. Thus, it has been
held, that presentment or notice of dishonour is not
necessary to keep alive the liability of a person, not a
party to the instrument, who has guaranteed that a bill
or note shall be paid (i). But where a debtor indorsed
a bill of exchange, of which he was the indorsee, over
to his creditor by way of collateral security for his debt,

Margin notes: Nor need surety him-self be re-quested to pay in ab-sence of ex-press stipula-tion on the subject.

Nor is it necessary even to in-form surety of default having been made.

(e) In *Sicklemore* v. *Thistleton*, 6 M. & S. 9, there was such an
express stipulation as that alluded to in the text. See also
Batson v. *Spearman*, 9 Ad. & E. 298.
(f) *Hitchcock* v. *Humfrey*, 5 M. & G. 559.
(g) *Payne* v. *Ives*, 3 D. & Ry. 664.
(h) *Cutler* v. *Southern*, 1 Wms. Saund. 115 ; *Ker* v. *Mitchell*, 2
Chit. Rep. 487 ; Com. Dig. Condition (T) ; Hurlstone on Bonds,
p. 83 et seq.; *Sicklemore* v. *Thistleton*, 6 M. & S. 9 ; *Batson* v.
Spearman, 9 Ad. & E. 298 ; and see *Carr* v. *Browne*, 12 Moore,
12; *Phillips* v. *Fordyce*, 2 Chit. 676.
(i) *Hitchcock* v. *Humfrey*, 5 M. & Gr. 559 ♦ *Walton* v. *Mascall*,
13 M. & W. 72 ; *Holbrow* v. *Wilkins*, 1 B. & C. 10 ; *Van Wort* v.
Woolley, 3 B. & C. 439 ; *Warrington* v. *Furber*, 8 East 242.

and the creditor did not present it at maturity, nor give the debtor notice of its dishonour when presented, it was held, that the creditor could not recover in an action either on his original debt or upon the bill of exchange (*k*). And it would seem that if such want of presentment or notice of dishonour, owing to the peculiar circumstances of the case, were to amount to *unreasonable* neglect on the part of the holder of the bill or note, the guarantor would be discharged from all liability (*l*). Cases of this kind would seem to depend upon the circumstances peculiar to each (*m*).

Where guarantee to operate on certain events notice of occurrence of such event necessary.

[*190] * Where the guarantee is only to operate on the occurrence of a certain event, it may become necessary for the creditor to give notice to the surety of the occurrence of such event, before proceeding upon the guarantee (*n*).

Liability of surety may depend on performance of conditions precedent. Examples.

The liability of the surety—like any other liability arising on a contract—may, by express stipulation, be made to depend on the performance of *conditions precedent* to its accrual (o). And when this is the case, the liability of the surety is, of course, not complete until all *conditions precedent* to his liability have been fulfilled (*p*). Thus, a contract by way of guarantee, to pay over to the creditor moneys received as the proceeds of the property of the debtor, is conditional, not only upon the receipt of money, the proceeds of such property, but on the receipt of such money properly payable to him; and does not apply to money received only subject to a prior claim of a third party, and which, therefore, is not payable to the creditor (*q*). Again, where the vendor of a business to a company guaranteed to the shareholders thereof a minimum dividend for the term of five years, it was held, that the guarantee was given upon the implied condition that the company

---

(*k*) *Peacock* v. *Pursell*, 14 C. B., N. S. 728 ; 32 L. J., C. P. 266; 10 Jur., N. S. 178 ; 8 L. T 636; 11 W. R. 834.

(*l*) *Phillips* v. *Astling*, 2 Taunt. 206; and see Chitty on Bills, 10th ed., note 3, p. 308.

(*m*) Per *Abbott*, C. J., in *Van. Wort* v. *Woolley*, 3 B. & C. 439, 448.

(*n*) See *Morten* v. *Marshall*, 9 Jur., N. S. 651.

(*o*) It has already been seen, when the nature of the surety's liability was described, that the existence of a principal debtor is a condition precedent to the very existence of a guarantee, and therefore essential to the surety's liability, *ante*, p. 183 *et seq.*

(*p*) *Elworthy* v. *Maunder*, 2 Moo. & P. 482; *Pearse* v. *Morrice*, 2 Ad. & E. 84; *Lawrence* v. *Walmsley*, 31 L. J., C. P. 143; 10 W. R. 344; 5 L. T. 790 Phillips v. Fordyce, 2 Chit. 676; *Burton* v. *Gray*, L. R., 8 Ch. App. 932.

(*q*) *Jupp* v. *Richardson*, 26 L. J., Ex. 281.

should carry on the whole concern as it existed at the first, and that the company having broken the contract, or its part, the vendor was discharged from his guarantee (r). So, where in consideration *of the [*191] plaintiff agreeing to supply A. with goods, to enable him to carry out his contract with the government, the defendant guaranteed to the plaintiff the payment of the goods *when the government paid A. the amount of the contract,* it was held, that the government having, before the performance of the contract, dismissed A. and employed some one else in his place, and not having therefore paid to A. the *whole amount* of the contract, the plaintiff was not entitled to recover (s). So also, in another case, H. & Sons being engaged, under a contract in writing, in the erection of certain engineer's work for N., for which iron and brass castings were required, and *Hill,* the founder from whom the castings were procured, having a claim against H. & Sons to the amount of 218l. for goods already supplied, and refusing to continue the supply without obtaining payment or security for that sum, N. consented to give *Hill* a guarantee in the following terms:—

"May 22nd, 1861. Mr. J. N. agrees to pay to Mrs. *Hill,* ironfounder, on H. & Son's account, the sum of 218l., being the amount owing to her by them, together with interest, in six months from the above date, *providing he has work done as security for the same.*" In an action by the representatives of *Hill* against N. upon this guarantee, it was held, that it was *a condition* of N.'s liability thereon, that, at the end of the six months, work should have been done by H. & Sons for him in respect of which a debt should be due from him to them ; and that the plaintiffs could not recover without producing the contract between H. & Sons and N. under which the work was done (t). In *London Guarantee and Accident Co.* v. *Fearnley* (u), the following were the *facts :—By an agreement, and a policy of in- [*192] surance, the defendants agreed to reimburse the plaintiff any pecuniary loss, to the amount of 1,000l., which he might sustain by reason of any such fraud or dishonesty of A. in connection with his employment by the plaintiff, as should amount to embezzlement, and

---

(r) *Brown & Co.* v. *Brown,* 35 L. T. 54.
(s) *Hemming* v. *Trenery,* 2 Cr. M. & R. 385. See also *Moor* v. *Roberts,* 3 C. B., N. S. 830.
(t) *Hill* v. *Nuttall,* 17 C. B., N. S. 262. See also *Burbridge* v. *Child,* 10 Jur., N. S. 106.
(u) 5 App. Cas. 911 ; 43 L. T. R. 390 ; 28 W. R. 893.

should be committed and discovered during the continuance of the policy. The policy provided (among other things) "that the employer shall, if and when required by the company [but at the expense of the company if a conviction be obtained] use all diligence in prosecuting the employed to conviction for any fraud or dishonesty as aforesaid, which he shall have committed, and in consequence of which a claim shall have been made under the policy, and shall, at the company's expense, give all information and assistance to enable the company to sue for and obtain reimbursement by the employed, or by his estate, of any moneys which the company shall have become liable to pay." It was held by Lords *Blackburn* and *Watson* (*Selborne*, L•C., *diss.*), that the prosecution of A. for embezzlement was a condition precedent to the plaintiff's right of action upon the policy. But where, in consideration of the plaintiff agreeing to stay proceedings in an action against A. until a given day, and proceeding to trial with an action against B., the defendant promised to indemnify the plaintiff against all costs and expenses connected with the action against B., *whether the same should be decided in favour of the plaintiffs or of B.:* it was held, that the *final* determination of the action against B. was not a condition precedent to the plaintiff's right to sue for costs, and that the consideration was satisfied by the plaintiff staying proceedings against A. and going to trial against B. (*x*).

[*193] *In *Lewis* v. *Hoare* (*y*), the facts were as follow :—The respondent advanced money to the appellant on a guarantee "to be repaid on the completion of six houses in accordance with a contract between myself and T." One of the terms of the contract was that the houses were to be built to the satisfaction of a surveyor, and payment was to be made upon his certificate. No such certificate had been given. In an action on the guarantee brought by the respondent against the appellant, the jury found, that as a matter of fact the houses were completed. It was held, that the respondent was entitled to recover, notwithstanding the absence of the certificate. Where, a plaintiff having given the defendant promissory notes and a cognovit for 500*l.* as a

(*x*) *Wilson* v. *Bevan*, 7 C. B. 673. See also *Christie* v. *Borelly*, 7 C. B., N. S. 561 ; *Morten* v. *Marshall*, 9 Jur. N. S. 651 ; *Coyte* v. *Elphick*, 22 W. R. 541 ; *Crick* v. *Warren*, 2 F. & F. 348 ; *Dimmock* v. *Sturla*, 14 M. & W. 758 ; 15 L. J., Ex. 65, which are instances of conditions precedent.
(*y*) 29 W. R. 357 ; 44 L. T. R. 66. See also *Ex parte Ashwell*, 2 Dea. & Chit. 281.

composition for certain claims, the defendant, *in consideration of the money so secured to be paid*, engaged to indemnify him against certain liabilities, it was held that the security, not the actual payment, was the consideration, and that the plaintiff might sue on the guarantee, though he had not paid the 500*l*. (z). In *Russell* v. *Trickett* (a), the facts were as follow :—By a deed between a local board of the first part, certain contractors of the second part, and the defendant of the third part, the contractors covenanted to do work upon the basis of a specification ; and the defendant covenanted to pay any losses that might be sustained from the non-performance of the work. The deed recited that the specification had been signed by five members of the local board, as was required by the Local Act. In point of fact, the specification had never been signed, although it had been acted upon. Held, *that [*194] the mere fact of the specification not having been signed did not release the sureties from their liability.

The most common examples, perhaps, of the existence of a condition precedent to the liability of the surety, are cases in which a guarantee is given in consideration of time being given to the principal debtor ; or, in which a guarantee is given in which it is intended that others shall join.

Where a guarantee is given in consideration of the plaintiff undertaking to forbear to sue a third person for a certain period, or where the nature of the transaction shows that this was the intention of the parties, forbearance to sue before the expiration of the period agreed upon is a condition precedent to the plaintiff's right of action on the guarantee (b).

In a similar manner, where a person executes a surety-bond on the faith of its being at some subsequent time also executed by another person as co-surety, or by the principal debtor himself, the execution by such co-surety or principal debtor is a condition precedent to the liability of the person who thus executes. Consequently he is not bound by the bond unless this condition be fulfilled (c). However, where there are more than one surety on the face of a deed, it does not follow that one is not bound by his signature unless the others sign. That is not the law, and unless either

Execution of guarantee by co-surety is sometimes a condition precedent to surety's liability.

(z) *Ikin* v. *Brook*, 1 B. & A. 124.
(a) 13 L. T. 280.
(b) *Rolt* v. *Cozens*, 18 C. B. 673.
(c) *Bonser* v. *Cox*, 4 Beav. 379; *Evans* v. *Bremridge*, 2 K. & J. 174; 8 De G., M. & G. 101.

the parties expressly stipulated that one surety should
not be bound unless the others were, or the deed was
delivered as an escrow, the omission of one surety to
sign would not relieve the others from liability (d).

A very good example of the rule, that a suretyship may be made dependent on the execution of a
deed by others, is afforded by the well-known case
[*195] *of *Emmet* v. *Dewhurst* (e). There W. D., by
indenture, agreed to guarantee a certain composition
to all the creditors of J. D. who should, before a fixed
day, execute a release of their debts. The plaintiff,
who was a creditor of J. D., did not execute by the
time named, but insisted that this delay had taken
place in consequence of an arrangement entered into
between him and the agent of W. D., the effect of
which was to bind the plaintiff to accept the composition, but to allow him to postpone his execution of the
release. It was held, dismissing a bill filed by the
plaintiff against W. D. for specific performance of
agreement to pay the composition, that there was no
evidence that the agent of W. D. had authority to
enter into any new agreement; that if such authority
had been proved, the agreement being within the 4th
section of the Statute of Frauds, any alteration in its
terms must have been evidenced by writing; that the
condition in the original agreement not having been
performed by the plaintiff, the agreement never took
effect so far as he was concerned, and that in the absence of fraud no parol agreement could be substituted.

To relieve
surety,
omission by
another to
execute an
instrument
must amount
to a breach of
a condition
precedent.

It should, however, be here observed that it has been
decided that a surety, who has executed a bond on the
faith of its being executed by the principal debtor also,
cannot be released from his obligation on the ground
that the principal has never executed it, if the principal has executed an instrument on which the surety
may sue him, and become a specialty creditor of his (f).
Moreover, where a defence of this kind is relied upon,
there must be some evidence, either of an agreement
by the plaintiff with the defendant that such co-surety
should execute, or that the defendant executed the
instrument on the faith of the others doing so. Thus,
[*196] *where in an action against a surety the defendant had pleaded an equitable plea, founded on the
non-execution of the security by a co-surety, and it appeared that the proposal of another surety came from

(d) *Coyle* v. *Elphick*, 22 W. R. 541, 544.
(e) 3 Mac. &G. 587.
(f) *Cooper* v. *Evans*, L. R., 4 Eq. 45.

the plaintiff, and was not at the time made a *condition* by the defendant, it was held that the defence failed (g).

In the case of *Horne* v. *Ramsdale* (h), it was also held that the existence of the alleged condition precedent was not made out. In that case the declaration stated that one T. was the lessee of certain tolls, and that one S. and the defendant agreed to join with T. in a bond conditioned for payment of the rent under the lease, and it alleged as a breach that the defendant refused to join T. in the bond. The defendant pleaded, first, that at the time of tendering the bond to him, S. had not executed the same, nor was he present ready to execute it jointly with the defendant; secondly, that S. died before the commencement of the suit, and that before his death the bond was not tendered to the defendant for execution, nor was he requested to execute it. It was decided that the pleas were bad. Lord *Abinger*, C. B., thus described the nature of the contract: "It is a contract by each of the intended sureties to join in the bond with T. the principal; *i. e.*, to execute the bond in the character of surety. It is not a contract that they shall execute it in the presence of each other, or that if one die the other shall be at liberty to refuse to execute it." Again in *Dallas* v. *Walls* (i), the following were the facts: A bank, having advanced certain sums to a company, made a further advance upon the personal security of three of the directors. Five of the guarantors for the amount secured by an earlier bond signed an agreement that they would join the three directors in guaranteeing *repayment [*197] to the bank of the further advance in equal proportions with the three directors. One of the five who signed this agreement stated by his affidavit that his signature (if he did sign) was obtained "on the express agreement and understanding" that the agreement should be signed by all the guarantors for the sum secured by the bond. It was held that the words "express understanding" were utterly unmeaning, and that the Court would never pay any attention to a statement that something was done on an express engagement unless the engagement was deposed to in a manner which was admissible in evidence.

(g) *Traill* v. *Gibbons*, 2 F. & F. 358. See also *Austin* v. *Howard*, 7 Taunt. 24; *Cumberlege* v. *Lawson*, 1 C. B., N. S. 709; but see *Barry* v. *Moroney*, 8 Ir. C. L. R. 554.

(h) 9 M. & W. 329.

(i) 29 L. T. R. 599. And see *Dodge* v. *Pringle*, 29 L. J., Ex. 115.

Thirdly.   *Thirdly.* The nature of the surety's liability having
How surety's been indicated, and *when* it is that such liability arises,
liability may it is now necessary to consider *how such liability may*
be enforced. *be enforced against the surety.*

The liability   It is important to bear in mind that the surety is en-
must be titled to have the liability proved as against him in the
proved same way as against the principal debtor. Therefore,
against in the absence of special agreement, a judgment or an
surety in award against a principal debtor is not binding on the
same way as surety, and is not evidence against him in an action by
against prin- the creditor (*k*). And, on a guarantee to pay for goods
cipal debtor. sold and delivered to a third person, what such person
has said respecting the goods sold to him is not evidence
to charge the person giving the guarantee; but independent proof must be given of the delivery of the
goods (*l*).

Action the   In the majority of cases, of course, the creditor, as
usual way of plaintiff, seeks to enforce his liability by means of an
enforcing action against the surety as defendant.
surety's   In an action brought for this purpose, one of the
liability. first things which, before the passing of the Judicature
Act, had to be considered was the form of action to be
[*198] adopted. *With regard to this, it was held,
that the surety must be sued *specially* on the guarantee,
and not on the common counts (*n*). However, where, on
the trial of an action upon a guarantee for the payment
of work done for a third person, the plaintiff at first
shaped his case upon a guarantee, but afterwards re
sorted to the common counts, and made out the defendant's liability *as a principal,* and recovered a verdict on
those counts, it was held that the verdict could not be
disturbed (*o*). So, also, in *Wilson* v. *Marshall* (*p*),
where a *verbal* guarantee was given for the supply of
goods to a third person, and, subsequently, to the supply of the goods, the defendant admitted his liability
under the guarantee, it was held that the plaintiff was
entitled to recover on accounts stated.

Plaintiff may   It is now provided by the Rules of the Supreme
now proceed Court, 1883, that where the plaintiff seeks only to re-
against cover a debt or liquidated demand in money payable by
surety by the defendant, with or without interest, arising on a
specially in-
dorsed writ.

(*k*) *Ex parte Young, In re Kitchner,* 17 Ch. Div. 668; 50 L. J.,
Ch. 824; 45 L. T. 90, following the American case of *Douglas* v.
Howland, 24 Wendell, 35.

(*l*) *Evans* v. *Beattie,* 5 Esp. 26.

(*n*)*Mines* v. *Schulthorpe,* 2 Camp. 215. See also *Jones* v. *Fleming,*
7 B. & C. 217.

(*o*) *Edge* v. *Frost,* 4 D. & R. 243.

(*p*) 15 Ir. C. L. R. 467.

guarantee, whether under seal or not, where the claim against the principal is in respect of a debt or liquidated demand only, the writ of summons may, at the option of the plaintiff, be specially indorsed with a statement of his claim, or of the remedy or relief to which he claims to be entitled. Such special indorsement shall be to the effect of such of the forms in Appendix C., sect. 4, as shall be applicable to the case (q). Where the writ is specially indorsed, it is provided that no further statement of claim shall be delivered, but the indorsement on the writ shall be deemed to be the statement of claim (r). After the defendant has appeared to such a writ, the plaintiff may make summary application for judgment in manner provided by Ord. XIV. of the *Supreme Court Rules 1883. The [*199] defendant may, however, show cause why judgment should not be signed and obtain leave to defend. Where, in an action against a surety on a specially indorsed writ, it was not shown that the debt had been acknowledged by the principal debtor, or that particulars had been furnished to the defendant, or that he had admitted his liability, it was held that the defendant might reasonably call on the plaintiff to prove his claim, and should be allowed to defend without paying money into court or giving security (s).

In cases where the plaintiff does not or cannot proceed against the surety by means of a specially indorsed writ the statement of claim must be framed in accordance with the rules of pleading contained in the Supreme Court Rules, 1883 (t).

As regards the question, who must be joined as plaintiffs or defendants in an action upon a guarantee, the following principles and decisions are of importance :— *Parties to actions on guarantees.*

First, as regards the persons who may enforce a guarantee, that is to say, under ordinary circumstances, *the plaintiffs* (u). It has been decided that where the interest of persons in a guarantee is *actually joint*, but *in terms, is joint and several*, the action must be brought in the names of *all* the persons to whom the guarantee *The plaintiffs to action on the guarantee.*

(q) Ord. III, r. 6. And see Jud. Act, 1875, App. C. s. 4, Forms 10 and 11.

(r) Supreme Court Rules, 1883, Ord. XX. r. 1 (a).

(s) *Lloyd's Banking Co.* v. *Ogle*, 1 Ex. D. 262; 45 L. J., Ex. 406; 34 L. T. 584; 24 W. R. 678.

(t) See Jud. Act, 1875, App. C. s. 4, Forms 10 and 11.

(u) Ord. XVI. of the Supreme Court Rules, 1883, governs the subject of parties to High Court actions.

was given (v). In an action by persons, jointly interested in a guarantee, it is not necessary that, as between themselves, their interest in the sum sought to be [*200] *recovered from the surety should be *joint;* but, as between the plaintiffs and defendants, the damages to be recovered under the instrument must be joint (x). And, on the one hand, it seems that where a guarantee is addressed to, among other persons, one who has no interest whatever in the subject-matter guaranteed, such person need not be joined as a plaintiff. Thus, in *Place* v. *Delegal* (y), E., as attorney for the plaintiffs, who were executors of M., sold an estate, to a share of the proceeds of which W. was entitled as legatee of M. The defendant claimed W.'s share of such proceeds under an agreement with W. Thereupon the plaintiffs paid the amount to the defendant on receiving from him a guarantee addressed to E., and also to the plaintiffs as executors of M., and undertaking to indemnify them, and each of them, against any action by W. It was held, that the plaintiffs might sue on this guarantee without joining E. On the other hand, moreover, persons who are actually interested in the subject-matter of the guarantee, but to whom it is not addressed, need not be joined as plaintiffs in an action brought against it. Thus, in *Agacio* v. *Forbes* (z), the plaintiff was a member of a partnership, and in consideration of the plaintiff's undertaking not to sue B. & Co., who were debtors to his firm, the defendant gave a guarantee to the plaintiff. It was held, that the contract being entered into with the plaintiff *personally* upon his undertaking not to sue B. & Co., it constituted a personal agreement, and that the plaintiff was entitled to sue the defendant in his own name without joining his partners as plaintiffs in the action.

The defendants to action on a guarantee. Next, as regards the persons against whom a guarantee may be enforced, that is, under ordinary circumstances, the defendants. It sometimes occurs that a [*201] *guarantee which, at first sight, would appear joint, is really joint and several. Thus, in *Fell* v. *Goslin* (a), the plaintiffs sued the defendants jointly upon

(v) *Pugh* v. *Stringfield*, 3 C. B., N. S. 2. The Supreme Court Rules, 1883, Ord. XVI. r. 1, provide that all persons may be joined as plaintiffs in whom the right to any relief claimed is alleged to exist, whether jointly, severally, or in the alternative.
(x) *Pugh* v. *Stringfield*, 4 C. B., N. S. 364.
(y) 4 Bing. N. C. 426. And see *Palmer* v. *Sparshott*, 4 M. & J. 137.
(z) 14 Moore, P. C. C. 160.
(a) 7 Exch. 185. See also *Collins* v. *Prosser*, 1 B. & C. 682. And see *Palmer* v. *Sparshott*, 4 M. & J. 137.

the following guarantee : "In consideration that you will sell to Mr. F. the distillery situate at, &c., and will take Mr. F's acceptance, to be dated 29th September, 1849, for 400l. (the amount of the purchase-money), and interest payable at six months after the date, we undertake and guarantee that the said sum of 400l. and interest shall be duly paid to you when the said acceptance arrives at maturity, in the proportion of 200l. each." It was held, that the defendants were severally liable to the plaintiff to the extent only of 200l. each.

Again, in the *Irish* case of *Armstrong* v. *Cahill*(b), where A., as principal, and three sureties, B., C. and D., executed a bond to E. for the fidelity of A. in certain duties for which he was employed by E., the bond was in the following form: "We, A., B., C. and D., are held and firmly bound to E in the sum of 50l. each, to be paid to E, his executors, administrators and assigns ; to which payment well and truly to be made, we hereby bind us and each of us, our and each of our heirs, executors and administrators, and every of them by these presents." It was held that the bond was the separate bond of each obligor, binding each to pay the sum of 50l. in the event of default by the principal; and that, therefore, the payment of 50l. by E., one of the obligors, after breach, was no answer to an action on the bond against another obligor, C.

The plaintiff may now, at his option, join as defendants to the same action all or any of the persons severally, or jointly and severally, liable on any one contract, including parties to bills of exchange and promissory notes (c). *Who may now be joined as defendants.*

*It is now necessary to consider how far the [*202] liability of a surety can be enforced against him by way of set-off. For, although the persons entitled to the performance of a guarantee usually seek to enforce it as plaintiffs, it, in some cases, happens that they wish to avail themselves of their rights under the guarantee, by way of defence to some action brought by the person liable as surety. And it then becomes important to consider whether rights existing under a guarantee can be enforced against a surety by way of set-off. *Right of set-off founded upon plaintiff's guarantee.*

Formerly, where *a mere liability* under a guarantee existed on the plaintiff's part, such *mere liability* could not have formed the subject of a set-off (d).

(b) Ir. L. R., 6. Q. B., C. P., and Ex. Divs. 440.
(c) Supreme Court Rules, 1883, Ord. XVI. r. 6.
(d) *Crawford* v. *Stirling.* 4 Esp. 207; *Morley* v. *Inglis,* 4 Bing. N. C. 58; 5 Scott, 314, 333.

However, it was decided in the case of *Hutchinson* v. *Sydney* (e), that though a mere liability under a guarantee could not be set off, yet money that had *actually been paid* for another under an indemnity might be set off as money paid to the use of the plaintiff (*f*).

Set-off now regulated by Judicature Rules.

The whole law relating to the right of set-off is now regulated by the Judicature Rules (g), which extend the right of set-off to cases in which it was not formerly available. Thus, in the case of pecuniary claims, the power of set-off is no longer, as was formerly the case, limited to debts. Claims for unliquidated damages may now be set off against debts, and debts against damages, and damages against damages (h). Moreover, the Judicature Act likewise enables the defendant to set up a counterclaim, which, as distinguished from a set-off, is the assertion of a separate and independent demand; but does not answer or destroy the original claim of the plaintiff (i).

Fourthly. The extent of the surety's liability.

[*203] *Fourthly.* Having now shown what is the nature of the surety's liability, *when* it arises, and *how it is enforced*, it remains to consider the question, *what is the extent of the surety's liability ?*

Was the same both at law and in equity.

Upon this point it is to be observed, that the liability of the surety was always, it seems, the same both at law and in equity (k).

Not necessarily co-extensive with that of principal debtor.

It is obvious that the extent of the surety's liability must vary in each case. Sometimes it is co-extensive with that of the principal debtor. Sometimes it is not co-extensive. The surety, however, can never be obliged to a greater extent than the principal debtor. He may be obliged for less than the debtor ; but one who obliges himself in favour of another, for more than the other is obliged for, is not a surety (l), at all events, so far as the excess is concerned. Where the liability is co-extensive the question as to the extent is a very simple one. For *the measure* of the surety's liability is the loss sustained by the creditor through the default of the principal debtor. A good instance of this kind is furnished by the case of *Oastley* v. *Round* (m). There

---

(e) 10 Exch. 438, 24 L. J., Ex. 25.
(f) As to right of set-off possessed by surety, see *post*, p. 289.
(g) Rules of Supreme Court, 1883, Ord. XIX. r. 3.
(h) Wilson's Judicature Acts and Rules, 4th ed. pp. 249 *et seq.*
(i) County Court Practice, by G. Pitt-Lewis, assisted by H. A. de Colyar, 2nd ed. Vol. I. p. 347. And see *Stooke* v. *Taylor*, 5 Q. B. D. 569.
(k) Per Lord *Eldon* in *Samuel* v. *Howarth*, 3 Meriv. 277, 278.
(l) Theobald on the Law of Principal and Surety, pp. 3, 66.
(m) 11 W. R. 518.

the plaintiff entered into a sub-contract with one B., a government contractor, to supply B. with certain articles within the period stipulated in a certain government contract. In the government contract there were penalties and deductions for delay in delivery, but these were not contained in the sub-contract. The defendants guaranteed the plaintiffs "the payment of the value" of the articles thus to be supplied by the plaintiffs to the government contractor "so soon as he should have received payment from the government." The plaintiffs supplied the goods, but did not supply them within the time named in the government contract held by B., and there was delay *in delivery under [*204] both contracts. The government, however, did not exact any penalties, and paid B. (their contractor) at the full contract price. Obviously by accepting and keeping the goods supplied, B. became liable to the plaintiffs to pay for them, subject perhaps to any question with the government. Accordingly it was held that B. was liable to pay the plaintiffs the full contract price under their contract with him, and that, therefore, the defendant was liable on his guarantee to the same amount.

In many cases, however, it is by no means obvious, Division of or agreed, that the liability of the surety and of the the subject principal debtor are co-extensive. And, in such cases, under con-it often becomes a matter of some difficulty to deter-sideration. mine the exact extent of the surety's liability. The most convenient mode of discussing the subject will probably be to separately consider—(I.) As from what time a guarantee comes into operation, and the liability of the surety commences ; (II.) To what things, and how far, a guarantee extends ; (III.) How long a guarantee continues in operation ; (IV.) The liability of the surety for fraud committed by himself ; (V.) The effect of the surety's liability of a change in constitution on persons to or for whom the guarantee is given ; (VL) The effect of bankruptcy of the surety.

First, then, as to the time from which a guarantee (I.) From comes into operation and the liability of the surety what time commences. This depends upon the agreement made a guarantee by the parties themselves. A guarantee only operates comes into as from the time at which the parties intended that it operation. should do so. Thus the liability of a surety for the good behaviour of a third person in an office extends only to defaults committed after such third person has

11　　　　(1395)

been *legally* appointed to the office (*n*). And, even if the [*205] *condition of surety bonds recite the due appointment of such third persons to the offices contemplated, the sureties are not estopped by these recitals from showing that there had been no complete appointment (*o*). But, upon the other hand, a guarantee for the payment of goods supplied to a third person, if given on the 7th, will cover goods contracted for on the 6th, but not delivered till the 7th, and then supplied on the credit of the guarantee (*p*).

(II.) To what things, and how far guarantee extends.

It is now, in the second place, necessary to consider to what things, and how far, a guarantee extends.

Now, in some cases, by the instrument of guarantee itself, a limit is placed upon the extent of the liability of the surety. Where this is done the surety is liable up to such amount, but of course not beyond it. The rule as laid down by a modern text-writer and approved by the courts is this: "If a bond or guarantee is given by a surety to secure the repayment of advances of money to the principal, provided such advances do not exceed in the whole, at any one time, a certain limited amount, the proviso protects the surety from being answerable beyond the amount named, but it does not render the obligation void if the advances go beyond it, unless that clearly appears to have been the intention of the parties" (*q*).

Where the guarantee imposes a limit on surety's pecuniary liability.

Difficult sometimes to determine whether a guarantee limited in amount is applicable to *whole* debt or to *part* thereof.

Where a surety gives a continuing guarantee, limited in amount to a certain fixed sum, the question sometimes arises whether the suretyship is in respect of the *whole* debt, with a limitation on the liability of the surety, or is applicable to a *part* only of the debt co-extensive with the amount of the guarantee. On this [*206] question the *following principles were laid down in *Ellis* v. *Emmanuel* (*r*), namely: where a surety gives a continuing guarantee, limited in amount, to secure the floating balance which may from time to time be due from the principal to the creditor, the guar-

---

(*n*) *Kepp* v. *Wiggett*, 10 C. B. 35. See also *Nares* v. *Rowles*, 14 East, 510; *Webb* v. *James*, 7 M. & W. 279; *Holland* v. *Lea*, 9 Exch. 430.

(*o*) *Kepp* v. *Wiggett*, *ubi supra*.

(*p*) *Simmons* v. *Keating*, 2 Stark. 426.

(*q*) Addison on Contracts, 8th ed. p. 656. Approved of in *Laurie* v. *Scholefield*, L. R., 4 C. P. 622. See also *Seller* v. *Jones*, 16 M. & W. 112; *Gee* v. *Pack*, 33 L. J., Q. B. 49; *Backhouse* v. *Hall*, 6 B. & S. 507; 34 L. J., Q. B. 141; 12 L. T. 375; 13 W. R. 654; *Parker* v. *Wise*, 6 M. & S. 246; *Gordon* v. *Rae*, 8 Ell. & Bl. 1087.

(*r*) 1 Ex. Div. 157; 46 L. J., Ex. 25; 34 L. T. 453; 24 W. R. 832.

antee is, as between the surety and the creditor, to be construed (*primâ facie*, at least) as applicable to a part only of the debt co-extensive with the amount of the guarantee. But a guarantee, limited in amount, *for a debt already ascertained*, which exceeds that limit, is not *primâ facie* to be construed as a security for part of the debt only ; it is a question of construction on which the Court is to say whether the intention was to guarantee the whole debt with a limitation on the liability of the surety, or to guarantee a part of the debt only (*s*). Principles regulating this subject. *Ellis* v. *Emmanuel.*

As regards the liability of a surety for the payment of calls which may be made on shares in a company, it has been decided that he is not liable to be placed on the list of contributories of the company (*t*). Surety for payment of calls not a contributory.

In other cases, however,—indeed, probably in the majority of cases,—either no limit to the surety's liability is laid down at all, or, the limit mentioned is only a pecuniary one, and is of no assistance in determining whether losses which have occurred are of a class included within the guarantee or not. In such cases, the question whether or not the surety is liable, has to be determined by general principles. And the great leading principle, which applies to such cases, is, that a surety for the performance of a contract of a third *person can only be made liable for what is [*207] *strictly* loss sustained by breach of the contract (*u*). Accordingly, this principle is applied in determining whether a given loss is covered or not as answering the description of being what may properly be termed the principal thing guaranteed against, and the very subject-matter of the contract. For instance, a surety for the good behaviour of another in an office or employment is only liable to answer for those *defaults*— or rather for breaches of those duties only—which are strictly within the *scope* of the office or employment. Surety never liable, excepting for loss sustained through default guaranteed against. Surety for another's good conduct in an office liable only for default within scope of office.

Thus, in *Leigh* v. *Taylor* (*x*), it was held, that, as an overseer has not, by virtue of his office, any authority

<hr>

(s) And see *Hobson* v. *Bass*, L. R., 6 Ch. App. 792 ; *Ex parte Rushforth*, 10 Ves. 409 ; *Paley* v. *Field*, 12 Ves. 435 ; *Bardwell* v. *Lydall*, 7 Bing. 489 ; *Ex parte Holmes*, Mont. & Ch. 301 ; *Gee* v. *Pack*, 33 L. J., Q. B. 49 ; *Thornton* v. *M'Kewan*, 33 L. J., Ch. 69 ; *Gray* v. *Seckham*, L. R., 7 Ch. 680.

(t) *In re Bank of Hindostan, China and Japan, Harrison's case*, L. R., 6 Ch. App. 286.

(u) *Warre* v. *Calvert*, 7 A. & E. 154 ; *King* v. *Norman*, 4 C. B. 884.

(x) 7 B. & C. 491. See also *Napier* v. *Bruce*, 8 C. & F. 470 ; *Pattison* v. *Guardians of Belford Union*, 1 H. & N. 523 ; 26 L. J., Ex. 115 ; *Jephson* v. *Hawkins*, 2 Scott, N. R. 605.

to *borrow* money, therefore, in an action against a
surety on a bond, conditioned for the overseer's faithfully accounting for all sums received by him by virtue
of his office, the surety is not liable for a sum lent to
the overseer, and applied by him to parochial purposes.
Upon the other hand, the liability of the surety extends
to transactions, which, in the natural and usual order
of things, take place on the faith of the guarantee.
Thus where the defendant entered into a bond as surety
for the due and faithful performance by one C. of his
duty as clerk to a provincial bank, and C. being sent
by the manager of the bank, at the request of a customer, to his residence about eleven miles distant from
the bank, for the purpose of receiving a large sum of
money to be placed to his account—a considerable portion of it being in gold and silver—on his way back
dropped the money from his pocket and lost it, it was
held that the money was received by C. in the course
of his employment as clerk to the bank; that the de-
[*208] fendant was liable *as surety, notwithstanding
the finding of the jury that it was not the custom of
bankers in that part of the country to send for their
customers' money in the manner adopted; and that
the loss of the money was *primâ facie* evidence of
gross negligence on the part of C. (y). So, in *Ogden
v. Aspinall* (z), A. gave B. the following guarantee:—
"I have given C. an order to purchase cotton, and,
as it may be to my advantage to have his bills on me
negotiated through your house, I have in such case to
request that you will honor his drafts to the amount of
those we may send to you for sale, on my account, and
I engage that his bills on me, so transmitted, shall be
regularly accepted and paid." It was held, that, under
this guarantee, B. was justified in honouring C.'s draft
to the amount of a bill drawn by C. on A., and represented by C. to B. as being drawn on account of A.,
though such bill was in fact drawn by C. on his *own*
account. And, on the same principle, it is settled that
the creditor is entitled to recover loss actually sus
tained, although he may have entered into a compromise of the liability. This was settled by *Smith* v.
Compton (a), where it was held that, in an action on a

(y) *Melville* v. *Doidge*, 6 C. B. 450. See also *Saunders* v. *Taylor*,
9 B. & C. 35; *Hornsby* v. *Slack*, 1 Ir. C. L. R. 126.
(z) 7 D. & R. 637. See also *Pattison* v. *Guardians of Belford
Union*, 1 H. & N. 523; *Loveland* v. *Knight*, 3 C. & P. 106;
Gwynne v. *Burnell*, 7 Cl. & F. 572.
(a) 3 B. & Ad. 407. See also *Lewis* v. *Smith*, 9 C. B. 610.

general guarantee, the only effect of a party receiving the guarantee compromising a suit commenced against him without notice to the surety is to let in proof on his part, that the compromise was improvidently made, and it lies on him to establish that fact.

The doctrine, that the principal is liable for what is strictly loss caused by the default guaranteed against, is also applied to what may, perhaps, be called *matters incidental* to the principal subject-matter of the guarantee. *Liability of surety for incidental losses, &c.*

*Thus, upon the one hand, whenever the [*209] principal debtor was liable to pay interest on what he owed the creditor, his surety is also liable, on his default, for interest. So, a party who guarantees the *due payment* of a bill of exchange (which is an instrument carrying interest by law) by the acceptor, is liable for interest upon it if it be not paid when due (b). *For interest.*

Where the defendant agreed to indemnify the plaintiff against all liability which he might incur in giving a certain bond to the Treasury, and the plaintiff, under a statute passed subsequently to the giving of the indemnity, made a payment to obtain the cancelling of the bond, it was held that such payment was covered by the indemnity of the defendants (c). *For sum paid in pursuance of a statute passed after guarantee given.*

Upon the other hand, it sometimes happens that a person to whom a guarantee has been given, incurs costs by reason of his having enforced or resisted legal proceedings. The question then arises, is the surety liable for such costs? Can their amount be recovered from him? Upon this point, in *Gillett* v. *Rippon* (d), Lord *Tenterden*, C. J., said: "A man has no right, merely because he has an indemnity, to defend an action and to put the person guaranteeing to useless expense" (e). And this principle was applied and acted upon in the case of *Colvin* v. *Buckle* (f). There, in consideration of a further advance by the plaintiffs to G., on his consignment, the defendants undertook to reimburse them the amount on demand, with interest, *in the* event of the plaintiffs finding it necessary to call upon the defendants to do so, either from the state of G.'s pending account with the plaintiffs, *or [*210] *For costs incurred by creditor.*

(b) *Ackermann and others* v. *Ehrensperger*, 16 M. & W. 99.
(c) *Webster* v. *Petre*, 4 Ex. Div. 127.
(d) 1 M. & M. 406; *Spark* v. *Heslop*, 1 El. & El. 563. And see *Caldbeck* v. *Boon*, 7 Ir. C. L. R. 32; *Howard* v. *Lovegrove*, L. R., 6 Ex. 43; *Baker* v. *Jarratt*, 3 Bing. 56.
(e) See also *Ronneberg* v. *Falkland Island Co.*, 17 C. B., N. S. 1; *Fisher* v. *Val de Travers Asphalte Paving Co.*, 1 C. P. D. 511.
(f) 8 M. & W. 680.

from any other circumstances. On the arrival in England of the consignment on which the advances had been made, the East India Company sold the goods consigned, and out of it paid the freight, and in consequence of conflicting claims from the assignees of G. (for G. had become a bankrupt), filed an interpleader bill and paid the balance of the proceeds into Court. Proceedings, at law and equity, were carried on between all the above parties, for several years, and ultimately the plaintiffs were obliged to pay the costs of the owner of the vessel. It was held that the defendants could not be made liable, under the guarantee, for the expenses incurred by the plaintiffs in the law proceedings.

Credit must be given by creditor for sums paid by the principal debtor.
While the surety is thus held liable for all losses, which are strictly losses arising from his principal's default, he, of course, cannot be held liable for anything beyond the actual and real extent of such losses. Consequently, the creditor is bound, in estimating the liability of the surety to him, to give the surety credit for what the principal debtor may have paid towards the liquidation of the amount due to the creditor. Thus, where the creditor, with the privity of the surety, accepts from the principal debtor a composition on the whole of the debt due, the surety is entitled to a proportional reduction of his own liability (*g*).

(III.) How long a guarantee continues in operation.
The third matter to be considered, in inquiring into the extent of the surety's liability, is the question, How long a guarantee continues in operation ? It is sometimes by no means easy to determine what is the *extent, in point of time*, of the surety's liability. Thus, supposing goods to be supplied, or advances made to a third person, on the faith of a guarantee, the question often arises, Is the guarantee intended as a security for more than the *first* advance or supply ? Is it a *continuing* guarantee or not ?

Necessary sometimes to determine whether guarantee continuing or not.

Two classes of continuing guarantees.
[*211] *The cases in which this question, whether a guarantee is a continuing one or not, most commonly arise, may be considered as being of two classes. The first class of cases consists of ordinary mercantile guarantees for a current account, either for goods sold, or for money advanced, or some consideration of the like nature. The second class of cases arises where guarantees have been given for the good behaviour of a person in some office or employment.

First class of continuing guarantees.
With regard to the first class of cases, no fixed rules have been laid down for determining whether a guar-

(*g*) See *Bardswell* v. *Lyd ll*, 7 Bing. 489. See also *Gee* v. *Pack*, 33 L. J., Q. B. 49.

antee is to be considered a continuing one or not. All, therefore, that can be done is to give a selection from some of the more important of the decided cases as they are found in the reports. In such cases the language of one guarantee affords little or no guide to the construction of another which is given under other and different circumstances (*h*). Probably this is the reason that no fixed rules are to be found with regard to them. *[sidenote: Ordinary mercantile guarantees.]*

In the following cases the instrument was held to be a *continuing guarantee.* *[sidenote: Cases in which guarantee held to be continuing.]*

In *Laurie* v. *Scholefield* (*i*), R. & Co. being about to open an account with the Union Bank, the defendant and one *Black* signed the following guarantee:— *[sidenote: Laurie v. Scholefield.]*

"In consideration of the Union Bank agreeing to advance, and advancing, to R. & Co. any sum or sums of money they may require, during the next eighteen months, not exceeding in the whole 1,000*l.*, we hereby, jointly and severally, guarantee the payment of any such sum as may be owing to the Bank at the expiration of the said period of eighteen months." 1,000*l.* was placed by the Bank to the credit of R. & Co.'s drawing account, and R. & Co. were debited with 1,000*l.* in a loan account. R. & Co. from time to time drew cheques against, and paid money to the credit of their drawing account. Over *1,000*l.* was thus paid in [*212] by R. & Co., and they were not debtors on the drawing account when it was finally closed. The loan account remained unaltered. The Bank sued the defendant for 1,000*l.* on the guarantee, and after the commencement of the action, *Black* paid the Bank 500*l.* in discharge of his liability. The defendant did not plead this payment. It was held that the guarantee was a continuing one, and that the defendant's liability was not discharged by the payments made by R. & Co. It was held, also, that (by rule 14 of Hilary Term, 1853), the defendant could not, in the absence of a proper plea of payment, give the payment by *Black* in evidence in mitigation of damages; and that the Bank was therefore entitled to recover the full amount claimed; but that the Court having power to amend the pleadings, would reduce the verdict by 500*l.* on payment by the defendant of the costs of the rule.

In the case of *Heffield* v. *Meadows* (*k*), W. York's *[sidenote: Heffield v. Meadows.]*

(*h*) Per *Bovill*, C. J., in *Coles* v. *Pack*, L. R., 3 C. P. 65, 70.
(*i*) L. R., 4 C. P. 622.
(*k*) L. R., 4 C. P. 595. But see *Walker* v. *Hardman*, 11 Cl. & F. 258; 11 Bligh, 299.

father had failed in his business of a butcher, and was
succeeded by his son, *W. York*, who had been supplied,
from time to time, as his father had been, with stock,
by the plaintiff, who was a grazier. At the time the
guarantee was given, *W. York* owed the plaintiff 9*l*. 9*s*.
9*d*., and wished to purchase from the *plaintiff* some
stock for 91*l*. The plaintiff, not wishing to trust *W.
York* to such an extent, went to the defendant and
asked him to give him a guarantee, saying, that if he
would give one for 50*l*. he would *still keep supplying
W. York*, as he had supplied *York's* father. The defendant consented, and signed the following guarantee:
—"£50. I, *John Meadows* (the defendant), of *Barwick*, in the county of *Northampton*, will be answerable
for £50 sterling, that *William York*, of Stamford,
butcher, may buy of Mr. *John Heffield* (the plaintiff),
of Donnington." The defendant desired the plaintiff
[*213] not *to let *W. York* know that he had given this
guarantee. The plaintiff delivered the stock to *W. York*
accordingly. Payments were subsequently made by *W.
York* to the plaintiff, to an amount exceeding 91*l*. It
was held, that the surrounding circumstances showed
that the object the parties had in view was to keep up
W. York in his business of a butcher, and that, as the
language of the guarantee was general, and capable of
meaning that the defendant intended to be answerab e
for goods, at any time supplied, to the extent of 50*l*. it
was a continuing guarantee. *Willes*, J., in his judgment, says: "The question in this case is, whether the
guarantee declared on was a continuing guarantee for
50*l*., so as to be a security to the plaintiff to that extent
for any balance which might become due to him in the
course of his dealings with *York* (*l*), or whether the
security was limited to a single transaction between the
plaintiff and *York*. It is obvious that we cannot decide
that question, upon the mere construction of the document itself, without looking at the surrounding circumstances to see what was the subject-matter which the
parties had in their contemplation when the guarantee
was given. It is proper to ascertain that, for the purpose of seeing what the parties were dealing about, not
for the purpose of altering the terms of the guarantee
by words of mouth passing at the time, but as part of
the conduct of the parties, in order to determine what
was the scope and object of the intended guarantee.
Having done that, it will be proper to turn to the lan-

(*l*) The principal debtor.

guage of the guarantee to see if that language is capable
of being construed so as to carry into effect that which
appears to have been really the intention of both parties." And *Montague Smith*, J., in the same case, said:
"The consideration is defectively stated. It does not
show in what the supply is *to consist. We [*214]
may, therefore, look at the surrounding circumstances,
in order to see *for what* it was given, and *to what* transactions or dealings it was intended to apply, *not to alter
the language*, but to fill up the instrument where it is
silent, and to apply it to the subject-matter to which the
parties intended it to be applied."

In *Coles* v. *Pack* (m), in April, 1867, in order to in- *Coles* v. *Pack.*
duce the plaintiff to continue his dealings with one F.,
who was then largely indebted to him, the defendant
gave the plaintiff a guarantee as follows:—

"Holborn Wharf, *Chatham*, April 3, 1867.
"Memorandum. In the event of your supplying
Mr. D. French, of *Chatham*, any coals, during the next
twelve months, from the 1st April last past, I do hereby
guarantee the payment to you of the amount, for the
time being, due from *Mr. D. French* to you, for coals
sold by you to him. This guarantee to expire at the
end of twelve months, viz., 1st April, 1868.
(Signed)   "*T. H. Pack.*"

Before the expiration of the twelve months mentioned
in the above guarantee, viz., on the 23rd of July, 1867,
the debt due from F. to the plaintiff having greatly
increased, and the plaintiff pressing for a settlement,
the defendant gave him a further guarantee, as follows:

"*Ditton*, July 23rd, 1867.
"To *E. R. Coles*, Esq.
"Whereas *Mr. D. French* of *Chatham, Kent*, coal
merchant, is and stands indebted to you, the said *E. R.
Coles*, in the sum of 2,205*l.* 3*s.* 9*d.*, upon an account
this day stated and settled between you and the said
D. French, in addition to his liability upon two certain
acceptances of mine to his drafts, each for 750*l.*, dated
3rd July, 1867, and payable three and four months
*after date, and respectively indorsed to you [*215]
by the said *D. French:* And whereas you are pressing
for the immediate payment of the said sum of 2,205*l.*
3*s.* 9*d.*: Now, I do hereby, in consideration of your

(m) L. R., 5 C. P. 65.
(1403)

forbearing to take immediate steps for the recovery of
the said sum, guarantee the payment of, and agree to
become responsible for, any sum of money for the time
being, due from the said *D. French* to you, whether in
addition to the said sum of 2,205*l.* 3*s.* 9*d.* or no.

(Signed)   "T. H. Pack."

It was held that this was a *continuing* guarantee, unlimited both as to time and amount (*n*).

Burgess v.
Eve.

In *Burgess* v. *Eve* (*o*), a father, being desirous of
obtaining advances for his son from a bank, gave the
son a promissory note for 2,000*l.*, and gave the bank
the following agreement under seal:—

"To *W. McKewan* and *W. J. Norfolk*, Esqrs., public
officers of the *London and County Banking Company.*

"Gentlemen,—In consideration of your discounting
for Mr. *William Henry Maeers* my promissory note to
him for 2,000*l.*, dated this day, and payable four months
after date, and of the sum of 5*s.*, the receipt of which
I hereby acknowledge, I deposit with you the several
documents mentioned in the schedule hereunder written,
which I agree shall remain with you, or other the
public officers, for the time being, of the said company,
as a security for the payment to you, or other such public
officers as aforesaid, of all moneys due, or to become
due, from him to the said company, of whatsoever
members or proprietors it shall from time to time consist, on any account whatsoever, including charges for
interest, commission and all costs, charges and expenses
which you may incur in enforcing or obtaining payment
[*216] * of such money, or in realizing this or any
further security. And I agree to pay you, or such
public officers aforesaid, upon demand, all such money.
And I hereby charge the hereditaments and premises
comprised in such documents respectively and all fix-
tures now or hereafter therein, with the payment thereof."
It was held that the payment was not limited to the
2,000*l.*, but was a continuing guarantee for all money
already due, or which should become due from the son
to the bank.

Wood v.
Priestner.

In the case of *Wood* v. *Priestner* (*p*), the guarantee
was as follows: "In consideration of the credit given
by H. G. C. & Co. to my son, for coal supplied by them

(*n*) The able judgment of *Bovill*, C. J., in this case is well
worth perusing.
(*o*) L. R., 13 Eq. 450.
(*p*) L. R., 2 Exch. 66.

to him, I hereby hold myself responsible as a guarantee to them for the sum of 100l., and in default of his payment of any accounts due, I bind myself by this note to pay to the H. G. C. & Co., whatever may be owing to an amount not exceeding the sum of 100l." When the guarantee was given, the defendant's son owed the plaintiff a debt of more than 100l. for goods supplied. It was held to be a continuing guarantee. *Kelly*, C. B., in delivering judgment, said: "I think this is clearly a continuing guarantee. The question in these cases depends not merely on the words, but when the words are at all ambiguous, requires a consideration of the circumstances to aid the construction."

In *Simpson* v. *Manley* (q), the guarantee was as follows:— *Simpson* v. *Manley.*

"May 26th, 1830.

"Our relation, Mr. *Thomas Manley*, having intimated to us that he is about to make some purchases of goods from you, we beg to say, that if you give him *credit*, we will be responsible that his payments shall be regularly made to the extent of 1,000l., from this period to the 1st of June, 1831."

*It was admitted by counsel, and stated by [*217] the court, to be clear, that this was a continuing guarantee.

In *Mason* v. *Pritchard* (r), it was held, that a guarantee by the defendant to the plaintiff "for any goods he *hath* or *may* supply W. P. with, to the amount of 100l.," is a continuing or standing guarantee to that extent for goods which may at any time have been supplied to W. P., until the credit was recalled, although goods to more than 100l. had been before supplied and paid for. In *Allan* v. *Kenning* (s), the following *Allan* v. *Kenning.* guarantee was given: "Whereas W. C. is indebted to you in a sum of money, and may have occasion to make further purchases from you, as an inducement to you to *continue* your dealings with him, I undertake to guarantee you in the sum of 100l., payable to you in default on the part of the said W. C. for two months." It was held to be a continuing guarantee, and that it was binding on the defendant till the parties came to an understanding that they would be off, and that, on default of W. C. for two months, the defendant would immediately be liable.

Mason v. *Pritchard.*

(q) 2 C. & J. 12.
(r) 12 East, 227. See observations on this case in *Melville* v. *Hayden*, 3 B. & Ald. 593.
(s) 9 Bing. 618 ; 2 M. & Scott, 762.

Bastow v.
Bennett.

In *Bastow* v. *Bennett* (t), the guarantee was as follows:

"*London*, 7th March, 1810.

"I hereby undertake and engage to be answerable to the extent of 300l., for any tallow or soap supplied by Mr. *Bastow* to *France & Bennett*, provided they shall neglect to pay in due time." It was held to be a continuing guarantee. Lord *Ellenborough*, in his judgment, says : "The defendant here became answerable for *any* soap or tallow supplied by the plaintiff to *France & Bennett.* Without the word *any* it might perhaps have been confined to one dealing to the amount of 300l. ; but, as it is actually worded, I am of opinion it remained in force while the parties continued to deal on the footing established when it was given. But I [*218] *think the goods supplied after the new arrangement (u) were not within the scope of the guarantee, and that the defendant is only answerable for the unsatisfied balance of the old account."

Merle v.
Wells.

In *Merle* v. *Wells* (x), the guarantee was as follows:—

"Gentlemen,—I have been applied to by my brother *William Wells*, jeweller, to be bound to you for any debts he may contract, not to exceed 100l. (with you), for goods necessary in his business as a jeweller. I have wrote to say by this declaration I consider myself bound to you for any debt he may contract for his business as a jeweller, not exceeding 100l. after this date.

"(Signed)   *John Wells.*"

It was held to be a continuing guarantee. Lord *Ellenborough*, in his judgment, said : "I think the defendant was answerable for any debt, not exceeding 100l., which *William Wells* might from time to time contract with the plaintiffs in the way of his business. The guarantee is not confined to one instance, but applies to debts successively renewed. If a party means to be surety only for a single dealing, he should take care to say so."

Martin v.
Wright.

In *Martin* v. *Wright* (y), the guarantee was as follows: "In consideration of your agreeing to supply goods to K., at two months' credit, I agree to guarantee

(t) 3 Camp. 220.
(u) The new arrangement alluded to was one which *altered* the credit on which the plaintiff supplied the goods to France & Bennett, substituting for a two months' credit, payment in ready money.
(x) 2 Camp. 413.
(y) 6 Q. B. 917.

(1406)

his present or any future debt with you to the amount of 60*l.* Should he fail to pay at the expiration of the above credit, I bind myself to pay you within seven days of receiving notice from you." It was held that this was a continuing guarantee.

In *The Nottingham Hide, Skin & Fat Market Co. (Limited)* v. *John Bottrill and another* (z), the [*219] facts were as follows : The plaintiffs were in the habit of holding weekly sales of hides, skins, &c., the course of business being that the goods bought at each sale were paid for in the following week. One *Dyson,* who had for some time bought skins at these sales, on the 29th of December, 1871, bought to the extent of 34*l.* 7*s.* 6*d.* Having heard that *Dyson* had executed a bill of sale, the plaintiffs declined to deliver the skins unless the defendants would engage to be responsible for the price. This being communicated by *Dyson* to the defendants, the latter on the 1st of January, 1872, telegraphed to the plaintiffs, "We agree to be answerable for the skins," and on the same day sent them a covering letter, in which, after stating that they had had dealings with *Dyson* for five years, and had never known anything dishonourable or dishonest in any of his transactions, they wrote, " What you have heard was done to protect him from a dishonest tradesman, and will in no way, we hope, be to the injury of his creditors. Having every confidence in him, he has but to call upon us for a cheque, and have it with pleasure, for any account he may have with you." The plaintiffs accordingly sent *Dyson* the goods, and continued to deal with him down to the 3rd of May, 1872, at which time he was indebted to them in 92*l.* 1*s.* 10*d.*, which he was unable to pay, the defendants, who were the holders of the bill of sale, having seize'd and sold all his effects under it. It was held that the defendants' letter of the 1st of January was a continuing guarantee. In his judgment in this case, *Keating,* J., said: "Each case must, no doubt, depend entirely upon the language used, and the document must be looked at with reference to the special circumstances under which it is given. Now, what did the writers of that letter of the 1st January mean, and what would the plaintiffs naturally understand from it ? The defendants *were aware of the state of [*220] things between the plaintiffs and *Dyson,* and sent that letter in order to remove the unfavourable impression the plaintiffs had of *Dyson's* credit and ability. The

Nottingham Hide, &c. Co. Limited v. *Bottrill.*

(z) L. R., 8 C. P. 694.

letter does not confine itself to the transaction alluded
to in the telegram ; but it goes on—'Having every confidence in him, he has but to call upon us for a cheque,
and have it with pleasure, for any account he may have
with you ; and when to the contrary we will write you.'
What would any man of business understand by that?
The only reasonable construction of the letter, as
it strikes me, is this : Our opinion of *Dyson* is so
high, that we are ready to become sureties for any account for which he may become indebted to you ; and,
if we see reason to change our mind, we will let you
know.   That amounts to a guarantee, and a continuing
guarantee.   It was calculated to induce the plaintiffs
to give credit to a man to whom they would not otherwise have given it " (*a*).

Mayer v.
Isaac.

In *Mayer* v. *Isaac* (*b*), the guarantee was as follows:
"In consideration of your supplying my nephew V.
with china and earthenware, I guarantee the payment
of any bills you may draw on him on account thereof
to the amount of 200*l.*"   It was held that the guarantee
was a continuing one, and that the defendant was liable
upon it, although, after the guarantee, goods to a greater
amount than 200*l.* had been supplied to and paid for
by V.   "It contemplates" (says Baron *Alderson* in his
judgment in this case) "the continuance of a supply on
the one side, and on the other, a liability for any default during that supply, and then it defines the extent
to which the defendant will be bound upon this continuing or running guarantee" (*c*).

*Cases in
which guar-
antee held
not to be
continuing.
Walker* v.
Hardman.

[*221]   *The following cases have been selected as instances of instruments which have been held *not* to be
continuing guarantees.

In *Walker* v. *Hardman* (*d*), it was laid down by the
House of Lords that where a bond, which, on the face
of it, appears to be a simple money bond, is given to
secure a sum certain with interest, it must be construed, so far at least as regards the surety, as given to
secure the debt then existing, and not to cover floating
balances.

(*a*) The judgment of *Brett*, J., in this case will also well repay
perusal.
(*b*) 6 M. & W. 605.
(*c*) For other instances of continuing guarantees, see *Tanner* v.
Moore, 9 Q. B. 1 ; *Hargreave* v. *Smee*, 6 Bing. 244 ; *Williams* v.
Rawlinson, 3 Bing. 71 ; *Hitchcock* v. *Humfrey*, 5 M. & G. 559 ;
Henniker v. *Wigg*, 4 Q. B. 792. See also *Woolley* v. *Jennings*, 5 B. &
C. 165 ; *Hoad* v. *Grace*, 7 H. & N. 494 ; *In re Booth, Browning* v.
Baldwin, 40 L. T. N. 248 ; 27 W. R. 644 ; *Hortor* v. *Carpenter*, 3
C. B., N. S. 172.
(*d*) 11 Cl. & F. 258 ; 11 Bligh, 299.

In *Nicholson* v. *Paget* (e), the guarantee was in the following words :— *Nicholson* v. *Paget.*

"Sir,—I hereby agree to be answerable for the payment of 50l. for T. Lerigo, in case T. Lerigo does not pay for the gin, &c., which he receives from you, and I will pay the amount." It was held that this was *not* a continuing guarantee, for that it referred to a particular quantity of gin which the party was to receive from the plaintiff.

In *Tayleur* v. *Wildin* (f) one M., being yearly tenant to the plaintiff on the terms of a written agreement, the defendant, in consideration of the plaintiff's continuing M. as such tenant, gave the plaintiff a guarantee for "the rent of the Leese Farm, in the occupation of M." The plaintiff afterwards gave M. notice to quit, but, on the payment of arrears of rent, withdrew it before the expiration of the current year. The next year the rent became in arrear, and the plaintiff sued the defendant on his guarantee. It was held that the old tenancy was determined by the notice to quit ; that the guarantee applied only to the tenancy which existed at the time *when it was given; and that [*222] the defendant was, therefore, not liable. *Tayleur* v. *Wildin.*

In *Chalmers* v. *Victors* (g), the defendant gave the following guarantee :—" J. V. hereby engages to be responsible for liabilities incurred by M. and V. to the extent of 50l." At the time the guarantee was given, 41l was due from M. and V. to the plaintiffs. It was held that the guarantee contemplated future credit, but only to such an amount as, with the existing liability, made up 50l, and that amount having been paid off by M. and V., it was held that the guarantee did not cover goods subsequently supplied. *Bovill*, C. J., in his judgment in this case, says : "It is difficult, if not impossible, to reconcile all the cases cited. The documents in them vary from each other, and the document in the present case varies from all those that have been cited. Taking the documents simply without reference to the surrounding circumstances, and reading it in the ordinary sense, it would apply only to past liabilities, and if there were nothing further, the guarantee would be altogether bad, but we are at liberty to look at the facts as they were on the day when the guarantee was given." *Byles*, J., in the same case, said : "The words of this guarantee are 'for liabilities incurred,' and we *Chalmers* v. *Victors.*

(e) 1 C. & M. 48.
(f) L. R., 3 Ex. 303. See *Holne* v. *Brunskill*, 3 Q. B. Div. 495.
(g) 16 W. R. 1046.

It appeared at the trial before *Tindal*, C. J., that on the 19th November, plaintiff delivered to *Taylor* five sacks of flour, and on the 21st November five more. On the 24th, *Taylor* sent back three and a half sacks out of the first five, as being of a bad quality; and three and a half other sacks were supplied that day. The defendant paid into Court the price of a sack and a half of flour. Chief Justice *Tindal* observing, that plaintiff had proved no second order from the defendant, nor any agreement on his part that three and a half sacks should be substituted on the 24th November, for three and a half delivered on the 19th, and to be paid for within a month from that day, left it to the jury to say whether the delivery on the 24th was made under the defendant's guarantee, and in substitution of any part of the delivery on the 19th, or whether it was made under a new contract. Verdict for defendant.

Second class of continuing guarantees. The *second* class of cases, in which the question, how long a guarantee continues in operation, - usually becomes important, consists of those cases in which a guarantee has been given for the fidelity of a person in some office or employment (*o*).

Bonds given for fidelity of official persons. Where a bond or other guarantee has been given for the good behaviour of third persons in offices or employments, very nice questions often arise as to whether the liability of the surety continues, after some change has taken place as to the circumstances of the appoint- **Rules for determining duration of surety's liability in such cases.** [*226] *ment; but (unlike the cases of mercantile guarantees), certain fixed rules appear now to be laid down for the determination of all such questions. We will, therefore, proceed to discuss in order (1) The liability of the surety after the third person's *re appointment* to the *same* office; (2) The surety's liability after the third person's appointment to another, though *similar* office or employment; (3) The surety's liability after a *change* has taken place *in the duties* or length of term of the third person's office. These cases well exemplify the rule that a surety's liability is not to be extended beyond the precise terms of his engagement. In determining the extent of this liability under a surety bond, it must be borne in mind that the words of the *condition* of the bond are to be restrained by the *recitals*.

(*o*) It has recently been held that a "guarantee society" may be accepted as surety to a bond given by an administrator pending suit, even though the directors do not by the bond render themselves personally liable : *Carpenter* v. *Solicitor to the Treasury*, 7 P. D. 235.

And *first*, let us consider those cases, where subsequently to the execution of the surety bond, the third person for whom the surety has agreed to be answerable is re-appointed to the *same* office which he filled at the time of the execution of the bond. To such cases, the rule applicable appears to be, that, though the words of the condition of the bond be *general* and *indefinite* as to the time during which the surety is to remain liable, yet such liability is not to extend beyond the time for which the office *recited* in the condition is limited to be holden, because such a construction is most agreeable to the intent of the condition. Moreover, it appears from the reported cases that even where the recital in the condition of the bond does not state the office to be for a *specific time*, yet, if this be shown by the pleadings to be the case, the liability of the surety must be confined to such specific time (*p*). We will now illustrate what we have just stated by one or two examples.

(1.) Cases where, after guarantee given, the third person is re-appointed to same office. Rule applicable to such cases.

*In the celebrated case of *Lord Arlington v.* [*227] *Merrick* (*q*), the bond was conditioned for the performance of the duties of deputy postmaster, by A. B., "*for and during all the time that he shall continue deputy postmaster of the said stage.*" It appeared, however, from a recital in the bond, that the plaintiff had appointed A. B. to act as deputy postmaster *for the term of six months*. It was accordingly held, that the general words of the condition was restrained by this recital, and that therefore the liability of the defendant under the bond as surety for A. B., endured only during the six months recited in the bond, and did not extend to subsequent re-appointments to the same office.

Lord Arlington v. Merricke.

In *Bamford v. Iles* (*r*) a bond reciting that A. was appointed assistant overseer of the parish of M. was conditioned for the due performance of his duties "thenceforth from time to time, and at all times, so long as he should continue in such office." Before the date of this bond, namely, on the 25th June,

Bamford v. Iles.

(*p*) In a recent American case it was held that a surety on the bond of a re-elected county treasurer is liable only for default during the term for which the bond was given: *Van Sickel* v. *County of Buffalo*, 42 Amer. R. 753 (U. S.)

(*q*) 2 Wms. Saund. 813. See also *Liverpool Waterworks Co.* v. *Atkinson*, 6 East, 507.

(*r*) 3 Exch. 380. It appears, however, from the case of *Frank* v. *Edwards*, 8 Exch. 214, that a mere reduction of salary, where the original appointment is *not revoked*, will not discharge the surety unless indeed the bond contain a stipulation to that effect. See the judgment of *Parke*, B., in this case, where the distinction between it and *Bamford* v. *Iles*, *supra*, is pointed out.

1840, a vestry meeting was held at which A. was *elected* assistant overseer until the 25th March, 1841. at a salary of 8*d.* in the pound on some sums collected, and 4*d.* on others. On the 9th July, 1840, the justices by their warrant, which recited the resolution of the vestry, *electing* A. at the aforesaid salary, *appointed* A. assistant overseer in pursuance of 59 Geo. 3, c. 12. On the 25th March, 1841, he was *again* elected to the *same* office, at a salary of 50*l.* per annum, and was reappointed by the justices, and continued to be so re-elected and re-appointed by the justices till March, [*228] 1846. On ceasing to hold office *he retained monies in his hands. It was held that the sureties were not liable on the bond.

Peppin v. *Cooper.*

In *Peppin* v. *Cooper* (*s*), a bond was given, which, after reciting the appointment of *Henry Warren* to be a collector, under an act of parliament which made the office an annual one, was conditioned for the due collection by *Henry Warren*, of the rates and duties "*at all times hereafter* ;" and it was holden that the due collection of the rates for one year was a compliance with the condition of the bond. *Abbott*, C. J., said, "I am of opinion that the condition of the bond is satisfied by the faithful collection of rates and duties for the space of one year. It is true that the words '*at all times hereafter*,' in the condition of the bond, would, taken by themselves, extend the liability of the surety beyond that period. But these words must be construed with reference to the recital, and to the nature of the appointment there mentioned, and the recital is, that *Warren*, together with *Peppin*, had been appointed collectors under the said act of parliament. Now, the nature and duration of that office must be learnt from the act of parliament itself; for if the statute make it an annual office, it is unnecessary to state that fact either in the bond or in pleading" (*t*).

In the three following cases the recitals of the bonds did not indeed state the office to be holden for a *specific time*, but, as this appeared from the pleadings, it was held that this was sufficient to control the general and indefinite language of the conditions of the bonds.

Kitson v. *Julian.*

In *Kitson* v. *Julian* (*u*), the defendants J. and S. gave a joint and several bond to the plaintiff, the condition whereof recited, that J. had been appointed clerk

(*s*) 2 B. & A. 431.
(*t*) And see *Savings Bank of Hannibal* v. *Hunt*, 37 Amer. R. 449 (U. S.)
(*u*) 4 Ell. & Bl. 854.

to plaintiff, and, that upon such appointment being made, it was agreed that J. and S., as surety for J., should *enter into the bond for the due execution of [*229] his said office, and the condition was declared to be, that if J. should "from time to time," and at all times, so long as he shall continue to hold the said office or employment," duly account for and pay to the plaintiff all sums of money received by him, "by virtue or in execution of his said office," and account for and deliver to the plaintiff all books and things "which shall at any time or times, be received by, or come to his hands, by virtue or in execution of his said office or employment," and "at all times" regularly keep accounts of such sums, books, &c., and "faithfully and diligently, in all respects, demean and conduct himself in the said office or employment, and in all matters and things relating to or concern the same," the bond should be void. The plaintiff declared on the bond against the defendants J. and S. The defendants' principal plea (after setting out the condition) alleged that the appointment of J. to the said office and employment was for one year, and no longer, and that J. did well and truly observe, perform, &c., all the articles, &c., in the condition specified. The replication to this plea alleged, that J., with the assent of the defendants and the plaintiff, remained in the said office and employment after the expiration of the year, for a long period, and during such last-mentioned period, and before the commencement of the suit, omitted to account, &c., for sums received by him "under and by virtue and in execution of his said office during such period." On demurrer to this replication, it was held : *That* the allegation in the plea, as to the time for which J. was in fact appointed, had the same effect as if the period of the appointment were recited in the condition. *That* the plea showed a good defence, the liability of the defendants on the bond not extending beyond the specified year. *That* the replication did not answer the plea, for that it did not show more than a fresh appointment by parol, which would not be comprehended in the condition of the bond.

*In *Hassell* v. *Long* (x), a bond was given by [*230] the defendant's testator as surety for E. The condition of the bond recited that E. had been, and still was, collector of the land tax, and all other taxes and duties imposed by several acts of parliament on the inhabitants

Hassell v. *Long.*

(x) 2 M. & Selw. 362. See also *Wardens of St. Saviour's* v. *Bostock,* 2 N. R. 175, *infra.*

of the parish of C., by means whereof he received from the inhabitants divers sums of money. The condition, in its operative part, depended on the due payment by E. from time to time, and at all times thereafter, to the Receiver-General of Taxes, &c., all and every sum which he (E.) should from time to time collect and receive from the inhabitants of the parish, for or on account of any tax or taxes then imposed, or which should or might thereafter be imposed on them by any act of parliament. It was held that this bond was confined to the current year for which E. was, at the date of the bond, collector, although it did not appear on the condition that he was only appointed for a year: it being shown, *by the defendant's plea*, that the said office of collector was an annual one, and held as such by E. at the date of the bond (*y*).

Wardens of St. Saviour's, Southwark v. Bostock.

In *The Wardens of St. Saviour's, Southwark* v. *Bostock* (*z*), A., B. and C. entered into a bond, as sureties for D. and E. The condition of the bond *recited* that D. was, on a certain day, appointed collector of the church rate of the parish of St. Saviour's, Southwark, by virtue of which office he was empowered to collect and receive all such monies as were rated and assessed on the inhabitants by virtue of the said rate, and for which he was accountable to the wardens of the grand account. It *bound* the sureties that D. should duly account for all monies collected or received by him, on account of the above rate, and also on every other rate [*231] *or rates thereafter to be made and collected by him, the said D. It being *admitted by the replication* that the office was an annual one, it was held that the sureties were only answerable for D. in that single appointment, and not on his appointment in the ensuing year.

Sometimes liability of surety is co-extensive with duration of third person's office.

Where, however, it does not appear from the recital of the bond itself, or in any other way, that the office, for the due fulfilment of which another is surety, is limited in duration, then, there being nothing to control the general and indefinite language of the condition of the bond, the liability of the surety is co-extensive in duration with the length of the third person's office.

Mayor of Birmingham v. Wright.

Thus, in the case of *The Mayor of Birmingham* v. *Wright* (*a*), certain parties had become sureties by bond.

(*y*) See, further, as to alleging in the defendant's pleading that the office is limited in duration, the cases of *Curling* v. *Chalkies*, 3 M. & S. 502, and *Leadley* v. *Evans*, 2 Bing. 32.

(*z*) 2 N. R. 175.

(*a*) 16 Q. B. 623. See also *Sansom* v. *Bell*, 2 Camp. 39.

The bond recited that R. had been appointed to act as overseer for making and levying borough rates in that part of the parish, A., which lay within the borough of B., during the pleasure of the council of the borough. It was conditioned for performance of the duties during such time as A. should act as overseer. Upon this bond it was held, that the sureties were liable beyond the expiration of the year, A. continuing in office ; for that there was no law limiting the duration of the office to a year, so as to control the express stipulations of the bond.

In *Curling* v. *Chalklen* (*b*), debt was brought on a *Curling* v. bond made by one *Chalklen* and his sureties. The con- *Chalklen.* dition recited statute 27 Geo. 2, c. 38, and that *Chalklen* (four years before the date of the bond) was appointed by the churchwardens and parishioners of *Deptford*, in pursuance of the statute, collector of the poor rates *to be levied and raised* in the parish. And the condition itself was that *Chalklen* should account, as often as required, for all monies *so collected and received by him, by virtue of the act*, &c. The *breach* alleged was not accounting for monies collected and received by *Chalklen before* the making of the bond

*The defendant pleaded, *first*, that C. ac- [*232] counted for all the monies collected and received by him before the making of the bond ; *secondly*, that the office of collector is an annual office, and that C. accounted for all the monies collected and received by him within the current year of office in which the bond was made. Upon demurrer, it was held that both the pleas were ill, for, by the words of the statute, the appointment was prospective, to collect future rates, and not retrospective only, and the condition was in the words of the statute, without any restraining words ; and it was not pleaded that the office was an annual office at the time of making the bond, and if it had been, yet it appeared by the statute not to be an annual office, though concerning rates which are raised in the course of the year. Lord *Ellenborough*, C. J., in his judgment in this case, said : "Here is a duty, not limited by the act to a year, so that it shall extend to that period and no longer, but a continuing duty on the party so long as he shall remain collector, without regard to any definite time, though it may be that the rates which he is to collect are, in form, limited to a less or not a greater period than a year. It appears, then, that there is nothing on the face of the act of parliament, nor of the condition, directly or indirectly, to limit the period of office to a year. Therefore, the obligation of the surety cannot be so narrowed ; it is indefinite in its language relating to a period before and after. As to the allegation in the plea that this is an annual office, I consider that as impertinent. The allegation should have been, that it was an annual office at the time when the obligation was made ; but that would not have been supported by the act."

Sometimes surety's liability, by express agreement, does not terminate on subsequent re-appointment of third party to same office.

Augero v. Keen.

Of course, by the use of proper words, a surety may provide for a continuance of his liability, on subsequent re-appointments to the same office, of the person whose default or miscarriage is guaranteed against. [*233] Thus, in *Augero* v. *Keen* (c), a bond given to secure the faithful performance of the office of a collector of parochial rates (who was by act of parliament to be appointed by trustees for a year, and then to be capable of re-election) was *conditioned* that "from time to time, and at all times thereafter, during such time as he should continue in his *said* office, whether by virtue of his said appointment, or of any re-appointment thereto, or of any such retainer or employment by or under the authority of the said trustees, or their successors, to be elected in the manner directed by the said act, he should use his best endeavours to collect the monies received by means of the rates in the then present or in any subsequent year," &c., &c. It was held, that the obligation of the bond was not confined to the year for which he was originally appointed, but extended also to all subsequent years in which he was continuously re-appointed. Lord *Abinger*, C. B., in giving judgment in this case, said : "It would be difficult to find any words more clear than those employed in this case to show that the parties meant to provide for the continuance of the party in office. In order to save expense, as long as he continues in office under his original appointment, or any continuing re-appointment, only one bond is to be required."

(2.) Where, after surety bond given, third person

We now come, in the *second* place, to cases where, after the execution of the surety bond, the third person has been appointed to *another*, though *similar* office (d).

(c) 1 M. & W. 390.

(d) These cases *might* certainly, without impropriety, be discussed with the cases which we shall next discuss, and which they *to a certain extent resemble*. It is, however, thought desirable, in order to prevent all possible confusion, to treat these cases separately.

An instance of this kind is furnished by the case of *re-appointed*
The Guardians of the Portsea Island Union v. *Whillier to another*
(*e*). In that case a bond, dated the 16th December, *but similar*
1852, recited an order of the Poor Law Commissioners *office.*
in *1836, by which it was ordered that the [*234] *Guardians of*
plaintiffs (guardians of the *Portsea Union*) should ap- *Union v.*
point one or more fit and proper persons to be the col- *Whillier.*
lector or collectors of the poor rates of such of the
parishes as the guardians might deem to require a collector, and that every person appointed a collector
should give security for the due discharge of the duties
of the office, and further recited that W. was duly appointed to be a collector under the said order. The
bond was then conditioned (among other things) that
W. should during his continuance in his said office, and
whether the district for which he was appointed were
or were not changed, faithfully discharge the duties
thereof, and obey the lawful directions of the guardians.
In the first instance the guardians had elected three
persons to be collectors of the poor rate in *Portsea*, to
each of whom was assigned a portion of the parish.
In 1848 the guardians had divided the parish into four
districts for collection of the poor rates, and appointed
an additional collector. After the passing of statute
13 & 14 Vict. c. 99, it was determined to appoint a fifth
collector. At this time one of the four collectors resigned, and an advertisement was published that the
guardians should appoint " two persons to be collectors
of the poor rates of the parish of *Portsea*, to one of
whom would be assigned a collection of such rates from
the owners of small tenements." W. had applied,
offering himself as a candidate for one of them, and
had been elected for the purpose of collecting the rates
from the owners of small tenements. The bond mentioned above was then executed by the defendant
Whillier, and as his surety. Some years after the execution of the bond, in the year 1855, one of the collectors having resigned, W. applied to the plaintiffs,
to transfer him to that district, which application was
acceded to. In an action upon this bond it was held,
that the appointment of *Whillier* was a general one as
collector of poor rates for the parish. and that there
*being only a change of duties in 1855, the [*235]
obligation of the surety was not discharged. *Cockburn*,
C. J., delivered the following judgment in the case:—
" The question which we have to determine in the first

(*e*) 6 Jur., N. S. 887.

instance is, whether the appointment of the collector, for whose default the defendant is sought to be made responsible, was an appointment of him as collector of rates generally, or of rates payable in respect of small tenements exclusively. If the latter, then, inasmuch as by the subsequent act of the guardians he was employed for a different purpose, and the default arose in respect of that appointment, it follows, according to well-established authorities, that the surety cannot be made responsible for his default; in justice and law his responsibility ceases. The question is not altogether free from doubt, but, upon the whole, I think that the right conclusion to arrive at is, that the appointment of *James William Whillier* was as collector of the rates of the parish of *Portsea* generally. In the first place, the order of the Poor Law Board was for the appointment of a collector of the parish generally. Then the advertisement, which led to the appointment of *James William Whillier*, as collector, was for two collectors of the parish, with an intimation that to one of them would be assigned a collection of the rates from the owners of small tenements. *James William Whillier* applies to be appointed as one of them, and then the bond, from beginning to end, treats the appointment, not as a special appointment, but as an appointment for collecting the rates of the parish of *Portsea* generally. Looking at the whole of the order, the advertisement, and the bond, there is sufficient evidence to lead us to the conclusion that the appointment was treated as, and was in effect, an appointment generally, and not for a limited or special purpose. It is true that at the time of the appointment the resolution is couched in language which, at first sight, appears to have reference to a more limited purpose, but, looking at the whole, I [*236] *think that much weight is not to be attached to that, because it being convenient to assign to each collector certain duties, they would, on the appointment, declare at once the particular duties which each was to discharge. Suppose, without reference to the collection of rates from the owners of small tenements, the guardians had thought proper to transfer one of the district collectors to another district, there is nothing in the appointment to justify the collector in refusing to acquiesce in the transfer. Suppose there was illness, or any other disability in a collector, can it be said that one collector could not discharge the duties of the other so disabled ? I think that this was the appointment of a collector generally, and then it would be competent to the guardians to determine which set of duties each collector should discharge. That is the good sense and justice of the case. It cannot be that because the principal is transferred to another department, with other duties, his surety is to be allowed to avoid his liability. Therefore I think that this was a general appointment for the whole parish, and that the defendant is liable."

In *Holland* v. *Lea* (*f*) the facts were as follows:— *Holland* v. In March, 1845, R. L. was nominated and elected assis- *Lea.* tant overseer of the poor of the parish of W. by the inhabitants in vestry assembled, at the yearly salary of 27*l.* In May following he entered into a bond, with two sureties, for the faithful execution of the office, under the 59 Geo. 3, c. 12. The condition of the bond recited that statute, and that R. L. had been duly nominated and elected at the annual salary of 27*l.* R. L. then proceeded to perform the duties of the office. In March, 1846, at a vestry duly held, a resolution was come to, that the permanent overseer's salary (meaning R. L.'s) should be raised from 27*l.* to 35*l.* a year, including all other extra charges. In June, 1846, a *warrant of the appointment of R. L. as assist- [*237] ant overseer was signed and sealed by two justices of the peace. This warrant recited that R. L. had been nominated and elected in March, 1846, at the yearly salary of 35*l.* Subsequently to June, 1846, R. L. had acted as assistant overseer, but had become a defaulter to a considerable amount. In an action on the bond by the succeeding overseers against the sureties, it was held (*Pollock*, C. B., *Parke*, B., and *Alderson*, B., *Martin* B., diss.), that R. L. had never been duly appointed assistant overseer, and that the sureties were not liable.

It seems that where a person is surety for another's Subsequent good behaviour in a particular office, and subsequently appointment such other person is appointed to a perfectly distinct of third party office, which is *incompatible* and *inconsistent* with (*g*) office which the first appointment, the surety is discharged; even is inconsist-though the duties under the two appointments be sub- ent with first stantially the same. This was decided in the case of appointment discharges *The Malling Union* v. *Graham* (*h*). There A., in 1865, surety. was duly appointed by a vestry of the parish of Mal- *Malling* ling assistant overseer of the said parish at a fixed *Union* v. salary. This appointment was made in pursuance of *Graham*

(*f*) 9 Ex. 430.
(*g*) *Worth* v. *Newton*, 10 Ex. 247.
(*h*) L. R., 5 C. P. 201.

59 Geo. 3, c. 12, s. 7 (*i*). B. became A.'s surety. Subsequently under 7 & 8 Vict. c. 101, s. 62 (*k*), A. was
[*238] appointed *by a board of guardians of a union,
on the recommendation of the.vestry of the parish of
West Malling, collector of poor rates for the said
parish, at a poundage of 6*d.* The Poor Law Board
duly confirmed this appointment. The duties under the
two appointments were substantially the same. After
the last appointment A. continued to perform the same
duties as he had before performed, and the appointment of 1865 was not otherwise resigned or revoked.
A. having made default after the last appointment in
keeping books and in paying over money, B. (the defendant), was sued on the bond. It was held, that the
two appointments were inconsistent and incompatible:
that the appointment of 1865 ceased by virtue of 7 &
8 Vict. c. 101, s. 62, on A.'s acceptance of the appointment by the guardians, and consequently that the liability of B., as surety on the bond, was at an end. It
would *seem* that there was under the circumstances both
a revocation of the first appointment by the vestry, and
a resignation by A.

Aliter, where the two offices are not inconsistent.

Where a person, for whose good behaviour another
is surety, is, subsequently to the execution of the surety
bond, appointed to an *additional* office or employment,
the liability of the surety does not in consequence
necessarily cease (*l*). Of course, however, in such a
case the liability of the surety would not extend to
anything done or omitted by the principal in respect to
such *additional* office or employment.

In a recent American case it was held that sureties
for the faithful performance of the duties of the bookkeeper of a bank are liable for his errors in that capacity, although he also performs the duties of teller, un-

---

(*i*) This enactment in substance provides, that the inhabitants
of a parish in vestry assembled may elect, and that two justices
of the peace may appoint, assistant overseers with a salary; and
that the person so appointed assistant overseer shall continue in
such office until he shall resign the same, or until revocation of
his appointment by the vestry.

(*k*) This enactment in substance provides, that the poor law
commissioners, on the application of the board of guardians of
any parish or union, may direct the appointment of a paid collector of poor rates. And all powers of the inhabitants of any
parish in vestry assembled, or of justices of the peace, or of any
persons other than the board of guardians of such parish or union,
to appoint any collector for any such parish as aforesaid, and
(except when otherwise directed by the commissioners), all appointments under such powers shall cease.

(*l*) *Skillett* v. *Fletcher*, L. R., 2 C. P. 469; *S. C.*, 1 C. P. 217;
Worth v. *Newton*, 10 Ex. 247.

less the errors were connected with or induced by the latter employment (m).

Thirdly, we come to those cases where, after the execution *of the surety bond, a change has taken [*239] place in the duties or length of term of the third person's office or employment, or in the mode of remunerating such third person for his services.

It seems to be well established, that, where the change made *materially* alters the duties of the office, and this affects the peril of the sureties, they are released from liability.

Thus, in the case of *Pybus* v. *Gibb* (n), sureties gave a bond to the high bailiff of a county court, conditioned for the good behaviour in his office of one of the bailiffs appointed by the high bailiff. After the execution of the bond, and before the breach of the duty complained of, several acts of parliament came into operation which *materially* altered the nature of the office of bailiff. It was held, that the surety was discharged, even *though the misconduct of the bailiff was in a matter not altered by the said acts of parliament.*

So, also, in *Bartlett* v. *The Att.-Gen.* (o), one *Clarke*, in 1691, was made collector of customs in the port of Boston; *Bartlett* and others were security for him. In 1698 (p), the duties were granted upon coals, &c., which by the statute were to be under the management of the commissioners of the customs, and several clauses for that purpose were contained in the act. The commissioners gave *Clarke* a deputation for that purpose, and took security. Afterwards *Clarke* died; the customs were paid; but, on this new coal duty, 1,000l. remained unpaid; upon which the bond was put in suit against *Bartlett*, the widow and executrix of *Bartlett*, the surety, and she brought her bill, and the question was, whether the bond in which *Bartlett* became surety extended to this future duty on coals. After adjournment, the barons delivered their opinions *seriatim*, and unanimously held, that the said bond did not extend to the future *duty on coals, and that [*240] the plaintiff ought to be relieved; and accordingly ordered a perpetual stay of process on the said bond.

Another case, which depends on the same principle, is *Bonar* v. *Macdonald* (q). There A. became surety,

(3.) Subsequent alteration in duties or duration of third party's office. Material alteration in duties of the office discharges the surety. *Pybus* v. *Gibb.*

Bartlett v. *The Att.-Gen.*

Bonar v. *Macdonald.*

(m) *Home Savings Bank* v. *Traube,* 42 Amer. R. 402 (U. S.).
(n) 6 E. & B. 902.
(o) Parker's Reports, p. 277.
(p) 10 Will. 3.
(q) 3 H. L. 226.

by bond, for B.'s conduct as a clerk in a bank. B. was subsequently appointed to a better situation in a branch of the same bank, and A. extended his suretyship to the new situation. B. afterwards, while remaining in the same situation, undertook on having his salary raised, to become liable to one-fourth of the losses on discounts. No communication of this new arrangement was made to A. B. allowed a customer considerably to overdraw his accounts, and thereby the bank lost a sum of money. It was held, that the surety could not be called on to make good the loss, though it fell within the terms of the original agreement, as the fresh agreement was the substitution of a new agreement for the former one, and A. was thereby discharged.

It appears, too, that in construing an agreement in the form of a bond in which a surety becomes liable for the due fulfilment of an agent's duties, therein particularly enumerated, a general clause in the obligatory part of the bond must be interpreted strictly, and controlled by reference to the prior clauses, specifying the extent of the agency. It was held, accordingly, in *Napier* v. *Bruce* (r) (affirming the judgment of the Court of Session), that monies received by an agent on account of his employers, during the time of his agency, but not in pursuance of the particular agency disclosed to the surety by the specified conditions in the bond, were not covered by the surety's obligation "that during the whole time the said J. D. B. (the agent) shall continue to act as agent aforesaid, in consequence of the above-recited agreement, he shall well and truly [*241] *account for and pay to us (the employers) all sums of money received by him on our account."

If a material change in the duties of the principal were relied on as a defence, such change must formerly have been clearly and distinctly alleged by the defendant in his plea. Thus, for instance, where the defendant became surety for G., so long as he continued in that service of the bank, and at the time the guarantee was given G. was *clerk* to the bank : it was held, that a *plea* stating that G. had, subsequently to the execution of the guarantee, been appointed *manager* of the bank, was bad, as not showing conclusively that G. had ceased to be *clerk* when he became *manager* (s).

Where, however, the change made in the duration of

Napier v *Bruce.*

Immaterial or contem-

(r) 8 C. & F. 470.
(s) *Anderson* v. *Thornton*, 3 Q. B. 271.

the office does *not materially* alter the duties, or is *contemplated* by the parties, tho bond is not avoided.

In *Oswald* v. *The Mayor of Berwick* (t), the facts were as follows :—Sureties by deed, in 1842, covenanted with the Mayor and others of Berwick that *David Murray*, who had been appointed treasurer to the corporation under stat. 5 & 6 Will. 4, c. 76, s. 58, "should well and truly pay to the Mayor, &c. of Berwick, or to their successors all such sums of money as the said *David Murray* should or might recover or receive in virtue of his said appointment as treasurer as aforesaid during the whole time of his continuing in the said office in consequence of the said election, or under *any annual or other future election*, of the said council to the said *office." At the time of the appoint- [*242] ment of *David Murray* the office was an annual one under 5 & 6 Will. 4, c. 76, s. 58; but in 1843 was passed the 6 & 7 Vict. c. 89, which, by sect. 6, repealed that enactment as inconvenient and unnecessary, and directed that the treasurer should "thenceforth hold his office during the pleasure of the council for the time being." It was held by the House of Lords (affirming the judgment of the Exchequer, from which, however, *Jervis*, C. J., *Pollock*, C. B., and *Maule*, J., had dissented), that there was not such a variation of tenure of the office as to discharge the sureties, and that the change from an annual to a perpetual appointment during pleasure was provided for by the words of the bond "annual or other future elections." Baron *Alderson* in this case delivered the unanimous opinion of the judges on the questions put to them by the House of Lords. He stated, that even assuming that an alteration of risk necessarily followed from a change in the duration of the office, yet as that change was contemplated this increase of risk must have been contemplated also. Baron *Alderson* then proceeds to distinguish in the following words the case before him from *Arlington* v. *Merricke:* "It was said that words such as these with which we have to deal are, according to *Arlington* v. *Merricke* and various other cases, to be modified and construed ac-

plated alteration in tenure or duties of office does not discharge the surety. *Oswald* v. *Mayor of Berwick.*

(t) 5 H. L. 856 ; *Mayor of Berwick* v. *Oswald*, 1 E. & B. 295 ; 6 E. & B. 695. This case is cited in 2 Jur., N. S. 743, as *Dobie* v. *The Mayor of Berwick*. There were in fact three actions in the court below, and three writs of error in the House of Lords. The first of these writs was brought in the name *Dobie* v. *Mayor of Berwick*, and under that name the case was argued. The other cases, involving precisely the same point, were made to depend on the decision of the first. See note (a), 5 H. L. C., p. 856.

cording to the words of the recital of the deed, and then it is suggested that the deed must be construed as containing a recital that the future appointments must be made according to the law which was in force when the deed was executed. But this is a mere fallacy; wholly inconsistent, we think, with the words of the covenant, which are quite general. The reason for referring to the recitals in a deed is, because from the circumstances and facts there stated, the parties themselves have plainly expressed their intention; and, consequently, in accordance with that express and specific [*243] intention, the Courts construe *and modify the more general words of their covenant. But it is somewhat strange to propose that the Court should construe their covenant by what must be at most an implied recital suggested by the counsel, and that where there is no express recital on this subject at all. And, therefore, after all, we can only in the present case construe the words of the covenant without any such light being thrown upon them; and, doing so, we cannot doubt that the natural and reasonable construction of the words 'under any annual or other future election' is 'under any future election, whether annual or other than annual'" (u).

Frank v. Edwards.

So, too, in the case of *Frank* v. *Edwards* (x), the bond was conditioned that T. R. should from time to time, and at all times thereafter during the continuance of his said appointment, faithfully account for the collection of the rates, &c., and duly execute all the duties of the office of permanent assistant overseer to the parish of W. F. Subsequently to the execution of the bond, the duties of the office filled by T. R. *became lessened* in consequence of the appointment of a relieving officer, and the vestry, with the consent of T. R., thereupon came to a resolution that T. R. should continue his office, at a reduced salary. It was held, that the surety was not discharged by this action on the part of the vestry, as it did not amount to a revocation of the office filled by T. R.

Skillett v. Fletcher.

Another case of the same class is the recent one of *Skillett* v. *Fletcher* (y). There an action was brought on a bond, conditioned for the due performance by A.

(u) See also *Mayor of Dartmouth* v. *Silly*, 7 E. & B. 97, in which the point raised was precisely the same as that determined in *Oswald* v. *Mayor of Berwick.*
(x) 8 Exch. 214; *Holland* v. *Lea*, 9 Ex. 430.
(y) L. R., 2 C. P. 469; *S. C.*, 1 C. P. 217; followed in *Home Savings Bank* v. *Traube*, 42 Amer. R. 402 (U. S.).

of his duties as collector of the poor rates, and of the
*sewers rates for the parish of St. Anne; the [*244]
bond to continue in force if A. held either office separately. The *breach* alleged was, that A. received money
in both capacities and failed to pay it over. To this
the defendant pleaded, that before breach an act was
passed increasing A.'s duties as collector of sewers rates,
and under which he was also elected collector of main
drainage rates, by the persons under whom he held his
other appointments. This plea was held bad on demurrer, on the ground that the bond was divisible, and
that the plea afforded no answer to the defendant's
liability for A.'s breaches of duty as collector of poor
rates. It was also held, that the appointment of A. to
the new office of collector of main drainage rates did
not avoid the bond, and also that the changes introduced
by the acts did not amount to an alteration of the office
of collector of sewers rates to which A. was originally
appointed, and, therefore, did not avoid the bond. In
this case *Lush*, J., delivered the following judgment
(z): "There is no doubt about the principle that governs these cases; the only doubt is as to its application
in the present instance. If the office is altered by the
addition of new duties, the surety is discharged; and
it is no answer to say, that if the old office had remained, the principal would have incurred the same
debts, and the surety have been responsible, because
the old office does not exist, and it was only for wrong
acts committed by the principal in the old office that
the surety is liable. I think the present case does not
come within the rule, for I think the acts referred to
did not alter the office of collector of sewers rates : and
the addition of a new office, that of collector of the
main drainage rate, could not do so. Even, however,
if the sewers rate had been altered by the act, I think
the plea would be bad, for the reasons given by the
*Court of Common Pleas (a), the offices of col- [*245]
lector of poor rates and collector of sewers rates being
distinct, and the plea affording no answer to the liability
arising from the breaches of duty committed by *Skillett*
as collector of poor rates."

If, indeed, the words of the condition of the surety· Surety may
bond show that the surety intended that his liability stipulate that

(z) See also the judgments of *Blackburn*, J., *Bramwell*, B., and
Martin, B., in this case.
(a) That the bond sued upon was *divisible*. See *S. C.*, L. R.,
1 C. P. 217. See also *Croydon Commercial Gas* v. *Dickinson*, 2 C.
P. D. 46; 46 L. J., C. P. 157; 36 L. T. 135; 25 W. R. 157.

his liability shall not continue after any change made in tenure of third party's office.

should *not* continue, after a change in the tenure, then his liability will be discharged, if subsequently to the execution of the bond the office for the due fulfilment of which he is surety is converted from being an *annual* one into one *during pleasure*. This appears from the case of *The Mayor of Cambridge* v. *Dennis* (b). There the condition recited that S. had been appointed, under a certain statute, treasurer to a borough, and declared that it had been agreed that the obligor should join S. in the bond for the due performance of the office. The condition of the bond was declared to be that if S. should duly perform the office according to the provi-sions of the said statute, *and of such statutes as might be thereafter passed relating to the said office*, then the bond should be void, &c. At the time the bond was given, the office filled by S. was an *annual* office, but it was *subsequently* converted into an office "during pleasure." It was held, that the surety was discharged, and that the words in the condition, which provided that S. should duly perform the office according to the provisions of a certain statute, *and of such statutes as might be thereafter passed relating to said office*, applied only to statutes that might be passed *during the year of office*. In this case, the decision in *Oswald* v. *Mayor of Berwick* (c) was approved of, but considered to be inapplicable, owing to the difference in the language of the bonds in the two cases.

Surety may be discharged from liability by alteration in mode of paying the third party.

[*246]   *The liability of the surety may also be de-stroyed by an alteration in the mode of payment, as well as by an alteration in the duties of the office. For, where a bond, given by a person as surety for the good behaviour of a third person in an office or employment, *recites* that such third person is to be remunerated for his services in a particular way, the surety is discharged from all liability, if, subsequently to the execution of the bond, any change be effected in the mode of remuner-ation. This was decided in *The London and North Western Railway Co.* v. *Whinray* (d). These were the facts of the case: In January, 1851, the defendant, as surety, executed a bond to a railway company, which, after reciting that the company had agreed to appoint L. as their clerk or agent for the purpose of selling coal, *at a yearly salary of* 100l., was conditioned for the due accounting by L. of all monies received by him for the use of the company. L. performed the duties of

London & N. Western Rail. Co. v. *Whin-ray.*

(b) Ell., Bl. & Ell. 660.
(c) *Ante*, p. 241.
(d) 10 Exch. 77.

such clerk or agent at the above salary until May, 1851, when it was agreed between L. and the company to substitute for such salary a commission of sixpence per ton on all coal for which he should obtain orders. From that time L. was paid for his services by such commission which amounted to a larger sum than the fixed salary. In 1852, L. was indebted to the company for sums which he did not pay over, and the company having sued the defendant on his bond, it was held (among other things), that the condition of the bond was restrained by the recital, so that the defendant, as surety, only undertook to be responsible for the faithful conduct of L. whilst he continued clerk at such fixed salary, and consequently that the defendant was not liable after the change in the mode of remuneration.

Having considered from what time a guarantee operates, to what things it extends, and how long it *continues, we may now conveniently notice the [*247.] rule that beyond the mere letter of the guarantee contained within its four corners, a surety may be liable for *fraud*. Thus, a surety who gives a guarantee which he knows to be worthless, and thereby induces a person to supply goods to a third person, is liable as for a fraud. This is shown by the case of *Barwick* v. *The English Joint Stock Bank* (e). In that case, the plaintiff having for some time, on a guarantee of the defendants, supplied J. D., a customer of theirs, with oats on credit, in order to enable him to carry out a government contract, refused to continue to do so unless he had a better guarantee. The defendants' manager thereupon gave him a written guarantee, to the effect, that the customer's cheque on the bank in the plaintiff's favour, in payment for the oats supplied, should be paid on receipt of the government money, in priority to any other payment "except to this bank." J. D. was then indebted to the bank to the amount of 12,000*l*., but this fact was not known to the plaintiff, nor was it communicated to him by the manager. The plaintiff thereupon supplied the oats to the value of 1,227*l*. ; the government money, amounting to 2,676*l*., was received by J. D. and paid into the bank ; but J. D.'s cheque for the price of oats, drawn on the bank in favour of the plaintiff, was dishonoured by the defendants, who claimed to retain the whole sum of 2,676*l*. in payment of J. D.'s debt due to them. The plaintiff having

(IV.) Liability of a surety for fraud.

Barwick v. *English Joint Stock Bank.*

(e) L. R., 2 Exch. 259 ; 36 L. J., Exch. 147 ; 16 L. T. 461 ; 15 W. R. 877.

brought an action for false representation and for money had and received, it was *held, first*, that there was evidence to go to the jury that the manager knew and intended that the guarantee should be unavailing, and fraudulently concealed from the plaintiff the fact which would make it so. *Secondly*, that the defendants would be liable for such fraud in their agents. *Thirdly*, [*248] that the fraud was properly *charged in the declaration as the fraud of the defendants.

Voluntary settlement made by surety whether fraudulent and void against creditors within 13 Eliz. c. 5. The question of whether a voluntary settlement made by a surety of the whole of his property can be supported by showing that when he made it, the principal debtor had assets enough to pay the amount guaranteed, was considered in the recent case of *In re Ridler, Ridler* v. *Ridler*, (*f*). The Court there held that where a surety, whose guarantee is one which he must know will probably be enforced, makes a voluntary settlement, without leaving enough property to pay his creditors, he must be considered to do it with an intent to defeat or delay them, so as to make the settlement a fraudulent one within 13 Eliz. c. 5. In his judgment in this case, Lord Chancellor *Selborne* thus expresses himself:—"I do not think that any close inquiry as to the supposed capacity of the person guaranteed to pay the debt ought to be entered into. I do not say that there might not be a state of things in which the liability of the guarantor might be so remote that it need not be regarded; but if he conveys away all his property by a voluntary settlement, I think it doubtful whether the settlement could in any case be supported in the event of his being ultimately called on under his guarantee."

(V.) Effect on surety's liability of a change in constitution of persons to or for whom the guarantee is given. In the cases which we have hitherto been considering, it will be observed that the liability of the surety depends upon the circumstances as they exist or were contemplated at the time the guarantee was given. But, in some cases, the surety's liability may be considerably affected by events, not at all contemplated by the parties, occurring subsequently to the execution of the guarantee, and altering the position of the parties. The most common cases in which this happens are, where a change takes place in the constitution of a [*249] *firm *to* whom or *for* whom the guarantee is given, or where a bankruptcy takes place. In addition to the classes of cases as to the surety's liability, which have already been discussed, it is proposed, now, to

---

(*f*) 22 Ch. Div. 74.
(1430)

consider the effect of a change in the persons (usually, as will be found, a partnership firm) to whom or for whom a guarantee is given; and lastly, the effect of a bankruptcy. We will commence by noticing those cases where, subsequently to the execution of the surety-bond, the obligees of the bond have ceased to occupy the·positions filled by them at the time of the execution of such bond.

In *Leadley* v. *Evans* (g), a bond, after reciting the appointment of J. B. by churchwardens and overseers as a collector of church and poor rates, was conditioned for the duly accounting to the obligees and their *successors* for money received pursuant to, and in execution of, the office of collector. It was held, that the obligors were not responsible for receipts on account of any year subsequent to that during which the obligees were in office. It is to be observed that, in this case, the offices of churchwarden and overseer were shown to be *annual* offices. Indeed, the court took *judicial notice* of the fact. Now J. B., as collector, was nothing more than *deputy* to the overseer, and it was therefore held by *Best,* C. J., that as the office of overseer was annual, so must be that of deputy. In *M'Gahey* v. *Alston* (h), however, which was much the same sort of case as *Leadley* v. *Evans*, it appeared that the office, for good behaviour in which security was given by bond, was not, according to the construction of an act of parliament, merely co-existent with that of the obligees of. the bond. If was, therefore, held that the bond continued in force after the obligees, to whom it was given, had gone out of office.

*When guarantees are given *to* partners, or as[*250] security for the debt, default or miscarriage *of* partners, it frequently becomes a very nice question for decision, whether the surety continues liable *after* a change has taken place in the firm *to* or *for* whom he has consented to become answerable.

The 4th section of the Mercantile Law Amendment Act, 1856 (i), enacts, that "No promise to answer for the debt, default or miscarriage of another made *to* a firm consisting of two or more persons, or to a single person trading under the name of a firm, and no promise to answer *for* the debt, default or miscarriage of a firm consisting of two or more persons, or of a single person trading under the name of a firm, shall be bind-

Marginal notes:
- *Leadley* v. *Evans*.
- *M'Gahey* v. *Alston*.
- Effect on liability of surety of change in the firm *to* or *for* whom guarantee given.
- 19 & 20 Vict. c. 97, s. 4.

(g) 2 Bing. 32. See also *Metcalf* v. *Bruin*, 12 East, 400.
(h) 1 M. & W. 386.
(i) 19 & 20 Vict. c. 97.

ing on the person making such promise in respect of
anything done or omitted to be done after a change
shall have taken place in any one or more of the per·
sons constituting the firm, or in the person trading under the name of the firm, unless the intention of the
parties that such promise shall continue to be binding,
notwithstanding such change, shall appear either by
express stipulation or by necessary implication from
the nature of the firm or otherwise."

*This enact-
ment declara-
tory of the
common law.
Backhouse v.
Hull.*

This enactment appears merely to affirm the common
law. This was decided in *Backhouse* v. *Hall* (*k*).
There three persons carried on the business of ship-
builders under the name of "*G., W. & W. J. Hall.*"
No person of that name had been in the partnership
for some time, and the plaintiff and defendant being
both aware of the constitution of the partnership, the
defendant gave the plaintiff the following guarantee:
"In consideration that you have at my instance and request consented to open an account with the firm of *G.,
W. & W. J. Hall*, ship·builders, I hereby guarantee
the payment to you of the monies that at any time may
[*251] become due, not *exceeding 5,000*l.*" It was
held, that the guarantee ceased on the death of the ·
partners, as a contrary intention did not appear by ex·
press stipulation, or by necessary implication from the
nature of the firm or otherwise.

As the 4th section of the Mercantile Law Amendment Act merely *affirms* the common law, those cases
which were decided *before* the passing of this enactment,
upon the subject which we are now considering, are,
consequently, as binding now as ever they were. We
propose, therefore, to examine them, and in doing so,
we shall not confine ourselves exclusively to cases where
guarantees were given to or for *partners*, but we will
also examine those strictly analogous cases where guar·
antees were given to or for *individuals* who have subsequently altered their condition.

In the following examples it will be observed that
the judges were very careful not to bind the surety
beyond the scope of his engagement; and that, in the
absence of express stipulation or necessary implication
to the contrary, they have always held his liability to
determine on any change taking place in the persons,
to or *for* whom the guarantee was given (*l*).

_____

(*k*) 6 B. & S. 507; 34 L. J., Q. B. 141.
(*l*) Many of these cases are collected and commented upon in
note (*d*), at p. 326 of 3 Douglas' Reports.

We will *first* examine those cases where, after the
execution of the guarantee, a change took place in the
persons *to whom* such guarantee was given.

(1.) *Where the change consisted of an increase in
the number of persons to whom the guarantee was
given.*

Whether an increase in the number of partners to
whom a guarantee was given discharged the surety
seems to have been somewhat unsettled before the
passing of the Mercantile Law Amendment Act.

In *Wright* v. *Russell* (m), a bond, conditioned for the
honesty of one *Baird*, a clerk, was given by the defend-
*ant to one *Wright*, the employer of the clerk. [*252]
Wright, subsequently to the giving of the bond, entered
into partnership with one J. D. It was *held* that the defendant was no longer liable on the bond. It was said, in
the judgment in this case: "It is truly said that the
defendant (the *surety*) ought not to be bound beyond
the scope of his engagement, which was to be answerable for the fidelity of *Baird* to *Wright* only, not to
Wright and any other person or persons. . . . . . .
The defendant *Russell* engaged for *Baird's* faithful
service to *Wright*. When *Wright* took in a partner
there was an end of the obligation; the condition was
confined to *Wright* only, and the breach assigned is for
non payment of the money to *Wright* and *Delafield*, or
either of them, which is not within the condition. The
defendant *Russell* and the other surety might have
confidence in *Wright*, that he would be careful with
respect to the conduct of *Baird* in his office of *broad
clerk*, which they might not have in any partner with
Wright, and, for anything that appears to the Court,
the defendant *Russell* had no conception of being engaged for *Baird's* fidelity to any other person besides
Wright."

It appears that, in the case just cited, the breach
assigned was for embezzling the *partnership* money, not
the money of Mr. *Wright* only. This circumstance is
commented on in *Barclay* v. *Lucas* (n). In this latter
case, debt was brought on a bond (reciting that the
plaintiffs, at the recommendation of the obligors, had
agreed to take one *Philip Jones into their service and
employ as a clerk in their shop and counting-house*, and
that the obligors had agreed to become security for

I. Where, after guarantee given, change has taken place in persons to whom guarantee is given.
(1) By increase in the number of persons to whom the guarantee is given.
Wright v. *Russell.*

Barclay v. *Lucas.*

(m) 3 Wils. 530; 2 Bl. Rep. 934.
(n) Cited in a note to *Barker* v. *Parker*, 1 T. R. at p. 291. But
see 1 N. R. 42; 4 Taunt. 681, from which it appears that the
decision in *Barclay* v. *Lucas* has been doubted.

his fidelity as far as 500l. each), which declared that if the said *P. Jones* should faithfully account for and pay [*253] *to the plaintiffs all sums of money he should at any time receive, &c. in the service of the plaintiffs, and did not embezzle, &c., then the bond was to be void. It was pleaded by the defendants that after the giving of the above bond, the plaintiffs received into partnership one *Robert Barclay*, and that *P. Jones* then quitted the service of the plaintiffs and entered into the service of the plaintiffs and *Robert Barclay*, and that *P. Jones*, all the time he remained in the service of the plaintiffs alone, well and faithfully accounted, &c. The plaintiffs replied in substance, that the said bond was given to the *house*, and not to the individual members of the firm. The following judgments were given in this case:—Lord *Mansfield*, C. J., said: "The question in this case turns upon the intention of the parties at the time of entering into the contract. In questions upon intention we must look to the subject-matter of the contract. It is notorious that there are many banking houses in the city which continue for generations. This can only be done by a constant succession of partners, and even if they should not bear the same name with the first proprietors, yet still the *house* frequently continues under the original firm. To carry on this business it is necessary to have a great number of clerks, whose office is extremely beneficial; for besides the present fees and emoluments, they are frequently taken into partnership in process of time. But it is of the utmost consequence to these houses that the clerks should behave honestly; and, therefore, a security is taken for their fidelity. The circumstance of taking in a new partner makes no difference either as to the quantity of the business, or the extent of the engagement. He continues to carry on the business of the plaintiffs; and this contract is co-extensive with his continuance in the house. This is a security to the *house* of the plaintiffs, and no change of partners will discharge the obligor." *Buller*, [*254] J., in the same case, said : * "This case is distinguishable from that in the Common Pleas (*o*); there the breach assigned was for embezzling the whole partnership money; and I observe from the report of that case, that Mr. J. *Gould* lays much stress upon the point that the breach assigned was for embezzling the partnership money, whereas it should have been for the plaintiff's money only. I confess I do not

---

(*o*) *Wright* v. *Russell*, cited *ante*, p. 251.

see the force of that objection: but, however, it is not
applicable to this case,—for here the plaintiffs have
confined the breach to the proportion of the money which
was actually their property."

In *Spiers* v. *Houston* (*p*) it was held that a guarantee
of monies advanced by a firm consisting of F. & Co.,
will not extend to a new firm into which H. is introduced as a partner. And payments made by the
principal, after the alteration of the firm, and in transactions with him, are applicable to the extinction of the
balance due to the old firm at the date of the alteration (*q*).

(2.) *Where the change consisted of a diminution in
the number of the persons to whom the guarantee was
given.*

(a) *By Death.*

The effect of a change by death in the firm to whom
the guarantee is given, generally speaking, was to discharge the surety. Thus, in *Strange* v. *Lee* (*r*), the
defendant's bond recited that A. intended forthwith to
open an account with C., D. & E. as his bankers, and
was conditioned for the payment to C., D & E. of all
sums from time to time advanced to A. at the banking
house of C., D. & E. It was held, that on C.'s death
the obligation ceased, and did not cover future advances made after another partner was taken in, and
that A., who was indebted to the house at C.'s death,
having *afterwards paid off the balance, which [*255]
was applied at the time to the old debt incurred in C.'s
lifetime, A. was wholly discharged from his obligation.
Lord *Ellenborough* distinguished this case from *Barclay* v. *Lucas* (*s*), on the ground that the words of the
bond in the latter case were different, for in that case
the bond provided that the clerk was to be taken into
the *service* of the obligees, as a clerk in their *shop and
counting house,* which might be supposed to mean the
same house, however the individual partners might
change.

So, again, in *Barker* v. *Parker* (*t*), it was held, that
a bond with a condition that a clerk should faithfully
serve and account for money to the obligee *and his executors,* did not make the obligor liable for money re-

Marginal notes: Spiers v. Houston. (2) Where number of persons to whom guarantee given is diminished— (a) By death. Strange v. Lee. Barker v. Parker.

(*p*) 4 Bligh, N. S. 515.
(*q*) Ib.
(*r*) 3 East, 484.
(*s*) *Ante*, p. 252.
(*t*) 1 T. R. 287.

ceived by the clerk in the service of the obligee's executor. Lord *Mansfield*, C. J., said : "The bond in
question is relative to the service with *Pyott*, the testator. It was given as an indemnity that the clerk
should be *faithful to him*, and should pay all the money
received on *his* account to him, or to his executors ;
because money might be in his hands at the time of the
testator's death, for which he could only account to the
executors. So that it was the intention of the parties
that the bond should not be extended beyond the life
of the testator."

Weston v.   To the same effect, also, is the case of *Weston* v.
Barton.   *Barton* (*u*). There the condition of the bond was for
the repayment to five persons of all sums advanced by
them, or any of them, to *Catterall & Watson*, in their
capacity of bankers. It was held, that the bond did
not extend to sums advanced after the decease of one
of the five by the four survivors, the four then acting
as bankers. *Mansfield*, C. J., delivered the following
judgment : "The question here is, whether the original
partnership being at an end, in consequence of the
[*256] death *of *Golding*, the bond is still in force as
security to the surviving four ; or whether that political personage, as it may be called, consisting of five,
being dead, the bond is not at an end. The case has
stood over in consequence of doubts which the Court
entertained on .particular expressions in the bond.
Many cases were cited at the bar, and the result of
them is, that, generally, when a change takes place in
the number of persons to whom such a bond is given,
the bond no longer exists. These decisions certainly
fall hard on the obligees ; for I believe the general understanding is, these securities are given to the *banking house*, and not to the particular individuals who
compose it ; and we should readily so construe the
bond, if the words would permit. The words of the
condition, on which the question depends [and which
his lordship now read over], again and again refer to
the obligees' capacity of bankers ; they were bankers,
only as they were partners in their banking house, as
it is called, and this security is conditioned to pay any
money advanced 'by them five, or any or either of
them.' Taking those last words by themselves, it
might at first be conceived, that, if any one of the five
advanced money this bond should secure it, but the
words are afterwards explained, when it is seen that

_____

(*u*) 4 Taunt. 673.

the money is to be paid to the five. Now it could never
be intended that money advanced by one of them singly
should be repaid to the five ; and this shows that the
words 'advanced by them, or any or either of them'
must be confined in their meaning to money advanced
by any or either of them in their capacity of bankers,
on behalf of all the five. This, then, being the construction of the instrument, from almost all the cases, in
truth, as we may say, from all (for though there is one
adverse case of *Barclay* v. *Lucas*, the propriety of that
decision has been very much questioned), it results,
that where one of the obligees dies, the security is at
an end. It is not necessary now to enter into the reasons of those *decisions, but there may be very [*257]
good reasons for such a construction ; it is very prob-
able that sureties may be induced to enter into such a
security, by a confidence which they repose in the integrity, diligence, caution and accuracy of one or two
of the partners. In the nature of things there cannot
be a partnership consisting of several persons, in which
there are not some persons possessing these qualities
in a greater degree than the rest; and it may be that
the partner dying, or going out, may be the very person on whom the sureties relied ; it would, therefore,
be very unreasonable to hold the surety to his contract
after such change. And, though the sum here is limited, that circumstance does not alter the case; for,
although the amount of the indemnity is not indefinite, yet 3,000l. is a large sum ; and, even if it were
only 1,000l., the same ground, in a degree, holds, for
there may be a great deal of difference in the measure
of caution or discretion with which different persons
would advance even 1,000l. ; some would permit one who
was almost a beggar to extend his credit to that sum ;
others would exercise a due degree of caution for the
safety of the surety ; and, therefore, we are of opinion,
that as to such sums only which were advanced *before*
the decease of *Golding* can an indemnity be recovered
by the plaintiffs ; and, as to the sums claimed for
debts incurred since his decease, the judgment must be
for the defendant."

A similar decision was also come to in the case of *Pemberton* v.
Pemberton v. *Oakes*(x). There a banking partnership *Oakes.*
was formed for fifteen years, between *Harding, Oakes*
and *Willington;* it was stipulated that, if *Oakes* or *Willington* should die during the term, the concern should

(x) 4 Russ. 154 ; and see *Bank of Scotland* v. *Christie,* 8 Cl. &
F. 214.

be continued by the survivors or survivor, the deceased's
share to be paid to his executors up to the death ; but
[*258] that if *Harding* should die, he might dispose *of
his share to his wife and children, and there was a provision for his appointing persons who should carry it
on as if he were living, during the minority of his
children ; and the business was, in that event, to be
carried on by the surviving partners and the appointee,
in the manner and on the terms and conditions directed
by the partnership articles, as if he had not died.
Harding made his will in favour of his children as to
his share, and appointed persons to carry on the concern with his partners ; and he dying, this was carried
into effect.   The question was, whether a surety for a
customer of the original firm, who had executed a deed
to the members of that firm to secure them for sums
already due or which should become due *to them for
advances made thence forward to the end of the fifteen
years,* was liable to any advance made after the death
of *Harding.* Lord Chancellor *Lyndhurst* held clearly
that he was not liable for advances by a new firm,
although he had stipulated to secure advances made
during the whole fifteen years ; and that the death of
Harding, with the substitution of the appointees, though
contemplated by the original articles, made a new firm.

Chapman v.   And yet another case in which the same view pre-
Beckington.   vailed is that of *Chapman* v. *Beckington,* (y). In that
case the plaintiff and one *William Chapman* entered into
partnership, by deed, with one *Potts. Potts* was to be
the acting partner.   In consideration of this trust he
and the defendant bound themselves by a bond of
guarantee to the plaintiff and the said *William Chapman,* for the observance by *Potts* of the covenants in
the partnership deed, and also that *Potts,* during such
time as he should continue the acting partner in the
said trade of the said co-partnership, should faithfully
make and deliver a true account in writing of all sums
[*259] of *money, notes, bills, and other partnership
effects, which should come to his hands, or which he
should be intrusted with by or on account of the said
co-partnership, and also make good, answer for and pay
over, the moneys due on the balance to the said plaintiff and *W. Chapman. Potts,* after the decease of *W.
Chapman,* rendered false accounts.   It was *held,* that
the co-partnership referred to in the condition of the
bond was determined by *W. Chapman's* death, and that

(y) 3 Q. B. 703.
(1438)

the defendant was therefore not liable for *Potts'* default happening after that event. In this case, Lord *Denman*, C. J., said : "Many cases were cited to show that, where the surety had covenanted with the house, and not the members of the firm, or had stipulated that his liability should not be effected by a change of the members, he would remain liable to the new firm. These cases we do not in the least question, our judgment proceeding on the language of this condition, making all due allowance for the effect which the language of the deed ought to have on its construction."

Even the circumstance that the guarantee was to be *Holland* v. for a fixed time, which had not expired when the change *Teed.* in the firm happened, made no difference as to the application of the rule. Thus, in *Holland* v. *Teed* (z), under a guarantee given to a banking house consisting of several partners, for the repayment of such bills drawn upon them by one of their customers as the bank might honour, and any advances they might make to the same customer, it was *held* that the guarantee *ceased* upon the death of one of the partners in the bank, before the expiration of the time to which the guarantee was expressed to extend. It was also *held*, that bills accepted before the death of the partner and payable afterwards, were within the guarantee; *that* the amount guaranteed could not be increased by any act of the *continuing firm and the customer after the [*260] death of the partner, although such amount might be diminished by such act.

Even before the Mercantile Law Amendment Act, By agree-however, the liability of the surety continued, if it ment surety appeared that the parties intended it should do so, not-may continue withstanding a change in the firm. Thus, in *Metcalf* v. change in *Bruin* (a), the bond was given to "seven of the trustees firm to whom of the Globe Insurance Company," or to their certain guarantee attornies, executors, administrators or assigns, to secure given. the faithful services of a clerk to the Globe Insurance *Metcalf* v. Company. The condition of the obligation was, that if *Bruin.* the clerk should, from time to time, and at all times thereafter, *during his continuance in the service of the said company*, faithfully serve *the said company*, and should, when required, deliver in writing a true account of all monies, &c. which in the said service should come to his hands on account of the said company, and pay over the balance to the said company, or to such person

(z) 7 Hare, 50. See also *Pemberton* v. *Oakes, ante,* p. 257.
(a) 12 East, 400. See also *Leadley* v. *Evans,* 2 Bing. 32, cited *ante,* p. 249.

as *the said company* or the court of directors thereof, *for
the time being*, should appoint; and should indemnify
the said company and the directors and *all other mem·
bers thereof* for all losses, &c., &c., which the company
or any of its members might sustain, by anything done
or neglected by the said clerk, during his said service,
then the obligation to be void. The Globe Insurance
Company was not a corporation. It was held, that
the said bond might be put in suit by the trustees, for a
breach of faithful service by the clerk, committed at any
time during his continuance in the service of the actual
existing body of persons carrying on the same business
under the same name, notwithstanding any intermediate
change of the original holders of the shares by death or
[*261] transfer; the intention of the parties *to the
instrument being apparent, to contract for such service
to be performed to the company as a fluctuating body,
and the intervention of the trustees removing all legal
and technical difficulties to such a contract made with, or
suit instituted by, the company themselves as a natural
body.

The following is the judgment of Lord *Ellenborough*,
C. J., in the case:—" We cannot enhance the obligation
beyond the terms of it; the only question, therefore,
is upon the fair meaning of the terms used in it, and
we must put upon the word *company* the sense in which
the parties themselves used it in this instrument. We
could not, indeed, invert the rules of law to enable
persons to sue as a body or company who are not a
corporation; but here the bond has been given to
trustees, who are under no difficulty of suing upon it
in their own names; and the only question is, as to the
description of persons meant to be designated under
the term *company*. I will begin, therefore, by translat·
ing that word according to the subject-matter, namely,
the *Globe Insurance Company*. Now, suppose a bond
given to a trustee to secure the performance of certain
services to the commoners of such a common, would
there be any difficulty in applying it, to the use of
the commoners for the time being, whoever they might
happen to be, during the period for which the services
were to be performed? There could be no doubt of it.
Now, the persons constituting this company laboured at
the time under an imperfection to contract from the
fluctuating nature of their body, and therefore they
constituted seven persons to be trustees for them; and
whether those seven were members of the body or not
is, for this purpose, indifferent. Those seven entered

into this contract for the benefit of the company, and
if it had not been understood by the contracting parties that the company therein mentioned meant a fluctuating company, we must suppose that they contemplated that *the bond might probably be gone [*262]
in twenty-four hours, which never could have been
meant. It must, therefore, have been intended to secure
the faithful performance of the service to a succession
of masters, who might from time to time constitute the
company. *Wilkinson* then was admitted into the service of the *Globe Insurance Company*, the parties well
knowing that a body so constituted would be continually
changing and fluctuating, and they looked to his *continuance* in the service of the said company, which
could not mean a continuance in the service of the same
individuals, some of whom might be changed before
the wax on the bond was cold, but must have meant tho
successors of the persons so called the *Globe Insurance
Company*. He is then to account to the said company,
that is, to the same successive body; and he is to indemnify 'the company and the directors and all other
members thereof, from all losses, actions, &c. which
may be sued against them, or which the said company,
or any member or members thereof, should bear,' &c.,
by reason of his neglect: all this looks to the change
that might take place in the body. There is nothing
contrary to any rule of law in such an agreement: a
man may well agree to serve the subscribers to the
rooms at *Bath*. A contract with the body itself at large
would not have done; but a contract with the trustees,
for the benefit of the body, gets rid of all the difficulty.
So, if the contract were. made with the commoners
themselves of a certain common, the successive commoners could not come into court and sue upon the
contract, but a trust may be created for such a body
which would extend to those who were successively
clothed with the right of the original body. However
anomalous, therefore, the body may be, if we can get
at the intent of the contracting parties in their description of it, there is nothing illegal in such a contract.
Nor does our opinion clash with any of the cases which
have proceeded upon the terms of the respective bonds. A
*bond to A. cannot be extended to A. and B., [*263]
unless, as in *Barclay* v. *Lucas*, the terms of the bond
may be taken to explain such an intention. It may even
be thought that there was greater difficulty in that case.
than in the present; but I only collect from it the principle on which it professes to proceed, which was the

apparent intention of the parties at the time of entering into the contract to provide for a service to a change-
able body carrying on the same concern. In the present case, the intent appears very clearly to look to the
service of a fluctuating body." In the same case, in
commenting on *Barclay* v. *Lucas*, Bayley, J., said: "In
Barclay v. *Lucas* the obligation was understood as intended to secure the service to such persons as should
become partners in the same house of trade. This
mode of considering the case gets rid of the difficulty
started in the argument, that if it were extended beyond the continuance of the then existing members of
the body, it should include all who then were or should
thereafter become members; but it meant only the company for the time being, which gets rid of the difficulty."

Kipling v
Turner

The case of *Kipling* v. *Turner* (b) proceeds much on
the same principle as *Metcalf* v. *Bruin* (c). In *Kipling*
v. *Turner*, the condition of a bond, after reciting that
A., B. and C. had filed a bill in equity against R. M.
and J. S., was that the obligor would pay all such costs
as the Court of Chancery should award *to the defendants* on the hearing of the cause. It was held by Bayley, J., *Holroyd*, J., and *Best*, J., (*Abbott*, C. J., *dubitante*), that the death of one of the defendants, before
any costs awarded, could not be pleaded in discharge of
the bond. *Bayley*, J., said, "This bond is not conditioned to pay such costs as the court of equity shall
award to R. M. and J. S. by name, but to pay such
costs as shall be awarded by the court *to those who,*
[*264] *at that time, fill the character of defendants in
equity.* The case is very different where persons are
described *by character* and where they are described *by
name.* If, for instance, a man make A., B. and C. his
executors, and directs that A., B. and C. shall sell
his property, then if A. dies, B. and C. cannot sell it;
but if he directs *his executors* to sell it, B. and C. may
do so. In this case, therefore, I think, that if any
costs were awarded to persons filling the character of
defendants in equity, they would be within the bond,
and here it appears by the replication that there were
costs so awarded. I am, therefore, of opinion that
there should be judgment for the plaintiff."

(b) Diminu-
tion by retire-
ment of per-
sons from

(b) *By one partner retiring from the firm.*
The voluntary retirement by a partner from the firm
had, even before the Mercantile Law Amendment Act,

(b) 5 B. & A. 261.
(c) *Ante,* p. 260 *et seq.*

the same effect as his death—it put an end to the surety's liability. Thus, in *Myers* v. *Edge* (d), it was held
that a promise in writing directed to A. B., &c. [a house
in trade]to pay for goods to be furnished to another,
cannot be enforced in an action by B. and C. to recover
,the value of goods furnished after A. had *withdrawn*
from the partnership. In *Pease* v. *Hirst* (e), however,
it was held, that as the instrument (a promissory note
payable to the five members of a banking house *or order*)
was framed so as to comprehend future as well as present partners, the maker of the note was liable notwithstanding a change in the firm by the retirement of a
partner from the firm.

margin: firm to whom guarantee given. *Myers* v. *Edge.* *Pease* v. *Hirst.*

(3.) *Where the change consisted of the incorporation or
consolidation of the persons to whom the guarantee was
given.*

Where the effect of the consolidation was entirely to
change the nature and circumstances of the creditors
*the surety was discharged, even before the [*265]
passing of the Mercantile Law Amendment Act (f).
Thus, in *Dance* v. *Girdler* (g), a bond was given to A.,
B., C., &c., payable to them and their successors as the
governors of the Society of Musicians, conditioned to
secure J. H.'s faithfully accounting with them and their
successors, governors, &c., as their collector ; *afterwards,*
the society was incorporated by letters patent, at which
time J. H. had duly accounted for all monies collected
by him, but after the incorporation he received monies
for which he did not account. It was *held*, that the
obligor was not liable for such default of J. H. in an
action on the bond. Lord *Mansfield*, C. J., in his judgment, while pointing out that it would be unreasonable,
under the circumstances, to hold the surety liable, inasmuch as a voluntary society, to which the bond was
given, is very different in character from the corporation which had been substituted for such voluntary
society, expressly bases his decision on the ground, that
according to all the cases which had been cited, as well
as others which might be found, the surety was not
bound to answer for sums received after the charter of
incorporation, which constituted a perfectly new body

margin: (3) Effect on surety's liability of incorporation or consolidation of the persons to whom the guarantee was given. *Dance* v. *Girdler.*

(d) 7 T. R. 254. See also *Dry* v. *Davy*, 10 A. & E. 30; *Solvency Mutual Guarantee Society* v. *Freeman*, 7 H. &. N. 17; 31 L. J. Ex. 197.
(e) 10 B. & C. 122.
(f) See 19 & 20 Vict. c. 97, s. 4, *ante*, p. 250.
(g) 1 N. R. 34.

of persons in point of law. But, where the consolidation makes no substantial difference in the situation of the creditor and the surety, the latter is not discharged. Thus where a surety became bound by bond for the good behaviour of a clerk to two railway companies, and, subsequently to the execution of such bond, these two companies were consolidated by act of parliament, it was held, that the surety was not discharged, as the consolidation of the two companies did not affect the duties or responsibility of the principal or surety, notwithstanding the new company possessed additional lines (h).

II. Where, after guarantee given, change has taken place in persons for whom it was given.

[*266] *We will *next* examine those cases where, after the execution of the guarantee, a change has occurred in the persons *for* whom such guarantee was given.

(1) By increase in the number of persons for whom the guarantee was given. Bellairs v. Ebsworth.

(1.) *Where the change consisted of an increase in the number of the persons for whom the guarantee was given.*

The general effect of an increase in the number of persons for whom a guarantee is given—as, for instance, an increase by the principal's entering into partnership with others—would seem always to have been, as it still is (g), to discharge the surety from liability for acts done by his principal jointly with such others. Thus, in the case of *Bellairs* v. *Ebsworth* (h), it was decided that, if A. become bound to B., under condition that C. shall truly account to B. for all sums of money received by C. for B.'s use, and C. subsequently to the giving of such bond, with B's knowledge, takes D. as his partner, the guarantee does not extend to sums of money received by C. for B.'s use, after the formation of the partnership. Lord *Ellenborough*, in his judgment, says: "The defendant was surety for *Philip Nott*, and not for *Mingay, Nott & Co.* When the plaintiffs intrusted their agency to the new firm, the defendant's responsibility was at an end. He by no means undertook for the good conduct of any future partner with whom *P. Nott* might associate. The recital and the whole scope of the condition show that the suretyship was confined to *P. Nott* individually" (i).

(h) *London, Brighton and South Coast Rail. Co.* v. *Goodwin,* 3 Exch. 320. See also *Eastern Union Rail Co.* v. *Cochrane,* 9 Exch. 197; *Wilson* v. *Craven,* 8 M. & W. 584.
(g) See 19 & 20 Vict. c. 97, s. 4, *ante,* p. 250.
(h) 3 Camp. 52.
(i) The bond sued upon, as far as is material, was as follows: "Whereas the above-bounden *Philip Nott* hath for some time past acted as the agent for the said *A.* and *J. Bellairs,* in the receiving

(1444)

*In *Montefiore* v. *Lloyd* (*k*), the facts were as [*267] *Montefiore* v.
follows : The defendant, as surety, executed a bond, *Lloyd*
the condition of which was declared to be, that L.
should pay to the plaintiffs, an insurance company, all
moneys received by him for assurances effected with the
said company, and should duly account for all monies
received by him for the said company. The defendant,
before signing the bond, received a letter stating that
L. was about to enter into partnership with F. as agents
of the said company. Four months afterwards L. duly
entered *into partnership with F. The firm of [*268]   •
F. & Co. having become indebted to the company as
such agents in a considerable sum, it was held that this
was a default for which the defendant was not liable.

Although, however, the general rule is as before Surety not
stated, yet the circumstances may be such—or the always discharged by

of various large sums of money for them, and the said *Philip Nott*
will continue to receive money and other things on their account:
And whereas the better to secure the said *A.* and *J. Bellairs* the
payment of all such sum and sums of money which at any time
hereafter shall be in the hands of the said *Philip Nott*, belonging
to the said *A.* and *J. Bellairs*, the said *Philip Nott* hath proposed
and agreed to execute this present bond of indemnity, and hath
prevailed on the said *John Nott* and *John Ebsworth* to become
surety for and to join with him, the said *Philip Nott*, in the execution thereof, and to guarantee the said *A.* and *J. Bellairs*, and
the survivor of them, against any loss they may happen to sustain on account of their confidence in the said *Philip Nott* touching
the matters aforesaid : Now the condition of the above-written
obligation is such, that if the above-bounden *Philip Nott*, his
heirs, executors and administrators, do and shall from time to
time, and at all times, as often as he or they shall be thereunto
required by the said *A.* and *J. Bellairs*, or the survivor of them,
make, draw out and deliver unto them, or the survivor of them,
a true and just account of all such sum and sums of money, bonds,
bills of exchange, promissory notes or other securities for money,
which he the said *Philip Nott* shall or may hereafter receive, or be
intrusted with, for or on account of the said *A.* and *J. Bellairs*,
or the survivor of them ; and if the said *Philip Nott*, his heirs, executors or administrators, shall and do from time to time, and
at all times hereafter when thereunto required, pay, or cause to be
paid, unto the said *A.* and *J. Bellairs*, or the survivor of them, all
such sum and sums of money which the said *Philip Nott* shall
hereafter receive, or be intrusted with, for or on account of the
said *A.* and *J. Bellairs*, or the survivor of them, and also shall,
when thereunto requested, deliver unto the said *A.* and *J. Bellairs*, or the survivor of them, all such bonds, bills of exchange,
promissory notes or other securities for money, which he the said
Philip Nott shall or may hereafter receive, or be intrusted with,
for, and on their account ; and if the said *Philip Nott* shall conduct himself truly, justly and honestly, towards the said *A.* and
J. Bellairs, and the survivor of them, in all his dealings and transactions with them, or the survivor of them, touching the matters
aforesaid, then the above-written obligation to be void, &c."

(*k*) 12 W. R., C. P. 83.

increase in number of persons for whom a guarantee is given.

Leathley v. *Spyer*.

transaction may be of so peculiar a nature—that the surety's liability is not affected by an increase in the number of persons acting in the matter guaranteed. This happened in the case of *Leathley* v. *Spyer* (*l*). The facts there were as follows : J. S. wished to carry on business as an insurance broker at *Lloyd's*. By the rules of *Lloyd's* he could only do this on being admitted a subscriber and giving security to the committee. Thereupon, in March, in 1858, the defendant and another person addressed the following letter to the committee : "We each of us hereby hold ourselves responsible to the extent of 750*l.* for any debts that J. S. (who has applied to your committee to be admitted a subscriber of your institution, to enable him to act as an insurance broker) may contract in his capacity of such broker, for two years from this date, and till notice." J. S. was, therefore, admitted and acted as a broker on his *sole account*, until January, 1860, when he took H. into partnership, with the knowledge of his sureties. In April, 1860, the defendant and his co-surety gave notice to the committee for the discontinuance of the guarantee ; but, upon being informed that J. S. could not be allowed to remain a member of *Lloyd's* without security, they, on the 17th of that month, addressed the committee as follows : "The letter we addressed to you, under date of the 11th instant, notifying the putting an end to our guarantee dated 24th March, 1858, on behalf of J. S., we now hereby withdraw, and declare that such [*269] *guarantee shall continue in force upon the same terms and conditions as are mentioned in such guarantee." By the rules of *Lloyd's*, one member only of a firm is allowed to act as a broker ; but he may obtain a "substitute's ticket," which enables his substitute to contract for him in the house. In January, 1862, J. S. appointed H. his substitute, and H., as such substitute, entered into contracts with underwriting members of *Lloyd's*. All the contracts made after April, 1860, whether by J. S. or his substitute, were made in the name and on account of the partnership. Many of these contracts resulted in debts due to members of *Lloyd's* from the partnership. It was held that the guarantee was to be construed with reference to the circumstances existing in April, 1860 ; that it included, therefore, all transactions by J. S. in his capacity of broker after April, 1860, whether by himself, personally, or by H., as his substitute, and whether for his own sole

(*l*) L. R., 5 C. P. 595 ; and see *Bank of British North America* v. *Cuvillier*, 4 L. T. 159.

benefit or for the benefit of the firm ; and, consequently, that the defendant was liable under the guarantee for these partnership debts. "I am of opinion," says *Willes,* J., in this case, "that the plaintiffs are entitled to judgment. Looking at the guarantee, without the light of the surrounding circumstances, it would appear to be a guarantee for the acts of J. S. only, and for debts incurred for himself alone ; and *Bellairs* v. *Ebsworth* (*m*) and *Montefiore* v. *Lloyd* (*n*) would have been applicable. It would have been as if a simple guarantee of debts due from A. had been sought to be extended and applied to debts incurred by A. jointly with B., whom he had afterwards taken into partnership. The short answer would have been, that the defendant agreed to become surety for A., but not for B. The character of the transaction would have been altogether different from that for *which the defendant undertook to be liable [*270] But, when the surrounding circumstances are looked at, it would appear that, though the persons liable for the transactions at *Lloyd's* were a firm, whereas the person originally contemplated by the guarantee was only an individual, yet that the guarantee was given, not with reference to the single individual being the person ultimately liable, but with reference to a course of business in a particular house, viz., *Lloyd's*, such business being carried on with the individual named ; and so the transactions in respect of which the defendant is sought to be made liable are not different in character from those to which the guarantee referred."

(2) *Where the change consisted in a diminution in the number of persons for whom the guarantee is given.*

(a) *By death.*

The effect of the death of one of the principal debtors was, before the Mercantile Law Amendment Act, and still is (*n*), to determine the surety's liability. Thus in *Simson* v. *Cooke* (*o*), a bond by which, after reciting the partnership of J. C. and T. C., one W. P. became surety for such sums as should be advanced to meet bills drawn by J. C. and T. C., or either of them, was held not to extend to bills drawn by J. C. *after the death* of T. C.

(b) *By one partner retiring from the firm.*

(side notes:)
(2) Diminution in number of persons for whom guarantee given.
(a) By death.
Simson v. *Cooke.*
(b) By one partner retiring from the firm.

(*m*) 3 Camp. 53, and see *ante*, p. 266.
(*n*) 15 C. B., N. S. 203 ; 33 L. J., C. P. 49, and see *ante*, p. 267.
(*n*) See 19 & 20 Vict. c. 97, s. 4, *ante*, p. 250.
(*o*) 1 Bing. 452.

The voluntary retirement of one of the principal debtors likewise had, and still has (n), the effect of putting an end to the surety's liability. In the case of *The University of Cambridge v. Baldwin* (p), the condition of a bond recited that the chancellor, masters and scholars of the University of Cambridge had appointed B., C. and J. *their agents* for the sale of books printed at their press in the university, and that the defendant had offered to enter into a bond with them as a [*271] *surety; and it was conditioned that if the said B., C. and J., *and the survivors and survivor of them,* and such other persons as should or might at any time or times thereafter, in partnership with *them or any or either of them, act as agent or agents* of the said chancellor, &c., and their successors, for all books delivered or sent to *them* or *any* or *either of them* for sale as aforesaid, and should pay all monies which should become payable to the said chancellor, &c., in respect of such sale, then the obligation to be void, &c. An action having been brought on this bond against the surety, it was *held* that, by the *retirement* of J. from the partnership of B., C. and J., the defendant, as their surety, was discharged from all further liability on this bond.

The extent of the surety's liability has now been dealt with so far as regards the time from which a guarantee operates, the things to which it extends, the period during which its operation continues, and the persons in whose favor and on whose account its operation will take effect.

Let us now consider the only remaining question which can affect the extent of the liability of the surety; namely, the liability of a *bankrupt* surety.

Before default on the part of the principal debtor, the creditor could not, formerly, prove against the estate of a bankrupt surety (q). So no proof was allowed in bankruptcy, upon an undertaking to pay, on one month's notice, the debt of another, where such notice was not given before the bankruptcy, for otherwise it was not a debt at the time of the bankruptcy (r).

The 56th section of 6 Geo. 4, c. 16, appears, however, to have given the creditor an enlarged right of proof

University of Cambridge v. Baldwin.

(VI.) The effect upon the surety's liability of his own bankruptcy. Formerly no proof allowed against surety's estate before principal's default.

Enlarged right of proof conceded by 6 Geo. 4, c. 16.

(n) See 19 & 20 Vict. c. 97, s. 4, *ante*, p. 250.
(p) 5 M. & W. 580.
(q) *Ex parte M'Millan*, Buck, 287; *Ex parte Gardom*, 15 Ves. 286; *Ex parte Adney*, Cowp. 460; *Also* v. *Price*, Dougl. 160; *Overseers of St. Martin* v. *Warren*, 1 Barn. & Ald. 491; *Hoffham* v. *Foudrinier*, 5 M. & S. 21.
(r) *Ex parte Minet*, 14 Ves. 189; *Ex parte Gardom*, *supra.*

*against the bankrupt surety (s). Under this [*272] enactment, it was decided that where a bond was given by a person as surety for the payment of money by another on a day named, and before such day the surety became bankrupt, and afterwards the principal debtor made default, the creditor could prove for what was due from the principal debtor under the commission against the surety (s). So, where a bond of indemnity was executed by a person, and before the amount of damage was ascertained the obligor became bankrupt, the court directed a claim to be entered, on the ground that a contingent debt was proveable under sect. 56 of 6 Geo. 4, c. 16 (u).

In the case of *Re Willis* (x), it was decided that a claim, under a guarantee, for a sum certain, *when* due, was proveable as a debt, and, *before* it was due, was proveable as a debt due on a contingency under 6 Geo. 4, c. 16, s. 56.

Where a person guaranteed to a banking company· "all current obligations in their hands to which B. may be a party, and also all his future obligations and engagements that may come into their hands," it was held that the banking company might, on the bankruptcy of the surety, prove for the amount of their advances to B. *subsequent* to the date of the guarantee (y).

The contingent debt clauses of the old Bankruptcy Acts did not, however, it seems, apply to cases where, from the nature of the case, there might never. be a debt due from the principal debtor for whom the bankrupt was surety (z). To constitute a debt payable on a contingency within the 56th section of 6 Geo. 4, *c. 16, it must have been a debt capable, *á priori*, of [*273] valuation (a). Where the defendant gave the plaintiff guarantee·to the extent of 200*l.*, but revocable at his option, on giving him notice in writing, and afterwards became bankrupt and obtained his certificate of conformity under 12 & 13 Vict. c. 106, but did not give notice to determine the guarantee, it·was held that his·

(s) Robson's Law of Bankruptcy, 5th ed. p. 305.
(t) *Ex parte Lewis,* M. & M. 426. See further, *Ex parte Myers,* Mont. & Bli. 229; *Ex parte Simpson,* 1 M. & Ayr. 451.
(u) *Ex parte Marshall,* Mont. & Bli. 242.
(x) 19 L. J. (N. S.) C. P. 30.
(y) *Ex parte Littlejohn,* 3 M., D. & D. 182. See also *Ex parte Hope,* 3 M., D. & D. 720.
(z) *Ex parte Thompson,* Mont. & Bli. 219, 229.
(a) Per *Erskine,* J., in *Ex parte Thompson;* and see *Amott* v. *Holden,* 18 Q. B. 593; 17 Jur. 318; *White* v. *Corbett,* 1 El. & Bl. 692.

liability was a contingent liability within sect. 178 of that statute, and that the certificate was a bar to all claims under the guarantee (b). However, the right of proof against a surety is now regulated by the 37th section of the Bankruptcy Act, 1883, which is quite as comprehensive in its terms as sect. 31 of the Bankruptcy Act, 1869, of which latter enactment it has been remarked that its words " are so general and so comprehensive as to include almost every transaction in which men can engage, from express contract to 'remote possibility' " (c).

Right of proof under Bankruptcy Act, 1883.

It is hardly necessary to state that the creditor's proof against the surety's estate will be rejected in cases where the surety has been discharged from liability by the conduct of the creditor (d).

Proof against estate of surety, who has been discharged by conduct of creditor, will be rejected.

It is important to bear in mind that no admission or acknowledgment by the debtor, or judgment obtained against him, can fix the surety with liability for an amount other than that which was really due, and which alone the surety has contracted to pay, should default be made by the debtor. Therefore, where a surety engaged to be answerable for any debt another person might owe for wines, and for any damages which might be sustained by breach of any other provisions of the [*274] *agreement it was held that the creditors were not entitled to prove against the surety for the amount found due by an award made in an arbitration between the creditors and the principal debtor (e).

Award against principal debtor does not dispense with necessity for strict proof of surety's liability by creditors against his estate.

The question sometimes arises whether the person seeking to prove in respect of a guarantee has really a sufficient interest in the guarantee to entitle him to do so. This point recently arose, under the following circumstances :—M. drew bills upon the B. & A. Co.; and a banking company, under an agreement with M., guaranteed the acceptors (also a company) that they would supply them with goods to meet the bills. S. discounted the bills, being informed by M. of the guarantee of the banking company, but he gave no notice to the banking company or to the acceptors. Afterwards the banking company and the acceptors suspended payment and were wound up. M. also executed a deed of composition with his creditors. It was held

Creditor seeking to prove in respect of a guarantee must have sufficient interest therein to entitle him to do so.

(b) *Boyd* v. *Robins*, 4 C. B., N. S. 749 ; 27 L. J., C. P. 299.
(c) See Robson's Law of Bankruptcy, 2nd ed., p. 242 ; and see *Ibid.* 5th ed., p. 305.
(d) The discharge of the creditor is dealt with on a subsequent page, *post* p. 323 *et seq.*
(e) *Ex parte Young, In re Kitchin*, 17 Ch. Div. 668 ; 50 L. J., Ch. 824.

that S. had no equity to rank as the creditor of the banking company in respect to the guarantee (f). *Wood,* L. J., in his judgment in the case, pointed out that the person who induced S. to discount the bills in question was the *drawer* of the bills, but that the guarantee was *not* given to the *drawer,* but to the *acceptors.* He also observed, that the present case did not resemble cases where a bank gives a letter of credit, intended to be exhibited to all the world, and on the faith of which money is advanced (g). In such cases all the world is invited to trust to the representations of the persons who have given the letter, and therefore those persons are bound. Moreover, as the Lord Justice also pointed out, in the present case, the person who had *secured the money* was *not in fact the person who was [*275] interested at all in the guarantee. If the money had been paid it would have been a different thing. Then, said the Lord Justice, the bill holder might have raised his equity ; but even then he could not raise it until he had given to the persons who so guaranteed notice of his claim, and until that time the persons who so guaranteed might deal with all the rights, as between them and the guarantors, in any way they thought fit.

While dealing with the subject of a surety becoming bankrupt, it should be observed that if the surety receives security from the principal debtor, and afterwards both these parties become insolvent, the creditors of the surety are entitled to regard such security as part of the property of the surety, and consequently are entitled to the benefit of it in discharge of their debts (h).

Right of creditors to benefit of securities received by surety from principal debtor when both insolvent.

(f) *Barned's Banking Co., In re Stephens,* L. R., 3 Ch. App. 753 ; S. C., 6 W. R. 1162.

(g) See *Re Agra and Masterman's Bank,* L. R., 2 Ch. App. 391.
(h) *Loder's case,* L. R., 6 Eq. 491.

[*276]   *CHAPTER V.

THE RIGHTS OF THE SURETY.

Division of this chapter.   IT is proposed to treat of the rights of the surety in the following order:—I. The Rights of the Surety against the Principal Debtor. II. The Rights of the Surety against the Creditor. III. The Rights of the Surety against his Co-sureties.

I. Rights of surety against the principal debtor.   I. *The rights of the Surety against the Principal Debtor.*

The surety possesses rights against the principal debtor, some of which exist before the surety has been compelled to pay anything under his guarantee, others of which exist after he has made payments under his guarantee, and before such payments have been repaid to him by the principal debtor; and others, again, which are given to him for the very purpose of enabling him to recover back from the principal debtor sums which he has paid on his account.

May compel debtor to exonerate him from liability.   The most important right which a surety possesses before any payment has been demanded of him is, that after the debt has become due he may compel the debtor to exonerate him from his liability, by at once paying the debt (a). To obtain this relief a surety must formerly have had recourse to a Court of Equity; and he should now resort to the Chancery Division, as being, since the Judicature Acts, the appropriate tribunal [*277] *in such cases. "Although," says Lord Keeper *North*, "the *surety* is not troubled or molested for the debt, yet at any time after the money becomes payable on the original bond, this court will decree the *principal* to discharge the debt, it being unreasonable that a man should always have such a cloud hang over him " (b).

(a) Per Sir *W. Grant*, M. R., in *Antrobus* v. *Davidson*, 3 Meriv. 569, 579; per Lord *Thurlow* in *Nisbet* v. *Smith*, 2 Brown, Ch. Ca. 579, 582; per Sir *Joseph Jekyll*, M. R., in *Lee* v. *Brook*, Moseley. 318; *Wooldridge* v. *Norris*, L. R., 6 Eq. 410. See also *Hayes* v. *Ward*, 4 Johns. Ch. Ca. 123, 132.

(b) In *Ranelagh* v. *Hayes*, 1 Vern. 189, 190.

The only state of circumstances, however, under which a surety could sue his principal in equity to be discharged from his liability, was where the creditor had a right to sue the principal debtor, and refused to exercise such right (c).

A mere surety for the price of goods cannot exercise the right of stoppage *in transitu* on the insolvency of the principal debtor (d). But if a surety for an insolvent buyer should pay the vendor, it would seem that he would now have the right of stoppage *in transitu*, if not in his own name, at all events in the name of the vendor, by virtue of the provisions of the 5th section (e) of the Mercantile Law Amendment Act (19 & 20 Vict. c. 97) (f). It has, moreover, been held in a recent case that a broker for an undisclosed principal, who is in the position of a surety, may, under certain circumstances, exercise this right (g).

Right of surety to stop goods in transitu on principal's insolvency.

After any actual payment on account of the debt of the principal has been made by him, the surety is entitled to rank as a creditor for the amount, though only as a simple contract creditor (h). As, however, *specialty debts and simple contracts now rank [*278] together in the administration of assets of a deceased person (i), the rank of debts to which the liability of a surety belongs is now of little importance. And now the Judicature Act, 1875 (k) provides that the insolvent estates of deceased persons are to be administered as in bankruptcy. Should he be made executor of the principal debtor, the surety is entitled to retain the amount which has been paid by him out of the assets

Right of surety after payment on account of debtor to rank as creditor for amount so paid.

(c) *Padwick* v. *Stanley*, 9 Hare, 627.

(d) *Siffken* v. *Wray*, 6 East, 371.

(e) See this section, *post*, p. 295.

(f) Benjamin on Sales, 3rd ed., pp. 819—820.

(g) *Imperial Bank of London* v. *The St. Katherine's Dock Co.*, 5 Ch Div. 195.

(h) A wife, married before the Dower Act, joined, for the purpose of releasing her dower, with her husband in mortgaging his freehold estate to secure his debt. The equity of redemption was reserved to the husband. Held, that the wife had no right, in character of surety for her husband's debt, to have the value of her dower made good after his death out of the surplus proceeds of sale of the property, which had been during his life sold by the mortgagee under a power of sale contained in the mortgage deed. *Dawson* v. *Bank of Whitehaven*, 6 Ch. Div. 218 ; *S. C.*, 25 W. R. 582 ; 46 L. J., Ch. 545 ; 36 L. T. 310. It is, however, to be noticed that in this case she had undertaken no personal liability on behalf of her husband, and therefore was not really a surety.

(i). 32 & 33 Vict. c 46.

(k) Sect. 10.

of the principal against all creditors of equal degree(*l*),
even though judgment for administration may have
been obtained against him (*m*). Moreover, a surety
who, after the death of the principal debtor, pays off
the debt, is, in case of intestacy, entitled to administration as a creditor (*n*).

Surety may compel debtor to repay him.

When the surety is desirous, however, of obtaining
repayment from his principal of the sum which he has
paid for him, the law provides him ample means of
obtaining it. "When the engagement of the surety is
made with the knowledge and consent of the principal
debtor, there is, in point of law, an implied request
from the latter to the surety to intervene on the principal's behalf if the latter makes default; and money paid
by the surety for the purpose of discharging the claim
against the principal is money paid for the use of the
principal, at his request, which may be recovered from
the latter" (*o*).

But the suretyship must have been under- taken at principal debtor's re- quest.

[*279] *The reason why the principal debtor is not
chargeable to the surety, unless the engagement of the
latter was made with the former's consent, is because
the *English law* does not allow a person to make himself the creditor of another by *volunteering* to discharge
his obligation (*p*). Where, however, the surety, having entered into the suretyship at the request of the
principal debtor, is called upon by the creditor to pay
the debt due from the principal debtor, the payment is
treated as so much money paid to the use of the
principal debtor. It can, therefore, be recovered
from him in an action, or may be proved against
his estate on his bankruptcy. In *Ex parte Bishop,
In re Fox, Walker & Co.* (*q*), it being proved to
be the common and almost invariable practice of

(*l*) *Boyd* v. *Brooks*, 34 L. J., Ch. 605; 13 W. R. 419; 12 L. T.,
N. S. 38.

(*m*) *Re Orme, Evans* v. *Maxwell*, 50 L. T. 51.

(*n*) *Williams* v. *Jukes*, 34 L. J., Prob. & Mat. 60.

(*o*) Addison on Contracts, 8th ed., p. 668, and see the judgment of Lord *Kenyon*, C. J., in *Exall* v. *Partridge*, 1 T. R. 308,
310; *Warrington* v. *Furbor*, 8 East, 242; judgment of Lord *Brougham* in *Hodgson* v. *Shaw*, 3 Myl. & Kee, 183, 190; *Morrice* v. *Red-
win*, 2 Barnard. 26; judgment of Lord *Eldon*, C., in *Wane* v. *Horwood*, 14 Ves. 28. And see *Huntley* v. *Sanderson*, 1 Cr. & Mee.
467; *Davies* v. *Humphreys*, 6 M. & W. 153; *Reynolds* v. *Doyle*, 1
M. & G. 753.

(*p*) *James* v. *Isaacs*, 12 C. B. 791; *Kemp* v. *Balls*, 10 Exch. 607;
Cook v. *Lister*, 13 C. B., N. S. 543, 594; *Jones* v. *Broadhurst*, 9
C. B. 173, 193 to 198; *Belshaw* v. *Bush*, 11 C. B. 191. See also
Walter v. *James*, L. R., 6 Exch. 124; 40 L. J., Exch. 104; 24 L.
T. 188.

(*q*) 15 Ch. Div. 400.

bill brokers in the City of London not to indorse each bill of exchange which may have been discounted for a customer when they re-discount it with their bankers, but to give the bankers a general guarantee for all bills which they re-discount with them, it was held that when an accommodation bill is drawn and accepted for the purpose of raising money for the drawer and acceptor, the drawer, in discounting the bill with bill brokers in the City of London, has an implied authority from the acceptor to deal with them in the ordinary course of their business ; and, consequently, that the bill brokers have an implied authority from the acceptor to make themselves liable on the bill under *their guarantee to their bankers, and are, in [*280] the event of the bankruptcy of the acceptor, entitled to prove against his estate for what they have paid to the bankers in respect of the bill under their guarantee. It was also held that the bill brokers were entitled to prove against the estate of the acceptor for interest upon the amount which they had paid under their guarantee.

As a general rule, as soon as the surety has paid any-thing for the principal debtor, the latter becomes chargeable to him (r) ; and since, as often as he pays any-thing, a right of action accrues to him for the recovery back of the sum so paid, the surety cannot *accelerate* the liability of the principal debtor by voluntarily paying the principal's debt before it is due (s).

Surety who has paid any portion of the debt has right of action against principal debtor.

Though, as just pointed out, the surety must have first paid something for the principal debtor in order to make the latter chargeable to him, yet it appears that, *by express contract*, the surety may, before payment, be entitled to recover *damages* from the principal debtor ; where, for instance, the principal debtor has covenanted with the surety to pay the amount due to the creditor on a day named, and makes default (t).

Sometimes surety may be entitled to recover damages from principal debtor before making any payment.

The right of the surety to sue the debtor the moment he has paid *anything* for the debtor is certainly calculated to produce a hardship upon the principal debtor, by exposing him to several actions at the suit of the surety.   But, however convenient it might be to limit the number of actions in respect of one surety-ship, there is certainly no rule of law which requires the surety to pay the whole debt of the principal debtor before he can call for reimbursement (u).

(r) See *Davies* v. *Humphreys*, 6 M. & W. 153.
(s) Addison on Contracts, 8th ed., p. 668.
(t) *Loosemore* v. *Radford*, 9 M. & W. 657.   See also *Penny* v. *Fox*, 8 B. & C. 11, 14.
(u) Per *Parke*, B., in *Davies* v. *Humphreys*, 6 M. & W. 153, 167.

The action by the surety for money paid on the [*281] *debtor's account lies, *even though the surety did not pay the debt by the desire of the principal debtor* (*x*). It frequently happens, however, that the surety takes from the principal debtor a bond as security or indemnity. If he do this, the remedy of the surety is on the bond.

What the surety can recover from principal debtor. With regard to *what* the surety can recover against the principal debtor, one or two points are to be noticed.

It is clear that the surety is entitled to recover the amount which he has actually paid with interest (*y*).

He can always recover the amount which he has actually paid. But a surety who compounds a debt, for which his principal and himself have become jointly liable, and takes an assignment of that debt to a trustee for himself, can only claim against his principal the amount which he has actually paid (*z*).

Is entitled to claim interest. A surety is entitled to recover *interest* from the principal debtor, because the surety is entitled to be indemnified against loss ●hich he has sustained through the default of the principal debtor (*a*). The cases upon direct contracts for the payment of money which omit mention of interest are well distinguished, on the ground that the intention of the parties is presumed●to be *expressed* in the terms of their contract (*b*).

Surety for a company which is being wound up entitled to interest. A surety for a company who pays money on behalf of the company is not in a worse position than a stranger who advances money, but is entitled on the winding-up of the company, to interest at 5*l.* per cent. on his debt (*c*). However, a surety for a *company* cannot, after an order to *wind up* the company has been made, be admitted to prove in respect of interest accruing *after* the said order upon payments [*282] made by the surety for the company (*g*). This is because an order to wind up a company fixes the right of its creditors and nullifies, as between them, all contracts for interest (*g*). After an order to·wind up has been made, the proper course for a surety for the company seeking to recover interest (subsequently accrued due) to adopt, is to take a claim into chambers for the established value of his right to indemnity at the time

(*x*) *Exall* v. *Partridge*, 1 T. R. 308; *Warrington* v. *Furbor*, 8 East, 242; but see note (*p*), p. 506, of Chitty on Contracts, 9th ed. See also *Allexander* v. *Vane*, 1 M. & W. 511.
(*y*) *Petre* v. *Duncombe*, 20 L. J. (N. S.), Q. B. 242.
(*z*) *Reed* v. *Morris*, 2 Mylne & C. 361; 1 Jur. 233.
(*a*) Per *Erle*, C. J., in *Petre* v. *Duncombe*, 20 L. J., Q. B. 242.
(*b*) *Ib.*
(*c*) *In re Beulah Park Estate, Sargood's claim*, L. R., 15. Eq. 43.
(*g*) I● re *International Contract Co., Hughes' claim*, L. R.,13 Eq.823.

when the winding-up order was made (g). It would
seem, too, that in such a case the claim for interest
should be made against the surplus assets of the company after all its debts (quâ principal moneys) are paid
(g).

The surety, cannot, it appears, recover from the prin- Right of a
cipal debtor the costs of *defending* an action unless he surety to re-
was authorized by the principal debtor to defend (h). cover from
However, it has recently been held, that when a man principal
has defended an action for a claim, for which another of defending
is liable over to him, his right to recover the costs in- actions.
curred in the defence depends on the *reasonableness* of
that defence, and that is a question for the jury (i).
Moreover, where the plaintiff guaranteed A. that the
defendant would, upon demand, from time to time, pay
to A. what should be due, and, upon defendant making
default, a writ was issued against the plaintiff for the
amount, the writ being the first notification to him of
the amount being due and unpaid : it was held that the
plaintiff having allowed judgment to go by default,
and an execution to be levied upon his goods, might
recover against the defendant the *costs of the writ* at
the suit of A., but *not* of the subsequent proceedings (k).

*If a surety make a payment in respect of a [*283] Surety can-
claim known by him to be illegal or void for fraud or net, *semble*,
immorality, he cannot, it seems, recover in respect of principal
such a payment from the principal debtor (l). debtor pay-

The defences which may be set up in an action by a ments know-
surety against the principal debtor are, of course, num- ingly made
erous, and vary with the circumstances of each case. by him in
The defences of payment and of the Statute of Limita- an illegal or
tions, however, require a few words of notice. fraudulent

Payment in full to the creditor by the principal claim.
debtor, if made in proper time, will, of course, always Defences by
afford a sufficient defence to an action brought by the principal
surety against the principal debtor. But, where there surety's
are several sureties, it is apprehended that payment by action.
the principal debtor to *another* of the sureties would Payment in
not be an answer to such an action (m). full made to
creditor.

(g) *In re International Contract Co., Hughes' claim*, L. R., 13 Eq.
623.

(h) *Gillett* v. *Rippon*, Mood. & M. 406. See also *Smith* v. *Compton*, 2 B. & Ad. 407 ; *Duffield* v. *Scott*, 3 T. R. 374, 377 ; *Roach* v.
Thompson, Mood. & Malk. 487.

(i) *Le Blanche* v. *Wilson*, 21 W. R. 109.

(k) *Pierce* v. *Williams*, 23 L. J., Exch. 322.

(l) *Bryant* v. *Christie*, 1 Stark. N. P. R. 239.

(m) See the American case of *Lowry* v. *Lumbermere's Bank*, 2
Watts. & Serg. R. 210.

Statute of Limitations may bar surety's right of action against principal debtor.	The Statute of Limitations may bar the surety's right of action against the principal debtor (n). It begins to run against a surety as soon as he has made a payment *in ease* of the principal debtor (o). The time runs from the time of *actual payment* by the surety, and not from the time when he became merely *liable to pay* (p).
Rights of surety against principal debtor on latter's bankruptcy:	Let us now see what are the rights of the surety against the principal debtor on the *bankruptcy* of the latter.
Could not formerly prove unless he paid debt before debtor's bankruptcy.	We have seen that the surety does not become a creditor of the principal debtor until he has paid something on his account. It was, therefore, formerly held, that, unless the surety paid the debt of the principal *before* the bankruptcy of the latter, he could not come in as a creditor under the commission (q). And, accord- [*284] *ingly, where a surety in a bond paid the debt *after* a commission of bankruptcy issued against his principal, it was held, that his right of action against his principal for the money so paid was *not barred* by the certificate, though the penalty of the bond was for-feited *before* the bankruptcy (r).
Right of proof conferred by 49 Geo. 3, c. 121, s. 8.	The statute 49 Geo. 3, c. 121, s. 8, first enabled a surety paying the debt of his principal *after* the bank-ruptcy of the latter, to prove against his estate. Subse-quent statutes re-enacted this provision (s).
The B. A. 1869 and 1883 do not expressly confer right of proof in respect of payments made by surety after principal debtor's bankruptcy.	The Bankruptcy Act, 1869 (32 & 33 Vict. c. 71) (t), did not contain any section enabling a surety to prove for a debt which he had paid *after* the bankruptcy of his principal. Nor is any such provision to be found in the Bankruptcy Act, 1883, or in the rules framed under it. A surety's right of proof would seem, therefore, still to depend upon previous enactments (u). We will, therefore, examine some of the cases decided under these older enactments.

(n) See American cases of *Eager* v. *Commonwealth*, 4 Mass. T. R. 182; *Thayer* v. *Daniels*, 110 Mass. 345.

(o) *Davies* v. *Humphreys*, 6 M. & W. 153.

(p) *Angrove* v. *Tippett*, 11 L. T., N. S. (Q. B.) 708.

(q) *Paul* v. *Jones*, 1 T. R. 599; *Brooks* v. *Rogers*, 1 H. B. 640; *Taylor* v. *Mills*, Cowp. 525. See also *Goddard* v. *Vanderheyden*, 3 Wilson, 362; *Young* v *Hockley*, 3 Wilson, 346.

(r) *Taylor* v. *Mills*, Cowp. 525; and see the judgment of Lord *Mansfield* in this case.

(s) 6 Geo. 4, c. 16, s. 52; 6 Geo. 4, c. 168; and 12 & 13 Vict. c. 106, s. 173 (B. A. 1849).

(t) Repealed by the Bankruptcy Act, 1883 (46 & 47 Vict. c. 52), s. 169, Fifth Sched.

(u) See observations on this subject in Robson's Law of Bankruptcy, 5th ed., p. 309.

Where a person who retired from a partnership upon an undertaking of his partner to pay the outstanding debts, was afterwards, upon the partner's becoming bankrupt, obliged to pay some of the partnership debts, it was held that he was a surety (x). Mere *liability* to pay the outstanding partnership debts would not, however, constitute the retiring partner a surety (y). And it was decided, in the case of *Hoare* v. *White* (z), that *sect. 173 of the Bankruptcy Act, 1849, applied [*285] only to persons under a *personal* liability to pay.

Moreover, under the enactments we are now considering, in order to entitle the surety to prove, it is necessary that the debt of the principal should be *actually due* at the time of the issuing of the commission. Thus, where a man was surety for the payment of a trader's rent, and no rent was due at the time of the bankruptcy, it was held, that, though the surety paid the rent afterwards accruing, he could not prove for the amount (a).

The surety, too, was not entitled to prove until the *whole* debt was satisfied, *i. e.*, either by payment in full or by payment of part in discharge of the whole (b). Where a surety in a bond for the bankrupts, after the bankrupts were certificated, joined with them and a new surety in a new bond to the representatives of the creditor and the old bond was delivered up to the surety: it was held, that this transaction did not amount to payment by the surety within Sir S. Romilly's Act (49 Geo. 3, c. 121, s. 8), so as to enable the surety to prove under the commission (c). So, again, where a surety paid part of the debt due from the principal, and thereupon the creditor gave him an indemnity from personal liability as to the remainder, it was held, that this did not operate as a payment of *part* in discharge of the *whole*, within 49 Geo. 3, c. 121, s. 8 (d). "The object of the statute is very plain. If the surety pays the whole of the debt, the original creditor is

Decisions on previous enactments must therefore be considered.

(x) *Wood* v. *Dodgson*, 2 M. & S. 195; 2 Rosc. 47. See also *Parker* v. *Ramsbottom*, 5 D. & R. 138; *Wallis.* v. *Swinburne*, 1 Ex. 203; *Ex parte Carpenter*, Mont. & M'A. 1.
(y) *Abbott* v. *Hicks*, 7 Scott, 715; 5 Bing. N. C. 579.
(z) 3 Jur. N. S. 445.
(a) *M'Dougal* v. *Paton*, 2 Moore, 644; 8 Taunt. 584. See also *Ex parte Minet*, 14 Ves. 189.
(b) *Young* v. *Taylor*, 8 Taunt. 315; *Ex parte Coplestone*, 4 Dea. 54. See also observations of *Buller*, J., in *Paul* v. *Jones*, 1 T. R. 599, 600; *Kittier* v. *Raynes*, Cox, 105; *Martin* v. *Brecknell*, 3 M. & S. 39.
(c) *Ex parte Serjeant*, 2 G. & J. 23.
(d) *Soutten* v. *Soutten*, 2 D. & Ry. 521; and see *Ex parte Turquand, In re Fothergill*, 3 Ch. Div. 445; 45 L. J., Bank. 153.

have been would restrain the creditor from proceeding at law
restrained by against the surety (p). But the Judicature Act, 1873,
injunction. now provides that no cause or proceeding at any time
Actions no pending in the High Court of Justice, or before the
longer to be Court of Appeal, shall be restrained by prohibition or
restrained by injunction; but every matter of equity on which an
Grounds on injunction against the prosecution of any such cause or
which in- proceeding might have been obtained if this Act had
junction not passed, either unconditionally or on any terms or con
formerly ditions, may be relied on by way of defence thereto (q).
granted now
available as a   In some cases, also, a court of equity would set *aside*
defence. and *cancel* the instrument under which the surety's lia-
Equitable [*289] bility arose (r). This jurisdiction is now *espe-
right to have cially assigned to the Chancery Division of the High
guarantee set Court (s).
aside and
cancelled.   The rights which the surety possesses when called
TheChancery upon to pay do not call for notice at length. Of course
Division of there are a great variety of defences, any one or more
High Court of which may be open to the surety; but, as such de-
will now fences are of common occurrence in other actions, they
exercise this need no special remarks here. There are only two mat-
jurisdiction. ters of defence which it is necessary to make special
The rights of
surety when mention of.
called upon   Formerly, if the creditor sued the surety on his
to pay. guarantee, the surety might have pleaded equitably a
Surety en- set-off which the principal debtor had against the
titled to ben- creditor (t). And now, by virtue of the Judicature
efit of set-off Act, 1873, where a defence shows grounds entitling the
which defendant in equity to be relieved against a contract
principal sought to be enforced by the plaintiff, any Division in
debtor had which the action is pending may give effect to the
against equitable defence, at least so far as to treat it as a
creditor. defense to the action (u).
Surety's   The other matter of equitable defence against a claim
right to com- under the guarantee requiring notice is, the surety's
pel creditor
to resort first right to compel a creditor having a claim upon two

(p) *Hawkshaw* v. *Parkins*, 2 Sw. 544; *Samuel* v. *Howarth*, 3 Mer. 272; *Small* v. *Currie*, 5 D., M. G. 141; 2 Drew. 102; *Allan* v. *Inman*, 7 Jur. 433. See also Story, Eq. Jur., 9th ed., pars. 883, 883a.

(q) 36 & 37 Vict. c. 66, s. 24 (5).

(r) *Blest* v. *Brown*, 3 Giff. 450.

(s) Judicature Act, 1873, s. 34 (3).

(t) *Murphy* v. *Glass*, L. R., 2 P. C. 408; *S. C.*, 6 Moo. P. C., N. S. 1; 20 L. T., N. S. 461; 17 W. R. 592. See also *Bechervaise* v. *Lewis*, 20 W. R., C. P. 726; *S. C.*, 41 L. J., C. P. 161; 26 L. T. 848; L. R., 7 C. P. 372.

(u) 36 & 37 Vict. c. 66, s. 24 (2); *Mostyn* v. *West Mostyn Coal Co.*. 1 C. P. D. 145; Wilson's Judicature Act, 4th ed., p. 20.

funds, one of which the surety cannot make available, to the fund
to resort to the latter fund *first* (x).

The rights which a surety possesses against the creditor
after he has been called upon to pay the debt are of
considerable importance.

If, in ignorance *of the facts*, he has paid the creditor
that which he was not liable to pay, the surety is entitled *to recover the amount so paid (y).* If, [*290]
however, a surety were to make an improper payment
in ignorance of law, and not of fact merely, it is presumed that he could not recover it back, for "*ignorantia
legis neminem excusat.*"

Assuming no such question as this to arise, another
right is, that he is entitled to the benefit of all the securities, whether known to him (the surety) or not (z),
which the creditor has against the principal (a). And
it is the duty of the creditor, as soon as the surety has
paid the debt, to make over to him all the securities
which he (the creditor) holds, in order that the surety
may recoup himself (b). In the case of a person who
becomes surety for a limited amount of a debt, he has,
on payment of the amount for which he is liable, all the
rights of a creditor in respect of that amount, and is
entitled to a share in the security held by the creditor
for the whole debt (c).

This right of the surety to the benefit of all the
securities held by the creditor is not necessarily dependent upon contract, but is the result of the equity

Margin notes:
to the fund which is not available to surety.

Rights of surety after payment demanded.

To recover sum paid to creditor in ignorance of fact.

To benefit of all securities held by creditor.

Nature of this right.

(x) *Ex parte Kendall*, 17 Ves. 514.

(y) *Mills* v. *Alderbury Union*, 3 Exch. 590.

(z) *Duncan, Fox & Co.* v. *North and South Wales Bank, ubi infra;
Mayhew* v. *Crickett*, 2 Swanst. 185, 191; *Pearl* v. *Deacon*, 24 Beav.
186. See also *Scott* v. *Knox*, 2 Jones (Ir.), 778; *Hodgson* v. *Shaw*,
3 Myl. & Kee. 183; *Yonge* v. *Reynell*, 9 Hare, 809; *Merchants'
Bank of London* v. *Maud*, 18 W. R. 312; 19 W. R. 657.

(a)*Ex parte Crisp*, 1 Atk. 135; *Sir Daniel O'Carrol's case*, Amb.
61; *Goddard* v. *Whyte*, 2 Giff. 449; *Brandon* v. *Brandon*, 3 De G.
& J. 524; *Parsons* v. *Briddock*, 2 Vern. 608. Observations of
Willes, J., in *Bechervaise* v. *Lewis*, 20 W. R., C. P. 726; 41 L. J.,
C. P. 161; 26 L. T 848; L. R., 7 C. P. 372. See also *Craythorne*
v. *Swinburne*, 14 Ves. 160; *Wright* v. *Morley*, 11 Ves. 12; *Ex parte
Rushforth*, 10 Ves. 409; *Pledge* v. *Buss*, Johns. 663; *Robinson* v.
Wilson, 2 Madd. 434; *Hotham* v. *Stone*, cited 2 Madd. 437; *Plumbe*
v. *Sanday*, 1 Madd. Princ. & Prac. 238; *Strange* v. *Fooks*, 4 Giff.408;
Hodgson v. *Shaw*, 3 Myl. & Kee. 183; *Swain* v. *Wall*, 1 Ch. Rep.
80.

(b) Per *Cockburn*, C. J., in *Wulff* v. *Jay*, 20 W. R., Q. B. 1030,
1031; *S.·C.*, L. R., 7 Q. B. 756; 41 L. J., Q. B. 322; 27 L. T.
118; 20 W. R. 1030.

(c) *Goodwin* v. *Gray*, 2 W. R. 312.

of indemnification attendant on the suretyship (d); and
[*291] *it can be exercised even where the only suretyship is created by indorsing a bill of exchange in order
to get it discounted (e). It seems, however, that, during
the currency of a bill of exchange, the indorsers are
not sureties to the indorsees, nor have they any equity
to prevent an indorsee from dealing as it may seem to
him most desirable with any other parties, unless thereby
he prevents himself from giving notice of dishonour,
so as to give them their remedy against prior parties to
the bill (f). Thus, it would seem, that, where bankers
are holders of a bill accepted by a customer, and indorsed by a third person, they will not be incapacitated
from carrying on their dealings with that customer, by
varying the securities received from him according to
the ordinary course of those dealings as long as he remains solvent, and before the acceptance has been dishonoured (g).

Surety en-titled to securities given *after* the contract of suretyship. This right extends, and the surety is entitled to
securities given *after* the contract of suretyship (h).
And, therefore, where the creditor has so dealt afterwards with such security that on payment by the
surety it cannot be given up to him in the same condition as it was when the creditor first acquired it, the
surety is discharged to the extent of such security (i).
And so, also, the surety is entitled to a transfer of any
mortgage which the creditor may have taken for his
debt, even though the surety was not originally aware
of its existence (k). But, upon the other hand, a
surety is sometimes not entitled to an assignment from
the creditor of a mortgage, unless he pays off, not only
[*292] the *sum for the payment of which he became
surety, but also such further sum as may have been advanced on the security of the same mortgage (l). This
does not, however, appear to be the case, where the surety
was wholly ignorant of the second advance, and such
advance was not contemplated at the time of the orig-

Right of surety to transfer of mortgages taken by creditor for the debt.

(d) *Duncan, Fox & Co.* v. *North and South Wales Bank*, 6 App.
Cas. 1; 11 Ch. Div. 88; 50 L. J., Ch. 355; 43 L. T. 706; 29 W.
R. 763.
(e) *Ib.*
(f) *Ib.*, per *Blackburn*, Lord, at p. 18 of 6 App. Cas.
(g) *Ib.*, per *Selborne*, L. C., at p. 15 of 6 App. Cas.
(h) *Forbes* v. *Jackson*, 19 Ch. Div. 615, 621; *Pledge* v. *Buss*,
Johns. 663; *contra Newton* v. *Chorlton*, 10 Hare, 646; 2 Drew.
333; *Pearl* v. *Deacon*, 24 Beav. 186.
(i) *Campbell* v. *Rothwell*, 47 L. J., Q. B. 124; 38 L. T. 33.
(k) *Mayhew* v. *Crickett*, 3 Swan, 185, 191.
(l) *Williams* v. *Owen*, 13 Sim. 597.

inal loan (m). Where, also, there is a special contract excluding the right to tack a subsequent debt, the creditor
would not be allowed to retain the mortgage, as against
the surety, until payment of such subsequent debt (n).
In the case of *Farebrother* v. *Wodehouse* (o), it was *Farebrother* v.
decided, that where two properties are mortgaged by *Wodehouse.*
A. to B. for distinct sums, and C. is surety for one
only, the right of B. to retain all the securities until
repaid both debts overrides the right of C. to have the
benefit of the securities for that debt for which he is
surety. There the defendant lent A., at the same time,
two sums of 2,000l. and 3,000l. on distinct securities,
and the plaintiff was surety for the first sum. It was
held that the plaintiff, on paying the 2,000l., was not
entitled to have a transfer of the securities held for that
sum until the defendant had also been paid the 3,000l.

This last-named case has been disapproved of in the *Forbes* v.
recent case of *Forbes* v. *Jackson* (p), in which the *Jackson.*
facts were as follows:—In December, 1854, S. assigned certain premises and a policy of assurance to
secure the repayment of a sum of 200l. advanced to
him by W. and interest. The proviso for redemption
was, that on payment of the money W. would re-as-
sign the premises and policy unto S., his executors,
administrators or *assigns, or as he or they [*293]
should direct. F., by the same indenture as surety,
covenanted, for himself only, with W. that while the
200l., or any part thereof, remained owing, he would
pay the interest and premiums, and he also assigned a
policy on his own life and covenanted to pay the premiums. W., at four different periods, between May,
1856, and May, 1866, advanced moneys amounting to
530l. to S., on security of the same premises. S. made
default in payment of the interest. W. died in 1878,
and his executors made a demand upon F. for all arrears, which he paid, and he also paid the premiums
on the policy of S. It was held that F. was entitled to
have a transfer of all the securities on paying what was
due upon the mortgage of December, 1854. Now, it is
to be noticed that in this case it was admitted that
the subsequent advances were made without the sure-

(m) *Forbes* v. *Jackson*, 19 Ch. Div. 615; L. J., Ch. 690; 30 W.
R. 252; *Newton* v. *Chorlton*, 10 Hare, 646; 2 Drew. 333; *contra*
Williams v. *Owen*, 13 Sim. 597.
(n) *Bowker* v. *Bull*, 1 Sim. N. S..29, where, however, *Williams*
v. *Owen*, *supra*, was not cited.
(o) 23 Beav. 28.
(p) 19 Ch. Div. 615; 51 L. J., Ch. 690; 30 W. R. 252; and see
In re Kirkwood, 1 Ir. L. R., Ch. 108.

ty's knowledge or consent. It is, therefore, submitted that this circumstance is quite sufficient of itself to support the judgment of *Hall*, V.-C., and that, consequently, his decision in no way conflicts with *Farebrother* v. *Wodehouse* (q), where, at the time the suretyship was entered into, the surety *knew* that the securities held by the creditor were intended to cover not only the sum guaranteed, but also another sum to which the promise of the surety did not extend. However, no such distinction was drawn by the learned Vice-Chancellor in his judgment, in which he states that his decision is founded on *Newton* v. *Chorlton* (r), and that he refuses to follow *Williams* v. *Owen* (s), though Lord *Romilly* followed it in *Farebrother* v. *Wodehouse*.

South v. *Bloxam.*   The case of *South* v. *Bloxam* (t), is also of much importance to sureties. There two funds were mortgaged to A., with a covenant by a surety. A second mortgage of one of these funds was made to B. B.'s fund [*294] having *been exhausted in part payment of A.'s debt, and A.'s mortgage having been transferred to the surety, on payment by him of the balance, it was held that B. had a right to marshal the securities as against the surety. It was also held that the surety could not tack, as against B., the costs of a defence to an action on his covenant from which B. derived no benefit, but that he might charge, as against B., all costs incurred for the common benefit of the persons interested in the estate after the first mortgage. *Semble,* also, that, as against the original mortgagor, the surety might have tacked to his security all costs not improperly incurred as surety. And in all cases, *as against the mortgagor,* a surety for a mortgagor who pays part of the mortgage is entitled to a charge on the estate (u). In an action for foreclosure one period only of six months for redemption will be allowed to the mortgagor and his surety for the payment of the mortgage debt, and not a period of six months to each in succession (x).

Formerly surety not entitled to have bond debt of prin-   There formerly existed a remarkable exception to the general right of the surety to have all securities held by the creditor made over to him on payment of the debt. This exception was founded upon highly tech-

(q) *Ubi supra.*
(r) 10 Hare, 646.
(s) 13 Sim. 597.
(t) 2 H. & M. 457.
(u) *Gedge* v. *Matson,* 25 Beav. 310 ; and see *Allen* v. *De Lisle,* 11 W. R. 158.
(x) *Smith* v. *Olding,* 25 Ch. Div. 462 ; 50 L. T. 357 ; 22 W. R. 386.

nical reasons. For it was held that, where a surety *cipal debtor* paid off the *bond* debt of his principal, for which he *assigned to* was bound, he could not require the creditor to assign *him on pay-* to him such bond debt, because it was satisfied and ex- *ment.* tinguished by the very act of payment by the surety (*y*). And it was held, that even an assignment of the bond, executed to a trustee for the surety at the time when the surety paid off the debt, would not keep *alive the instrument so as to make the surety [*295] in equity a specialty creditor of the principal (*z*). The *The right* law of England has in this respect been altered by the *conferred by* 5th section of the Mercantile Law Amendment Act (*a*). *c. 97, s. 5.* This enacts that, "every person who, being surety for the debt or duty of another, or being liable with another for any debt or duty shall pay such debt or perform such duty, shall be entitled to have assigned to him, or to a trustee for him, every judgment, specialty or security which shall be held by the creditor in respect of such debt or duty, whether such judgment, specialty, or other security, shall or shall not be deemed at law to have been satisfied by the payment of the debt or performance of the duty, and such person shall be entitled to stand in the place of the creditor, in any action or other proceeding at law or in equity, in order to obtain from the principal debtor, or any co-surety, co-contractor, or co-debtor, as the case may be, indemnification for the advances made and loss sustained by the person who shall have so paid such debt or performed such duty ; and such payment or performance so made by such surety shall not be pleadable in bar of any such action or other proceeding by him : provided always, that no co-surety, co-contractor, or co-debtor, shall be entitled to recover from any other co-surety, co-contractor or co-debtor, by the means aforesaid, more than the just proportion to which, as between those parties themselves, such last-mentioned person shall be justly liable."

This enactment has, in one or two instances, received *Construction* judicial interpretation. Thus, it has been decided, that *of this enact-* the act applies to contracts entered into before the *ment.* passing of the act, provided the breaches of them have

---

(*y*) *Copis* v. *Middleton*, 1 T. & R. 231 ; *Jones* v. *Davids*, 4 Russ. 277 ; *Armitage* v. *Baldwin*, 5 Beav. 278 ; *Dowbiggan* v. *Bourne*, 2 You. & Coll. 462 ; *Gammon* v. *Stone*, 1 Ves. sen. 339 ; but see *Hotham* v. *Stone*, 1 T. & Russ. 226 (note) ; *Robinson* v. *Wilson*, 2 Madd. 434 ; *Parsons* v. *Briddock*, 2 Vern. 608.

(*z*) *Jones* v. *Davids*, 4 Russ. 277.

(*a*) 19 & 20 Vict. c. 97.

taken place and payment has been made by the surety, after the passing of the act (b). It has also been [*296] *held that a surety is not entitled to have an assignment of the principal security, unless he pays the debt in full (c). And in the very recent case of *In re Russell—Russell* v. *Shoolbred* (d), it was held that a right of distress for rent in arrear is not a security held by a creditor in respect of a debt within the meaning of the act, and, therefore, that the act of the creditor, though it may have the effect of destroying such right, does not discharge the surety. The reasons for this decision were thus shortly expressed by the court:— "In the first place, the right of distress is not in common parlance, nor we think in legal phraseology, a security held for a debt, it is a particular remedy which arises on non-payment; in the second place, the section appears to be dealing with securities, which, according to the existing law, are in their nature assignable, which is not the case with a power of distress for rent in arrear, which, according to the common law, was only incidental to the immediate reversion; and, lastly, we think that the preamble is strong to show that the Legislature had no intention of effecting a great change in the law regulating the relations of landlord and tenant."

In re Russell, Russell v. Shoolbred.

As regards the mode of enforcing the surety's right under 19 & 20 Vict. c. 97, s. 5, to an assignment of securities, it was held, in a case decided before the Judicature Acts, that advantage cannot be taken of the act by *motion* (e), and that the only way, apparently, in which it can be made available is by *action* (f).

Mode of compelling assignment of securities under 19 & 20 Vict. c. 97, s. 5.

An exception to the rule which requires all securities held by a creditor for the debt guaranteed to be preserved for the benefit of the surety exists where, on the [*297] *bankruptcy of the debtor, the creditor elects to surrender his security and prove for the whole debt (g). For it must be taken that where three persons enter into the relations of creditor, debtor and surety, the possible bankruptcy of the debtor is an event which the surety has in his contemplation at the time of entering

Surety not discharged by creditor surrendering security on debtor's bankruptcy, and electing to prove instead for whole debt.

(b) *In re Cochran, De Wolf* v. *Lindsell*, L. R., 5 Eq. 209; 16 W. R. 324; 17 L. T., N. S. 487; 37 L. J., Chanc. 293, following *Lockhart* v. *Reilly*, 1 De G. & J. 464; 27 L. J., Ch. 54; *Batchelor* v. *Lawrence*, 9 C. B., N. S. 543; 30 L. J., C. P. 39.
(c) *Ewart* v. *Latta*, 4 Macq. H. L. R. 983.
(d) 29 Ch. Div. 254.
(e) *Phillips* v. *Dickson*, 8 C. B., N. S. 391.
(f) *ib.*
(g) *Rainbow* v. *Juggins*, 5 Q. B. D. 138, 422.

into the contract of suretyship, and that consequently it becomes an implied term of that contract, that in the event of the bankruptcy occurring, the creditor shall be entitled to exercise that option which the bankruptcy law gives him in the way which is most advantageous to himself (h).

It is submitted that if the surety, on payment of the debt guaranteed, does not insist on the securities held for it by the creditor being given up, and a long time afterwards credit is given to the debtor on the same securities, the surety cannot compel the delivery of them to him. Certainly, as against the debtor the right of the creditor to hold such securities is absolute (i). Whether if surety does not insist on securities being given up he can long afterwards demand them from creditor who has made advances to debtor.

Not only is a surety, who pays off his principal's debt, entitled to a transfer of securities held by the creditor, but he is also in all respects entitled to all the equities which the creditor could have enforced. And, this right prevails, not merely against the original creditor of the principal debtor, but also against all persons claiming under the latter (k). A. mortgaged his estate to C., and B. became A.'s surety for the debt. Afterwards A. mortgaged the estate to D., who had notice of the first mortgage. The first mortgage was subsequently paid off, partly by B., the surety, but D. got a transfer of the legal estate. It was held that the surety had still priority over D. for the amount paid by him under the first mortgage, as surety for A. (l). Again, on a *purchase of goods by a broker for an undis- [*298] closed principal, in a market according to the usage of which such a broker is personally liable in default of his principal, and is therefore a surety for the latter, the unpaid vendor's lien will pass to the broker, on default made by his principal, even though the latter may have pledged his interest in the goods to third persons, and indorsed the delivery order to them (m). Surety is entitled to all the equities which creditor could have enforced.

A surety who has paid the principal's debt, also has a right, upon the *bankruptcy* of the principal debtor, to stand in the place of the creditor himself. Right of surety to stand in creditor's place on principal debtor's bankruptcy.

Thus a surety may compel the creditor, on the bankruptcy of the principal debtor, to prove against his estate for the amount due, and the creditor will be a trustee of the dividends for the surety who has paid the whole The creditor is a trustee of

---

(h) *Ib.*
(i) *Waugh* v. *Wren*, 11 W. R. 244.
(k) *Drew* v. *Lockett*, 32 Beav. 499.
(l) *Ib.*
(m) *Imperial Bank* v. *London and St. Katherine's Dock Co.*, 5 Ch. Div. 195 ; 46 L. J., Ch. 335 ; 36 L. T. 233. .

dividends for debt (n). If the dividends on the bankrupt's estate are
surety who not sufficient to pay the creditor, and the surety pays
has paid what remains due, he is entitled to stand in the creditor's
debt. place as to future dividends (o). Where a limited
guarantee has been given, and the limit has been exceeded by the creditor, who afterwards receives from
the estate of the principal debtor a dividend, the surety
is entitled to the benefit of a part of that dividend,
proportional on the amount guaranteed, notwithstanding
that the unpaid debt greatly exceeds the amount of such
guarantee (p). And if, in such a case, the creditor has
recovered the whole sum guaranteed, in an action against
the guarantor, the right of the latter to file a bill for an
[*299] account and payment to him of such dividends, *is
not barred by the fact that he might have pleaded a
set-off to that extent in the action, and omitted to do
so (q). Such a claim was held not to be a mere "money
demand," within the meaning of the principal excluding actions for damages merely (r). And where a
creditor receives dividends upon a debt, partly secured
by the guarantee of a third person, the dividends must
not be appropriated to the excess of the debt, above the
sum guaranteed, but must be applied rateably to the
whole debt, and the surety is relieved from liability by
the amount of dividend on the part which is secured
(s). On the other hand, if the creditor accepts from the
surety a composition of so much in the pound, he can
only prove against the estate of the principal debtor
for the balance, after deducting part payment (t).

If bills be discounted in the market which are drawn
by one firm upon another firm and then both these firms
become bankrupt or agree to a conposition, the bill-
holder is entitled to prove against both estates and to
receive all the dividends or composition he can get from
both estates until he has received 20s. in the pound, and
whether it may turn out that the drawer is surety for

(n) Ex parte Rushforth, 10 Ves. 409, 414; Beardmore v. Crutten-
den, 1 Cooke, B. L. 211, margin. And see Jackson v. Magee, 3
Ad. & E. 57; Phillips v. Smith, cited 10 Ves. 412; Ex parte Turner,
3 Ves. 243; Paley v. Field, 12 Ves. 435.
(o) Ex parte Johnson, 3 D., M. & G. 218.
(p) Thornton v. M'Kewan, 1 H. & M. 525. See also Hobson v.
Bass, L. R., 6 Ch. App. 792.
(q) Thornton v. M'Kewan, supra.
(r) Ib.
(s) Raikes v. Todd, 8 Ad. & E. 846. But see The Liverpool Borough Bank v. Logan, 5 H. & N. 464.
(t) Oriental Commercial Bank, Ex parte Maxoudoff, L. R., 6 Eq.
582. See also Midland Banking Co. v. Chambers, L. R., 4 Ch.
App. 398.

the acceptor or the acceptor is surety for the drawer, yet the surety has no right to receive anything until the bill-holder has received altogether 20s. in the pound (u).

The right of the surety, under section 173 of the Bankruptcy Act, 1849, was to prove in the place of the creditor, or to have the benefit of the creditor's proof, and the sureties were bound by the election *of [*300] the creditor who had elected to prove against a particular estate (x). *Rights formerly possessed by surety under sect. 173 of B. A. 1849.*

A surety paying, after the bankruptcy of the principal debtor, to a creditor who has proved, can only stand in the place of the creditor upon the bankrupt's estate, and, in case of a surplus, cannot claim interest unless the creditor could have claimed it (y). Where, however, the surety had improperly proved for interest, subsequent to the *fiat* in bankruptcy, the Court of Chancery, sitting in bankruptcy, refused to reduce the proof after seven years had elapsed, and after the death of the surety (z).

The Bankruptcy Act of 1869 did not, it seems, contain any section equivalent to the 173rd section of the Bankruptcy Act, 1849, which enacted, that "sureties and persons liable for the debts of a bankrupt may prove after having paid such debts" (a); nor do the Bankruptcy Act, 1883, and the rules framed under it, contain any provision as to proof by sureties (a). *Subsequent Bankruptcy Acts do not repeat this provision.*

Where there are several sureties, it sometimes becomes a question which of them is entitled to the benefit of the creditor's proof. A bond was entered into by a principal and three sureties. The principal and one of the sureties compounded with their creditors, and the other two sureties became bankrupt. The obligee proved the full amount of his debt against the separate estates of the two bankrupts, and claimed under the compositions, and by these means received 20s. in the pound; but the estate of the compounding surety paid more than its contributive share. It was held that that estate was entitled to the benefit of the proof made by the creditor against the bankrupt surety (b).

(u) *Ex parte Turquand, In re Fothergill*, 3 Ch. Div. 445, 450; 45 L. J., Bank. 153.

(x) *Ex parte Carne*, L. R., 3 Ch. App. 463. See also *Ex parte Bevan*, 10 Ves. 107.

(y) *Ex parte Houston*, 3 G. & J. 36. See also *Ex parte Wilson*, 1 R. 137.

(z) *Ex parte Sanderson*, 8 D., M. & G. 849.

(a) Robson's Bankruptcy, 5th ed. 309.

(b) *Ex parte Stokes and another*, De Gex, 618; 12 Jur. 891.

Rights possessed by surety for a company which is being wound up.

[*301] *Akin to the rights possessed by a surety, on the bankruptcy of the debtor, are those devolving upon a person who has guaranteed the debt of a company which has afterwards been wound up. That is to say, where such a person has paid the debt for which he is surety, he is entitled to receive from the creditor a share of the dividend payable to the latter in the winding up, bearing the same proportion to the whole dividend as the sum paid by him bore to the sum proved for by the creditor (c). Moreover, the rule established by *Ex parte Turner* (d) that in similar cases in bankruptcy, the sum paid by the surety is, in calculating the proportions of dividend, to be considered as expunged, does not apply to cases in winding up (e).

Surety may waive his rights.

The rights which the surety possesses of standing in the creditor's place, as regards all the latter's securities and equities, and on the bankruptcy of the principal, may, however, be waived. The waiver may be made by express agreement in the contract of suretyship (f). Thus it may be agreed between the surety and creditor that the receipt by the latter of dividends in the bankruptcy of the principal debtor shall not diminish the liability of the surety to pay in full (g). But it need not of necessity be express (h). Thus, for instance, in the case of *Cooper* v. *Jenkins* (i), A. was tenant for life of lots 1 and 2, to which B. was entitled in remainder. B., and A. as his surety, mortgaged lot 2,—B. alone covenanting to pay. By a contemporaneous deed, B. conveyed his interest in the other lot on trusts to indemnify A. as his surety. A. [*302] paid large sums for interest *on the mortgage. It was held that he was entitled to the benefit of the deed of indemnity only, but not to stand in the place of the mortgagee on lot 2. Sir *John Romilly*, M. R., said, "The plaintiff cannot have the benefit of the mortgage on the principle of the Mercantile Law Amendment Act. He must proceed under one or other of the two rights which he claims. If he had bound himself to pay the mortgagee and had done so, he would then have

---

(c) *Gray* v. *Seckham*, L. R., 7 Ch. App. 680; 26 L. T. 233; 27 L. T. 290.
(d) 3 Ves. 243.
(e) *Gray* v. *Seckham, ubi supra.*
(f) See *Ex parte Hope*, 3 M. D. & D. 720 ; *Midland Bank* v. *Chambers*, L. R., 4 Ch. App. 398 ; *Earle* v. *Oliver*, 2 Exch. 71.
(g) *Ex parte National Provincial Bank, In re Rees*, 17 Ch. D. 98; 44 L. T. 325; 27 W. R. 796 ; *Ex parte Miles*, De Gex, 623.
(h) *Waugh* v. *Wren*, 11 W. R. 244.
(i) 32 Beav. 337.

been entitled to the benefit of the mortgage. He has not done so; he has bargained by a separate instrument for an indemnity which is perfectly distinct. This payment of interest was perfectly voluntary, but that does not affect the deed of indemnity, which is precise and entitles him to what he has paid, whether he was compelled to pay or not. If a surety pay off the mortgage, he is entitled to the benefit of all the securities. But here the plaintiff has contracted with the mortgagor, for whom he is surety, that he should receive a particular species of indemnity if he pay off any part of the principal or interest. That indemnity he is entitled to, and not to the benefit of the mortgage paid off."

Where a surety who is liable for the whole or part of another's debt has paid the whole of what he is liable for, and has expressly waived in the contract of suretyship his right to stand in the place of the creditor to that extent against the estate of the bankrupt debtor (j), the circumstance of the surety having received from the principal debtor a counter-security, makes no difference in the respective rights of the parties. This was decided in the recent case of *The Midland Banking Company* v. *Chambers* (k.) There, a bank permitted a customer to *overdraw his account upon hav- [*303] ing a guarantee from a surety to the extent of 300l., which guarantee provided that all dividends, compositions and payments received on account of the customer should be applied as payments in gross, and that the guarantee should apply to and secure any ultimate balance that should remain due to the bank. The customer gave the surety a mortgage on part of his estate by way of indemnity. Afterwards the customer compounded with his creditors by a deed which provided for the administration of the assets as in bankruptcy. His banking account was overdrawn 410l. The mortgage was realized, and the surety paid the bank the 300l. secured by it. It was held by the Lords Justices (affirming the decree of *Malins*, V.-C.), that the bank was not, as contended by the trustees of the composition deed, restricted to proof for the balance of 110l., but was entitled to receive dividends on the whole 410l.,

---

(j) As to this right, see *ante*, p. 298, and see *The Midland Banking Co.*, *Ex parte, In re Sellers*, 38 L. T. 395; *Ex parte Hope*, 3 M., D. & D. 720; *Midland Banking Co.* v. *Chambers*, L. R., 4 Ch. App. 398.

(k) L. R., 4 Ch. App. 398. See also *Ex parte Hope*, 3 M., D. & D. 720.

not receiving in the whole, including the 300*l.*, more than 20*s.* in the pound.

In a continuing limited guarantee there was a proviso, that, if the creditors received a dividend from any estate of the principal debtor, it should not be taken in discharge of the guarantee, but that the creditors should be entitled to recover on the guarantee to the full extent of the limit notwithstanding. On the bankruptcy of the principal debtor the creditors proved, and, before receiving any dividend, obtained payment of the sureties to the extent of the limit. It was held that the sureties were *not* entitled to stand in the place of the creditors as to so much of their proof as was equal to their payment (*l*).

Right of surety to the benefit of dividends received on principal debtor's bankruptcy often a nice question of construction of instrument of guarantee.

The right of the surety to reduce his liability, by deducting a rateable proportion of dividends paid under the bankruptcy of the principal debtor, may not only be wholly lost by reason of its express exclusion contained in some clause of the instrument of guarantee, [*304] but it is *often a nice question of construction whether, having regard to the form of the guarantee, this right of the surety can be exercised, in cases where the debt guaranteed exceeds the sum to which the liability of the surety is expressly limited, until the whole of the debt has been liquidated. The determination of this question would appear to depend upon whether the intention was to guarantee the whole debt, with a limitation on the liability of the surety, or to guarantee a part of the debt only (*m*). In the former case, the surety's right to stand in the place of the creditor remains in abeyance until satisfaction of the whole debt (*n*); while, in the latter case, his right can be exercised the moment the limit of his guarantee has been reached, and he has been obliged to make payments thereunder (*o*). To which class of guarantees a particular instrument belongs is determined by principles which have been explained on an earlier page of this work (*p*).

Previous course of dealing between parties

It would seem that a course of dealing between the parties, previous to the bankruptcy of the principal debtor, will not give rise to the presumption that the

(*l*) *Ex parte Miles*, De G. 623.
(*m*) *Ellis* v. *Emmanuel*, 1 Ex. Div. 157.
(*n*) *Ellis* v. *Emmanuel, ubi supra; Hobson* v. *Bass*, L. R., 6 Ch. App. 792; *Bardwell* v. *Lydall*, 7 Bing. 489.
(*o*) See *Gray* v. *Seckham*, L. R., 7 Ch. App. 680.
(*p*) *Ante*, pp. 205, 206.

surety has abandoned to the creditor his right of proof against the estate of the principal debtor (q).

III. The Rights of the Surety against the Co-sureties.

The rights of a surety against his co-sureties arise when he has been compelled to pay under the guarantee. And the principal rights which he then becomes entitled to are, the right of contribution from his co-sureties, and the right to the benefit of any securities which they may possess.

*The right of the creditor to contribution [*305] from his co-sureties arises thus.

It often happens that where there are more sureties than one for the *same* principal debtor, the creditor makes one surety pay the *whole* debt, or more than his just share or proportion of such debt. Whenever this occurs, the surety who has thus been made to pay has a right to recover from his co-sureties their respective shares of the sum which he has paid to the common creditor (r).

The Roman civil law never recognized the right of contribution among sureties (*fidejussores*) as it exists in England, and in most, if not all, European states. This is the more remarkable, because the *lex Apuleia* (a. c. 102) provided that in the case of *sponsores* and *fidepromissores* (s), if any one of them paid more than his share, he should have an action against the others for that which he had paid in excess. However, the *fidejussor* (surety), who was first sued by the creditor, though he had no remedy in his own right, against his

Side notes: may indicate an intention by surety to abandon right of proof against principal debtor's estate. III. Rights of surety against co-sureties. To obtain contribution from his co-sureties. How this right arises. Roman civil law did not recognize this right.

(q) Ex parte Johnson, 3 De G., M. & G. 218.
(r) Cowell v. Edwards, 2 B. & P. 268; Dering v. Winchelsea, 2 B. & P. 270; Kemp v. Finden, 12 M. & W. 421; Reynolds v. Wheeler, 10 C. B., N. S. 561; 30 L. J., C. P. 350; Morgan v. Seymour, 1 Ch. Ca. 64; Fleetwood v. Charnock, Nelson, C. R. 10; Davies v. Humphreys, 6 M. & W. 153, 167, Ex parte Snowdon, In re Snowdon, 17 Ch. Div. 44; 50 L. J., Ch. 540; 44 L. T. 830; 29 W. R. 654; Batard v. Hawes, 2 E. & B. 287; Brown v. Lee, 6 B. & C. 697; Ex parte Gifford, 6 Ves. 805; Dunn v. Slee, 1 Moore, 2; Turner v. Davies, 2 Esp. 479; Craythorne v. Swinburne, 14 Ves. 164; and see Macdonald v. Whitfield, 8 App. Cas. 733.
(s) Sponsores and fidepromissores differed in some particulars from fidejussores (sureties). Thus the former could not be attached to any but verbal obligations, whereas the latter could be attached to any obligation, whether contracted re, verbis, literis or consensu. Again, while the obligation of the fidejussor bound the heir, that of the sponsor and fidepromissor did not do so. So, too, the latter were freed from liability after two years by the lex Furia, while the former was bound in perpetuity. See, further, the Commentaries of Gaius, by Abdy and Walker, Book iii., 115, 126.

co-sureties, had, what was termed, the *beneficium ceden-darum actionum*, which enabled him, before paying the [*306] *creditor, to compel the latter to assign over to him all his rights of action againt the principal debtor and the co-sureties (*t*). Moreover, a rescript of the Emperor Hadrian gave to the *fidejussor* (surety), against whom the creditor demanded payment in full, the *beneficium divisionis* (*u*), that is to say, the right of forcing the creditor to divide his demand amongst all those *fidejussores* (sureties) who were solvent at the time of the *litis contestatio* (*x*). Again, as already pointed out (*y*), the creditor might have been compelled by the sureties to sue the principal debtor before having recourse to any of them. It cannot, therefore, be considered that the Roman civil law was harsh in its treatment of sureties.

From what date right of contribution recognized in England and by chancery courts. In *England*, the right of contribution among sureties seems to have been recognized by the courts of chancery, at all events from the time of Elizabeth (*z*). According to Lord *Eldon* (*a*), it existed in equity from the very earliest times. The courts of common law, however, did not anciently enforce contribution among sureties, and in *Offley and Johnson's Case* (*b*), it was held, that, at *common law*, one surety has no right to contribution from a co-surety.

Courts of common law eventually enforced contribution. It seems, however, that the right of contribution has always existed by the custom of London (*c*), and all the courts of common law eventually assumed jurisdiction in cases of contribution; but the courts of equity did not on that account abdicate their *original* jurisdiction (*d*). And [*307] even when *courts of law and equity alike recognized the right of contribution amongst sureties,

But jurisdiction in equity was more convenient and extensive. yet the jurisdiction in equity was, before the Judicature Acts, both more *convenient* and more *extensive* than that of the courts of common law. It was more *convenient*, because, where the sureties were numerous, and bound by separate instruments, by a single suit in

---

(*t*) Dig. xlvi. 1, 17. See also Mackeldeii Systema Juris Romani, § 438.
(*u*) Inst. 3, 20, par. 4.
(*x*) The ceremony by which litigants submitted the matter in dispute between them to the decision of the judge.
(*y*) *Ante*, p. 187.
(*z*) 1 Spence, Eq. Jur. of the Court of Chancery.
(*a*) In *Underhill* v. *Horwood*, 10 Ves. 208.
(*b*) 3 Leon. 166. See also observations of *Buller*, J., in *Toussaint* v. *Martinnant*, 2 T. R. 100, 105; and of *Tindal*, C. J., in *Edgar* v. *Knapp*, 6 Scott, N. R. 707, 713.
(*c*) *Layer* v. *Nelson*, 1 Vern. 456.
(*d*) *Wright* v. *Hunter*, 5 Ves. 794.

equity, to which all the sureties were made defendants, it was possible to achieve that, which, at common law, could only be attained by bringing separate actions against the different sureties for their respective contributions. It was more *extensive*, because, at common law, the proportion of the debt which each surety was liable to contribute was always regulated by the number of sureties originally liable, including any that were insolvent (e). But, in equity, the proportion of each surety's contribution was regulated by the number of solvent sureties.

These distinctions between law and equity, which formerly prevailed, are no longer of any practical importance, it having been provided by the Judicature Act, 1873, that where there is any conflict or variance between the rules of equity and those of the common law, with reference to the same matter, the rules of equity shall prevail (f). Moreover, in cases where no rule of practice is laid down by the new orders, and there is a variance in the old practice of the chancery and common law courts, that practice is to prevail which is considered by the court to be most convenient (g). *[Former distinctions between law and equity in regard to contribution abrogated by Judicature Act.]*

The doctrine of contribution, as has been remarked before, originally was only a doctrine of the courts of equity, and, as an equitable doctrine, it is not founded *in contract*, but is the result of *general* [*308] *equity*, on the ground of equality of burden and benefit (h). *[Foundation of doctrine of contribution.]*

The courts of law, however, having borrowed the equitable doctrine as to enforcing contribution amongst sureties, professed to give relief on the ground of implied *assumpsit*. The real principal, however, on which the right depends is, that it is an equitable right. It has long been settled, said Lord *Eldon*, in *Craythorne* v. *Swinburne* (i), "That if there are co-sureties by the same instrument, and the creditor calls upon either of them to pay the principal debt, *or any part of it*, the *[It is an equitable right.]*

(e) See *Brown* v. *Lee*, 6 B. & C. 699 ; *Cowell* v. *Edwards*, 2 B. & P. 265; *Dallas* v. *Walls*, 29 L. T. 599 ; *Batard* v. *Hawes*, 2 E. & B. 287, 291.
(f) 36 & 37 Vict. c. 66, s. 25 (11); and see White & Tudor's L. C. in Eq., 5th ed. p. 113.
(g) *Newbiggin-by-the-Sea Gas Co.* v. *Armstrong*, 13 Ch. Div. 310.
(h) *Dering* v. *Winchelsea*, 2 B. & P. 270. Per Lord *Redesdale*, in *Stirling* v. *Forrister*, 3 Bligh, 575, 590; *Craythorne* v. *Swinburne*, 14 Ves. 164.
(i) 14 Ves. 164; and see also *Macdonald* v. *Whitfield*, 8 App. Cas. 733.

surety has a right in this court, either upon a principle of equity or upon contract, to call upon his co-surety for contribution, and I think, that right is properly enough stated, as depending rather upon a principle of equity than upon contract, unless in this sense, that the principle of equity being in its operation established, a contract may be inferred upon the implied knowledge of that principle by all persons, and it must be upon such a ground of implied *assumpsit*, that in modern times courts of law have assumed a jurisdiction upon this subject,—a jurisdiction convenient enough in a case simple and uncomplicated, but attended with great difficulty where the sureties are numerous, especially since it has been held, that separate actions may be brought against the different sureties for their respective proportions."

When the right of contribution arises. The existence of the right of contribution being thus clearly established, and the principal on which it rests pointed out, it next remains to consider *when* such right arises. Now, we have already seen (k), that, in the case of principal and surety, the latter is entitled to sue the former for money paid to his use the moment he has [*309] *paid *anything* in ease of the principal debtor.

As soon as surety has paid more than his share of common debt. But the right of one surety to sue the other for contribution does not arise until the former has paid *more than his proportion or share of the common debt, i. e., more than he can ever be called upon to pay;* for, till then, it is not clear that he ever will be entitled to demand anything from his co-sureties, and, until he has a right to make this demand, he has no equity to receive a contribution, and, consequently, no right of action, since the right of action is founded on the equity to receive it (l). The co-surety cannot know what is the debt due to him by his co-surety until he knows what has been done in respect of the residue of the debt for which he is equally liable (m). Moreover, until the surety has paid more than his proportion of the guaranteed debt, his right of contribution does not arise, even though the co-surety has not been required by the creditor to pay anything, provided that the co-surety has not been released by the creditor (n).

(k) *Ante*, p. 280.
(l) *Ex parte Gifford*, 2 B. & P. 269; *Davies* v. *Humphreys*, 6 M. & W. 163, where a dubious expression in *Craythorne* v. *Swinburne*, 14 Ves. 164, is explained; and see *Ex parte Snowdon, In re Snowdon*, 17 Ch. Div. 44; 50 L. J., Ch. 540; 44 L. T. 830; 29 W. R. 654.
(m) *Ex parte Snowdon, In re Snowdon*, 17 Ch. Div. 44, 47; 50 L. J., Ch. 540; 44 L. T. 830; 29 W. R. 654.
(n) *Ib.*

The practical advantage of this rule is considerable, as it would tend to multiplicity of actions and great inconvenience if each surety might sue all the others for a rateable proportion of what he had paid, the instant he had paid any part of the debt (o).

Though, however, the right of contribution does not arise until the surety has paid more than his proportionate share of the common debt, yet it *seems* that when a surety is called upon to pay a part of the whole debt for which he is liable he may bring an action against his co-sureties to compel them to contribute towards the payment of the debt due to the creditor, just as he would be entitled to call on them for contribution if he *had been sued by the creditor, asking [*310] that he should be indemnified by his co sureties against paying the whole debt or whatever risk he ran (p). **But, *semble*, before paying more than his share of common debt surety may by action compel co-sureties to contribute towards payment of the debt to the creditor.**

A payment made by a surety on the default of the principal debtor cannot, under any circumstances, be regarded as a payment made *voluntarily* (q); though a surety has no right to sue his co-surety for contribution unless the sum paid by him, and in respect of which he sues, is his *own* money (r). Therefore, to entitle the surety to sue the co-sureties for contribution, he need not show that he abstained from paying the creditor until compelled or requested by the latter to do so (s). **Payment made by surety of common debt is not a voluntary payment.**

It seems that one of several co-sureties may recover contribution from the others in an action without proving the insolvency of the principal and the other sureties (t). **Contribution may be recovered without proving insolvency of principal**

The persons by and against whom the right to contribution—assuming it to exist—may be enforced, must next be considered. Now, as to this, it is well settled that a surety is entitled to enforce contribution, whether he knew or not at the time he became surety that he was co-surety with others (u); for, though one person becomes a surety without the knowledge of the others, the right of contribution exists (x). **principal debtor or of other co-sureties. Persons by and against whom contribution may be enforced.**

(o) Per *Parke*, B., in *Davies* v. *Humphreys*, 6 M. & W. 153.

(p) Per *James*, L. J., in *Ex parte Snowdon, In re Snowdon*, 17 Ch. Div. at p. 47.

(q) *Pitt* v. *Purssord*, 8 M. & W. 538.

(r) *Gopel* v. *Swindon*, 1 D. & L. 888; 13 L. J., Q. B. 113.

(s) *Pitt* v. *Purssord, ubi supra*.

(t) *Cowell* v. *Edwards*, 2 B. & P. 268; and see *Lawson* v. *Wright*, 1 Cox, Ch. Cas. 275.

(u) *Craythorne* v. *Swinburne*, 14 Ves. 160, 163; *Whiting* v. *Burke*, L. R., 10 Eq. 539; L. R., 6 Ch. App. 342.

(x) 14 Ves. 165.

In *Whiting* v. *Burke* (y), the following were the facts:—A bond was executed by a principal debtor and two sureties, which provided that the sureties should not be discharged by any new arrangement between the creditor and the principal. One of the sureties compounded with his creditors, and by the terms of the [*311] *bond the moneys secured became immediately payable. After this the plaintiff signed a separate undertaking to become liable for the whole amount, and, upon the principal becoming insolvent, the creditor sued the plaintiff and obtained payment of the amount due. The plaintiff sought to enforce contribution against the solvent surety in the original bond, and it was held that the plaintiff was entitled to such contribution.

Right of contribution where the sureties bound jointly, or jointly and severally. The right of contribution also exists whether the sureties be bound jointly, or jointly and severally (z). It exists also among sureties for the *same* principal and the *same* engagement, whether they are bound by the *same* instrument or by *different* instruments (a). However, where sureties are bound by *different* instruments for equal portions of a debt due from the same principal, and the suretyship of each is a separate and distinct transaction, there is no right of contribution between them (b). Where, too, sureties are bound by separate deeds and for *unequal* sums, no one can be called upon to contribute beyond the sum to which he is liable under his own deed (c).

No contribution where each surety bound for a given portion of one sum. So, again, if it be arranged by contract (which it may be) that each surety shall be answerable only for a *given portion* of one sum of money, in such case there is no right of contribution among the co-sureties (d). In short, "where the same default of the principal renders all the co-sureties responsible, all are to contribute ; and then the law superadds that which is not only the principle, but the equitable mode of applying the principle, that they should all contribute *equally, if each is a surety to an equal amount*, and if not equally, [*312] *then proportionably to the amount for which each is a surety" (e).

(y) *Ubi supra.*
(z) Per Lord *Eldon*, in *Underhill* v. *Horwood*, 10 Ves. 208.
(a) *Mayhew* v. *Crickett*, 2 Swanst. 185 ; *Craythorne* v. *Swinburne*, 14 Ves. 160, 169, 170 ; *Pendlebury* v. *Walker*, 4 Y. & C. 424; *Swain* v. *Wall*, 1 Ch. Rep. 80 ; *Dallas* v. *Walls*, 29 L. T. R. 599.
(b) *Coope* v. *Twyman*, 1 T. & Russ. 426.
(c) See *Craythorne* v. *Swinburne*, 14 Ves. 160 ; *Dering* v. *Winchelsea*, 2 B. & P. 270.
(d) *Pendlebury* v. *Walker*, 4 Y. & C. 424.
(e) Per *Alderson*, B., in *Pendlebury* v. *Walker*, 4 Y. & C. 424, 441 ; and see *Arcedeckne* v. *Howard*, 45 L. J., Ch. 622.

In case of the death of one of several co-sureties, a Former distinctions between law and equity as to right of contribution where one of several co-sureties died. surety, who had been compelled to pay the whole debt, could always have recovered in equity the proportionate amount payable by the deceased solvent surety from his representative (*f*). But as the liability at law of a co-surety to one who had paid the entire debt was to contribute an aliquot part, according to the number of persons *originally* liable, without reference to the number liable at law at the time of payment, it followed that the death of one of the co-sureties did not increase the amount of contribution payable by the rest (*g*), though in such a case, it would seem that an action at law might have been maintained for contribution against the representative of the deceased surety (*h*). These distinctions have been swept away by the Judicature Act, 1873, which, as already stated, provides that where there is any conflict and variance between the rules of law and equity with reference to the same matter, the rules of equity shall prevail (*i*). These distinctions abrogated by Judicature Act.

The right of a surety to call for contribution can, however, only be enforced against persons who are strictly and really co sureties with him. It does not exist against a surety for a surety. Such a person cannot be called upon to contribute. This was decided in *Craythorne* v. *Swinburne* (*j*). There A. and B. became sureties for C. and D. E., without the privity of A. and B., gave a distinct collateral security, limited to *default of payment by the principal and the* [*313] *other surety.* It was held that E. was not a co-surety, and therefore could not be made to contribute. In fact, E. was not liable in the *second* instance at all, but only in the *third* instance. Therefore E. could not be affected by the doctrine of contribution among sureties, which only arises where sureties are *equally* liable to the creditor. Right of contribution can only be enforced against persons who really are co-sureties. Surety for a surety not liable to contribute.

A person who becomes surety for a third person jointly with another surety, and at the latter's request, cannot be compelled by the latter to contribute (*k*). Person becoming surety at co-surety's request not

Where a defendant signed a guarantee upon a con-

(*f*) *Primrose* v. *Bromley*, 1 Atk. 89 ; *Simpson* v. *Vaughan*, 2 Atk. 37.

(*g*) *Batard* v. *Hawes*, 2 E. & B. 287.

(*h*) *Prior* v. *Hembrow*, 8 M. & W. 873 ; *Batard* v. *Hawes*; *supra*.

(*i*) 36 & 37 Vict. c. 66, s. 25, sub-s. 11, and see Supreme Court Rules, 1883, Ord. XVI., and Daniell's Chanc. Prac., 6th ed. p. 252.

(*j*) 14 Ves. 160. See also per Lord *Plunket*, in *Hartley* v. *O' Flaherty*, L. & G. (Ir. Ch.), 208, 217.

(*k*) *Turner* v. *Davies*, 2 Esp. 479.

liable to contribute.

Nor person becoming surety on condition of another signing as co-surety, which condition has not been fulfilled.

dition, orally agreed to, that M. should also sign as a co-surety, and M. did not sign, and subsequently, and without notice of that condition, the guarantee was signed by the plaintiff, who, having been obliged, upon the default of the principal debtor, to pay the whole debt, sought to recover contribution from the defendant, it was held by the Court of Appeal *in Ireland* (reversing the decision of the Common Pleas) that the non-performance of the condition was a good defence to the action (*l*).

How right of contribution enforced.

The mode of enforcing the right of contribution by co-sureties is either by action or (should a co-surety unfortunately have become bankrupt) by proceedings in bankruptcy against him. Particulars of demand will be required from a surety claiming payment of a definite sum by way of contribution from a co-surety, and not merely asking for an account (*m*).

Defendant can claim contribution from co-surety by means of third party notice under Judicature Rules.

In addition to the remedy afforded by means of an action against a co-surety for the recovery of contribution, a surety against whom an action has been brought upon his guarantee may assert his right to contribution in the mode indicated by Ord. XVI. of the Judicature Rules. Rule 48 of this Order provides that a defend- [*314] ant claiming contribution or indemnity *over against any other person may obtain leave from a judge to give notice to such other person, who, if desirous of disputing the plaintiff's claim, may appear as a party to the action (*n*). Should the party upon whom the notice is served elect not to appear, it is provided by Rule 49 of the same order, that he shall be deemed to admit the validity of the judgment obtained against the defendant, whether obtained by consent or otherwise, and his own liability to contribute or indemnify, as the case may be, to the extent claimed in the third party notice. In giving leave to a defendant to serve notice of claim for contribution or indemnity on a third party, the court will not consider whether the claim is a valid one, but only whether the claim is *bona fide*, and whether, if established, it will result in contribution or indemnity (*o*).

(*l*) *Barry* v. *Moroney*, 8 Ir. C. L. R. 554.
(*m*) *Blackie* v. *Osmaston*, 28 Ch. Div. (C. A.), 119.
(*n*) For form of third party notice by a surety claiming contribution against a co-surety, see Appendix B., Form No. 1 of Judicature Rules. The court has no power to give a third party, who has been served with a third party notice, leave to file a counterclaim against the original plaintiff. *Eden* v. *Weardale Iron & Coal Co.*, 28 Ch. Div. (C. A.) 333.
(*o*) *Carshore* v. *N. E. Rail.Co.*, 29 Ch. Div. 344, C. A.

In the next place, it is important to consider *what* the surety seeking contribution can recover from his co-sureties.

As a general rule, a surety, who defends an action brought for money deficient in the accounts of his principal, cannot claim contribution from his co-sureties, for the costs of the action, unless he was authorized by them to defend (*p*).

But where the plaintiff and defendant had executed, as sureties, a warrant of attorney, given as a collateral security for a sum of money advanced on mortgage to the principals, and, on default being made by the principals, judgment was entered up on the warrant of *attorney and execution issued against the [*315] plaintiff, it was held, that he was entitled to recover from the defendant as his co-surety a moiety of the costs of such execution (*q*).

Another general rule is this: in his claim for contribution from his co-sureties the surety must allow for all that he may have received either from the principal debtor or by a counter-security (*r*).

As already mentioned (*s*) in equity, the amount of contribution was regulated by the number of *solvent* sureties, though at law a different rule prevailed (*t*). An early case upon this point is that of *Peter* v. *Rich* (*u*); there the plaintiff, the defendant, and a third person were joint sureties for the payment of purchase money to *Lord Russell;* the plaintiff and the defendant had each paid their proportionate share, but, the third surety being insolvent, the plaintiff paid his share in addition. It was ordered by the court of equity, that such payment ought to be equally paid and borne by the plaintiff and defendant. So, also, in *Hitchman* v.

What can be recovered by way of contribution.

Costs of action defended by surety cannot, as a rule, be recovered.

Surety claiming contribution must give credit for sums received by him.

In equity amount recoverable by way of contribution was always regulated by number of solvent sureties.

(*p*) *Knight* v. *Hughes*, 1 Mood. & Malk., N. P. C. R. 247; *S. C.*, 3 C. &. P. 467. See also *Roach* v. *Thompson*, 1 Mood. & Malk., N. P. C. R. 487; and *Gillett* v. *Rippon*, 1 Mood. & Malk., N. P. C. R 403.

(*q*)*Kemp* v. *Finden*, 12 M. & W. 421.

(*r*) *Knight* v. *Hughes*, 1 Moo. & Malk., N. P. C. R. 247; *S. C.*, 3 C. & P. 467; *Steel* v. *Dixon*, 17 Ch. Div. 825; 50 L. J., Ch. 591; 45 L. T. 142; 29 W. R. 735 ; *In re Arcedeckne, Atkins* v. *Arcedeckne*, 24 Ch. Div. 709; 53 L. J., Ch. 102; 48 L. T. 725.

(*s*) *Ante*, p. 307.

(*t*) *Ib.*

(*u*) 1 Ch. Ca. 34. But see *Swain* v. *Wall*, Com. Dig. Chancery, 4 D. 6, contradicting this, and for observations upon last-named case, see Fell's Law of Mercantile Guarantees, 2nd ed., p. 212. See also, further, *Hole* v. *Harrison*, 1 Cas. in Ch. 246; and *Mayor of Berwick-upon-Tweed* v. *Murray*, 7 De G., M. & G. 497.

Stewart (*v*), it was decided, that when one of several sureties has paid the principal debt, and some of the co-sureties are insolvent, he is entitled in equity, as against the solvent sureties, to be repaid their numerical shares of what he has paid, with interest (*x*) from the [*316] time of payment, although the *instrument does not contain any express indemnity so as to carry interest as on a specialty. And it was there further held, that the insolvent sureties must pay their own costs of being brought before the court to the final hearing of the cause. "It appears to me," said Vice-Chancellor Kindersley, in this case, "that it is just, that when several persons concur in being sureties for a principal debtor, whatever view a court of law may take, on which I give no opinion, a court of equity will take this view; that there is among them all an implied agreement to indemnify each other; each agrees that, as among them, he will bear his aliquot part of the debt, and on that principal it is, I think, that *Lawson* v. *Wright* (*y*) must have been decided; finding that decision and finding it founded on what I think a sound equity, and no decision against it, I cannot do better than to follow it."

Who should be made parties to action for contribution. In an action by a surety for contribution the principal and co-sureties or their personal representatives, should, although they may have become *insolvent*, be made parties; unless the fact of their insolvency is clearly proved or admitted, and even in that case it seems that the plaintiff has his election whether he will not bring the insolvent co-obligor or his representative before the court (*z*).

Contribution may be enforced against bankrupt co-surety. Should one of the co-sureties have become bankrupt, the surety requiring contribution will have to seek it not at common law, or in equity, but in bankruptcy. And it therefore is of importance to see what his rights, in such a case, will be.

Surety cannot petition in bank- [*317] *As has already been stated (*a*), the right to contribution does not arise until a surety has paid more than his share of the common debt. Consequently, a surety

---

(*v*) 2 Drew. 271; and see *Ex parte Bishop, In re Fox, Walker & Co.*, 15 Ch. Div. 400; *Dallas* v. *Walls*, 29 L. T. R. 599.

(*x*) It was formerly held in equity that a surety could not claim interest on the money paid by him, or on any part thereof. See *Onge* v. *Truelock*, 2 Mollny, 44; *Bell* v. *Free*, 1 Swanst. 90; but there is no doubt now that it is recoverable. See *Swain* v. *Wall*, 1 Ch. Rep. 81; *Lawson* v. *Wright*. 1 Cox, Ch. Cas. 275, 277; *Petre* v. *Duncombe*, 15 Jur. 86; 20 L. J., N. S. (Q. B.), 221; *In re Swan's Estate*, 4 Ir. Rep., Eq. 209.

(*y*) 1 Cox, Ch. Cas. 275.

(*z*) Daniell's Chanc. Prac., 6th ed., Vol. I., p. 252.

(*a*) *Ante*, pp. 308, 309.

RIGHTS OF THE SURETY.

who has only paid his proportion of the common debt has no debt capable of supporting a petition in bankruptcy against his co-surety (b). For, "until the whole debt has been paid by one surety, or so much of it as to make it clear that, as between himself and his co-sureties, he has paid all that he ever can be called upon to pay, there can be no equitable debt from them to him in respect of it. There is nothing ascertained as a debt which would give him a right to proceed against his co-sureties" (c).

If the amount has been paid before bankruptcy, the surety always could, and still may, prove for it in the usual way.

A surety, however, who was compelled to pay the debt of the principal debtor *after* the bankruptcy of a co-surety, could not prove under the 52nd section of 6 Geo. 4, c. 16, which provided, that sureties and persons liable for the debts of bankrupts might prove *after* having paid such debts as therein mentioned. In *Wallis* v. *Swinburne* (d), which is a decision upon this enactment, *Parke*, B., in giving judgment, observed, that it had been properly admitted by the counsel for the defendant (the bankrupt co-surety), that the plaintiff was not a surety for the debt of the bankrupt, but that it had been contended that, though not a surety, he was a *person liable* for the bankrupt's debt by reason of the instrument (a promissory note), on which he as well as the bankrupt was indebted to the creditors, having become due before the bankruptcy. After reviewing the various authorities, he went on to say, that no case *had extended the construction of the statute so [*318] as to include persons who were co-sureties for a debt due, not from the bankrupt, but from a third person. That it was not correct to say that one co-surety was liable for the debt of another at the time of the bankruptcy. "The bankrupt had not at that time engaged with his co-surety to provide any part of the money, but the third party, the principal, had engaged with both so to do, and it is then quite a contingency whether the co-surety will be called on by the creditor to pay more than his own share, and until then he has no claim upon the bankrupt" (e). The language of the 177th

Marginal notes:
ruptcy against co-surety until he has paid more than his share of common debt.

Proof in respect of payments made *before* the bankruptcy.

Proof in respect of payments made *after* the bankruptcy.

(b) *Ex parte Snowdon, In re Snowdon*, 17 Ch. Div. 44; 50 L. J., Ch. 540; 44 L. T., 830; 29 W. R. 654.
(c) *Ib.*, per *James*, L. J.
(d) 1 Exch. 203.
(e) See also *Clements* v. *Langley*, 2 Nev. & Mann., and the judgment of *Denman*, C. J., at p. 277.

section of the Bankruptcy Act, 1849 (*f*), is very similar
to that of the 52nd section of 6 Geo. 4, c. 16. Accordingly, in *Adkins* v. *Farrington* (*g*), where a surety, who
had paid more than his share of the common debt after
the bankruptcy of his co-surety, commenced an action
against him (after he had obtained his certificate) to
recover contribution, it was admitted in the argument
that *Wallis* v. *Swinburne* (*h*), though a decision on the
52nd section of 6 Geo. 4, c. 16, was an authority applicable to the 177th section of 12 & 13 Vict. c. 106 (*i*). It
was, however, held that, as the right of contribution
actually accrued before the expiration of six months
after the filing of the petition by the bankrupt co-
surety, it was proveable " as a liability to pay money
on a contingency " within the 178th section of 12 & 13
Vict. c. 106, and consequently, that the bankruptcy
and certificate of the defendant were an answer to the
action.

In the case of *Cary* v. *Dawson* (*k*) the facts were as
follows:—In January, 1869, a company lent a sum in
[*319] *consols to be deposited by the promoters of a
bill then before parliament ; and the two plaintiffs, the
defendant, and three others, entered into an undertaking with the company that if the bill was thrown out
the consols should be returned, and if it passed, an
equal amount of stock should be transferred to the
company, and that a sum in the nature of interest on
the value of the consols at the time they were lent,
from the end of six months to the date of the transfer,
should be paid to the company. In April, 1866, the
defendant was adjudged bankrupt, and in July he obtained his order of discharge. In August the bill was
passed, but the consols were not transferred to the company till May, 1867, and the plaintiffs were compelled,
in June, 1867, to pay, under the undertaking, 500*l.* and
the interest. An action was then brought to recover
contribution from the defendant of one-sixth of the
500*l.*; the defendant pleaded his discharge in bankruptcy. It was *held*, that, as the liability under the
undertaking depended on an uncertain event, viz., the
date at which the consols should be transferred, the
amount of liability was not capable of being ascertained,

(*f*) 12 & 13 Vict. c. 106.
(*g*) 5 H. & N. 586.
(*h*) *Supra.*
(*i*) And also, it is submitted, to the 173d section of the same
act.
(*k*) L. R., 4 Q. B. 568; 38 L. J., N. S. (Q. B.) 300.

and the plaintiff's claim was, therefore, not a debt provable under 12 & 13 Vict. c. 106, s. 178, nor under 24 & 25 Vict. c. 134, s. 154, and the defendant was, therefore, not discharged.

"Whether a proof can be made under the 37th section of the Bankruptcy Act, 1883, in respect of a contingent right of contribution as between co-sureties is a question which will have to be determined when it arises. But it is certainly very difficult to conceive on what principle the amount of such a proof could be calculated. The liability would seem to be incapable of being fairly estimated within the meaning of the above section" (l). *Whether under B. A. 1883, proof can be made in respect of contingent right of contribution.*

The right to contribution cannot be enforced where *circumstances are proved in which it would be [*320] fraudulent to insist upon it (m). But where it is sought to resist contribution on the ground that the plaintiff has been guilty of fraudulent concealment, it should be remembered that one surety is certainly not under any larger obligation in this respect to his co-surety, than the creditor is under to both of them (n). *Right of contribution not enforceable when fraudulent to insist upon it.* B. and C. became co sureties for an advance to A. of 500l., of which 125l. was, in pursuance of a previous agreement, advanced by A. to C. without B.'s knowledge ; afterwards, A. having become bankrupt and absconded, B. and C. were called upon to pay the balance of the advance of 500l. B. then brought an action against C. claiming that C. should, as between them, be treated as principal debtor to the extent of 125l., and claiming the benefit of all securities given to him. It was held that the action must be dismissed, the arrangement between A. and C. not prejudicially affecting B.'s position and no material fact having been concealed from him (o).

The right of a surety to contribution from his co-sureties may, like other rights, be lost or destroyed in various ways. *How right of contribution may be lost, &c.*

After the lapse of six years, the right will be barred by the Statute of Limitations. But, as we have seen in a previous page, the right to contribution does not arise until the surety has paid *more* than his share. And as his right of action does not vest till then, it follows that the Statute of Limitations does not begin to *Statute of Limitations will bar it.*

(l) Robson's Law of Bankruptcy, 5th ed. p. 314.
(m) Per *Kay*, J., in *Mackreth* v. *Walmesley*, 51 L. T. 19; 32 W. R. 819.
(n) *Ib.*
(o) *Ib.*

run till the surety has paid more than his proper amount (p.) If, therefore, a surety, more than six years before action brought, had paid a portion of the debt due from a principal debtor, and the principal has paid the residue within six years, the Statute of [*321] *Limitations will not run from the payment by the surety, but from the payment of the residue by the principal; for until the latter date it does not appear that the surety has paid more than his share (q).

The surety's right of action for contribution after he has paid, is not lost or affected by the circumstance that the creditor may have given him (the surety) time for payment (r).

Whether right of contribution affected by release of one of several co-sureties, It seems never to have been decided in England whether a surety deprives himself of his right of action against the other co-sureties by releasing one of several co-sureties ·with him. However, from the American case of Fletcher v. Grover (s), it would seem that a discharge of one surety discharges the other sureties for such proportion only of the debt as, upon a payment of the whole debt, they would be entitled to have recourse to him for.

or by co-surety's discharge of principal debtor. Whether a surety who discharges the principal debtor can afterwards recover contribution from his co-surety has not yet been decided though the point has been raised (t).

Right of surety to benefit of securities held by co-surety. In addition to the right of contribution from his co-sureties which a surety who has paid the whole debt possesses (and which we have now discussed fully), such a surety has another important right ; for it is laid down that "sureties are not only entitled to contribution from each other for moneys paid in discharge of their joint liabilities for the principal, but they are also entitled to the benefit of all securities which have been taken by any one of them to indemnify himself against such liabilities" (u).

Co-surety is bound to bring into hotchpot whatever he receives from counter security obtained by him from principal debtor. It has recently been decided that a surety who has obtained from the principal debtor a counter security [*322] *for the liability which he has undertaken, is bound to bring into hotchpot, for the benefit of his co-sureties, whatever he receives from that source, even though he consented to be a surety only upon the terms of having such security, and the co-sureties were, when

(p) Per Parke, B., in Davies v. Humphreys, 6 M. & W. 153.
(q) Per Parke, B., in Davies v. Humphreys, ubi supra.
(r) Dunn v. Slee, 1 Moore, 2.
(s) 11 N. Hamp. R. 368.
(t) Vorley v. Barrett, 1 C. B., N. S. 225 ; 26 L. J., C. P. 1.
(u) 1 Story, Eq. Jurisprudence, par. 499 ; and see Done v. Whalley, 2 Ex. 198 ; 17 L. J., Ex. 225 ; 12 Jur. 338.

they entered into the contract of suretyship, ignorant of his agreement for security (x). So, where several persons joined in a promissory note as sureties for C., the payee of the note effecting policies on the life of C., and afterwards one of the co-sureties paid, with the assistance of his father E., the said promissory note, whereupon the policies were assigned to E. who, on C.'s death, received the amount due under them from the insurance office, it was held that the co-surety and his father must be treated as one person, and that the claim for contribution against a deceased co-surety's estate would be allowed only after the moneys received under the policies had been brought into account as a set-off (y).

(x) *Steel* v. *Dixon*, 17 Ch. Div. 825 ; 50 L. J., Ch. 591 ; 45 L. T. 142 ; 29 W. R. 735, following the American cases of *Miller* v. *Sawyer*, 30 Vermont, 412 ; and *Hall* v. *Robinson*, 8 Iredell, 56.
(y) *In re Arcedeckne. Atkins* v. *Arcedeckne* 24 Ch. Div. 709 ; 53 L. J., Ch. 102 ; 48 L. T. 725.

[*323]   *CHAPTER VI.

THE DISCHARGE OF THE SURETY.

THE persons who may be parties to a contract of suretyship; the mode in which such a contract is formed; the operation of the Statute of Frauds upon the contract of guarantee, and the liabilities and rights of the surety under it, have all been discussed in the preceding chapters. In this chapter it now only remains to consider, how the contract of suretyship may be put an end to, and the surety discharged from all liability under it.

No conflict ever existed between legal and equitable doctrines governing the discharge of the surety.   Before discussing the different grounds of discharge, it may be as well to mention that, even before the fusion of law and equity effected by the Judicature Act (a), the same principles which were held to discharge the surety in equity also operated to discharge him at law (b); and that, where equity had *concurrent* jurisdiction, a court of equity would not send a party suing there to a court of law for the discharge to which he was equally entitled in equity (c).

Ways in which surety may be discharged are very numerous.   The ways in which a surety may be discharged from his suretyship are exceedingly numerous, for a surety is a "favoured debtor." And, indeed, it is somewhat [*324] *difficult to state systematically all the different modes in which the surety's release may be effected, or to make such an arrangement of them as will show at once the various principles upon which they depend.

Division of this chapter.   It is believed, however, that all the modes in which a surety may be discharged group themselves under one or other of the following classes:—I. The surety is discharged by matters which invalidate the contract of suretyship *ab initio*. II. The surety may be discharged by a revocation of the contract of suretyship. III. The

---

(a) 36 & 37 Vic. c. 66, s. 25 (11).
(b) Per *Selborne*, L. C., in *In re Sherry, London and County Banking Co*, v. *Sherry*, 25 Ch. Div. at p. 703; 53 L. J., Ch. 404; 50 L. T. 227; 32 W. R. 394; *Samuel* v. *Howarth*, 3 Mer. 277, 278; 1 Story, Eq. Jur., 10th ed., par. 325, and note 3, par. 325; *Strong* v. *Foster*, 17 C. B. 201, 219; *Cooper* v. *Evans*, L. R., 4 Eq. 45; *Mackintosh* v. *Wyatts*, 3 Hare, 562; *Hawkshaw* v. *Perkins*, 2 Sw. 539; *Eyre* v. *Everett*, 2 Russ. 381.
(c) *Samuel* v. *Howarth*, *supra*.

surety may be discharged by the conduct of creditor.
IV. The surety may be discharged by the fulfilment of
the contract. V. The surety may be discharged by the
operation of the Statute of Limitations. It is proposed
to discuss all these classes of discharges of the surety
in the order in which they have just been named.

I. The surety may be discharged by matters invalidating the contract of suretyship *ab initio*. There
are certain things which put an end to all contracts,
whatever their nature, and make them void from their
very foundation; and guarantees, like all other contracts, are liable to be defeated by any of these means.
The principal things which thus avoid a contract as
from its very foundation are — 1. fraud; 2. an
alteration of the written instrument in which the contract is contained; and 3. failure of the consideration
on which the contract is founded. Let us consider
these in order.

(1) *Fraud of the creditor discharges the surety.*

Fraud vitiates all contracts; including, of course, the
contract of guarantee. It is not proposed to define
fraud, as it is impossible to frame a definition of fraud
that would be applicable to all cases, because what is
fraud in one case is not deemed to be so in another.
Courts of equity always avoided imprudently hampering
themselves by defining, or laying down as a general
*exclusive proposition, what should or should not
constitute fraud; for had they so done, human ingenuity
would have found
a means of evading any proposition that might have
been laid down.

A fraud affecting the contract of guarantee may be
either a fraud connected with the existence of the guarantee, or may be a fraud connected with the existence of
such contract.

First, then, as to fraud connected with the existence of
the contract of guarantee. This fraud may
consist either in the suppression of something which is
true, or in the assertion of that which is false.

*Suppression, or concealment, concerning a fraudulent
to the guarantee, is the most useful form of fraud by
which guarantees are affected.

It seems open to have been thought that the rule as to
to the disclosure of all material facts prevailing in the insurance

Id. Henderson & Treatise on the Practice to prevent fraud
vol. i., pp. 12, 14, and cases there cited.

of all mate-   surances upon marine and life risks, applies also to
rial facts not contracts of guarantee—the rule that, upon a policy to
applicable to   cover a marine or life risk, the assured is bound at his
guarantees.   peril to disclose all material circumstances to the as-
surer, and that their non-disclosure, though innocent
and not fraudulent, vitiates the contract. The impression that the rule in question applied also to guarantees
North British was created by a dictum of Lord *Truro* in *Owen* v.
Insurance Co. *Howman* (e). The erroneous impression thus created
v. *Lloyd.* was, however, corrected in the case of *The North British
Insurance Co.* v. *Lloyd* (f). In that case the plaintiffs
had lent to Sir *T. Brancker* 10,000l., payable in a year,
[*326] on the deposit of some *shares, with the further
stipulation that if the market value of the shares should
fall 20l. per cent. below 10,000l. he should furnish new
shares or pay their value, so as to leave a surplus of
20l. per cent. The shares having fallen in value, below that amount, when the time for the payment of the
loan arrived, the time was extended to a further period
on the deposit of additional shares and the acceptance
of Mr. *Brancker*, the brother of Sir *T. Brancker*. Before the loan became due, in pursuance of the terms of
this second arrangement, Mr. *Brancker* applied to be
released from his acceptance upon procuring the guarantee of the defendant and three others for 500l. each.
Sir *T. Brancker* then informed the defendant of the
loan and of its terms, and told him that unless he could
procure security his shares would be sold at a great loss;
but the arrangement as to the withdrawal of Mr. *Brancker's* acceptance was not communicated to the defendant,
and he was wholly ignorant of it. The defendant executed a guarantee which did not refer to Mr. *Brancker's*
acceptance, but recited the consideration to be the
original loan, and the plaintiffs not requiring any further
security in the event of the depreciation of the shares as
provided for by the original agreement. In an action
on the guarantee it was held, that the non-communication of the private arrangement between the plaintiffs
and Sir *T. Brancker* and Mr. *Brancker* did not amount
to constructive fraud, and afforded no defence to the
action. *Pollock*, C. B., in his judgment says, "The
non-disclosure of the circumstance of the change of
security even if it had been material, would not have

(e) 3 M'N. & G. 378.
(f) 10 Exch. 523. See also *Wythes* v. *Labouchere*, 3 D. & J.
593 ; and per *Fry*, J., in *Davis* v. *London & Provincial Marine Insurance Co.*, 8 Ch. Div. 469, 475 ; 47 L. J., Ch. 511 ; 38 L. T. 478 ;
26 W. R. 794.

vitiated the guarantee, unless it had been fraudulently
kept back ; and there was no ground to impute fraud,
in fact, to the plaintiffs or their agents. They might
well have supposed that the desire of Mr. *T. Brancker*
to get rid of his own guarantee did not indicate any
bad opinion of his brother's character or solvency, but
*arose from a wish on other grounds to contract [*327]
his liabilities."(*g*).

In this case, therefore, the court was of opinion, that
there was no fraud, that the circumstance not disclosed
was not a *material circumstance*, and that, even if it had
been, its concealment, unless *fraudulent*, would not have
the effect of vitiating the guarantee. Now it is somewhat difficult to reconcile this decision with the previous
case of *Railton* v. *Mathews* (*h*). There a party became *Railton* v.
surety in a bond for the fidelity of a commission agent *Mathews.*
to his employers. After some time the employers discovered irregularities in the agent's accounts and put
the bond in suit. The surety then instituted a suit to
avoid the bond, on the ground of concealment by the
employers of material circumstances affecting the agent's
credit *prior* to the date of the bond, and which, if communicated to the surety, would have prevented him
from undertaking the obligation. On the trial of an
issue, directed by the court, to try whether the surety
was induced to sign the bond by undue concealment,
or deception on the part of the employers, the pre-
siding judge directed the jury that the concealment,
to be undue, must be wilful and intentional, with a
view to the advantages the employers were thereby to
gain. It was held by the House of Lords (reversing
the judgment of the Court of Session) that the direction
was wrong in point of law, that the mere non-communication of circumstances affecting the situation of the
parties material for the surety to be acquainted with,
and within the knowledge of a person obtaining a surety
bond, is undue concealment, *though not wilful or intentional, or with a view to any advantage to himself.*

The only way in which this case can be reconciled
with *the decision given in *North British In-* [*328]
surance Co. v. *Lloyd*, is on the assumption that the
objection of the House of Lords must be confined to
that part of the judge's charge where he ruled, that a

(*g*) And see *Lee* v. *Jones*, 17 C. B., N. S. 482; *S. C.*, 14 C. B.,
N. S. 386.

(*h*) 10 Cl. & F. 935. See observations on this case by *Quain*, J.,
and *Blackburn*, J., in *Phillips* v. *Foxall*, L. R., 7 Q. B. 666; 41
L. J., Q. B. 293; 27 L. T. 231; 20 W. R. 900.

concealment does not vitiate a guarantee unless the party guilty of it had his own particular advantage in view. Certainly, Lord *Cottenham* seems to assert, in this case, that *unintentional* concealment would be sufficient to vitiate a guarantee. Lord *Campbell*, however, is careful to separate the alleged misdirection of the judge into *two* parts. He says, "Now, according to my notion of the issue, that is an entire misconception of it: according to this direction, although the parties acquiring the bond had been aware of the most material facts which it was their duty to disclose, and the withholding of which would avoid the bond, if they did not wilfully and intentionally withhold them, that is to say, if they had forgotten them, or if they thought by mistake, that, in point of law or morality, they were not bound to disclose them, then, according to the holding of the learned judge, it would not be a concealment. *But the learned judge does not stop there;* he goes on, with a view to the advantage they were thereby to receive; introducing those words conjunctively, and, in effect, saying that it was not an undue concealment, unless they had their own particular advantage in view. *That* appears to me a misconception." It would therefore *seem*, that Lord *Campbell might* have agreed with the learned judge if he had only laid down that concealment, if not wilful and intentional, will *not* vitiate a guarantee.

The decision in the case of the *North British Insurance Co.* v. *Lloyd* (*i*), is certainly quite in harmony with the doctrine which prevailed in courts of equity, namely, that, in order to entitle a surety to relief *in equity*, on the ground of misrepresentation or concealment, at the time of the contract, he must make out a case amounting to *fraud* (*k*).

What amounts to fraudulent concealment which will vitiate a guarantee.

[*329]   *When we speak of a *fraudulent* as distinguished from an *innocent* concealment, we speak of one which is *wilful* and *intentional.* However, it is necessary to observe, that though every *fraudulent concealment* is wilful and intentional, the converse of that proposition is not correct, and that *every wilful* and *intentional* concealment is not necessarily by the law of England *fraudulent.* But we have already shown that no concealment will vitiate a guarantee unless it be *fraudulent.* Therefore, it is not every wilful and intentional concealment that will have this effect, since every wilful and intentional concealment is not necessarily

(*i*) 10 Exch. 523.
(*k*) *Pledge* v. *Buss*, Johns. 663.
(1494)

fraudulent (*l*). Now it appears that there are certain things which it is *the duty* of the creditor *spontaneously* to disclose to the surety, and that there are certain other things which the creditor need not disclose unless and until requested to do so by the surety. If, therefore, the creditor, *wilfully* and *intentionally*, omit to disclose those things which he is bound *spontaneously* to disclose, he is of course guilty of a *fraudulent* concealment, which vitiates the guarantee, and relieves the surety from liability. But an intentional and wilful *concealment* (as distinguished from a *misrepresentation*) of those things which he need not disclose unless the surety requests him to do so, will not amount to a *fraudulent concealment*, and will not therefore vitiate the guarantee.

Having said thus much, we will endeavour to explain what things the surety is bound *spontaneously* to disclose, and what are the things which the surety must *ascertain for himself* from the creditor.

In *Hamilton* v. *Watson* (*m*), Lord *Campbell* lays down "that this might be considered as the criterion whether the disclosure ought to be made voluntarily, namely, whether there is anything that might not naturally be expected to take place between the parties who are *concerned in the transaction, that is, [*330] whether there be a contract between the debtor and the creditor to the effect that his position shall be different from that which the surety might naturally expect, and, if so, the surety is to see whether that is disclosed to him. But if there be nothing which might not naturally take place between these parties, then, if the surety would guard against particular perils, he must put the question, and he must gain the information which he requires."

In *Wythes* v. *Labouchere* (*n*) Lord Chancellor *Chelmsford* said: "The concealment, too, must be of some material part of the transaction itself between the creditor and his debtor, to which the suretyship relates. The creditor is under no obligation to inform the intended surety of matters affecting the credit of the debtor, or of any circumstances unconnected with the transaction in which he is about to engage, which will render his position more hazardous."

In the recent case of *Davies* v. *London and Provin-*

Marginal notes: What things the surety is bound to disclose spontaneously. General principles. *Hamilton* v. *Watson.* *Wythes* v. *Labouchere.* *Davies* v. *London and*

(*l*) See recent case of *Mackreth* v. *Walmesley*, 51 L. T 19; 22 W. R. 819.
(*m*) 12 Cl. & Fin. 109, 119.
(*n*) 3 D. & J. 593, 609.

Provincial
Marine Insur-
ance Co.

cial *Marine Insurance Co.* (o), *Fry*, J., thus lays down
the law as to disclosure of circumstances by parties to
contracts:—"Where parties are contracting with one
another each may, unless there be a duty to disclose,
observe silence even in regard to facts which he believes
would be operative upon the mind of the other, and it
rests upon those who say that there was a duty to disclose, to show that the duty existed. . . . . It has
been argued here that the contract between the surety
and the creditor is one of those contracts which I have
spoken of as being *uberrimæ fidei*, and it has been held
that such a contract can only be upheld in the case of
there being the fullest disclosure by the intending creditor. I do not think that that proposition is sound in
law. I think that, on the contrary, that contract is
[*331] *one in which there is no universal obligation
to make disclosure, and therefore I shall not determine
this case on that view. But I do think that the contract of suretyship is, as expressed by Lord *Wesbury* in
Williams v. *Bayley* (p), one which 'should be based
upon the free and voluntary agency of the individual
who enters into it.'"

Particular
examples
where non-
disclosure of
circum-
stances com-
plained of.
Surety ought
to be in-
formed of
every private
bargain be-
tween credi-
tor and prin-
cipal debtor,
varying
degree of
surety's re-
sponsibility.
Sometimes
also necessary
to disclose
agreement
between

We will now pass on to *particular* examples :—

Where an agreement between the vendors and the
vendee of goods, that the latter should pay 10s. per ton
beyond the market price, which sum was to be applied
in liquidation of an old debt due to one of the vendors,
was not communicated to the person guaranteeing payment of the goods, it was held, that on that account the
guarantee was void (q), for a party giving a guarantee
ought to be informed of every private bargain made
between the vendor and the vendee of goods which may
have the effect of varying the degree of his responsibility (r). It would seem, moreover, that it may, under
certain circumstances, be necessary to communicate to
the surety the existence and nature of an agreement
entered into by the person receiving the guarantee and
some third person other than the principal debtor. This
would appear to be so from the case of *Stiff* v. *The
Local Board of Eastbourne* (s). The facts of this case
are as follows :—By a memorandum of agreement between one *James Hayward* of the one part, and the de-

(o) 8 Ch. Div. 469, 474—475.
(p) L. R., 1 H. L. 200, 219.
(q) *Pidcock* v. *Bishop*, 3 B. & C. 605. See remarks on this case
in *Ex parte Sharp*, 3 M., D. & D. 504.
(r) Per *Abbott*, C. J., in *Pidcock* v. *Bishop, ubi supra.* See also
Stone v. *Compton*, 5 Bing. N. C. 142.
(s) 19 L. T., N. S , Ch. 408.

fendants of the other part, *Hayward* contracted to execute certain sewage works at Eastbourne, conditional-
ly, among other things, on his being from time to time
paid for the work done by him under the contract upon
the certificate of a surveyor, who was defined as being
the *surveyor of the defendants. By a bond of [*332]
even date with the above agreement, *Hayward* as principal, and the plaintiff and another as sureties, became
jointly and severally bound to the defendants in the
penal sum of 5,000*l.* for the due performance of the
contract on or before a certain day. Subsequently
Hayward became insolvent, was unable to complete the
contract, and the defendants thereupon commenced an
action against the plaintiff in order to enforce his
penalty under the bond. This action the plaintiff
sought to stay by injunction. It appeared that previously to the contract with *Hayward* the defendants had
entered into an agreement with the Duke of Devon-
shire, who, possessing a good deal of property in the
neighbourhood, was interested in the sewage works,
that the works should be executed "under the joint
superintendence and control of the engineer and surveyor of the duke and of the local board, or their surveyor or clerk, or clerk of the works." At the time of
the execution of the bond the plaintiff was kept in
ignorance of this agreement. It was held, that the
plaintiff was relieved from liability as surety under his
bond, because at the time of its execution by him a
material circumstance was concealed from him, and that
an injunction restraining proceedings at law against
the surety upon the bond must, therefore, be granted.
Vice-Chancellor *Stuart* delivered the following judgment in this case :—"In contracts of this description it
is of the utmost importance to know who is to be the
surveyor, for on him depends the payment. In the
contract between the defendants and *Hayward* it is
distinctly stated, as one of the conditions, that the surveyor is to be the surveyor of the Eastbourne Local
Board ; yet it now turns out that the Duke of Devon-
shire's surveyor is to be associated with him. The fact
of this circumstance having been concealed from the
plaintiff at the time of the execution of the bond is, in
my opinion, sufficient *to exonerate him from all [*333]
liability. The injunction must, therefore, be granted."
  In *Smith* v. *The Bank of Scotland* (*t*), a guarantee

(*t*) 1 Dow, 272. See observations on this case by *Quain*, J.,
and *Blackburn*, J., in *Phillips* v. *Foxall*, L. R., 7 Q. B. 666 ; 41 L.
J., Q. B. 293 ; 27 L. T. 231 ; 20 W. R. 900.

264　　　　　　　THE LAW OF GUARANTEES.

disclose to surety past misconduct of principal debtor.

Smith v. *Bank of Scotland.*

was given for the good behaviour of a bank clerk. The bank concealed from the surety—or rather neglected to disclose to him—the circumstance that the principal had, *previously to the giving of the guarantee,* misconducted himself in his office. It was held, that this concealment or omission to disclose ought to have been admitted to proof by the court below on the ground, apparently, that it was so little to be expected that a bank would continue in their service such a clerk, that the application for a security under these circumstances amounted to holding him forth to the sureties as a person of trust, and that this amounted to fraud (*u*).

Lawder v. *Simpson.*

The recent *Irish* case of *Lawder* v. *Simpson* (*x*) is very similar to the case last cited. There an action was brought by a county treasurer against a surety to a bond of a defaulting county cess collector. The surety pleaded *equitably* that the plaintiff knew that the cess collector, when previously engaged in that office, had misconducted himself, and yet that the plaintiff had not informed the defendant (surety) of this fact. It was held, that this defence was inadmissible, as there was no privity between the surety and the plaintiff in his official capacity.

Lee v. *Jones.* Whether principal debtor's indebtedness to creditor should be disclosed.

In *Lee* v. *Jones* (*y*), it was held by the Court of Exchequer Chamber, that the non-communication by the plaintiffs to defendant of the fact that the principal debtor was indebted to the plaintiffs, at the time the [*334] *defendant executed the contract of guarantee, was evidence in support of the defendant's plea of fraud. This, however, was a case of misrepresentation rather than one of mere concealment.

Roper v. *Cox.*

In *Roper* v. *Cox* (*z*), it was held by the *Irish* Common Pleas Division, that where a guarantee was given for the due payment of rent by H., the surety could not escape from his liability under it by proving that, prior to the making of the guarantee, H. had been tenant to the plaintiff of the lands at a rent, and had been guilty of gross irregularity and delay in payment of such rent, and at the date of the guarantee

---

(*u*) See also *Leith Banking Co.* v. *Bell,* 8 Shaw & Dunl. 721; 5 Wils. & Shaw, 703 ; *Fishmongers' Co.* v. *Maltby,* cited p. 294 of 1 Dow.

(*x*) C. P. (Ir.), I. R., 7 C. D. 57, 21 W. R. 439.

(*y*) 17 C. B., N. S. 482 ; *S. C.,* 14 C. B., N. S. 386; 11 Jur., N. S. 81; 34 L. J., C. P. 131; 13 W. R. 318. See also *Williams* v. *Rawlinson,* 3 Bing. 71.

(*z*) 10 L. R., Ir. 200, C. P. D.; and see *Home Insurance Co.* v. *Holway,* 39 Amer. R. 179 (U. S.).

was indebted to the plaintiff in a large sum for arrears of such rent, of which the surety was ignorant.

In the case of *The Guardians of the Stokesley Union* v. *Stroher* (a), the bond was conditioned for the faithful discharge of the duties of a relieving officer. At the time of the execution of the bond there was a balance of 206l. due from the relieving officer in respect of money which had been received by him as relieving officer. That fact was not communicated to the surety. It was held, that as the existence of the balance did not necessarily involve any imputation of misconduct against the relieving officer, it was not a material fact which the guardians were bound to communicate to the surety before he executed the bond. In this case, Coleridge, J., while admitting that fraud might be proved by the non-communication of any material fact, considered, that, inasmuch as the relieving officer, *from the nature of his office*, must be sure to have money in hand, the non-communication of this fact was no fraud upon the surety.

Guardians of Stokesley Union v. Strother.

It may sometimes be necessary to communicate to the surety subsequent changes which have occurred in the circumstances under which the suretyship was to be entered into.

In Davies v. London and Provincial Marine [*335] *Insurance Co.* (b), the facts were as follows :—The officers of a company believing that a felony had been committed by one of their agents in whose accounts there was an alleged deficiency, directed his arrest. Certain friends of the defaulting agent thereupon proposed to deposit money by way of security for any deficiency. Pending the negotiations, the officers of the company withdrew directions for the agent's arrest on being advised that his acts did not amount to felony. This fact was not communicated to the agents' friends, who subsequently agreed to make the deposit, and carried out such agreement. It was held, that the change of circumstances ought to have been stated to the intended sureties, and that, therefore, the agreement must be rescinded, and the money returned to the sureties. It was also held, that if the agreement to give security was illegal as compounding a felony, the Court would interfere in a case where the money was actually in the hands of trustees, and pressure had been exercised.

Subsequent change in circumstances as they existed when suretyship first contemplated should be disclosed.

Davies v. London and Provincial Marine Insurance Co.

(a) 22 L. T. 84.

(b) 8 Ch. Div. 469; 47 L. J., Ch. 511; 38 L. T. 478; 26 W. R. 794. See also *Williams* v. *Bayley*, L. R., 1 H. L. 200.

Discharge of surety by fraudulent misrepresentations.

What is misrepresentation.

Written misrepresentation.

Lee v. *Jones.*

The other class of frauds committed prior to the execution of a guarantee, by which its operation is destroyed, consists of *misrepresentations*.

Misrepresentation is the assertion of that which is false. It need not consist of *verbal assertion*, for a *false assertion in writing* will certainly also amount to misrepresentation. Thus, in the case of *Lee* v. *Jones* (c), which we have already cited (d), the majority of the judges considered that there was "cogent evidence of such a suppression of the truth by a partial, inaccurate and subdolous setting forth by the plaintiffs in the written agreement of facts within their knowledge, material for the proposed sureties to be informed of, as, along with the non-communication [*336] of other facts, *material for them to know, amounted to a *misrepresentation* to the proposed sureties" that the principal debtor during the five years he had acted as the plaintiff's commission agent, had proved himself to be a man worthy of trust and confidence, "a satisfactory guarantor of others, and himself the safe subject of a guarantee." *Blackburn*, J., in this case, said : "I think that it must in every case depend upon the nature of the transaction whether the fact not disclosed is such, that it is impliedly represented not to exist, and that must generally be a question of fact proper for a jury."

Verbal misrepresentation.

Blest v. *Brown.*

We now come to a case of *verbal misrepresentation* —the case of *Blest* v. *Brown* (e). There, the plaintiff, as surety, executed a joint and several bond to secure to B. and M. money which might become due to them from A. M. for flour to be supplied by them to A. M. for the purpose, as stated on the face of the bond, of enabling him to carry out a contract with the government. It appeared by the evidence, that B. and M. never supplied A. M. with flour for the purpose of the contract, and also, that, at the time when the bond was executed, the plaintiff had inquired of the agent of B. and M., whether there were any trade debts owing from A. M. to B. and M., to which the agent had answered, "No." It turned out, however, that there was a trade debt owing, but the period of credit had not expired. Sir *J. Stuart*, V.-C., held, that there had been a misrepresentation of a material fact which might have influenced the conduct of the plaintiff in executing the bond, and that, therefore, he was entitled to be relieved

(c) 17 C. B., N. S. 482.
(d) *Ante,* p. 333.
(e) 8 Jur., N. S. 603

from its consequences. On appeal, this decision was affirmed by Lord Chancellor *Westbury,* who said: "Now, it must always be recollected in what manner a surety is bound. You bind him to the letter of his engagement. Beyond the proper interpretation *of that engagement you have no hold upon [*337] him. He receives no benefit and no consideration. He is bound therefore, merely according to the proper meaning and effect of the written engagement that he has entered into. If that written engagement is altered in a single line, no matter whether it be altered for his benefit, no matter whether the alteration be innocently made, he has a right to say, 'The contract is no longer that for which I engaged to be surety; you have put an end to the contract that I guaranteed, and my obligation, therefore, is at an end.'"

Before quitting the subject of frauds *antecedent* to the contract of guarantee, it may be well to call attention to a class of cases which are sometimes examples of fraudulent concealment, sometimes of fraudulent misrepresentation, and sometimes partake of both these elements, namely, cases where the surety contends that the guarantee is not binding upon him because he did not rightly understand the nature of the contract he was entering into. It has been thought best to treat these cases together. The general principles deducible from the decisions which have been given in such cases may be shortly stated as follows:—Where a guarantee is obtained by a creditor from a person likely to be under the influence of the debtor, as in the case of a relative just come of age, the onus is thrown upon the creditor of showing that such person understood the transaction and that he did not act under undue influence, otherwise the transaction will be set aside (*f*). So if the creditor has been guilty of misrepresentation by framing the guarantee in a way calculated to mislead the surety, it would be contrary to equitable principles to allow advantage to be taken of a guarantee executed under such circumstances (*g*). On the other *hand, it seems that a guarantee will not be in- [*338] validated by the circumstances that the surety has not been informed, previous to its execution, of its tenor or effect, if he has had full opportunity not only of duly considering it himself, uninfluenced by the representa-

Guarantee obtained by undue influence or misrepresentation of its contents or effect liable to be set aside as fraudulent.

(*f*) White & T. L. C., 5th ed., vol. ii., p. 586; *Maitland* v. *Irving,* 15 Sim. 437.
(*g*) Per *Kindersley,* V.-C., in *Small* v. *Currie,* 2 Drew. 102, 114; *Squire* v. *Whitton,* 1 H. L. 333.

tions or presence of the person to whom the guarantee
is given, but also of procuring the advice and assistance of his own solicitor. A court of equity will not
interfere in such a case, because the surety should have
asked for information if he required it (*g*). And
though it is certainly true that, as a rule, whenever a
person can establish that he has been misled as to the
contents of a written document he is not bound thereby
(*h*), yet it remains doubtful whether if there be a false
representation as to the contents of an instrument, a
person who is an *educated* person and who might by
very simple means have satisfied himself as to what the
contents of the deed really were, may not, by executing
it *negligently*, be estopped as between himself and a
person who innocently acts upon the faith of its being
a valid instrument (*i*). Whether misrepresentation as
to the *legal effect of* an agreement in writing or under
seal will operate to relieve a party thereto from liability,
is doubtful (*k*); but it would seem that a *fraudulent*
misrepresentation as to the effect of an instrument may
be relied upon as a defence to an action upon it (*l*).
However, it appears that *a man of business* who executes
[*339] *an instrument of a short and intelligible description will not be permitted to allege that he executed
it in blind ignorance of its real character or under circumstances of haste, surprise or deception (*m*).

Frauds sub-
sequent to
the execu-
tion of the
guarantee.

Frauds, however, may not only be *prior* to the execution of a guarantee, but they may (as has been stated)
also be *subsequent to it.* It remains to deal with frauds of
this description. Fraud *subsequent* to the execution of the
guarantee does not often occur, and there are not, therefore, many examples of this species of fraud to be cited.

If the creditor *connives at* the default of the principal debtor, this will, of course, be quite sufficient to
discharge the surety (*n*).

(*g*) Per *Kindersley*, V.-C., in *Small* v. *Currie, ubi supra;* and see
Brown v. *Wilkinson*, 13 M. & W. 14.
(*h*) *Thoroughgood's case*, 2 Co. 9 a. b., note (B); *Edwards* v.
Brown, 1 C. & J. at p. 312; *Foster* v. *Mackinnon*, L. R., 4 C. P.
620, 711; *Simons* v. *S. W. Rail. Co.*, 2 C. B., N. S. 420.
(*i*) Per *Mellish*, L. J., in *Hunter* v. *Walters*, L. R., 7 Ch. App.
83, 87, 88; but see *Byles*, J., in *Swan* v. *North British Australian
Co.*, 2 H. & C. at p. 184.
(*k*) *Lewis* v. *Jones*, 4 B. & C. 506; per *Mellish*, L. J., in *Beattie*
v. *Lord Ebury*, L. R., 7 Ch. App. at p. 802; *Edwards* v. *Brown*, 1
C. & J. 307; *Ogilvie* v. *Jeaffreson*, 2 Giff. 353.
(*l*) *Hirschfeld* v. *L. B. & S. C. Rail. Co.*, 2 Q. B. D. 1.
(*m*) *Wythes* v. *Labouchere*, 3 De G. & J. at p. 601.
(*n*) *Dawson* v. *Lawes*, 23 L. J., Ch. 434. See also *Mactaggart*
v. *Watson*, 3 C. & F. 525; *Shepherd* v. *Beecher*, 2 P. W. 288.

We have already seen, that, in the case of a guarantee for the honesty of another person in an employment, if the person guaranteed *conceals* from the surety, that, previously to the giving of the guarantee, the person employed had committed defalcations in the service of the person guaranteed, the surety may be relieved on the ground of *fraud.* And, in the recent case of *Phillips* v. *Foxall* (o), it was decided, that if, *after the execution of such a continuing guarantee*, a similar concealment be made, the surety is equally discharged. Thus, if, after the execution of such a guarantee, the person employed is guilty of a dishonest act, or even of the breach (whether accompanied with dishonesty or not) of the duty for the due fulfilment of which another has become surety, and the employer continues to employ such person after knowledge of these facts, the surety is discharged (p). Where, however, the person to whom a *guarantee for good conduct of a rate collector [*340] had been given merely possessed the power of *suspending* the latter on his being guilty of neglect of duty, the power of *dismissal* being vested in another and higher official, it was held that the doctrine of *Phillips* v. *Foxall* (q) did not apply, and that the omission to exercise a power of suspension, as distinguished from a power of dismissal, did not terminate the liability of the sureties (r).

Fraudulent concealment from surety of subsequent misconduct of principal.

Omission by employer to suspend principal who has misconducted himself will not relieve surety where power of dismissal not vested in employer.

Another instance of wrongful conduct subsequent to the formation of the relationship of principal and surety discharging the latter is afforded by the case of *Burke* v. *Rogerson* (s), in which the facts were as follows:— The defendant agreed to sell two ships to the D. Co., to be paid partly in bills of exchange accepted by the company, with liberty to the defendant to freight one of the vessels. The plaintiffs agreed to indorse the bills by way of surety. Shortly afterwards the defendant, assuming to act as agent of the company, despatched one of the vessels to Constantinople laden, on his own account, with munitions of war, for the Circassians, who were then at war with Russia. This was not known either to the company or to the plaintiffs. It was held

Discharge of surety for payment of price of ships by subsequent improper employment of one of such ships by vendor.

(o) L. R., 7 Q. B. 666; 41 L. J., Q. B. 293; 27 L. T. 231; 20 W. R. 900.

(p) *Phillips* v. *Foxall, ubi supra: Sanderson* v. *Aston*, L. R., 8 Exch. 73. See also observations of *Malins*, V.-C., in *Burgess* v. *Eve*, L. R., 13 Eq. 450. See also *Peel* v. *Tatlock*, 1 B. & P. 419, 423.

(q) *Ubi supra.*
(r) *Byrne* v. *Muzio*, 8 L. R. (Ir.), 396, Ex. D.
(s) 12 Jur., N. S. 635; 14 L. T. 780.

that the defendant having exposed the ships to extraordinary risks, and having wrongfully concealed this
from the plaintiffs, it amounted to a release of the plaintiffs from their liability as sureties.

(2) Altera-   ,2.) *An alteration made in the instrument of guar*
tion in in-   *antee after its execution may discharge the surety.*
strument of   It was decided in *Pigot's case* (t), that the alteration
guarantee   of *a deed* by the *obligee*, in a *point material, or not ma-*
after its exe- *terial*, avoids the deed ; but the alteration by a *stranger,*
cution may   without the privity of the obligee, does not avoid the
discharge   [*341] *deed, unless the alteration is in a *material* point.
surety.   This doctrine has been, *in part*, at all events extended
               to written instruments not *under seal* and, among others,
Davidson v.   to guarantees.   Thus, in the case of *Davidson* v. *Cooper*
Cooper.   (u), a plea alleged that, after the making of the guar-
               antee sued on (which was *under seal*), and whilst it was
               in the hands of the plaintiff, it was, without the knowl-
               edge of the defendant, by some person, to him unknown,
               altered in a *material* particular, by affixing two seals
               by and near to the signatures of the defendants, as
               and for their seals, thereby causing the guarantee to
               purport to be the deed of the defendants.   It was held,
               that the guarantee become void in law, and that the
               plaintiff could not recover (x).   Again, in the case of
Bank of Hin-   *The Bank of Hindustan, China and Japan* v. *Smith* (y),
dustan, China an action was brought on a guarantee not under seal,
and Japan v.   whereby, as alleged in the declaration, the defendant
Smith.   promised that, if the plaintiffs paid a large sum of
               money to the liquidator of another bank, he (the de-
               fendant) would be responsible for the repayment of
               such sum and would indemnify the plaintiffs.   The plea
               to the declaration in this action set out the guarantee
               itself and alleged that the contract was to contribute
               aliquot parts, as the bank well knew, and that several
               of the names of the persons who had signed the guar-
               antee were struck out, whilst the instrument of guar-
               antee was in the plaintiffs' possession.   It was held,
               that this alteration alleged in the plea precluded the
               bank from recovering, and that as the alteration ap-
               peared to have been made by the bank secretary, it was
               just as if the bank itself had made it.
                   However, so far, at any rate, as instruments not un-

_____

(t) 11 Rep. 27 a.
(u) 11 M. & W. 778 : S. C. (Cam. Scacc.), 13 M. & W. 343, 352.
(x) The removal of the seal of one of the obligors to a several
bond does not render such bond invalid as to the others. See
Collins v. *Prosser.* 1 B. & C. 682.
(y) 36 L. J., C. P. 241.

der seal are concerned, the doctrine of *Pigot's case* is
*qualified by the modern case of *Aldous* v. [*342] *Aldous* v.
Cornwell (y). In this latter case the Court of Queen's *Cornwell.*
Bench held that in such a case (the instance actually
under consideration being that of a promispry note) an
immaterial alteration, though made by a party to it,
does not render it void (z). Now in *Pigot's case* it
was, as before observed, laid down that any alteration
in a deed, *whether material or not*, made by the obligee
avoided the deed. But as in *Pigot's case* it was found,
as a fact, that the alteration, which was not a material
one, was made by a *stranger*, the Court of Queen's
Bench, in *Aldous* v. *Cornwell* (a), did not consider
themselves bound by *Pigot's case* (b). Moreover, even
had this not been so, it is conceived that, inasmuch as
in *Pigot's case* the alteration was in a *deed*, whilst in
Aldous v. *Cornwell* it was in an instrument *not under seal*,
the Court of Queen's Bench, were, in deciding the latter
case, in no sense bound by the former case. And, in
all probability, even should the same question ever arise
in reference to a deed, our judges would be disposed to
follow *Aldous* v. *Cornwell.* And, in accordance with
the principal acted on in *Aldous* v. *Cornwell*, where an
alteration *not material* to the defendant's liability was
made in a guarantee by the plaintiff, with the consent of
the principal debtor, it was held that the guarantee was
not thereby avoided (c).

The ground on which an alteration avoids an instru- Why subse-
ment is explained in *Davidson* v. *Cooper* (d), to be" that quent alter-
a party who has the custody of the instrument made for ation of an
his benefit is *bound* to preserve it in its original state." instrument
In reference to this, a distinguished writer on English avoids it.
law (e) has said: "But although it is no doubt highly
*important that all legal instruments should be [*343]
preserved in their integrity, it may perhaps be doubted
whether the doctrine in question would ever have ex
isted, had there been no other reason for it than the
duty of a person having the custody of an instrument
made for his benefit to preserve it in its original state."

(y) L. R., 3 Q. B. 573.
(z) See also *Garrard* v. *Lewis*, 10 Q. B. D. 1; *Suffell* v. *Bank of
England*, 7 Q. B. D. 270; 9 Q. B. D. 555.
(a) *Ubi supra.*
(b) See the judgment in *Aldous* v. *Cornwell.*
(c) *Andrews* v. *Lawrence*, 19 C. B., N. S. 768.
(d) Per Lord *Denman*, C. J., 13 M. & W. at p. 352.
(e) Mr. J. Williams, Q. C. in his work entitled "The Principles of the Law of Personal Property," at p. 88 (7th edition).

272   THE LAW OF GUARANTEES.

(3) Failure of consideration antee was given discharges the surety. for which guarantee given discharges the surety. (8.) *Failure of the consideration for which the guarantee was given discharges the surety.*

Failure of the consideration for which the guarantee was given will of course discharge the surety, just as failure of the consideration in any other case releases the promiser. An instance of a failure of consideration for a guarantee is afforded by the case of *Cooper* v. *Joel* (f). In that case, upon the eve of a sale by the sheriff, a surety gave a written guarantee for payment of the judgment debts by instalments, in consideration of the judgment creditors consenting to postpone the sale under the execution. It turned out that the consent of another person was necessary in order to prevent the sale, and, in consequence the sale took place. The surety gave notice that the consideration having failed, the guarantee was at an end. It appeared that representations were made on behalf of the judgment creditors, when they took the guarantee, that they had power to stop the sale, and that it would be stopped. It was held that the surety was entitled to have the guarantee given up.

In the recent case of *Ex parte Agra Bank* (g), it was decided on the facts of the case, that there was no failure of consideration. There a bank granted a letter of credit to a company, *and agreed to accept bills drawn upon them by the company in respect of that credit,* on the terms that the company should ship tea and forward bills of lading, invoices and policy of insurance on the tea to the bank, and should also draw on B. & [*344] Co. bills *to be accepted by B. & Co. to an amount sufficient to cover the amount authorized by the letter of credit. B. & Co. guaranteed the performance by the company of these terms, "holding themselves responsible for the same." The company drew on the bank, and the bank accepted the bills, but owing to the failure of the bank after the dates when the bills were drawn, and before they became due, the company shipped no tea, and did not perform any of the terms agreed on. The bills accepted by the bank were, it would appear, *ultimately* paid. It was held that the failure of the bank was no reason for the default of the company to perform its part of the contract, and that B. & Co. were liable on their guarantee (h).

(f) 1 De. G. F. & J. 240.
(g) R. L., 9 Eq. 725.
(h) This case rests mainly upon another ground, though the question of failure of consideration was also involved. *Post,* p. 390.

(1506)

II. The surety may be discharged by a revocation of the contract of suretyship.

A revocation of the contract made arises either (1), by act of the parties, or (2), by death of the surety. Let us consider these two modes of revocation separately.

(1.) The most frequent cases in which a rescission of a contract of suretyship is made by act of the parties are, where (A) the surety revokes the guarantee; or (B) a new agreement is substituted for it by mutual consent.

(A.) *The surety may sometimes be discharged by notice of revocation of the guarantee given by the surety to the creditor.*

We have already seen (*i*), that a mere offer to guarantee may be revoked, by notice, at any time before it is expressly or impliedly accepted. Whenever it is *expressly* provided in the contract of guarantee that it shall be determinable, on notice, by the surety, it is, *of course, revocable in the way thus specified [*345] (*k*). It is, however, rather doubtful, whether in the absence of express stipulation to that effect, a guarantee may be revoked by the surety after it has been *even partially* acted upon. But it would seem that the power of revocation depends upon whether the consideration for the guarantee is given once for all, or whether the consideration be made up of separate advances of money or goods. In the former case, it has been decided recently that the guarantee cannot be determined either by the surety or his representatives (*l*); but, *semble*, that, in the latter case, the guarantee is revocable by notice so as to relieve the surety from subsequent liability in respect of any future advances made or further goods sold (*m*).

At one time it *seems* to have been thought that, under no circumstances, could a guarantee under seal be revoked (*n*). However, in the case of *Burgess* v. *Eve* (*o*), *Malins*, V.-C, expressed the opinion, that though in the case of a guarantee under seal for the good be-

II. Revocation of contract of suretyship.

Two modes of revocation.

(1) Revocation by act of the parties.

(A.) Where notice of revocation given by the surety to the creditor.

Where guarantee is silent on the subject, power of revocation depends on nature of guarantee.

Formerly considered that guarantee under seal could not be revoked.

(*i*) *Ante,* p. 2 ; *Offord* v. *Davies,* 12 C. B., N. S. 748.

(*k*) *Solvency Mutual Guarantee Company* v. *Froame,* 7 H. & N. 5. And see also *Boyd* v. *Robins,* 4 C. B., N. S. 749.

(*l*) *Lloyds* v. *Harper,* 16 Ch. Div. 290 ; 50 L. J., Ch. 140 ; 43 L. T. 481 ; 29 W. R. 452 ; *Calvert* v. *Gordon,* 3 Mann. & Ry. 124.

(*m*) *Lloyds* v. *Harper, ubi supra ; Bastow* v. *Bennett,* 3 Camp. 220.

(*n*) Per Lord *Ellenborough,* C. J., in *Hassell* v. *Long,* 2 M. & S. 363, 370, 371; *Gordon* v. *Calvert,* 2 Sim, 253. But see *Hough* v. *Warr,* 1 C. & P. 151; *Shepherd* v. *Beecher,* 2 P. W. 287.

(*o*) L. R., 13 Eq. 450.

18	(1507)

Contrary opinion expressed in *Burgess* v. *Eve.*

haviour of another in an office or employment, a surety might not arbitrarily and without the fullest justification withdraw that which he deliberately entered into; yet, as soon as the employed was guilty of an act which in the eye of a court of equity (*p*) is a dishonest act, the right of the surety to withdraw his guarantee attached. But it would seem that in this case the surety would not have been at liberty to withdraw his [*346] *guarantee but for the misconduct of the person employed, rendering it inequitable to hold the surety liable in the future (*q*). For the liability under the guarantee would have continued so long as the person for whom it was given retained the *status* which he acquired on the faith of it.

Guarantee for person employed cannot, as a rule, be revoked so long as he retains the *status* which he acquired on the faith of it.

(B.) Where a new agreement is substituted for original one before breach of latter.

Taylor v. *Hilary.*

(B.) *The surety may be discharged by substitution of a new contract before breach of the old one.*

The *substitution* of a new agreement for the former one, before any breach of the first, discharges the surety from all liability under the first. This was decided in *Taylor* v. *Hilary* (*r*). There the declaration stated that the defendant guaranteed the plaintiff in supplying goods to one H. H. The plea was, that before breach of the agreement declared on, it was agreed between the plaintiff and the defendant that the plaintiff should supply goods to H. H., and that they should be paid for at the end of three months by a bill at four months, to be accepted by the defendant, which agreement the plaintiff before breach, accepted in discharge of the former agreement and released the defendant from the performance thereof. It was held that the plea was good, and that the second agreement was a defence to the action, as being a substituted contract. "For," said the court, "before the breach of the first agreement a new agreement is entered into, varying the contract in an essential part, the time of payment. The latter, then, is a substituted contract, and is an answer to an action upon the former. The plea is not a plea of accord and satisfaction, and does not, therefore, require an averment of performance."

At common law a specialty could not be discharged

At common law an agreement under seal could not be discharged *before* breach by parol contract, whether executory or executed, nor could performance be waived [*347] *by parol (*s*). In the case of *The Mayor of*

(*p*) See also *Hough* v. *Warr*, 1 C. & P. 151.
(*q*) Per *Fry*, J., in *Lloyds* v. *Harper*, 16 Ch. Div. at p. 307; 50 L. J., Ch. 140; 43 L. T. 481; 29 W. R. 452.
(*r*) 1 C., M. & R. 741.
(*s*) Addison on Contracts, 8th ed. p. 1220.

Berwick v. *Oswald* (*t*), the plea was held to be bad, owing to this principle not having been observed. There, to an action on a guarantee *under seal*, it was pleaded that before breach, the plaintiffs accepted a fresh surety-bond in discharge of the deed sued on. It was held, on demurrer, that this plea was bad, as pleading accord and satisfaction to a *deed before* breach. The fresh surety bond, it must be observed, though nearly in the same terms as the deed on which the action was brought, *did not refer to the former deed.* — *before breach, by parol agreement. Mayor of Berwick v. Oswald.*

In equity, however, the rule of law was disregarded, and relief was often given there upon the principle that what was agreed to be done by a binding agreement was looked upon as done (*u*). — *Equity always disregarded.*

A parol license or dispensation may now be pleaded to an action on a deed (*x*). — *Common law doctrine on this subject and now parol dispensation, may be pleaded to action on a deed.*

As to the form in which a binding substitution of one guarantee for another can be made, and whether such substitution need be in writing or not is a somewhat doubtful point. Guarantees are of course within sect. 4 of the Statute of Frauds. And it seems therefore, to be *vexata quæstio* whether a contract within the Statute of Frauds can be *wholly* waived and abandoned, before breach, by a subsequent agreement not in writing (*y*). It is clear, however, that any *alteration*, before breach, in the *terms* of an agreement which falls within the statute, must be in writing (*z*). An alteration of a guarantee, therefore, is not binding unless it be in *writing. Thus, in *Emmet* v. *Dewhurst* ( ), a [348] composition was guaranteed by the defendant to all the creditors of A. B. who executed a certain release before a fixed day. The plaintiff, who was one of such creditors, alleged as a reason why he did not execute the release within the fixed time, that a *verbal* arrangement was entered into between him and the defendant's agent, the effect of which was to bind the plaintiff to accept the composition, but to allow him to postpone his execution of the release. It was not only decided that there was no evidence that the defendant's agent — *Whether, in the case of contracts within sect. 4 of Statute of Frauds, the substitution of one contract for another must be in writing.*

(*t*) 1 Ell. & Bl. 295.
(*u*) White & Tudor. L. C. Eq., 5th ed., vol. ii., p. 1031 ; *Brooks* v. *Stuart*, 1 Beav. 512 ; Benjamin on sales, 3rd ed. p. 184.
(*x*) Addison on Contracts, 8th ed. p. 1221.
(*y*) Chitty on Contracts, 9th ed. p. 107 ; Benjamin on Sales, 3rd ed. p. 183. And see per *Amphlett*, J., in *Sanderson* v. *Graves*, L. R., 10 Ex. 234.
(*z*) See *Noble* v. *Ward*, L. R.; 2 Ex. 135 ; *Sanderson* v. *Graves, ubi supra.*
(*a*) 3 Mac. & G. 587.

had authority to enter into any new agreement, but it was held, that if such authority had been proved, the agreement being within the 4th sect. of the Statute of Frauds any alteration of its terms must have been evidenced by writing. It would seem, moreover, from the observations of Lord *Truro*, in his judgment in this case, that whether what passed between the plaintiff and the defendant's agent could or could not be contended to be a variation of the old agreemnt, *or as the formation of a new agreement*, that it ought to have been evidenced by writing.

(2) Revocation by death of the surety.

(2.) *The death of the surety is sometimes a revocation of the guarantee.*

Surety's death does not affect his past liability.

The death of the surety does not, of course, affect his liability in respect of past transactons. Whatever liability had actually attached to the surety at the time of his death may be enforced against his representatives. With respect to subsequent transactions and liabilities, whether a guarantee is revoked by the death of the surety depends, it would seem, upon the nature of the guarantee given. If it be a guarantee which the surety could himself have determined by notice (*a*), then, it appears, that notice of his death will operate as a revocation (*b*). But if, on the other hand, the surety could [*349] *not himself have put an end to the guarantee by notice, then his death does not revoke the instrument, nor does it extinguish his liability thereunder (*c*). In cases where the guarantee is determinable by notice of the death, and no such notice is given by the surety's executor or administrator, the right of the creditor to the benefit of the guarantee in respect of advances made or liabilities incurred subsequent to the death, would appear to depend upon the creditor's knowledge of such death having taken place (*d*.) Where, however, there are co-sureties, under a joint and several continuing guarantee, the death of one of them does not determine the future liability thereunder of the survivors (*e*), unless, *it seems*, they have given *express*

Its effect on subsequent transactions depends on nature of the guarantee itself.

Result of decisions on this subject stated.

(*a*) *Ante*, p. 345.
(*b*) *Coulthart* v. *Clementson*, 5 Q. B. D. 42; *Harris* v. *Fawcett*, L. R., 8 Ch. App. 866. See also *Beckett* v. *Addyman*, 9 Q. B. Div. 783, 791; *In re Sherry, London and County Banking Co* , v. *Terry*, 25. Ch. Div. 692, 703, 705; 53 L. J., Ch. 404; 50 L. T. 227; 32 W. R. 394.
(*c*) *Lloyds* v. *Harper*, 16 Ch. Div. 290; 50 L. J., Ch. 140; 43 L. T. 481; 29 W. R. 452.
(*d*) See *Harris* v. *Fawcett*, L. R., 15 Eq. 311; L. R., 8 Ch. App. 866. See also *Bradbury* v. *Morgan*, 8 Jur. N. S. 918.
(*e*) *Beckett* v. *Addyman*, 9 Q. B. Div. 783.

notice to the creditor terminating their liability thereunder (f). It is, however, to be noticed that the mere
fact of the guarantee being " a *joint* and *several* " guarantee must of itself be taken as some indication that
the death of one of the co-sureties was a possible event
contemplated by the parties at the time of the execution of the guarantee. But if the guarantee is "*joint*,"
and not "*joint* and *several*," this indication of intention would seem to be wanting. Where, however, three
persons joined in the guarantee, which was *not* in terms
several, to a bank, it was held that the death of one of
the sureties did not discharge the liability of the survivors (g).

It would seem, that, in the case of a guarantee of a
current account at a bank, it deals only with the account between the bank and the creditor until the bank
receives notice of the surety's death, so that no further
*dealings can take place on the faith of the [*350]
guarantee after death (h).

III. The surety may be discharged by the conduct
of the creditor (k).

III. Discharge of the surety by the conduct of the creditor.

The instances in which the surety may be discharged
by the conduct of the creditor are very numerous. For
the law favours a surety and protects him with considerable vigilance and jealousy. The conduct of the creditor, which will discharge the surety (k), may conveniently be considered under the following heads :—(A)
where the creditor varies the terms of the original contract between himself and the principal debtor, or of
the contract between himself and the surety ; (B)
where the creditor takes a new security from the principal debtor in the place of the old one; (C) where
the creditor discharges the principal debtor ; (D)
where the creditor discharges a co-surety ; (E) where
the creditor gives time to the principal debtor ; (F)
where the creditor agrees with the principal to give
time to the surety ; (G) where loss occurs through the
negligence of the creditor. All the several modes in
in which an implied discharge is given to the surety
call for separate notice and discussion.

(f) Ib. at p. 791.
(g) Ashby v. Day, W. N. 1885, 67.
(h) In re Sherry, London and Counting Banking Co. v. Terry, 25
Ch. Div. 692; 53 L. J., Ch. 404 ; 50 L. T. 227 ; 32 W. R. 394.
(k) The discharge of the surety by the fraud of the creditor,
and by alteration of the instrument of guarantee, have already
been considered in dealing with matters invalidating the guarantee ab initio, ante, pp. 324 et seq., 340 et seq.

(A.) Varia-
tion by credi-
tor of terms
of contract
between him-
self and
principal or of
the contract
between him-
self and the
surety.

(A.) *The surety may be discharged by a variation by the creditor either of the terms of the contract between the creditor and the principal debtor, or of the terms of the contract originally made between the creditor and the surety.*

A variation of the terms of the original contract made between the principal debtor and the creditor will, generally speaking, discharge the surety. And this is the case, whether such variation be, *first*, of the original agreement between the principal debtor [*351] *and the creditor ; or, *secondly*, of the original agreement between the surety and the creditor. It will, however, be more convenient to consider these modes of making the variations separately. Let us *first* deal with the case of a variation being made of the original agreement between the creditor and the principal debtor. There are two states of facts under which a surety is discharged by a variation of the contract be-

1st. Varia-
tion of con-
tract between
creditor and
principal.

tween the principal debtor and the creditor.' For, 1st, any material variation of the terms of the contract between the creditor and the principal debtor will always discharge the surety; and 2ndly, a variation of those terms which is *not* material, will also discharge the surety if it clearly appears that he became surety on the faith of the original contract, or if he has made these terms part of his own contract. And if notice were given to the surety of the terms of the contract between the creditor and the principal debtor, and after such notice he executed the guarantee, he is held to have become surety on the *faith* of the original agreement (*i*). And where the surety has made the terms of the original contract between the creditor and the principal debtor part of his own contract, any variation will discharge the surety, because it amounts to a breach of the creditor's contract with the surety and not merely to a breach of the creditor's contract with the principal debtor.

Effect of
material
variation of
such con-
tract.

Let us consider, in order, both these states of facts under which the surety is discharged. 1st, as to a material variation of the terms of the contract between the creditor and the principal debtor. A good instance of the surety being discharged by a material variation of the terms between the creditor and the principal is

*General Steam
Navigation Co.
v. Rolt.*

furnished by the case of *The General Steam Naviga- tion Co.* v. *Rolt* (*k*). In that case A. contracted with B. to build for him (A.) a ship for a given sum, to be

(*i*) *Sanderson* v. *Aston,* L. R., 8 Exch. 73, 76.
(*k*) 6 C. B., N. S. 550.

paid by instalments as the work reached certain stages; and *C. became surety for the due performance [*352] of the contract on the part of B., the builder. A. allowed B. to anticipate the greater portion of the last two instalments. It was held that C. (the surety) was discharged, as A., by allowing B. to anticipate the instalments, had materially altered the terms of the contract with B., the principal.

Another and very similar instance of the discharge of the surety by a material variation as between the creditor and the principal of the original contract, occurred in the case of *Calvert* v. *The London Docks Co.* (*l*). There a contractor undertook to perform certain works upon the terms that three-fourths of the work as finished should be paid for every three months, and the remaining one-fourth on the completion of the whole work. Payments, *exceeding* three-fourths of the price of the work done, having, without the consent of the sureties ' for the due performance of the work, been made to the contractor before the completion of the contract, it was held that such sureties were discharged.

Calvert v. London Docks Co.

In order to have the effect of discharging the surety, however, the variation made must clearly appear to be a *material* one. Whether or not a variation be material is a matter depending almost entirely on the peculiar circumstances of each case. An instance of a variation being held to be not a material one, and therefore not to discharge the surety, occurred in the case of *Stewart* v. *M'Kean* (*m*). There the defendant executed the following guarantee, addressed to the plaintiffs :—

Stewart v. M'Kean.

"Gentlemen,—I hereby agree to guarantee my brother, Mr. W. M'Kean's intromissions (*n*), as your agent in Leith, to the extent of 5,000*l.* sterling; and I am, &c.,

"*H. McKean.*"

*Soon after the commencement of the agency [*353] it was agreed between the plaintiffs and W. M'Kean, that the latter should furnish to the plaintiffs every six months an account current of the stock sent by them and of cash received by him from customers. The

---

(*l*) 2 Keen, 638. See also *Warre* v. *Calvert*, 7 Ad. & E. 143.
(*m*) 10 Exch. 675.
(*n*) The word "intromission" is a term partly legal and partly mercantile, and signifies dealings with stock, goods and cash of a principal coming into the hands of his agent and to be accounted for by the agent to his principal.

practice continued for about a year and a half, when a new agreement was entered into between the plaintiffs and *W. M'Kean, without the defendant's knowledge or consent.* This new arrangement was to the effect, that *W. M'Kean* should, from time to time, make his promissory notes payable four months after date in favor of the plaintiffs, and that he should send them to the plaintiffs at the rate of about one note per month; and that, on the notes becoming due, *W. M'Kean* should transmit to the plaintiffs an account of all the debts or sums he had collected from their customers, and that the plaintiffs should send him such an amount of cash as would, when added to the money already in his hands enable him to take up the notes. This agreement was immediately acted upon, and was continued to be acted upon by the plaintiffs and *W. M'Kean* until the termination of his employment as their agent. The practical effect of this agreement was to cause *W. M'-Kean* to pay over the moneys collected by him more promptly to the plaintiffs than he would otherwise have done. When *W. M'Kean* ceased to be in the employment of the plaintiffs, it was found that he had received certain moneys for the plaintiffs for which he did not and could not account. In an action upon the above guarantee, it was held, per *Parke*, B., *Alderson*, B., and *Martin*, B. (*Pollock*, C. B., *dissentiente*); that, inasmuch as the guarantee left the mode of accounting open to the will of the employers (the plaintiffs) provided they adopted a reasonable one, the agreement between the plaintiffs and their agent, *W. M'Kean*, as to the mode of accounting by means of promissory notes, as above [*354] mentioned, did *not discharge the surety from his liability upon the guarantee.

Sanderson v. Aston.   The recent case of *Sanderson* v. *Aston* (o) is another instance of a variation being held to be not a material one. In that case the declaration was on a bond given to the plaintiff by the defendant. The bond, thus declared on, recited that by an agreement of even date the plaintiff had agreed to admit J. into his service as "clerk and employer" (not further stating the terms of the agreement), and was conditioned for J.'s accounting for and paying over to the plaintiff all moneys which he might receive on the plaintiff's account. The breach alleged was that J. had received moneys for the plaintiff, which he had not accounted for or paid over. Among other pleas the defendant pleaded, on equitable grounds,

(o) L. R., 8 Exch. 73.

that the original agreement between the plaintiff and J. was, that such agreement should be terminable by one month's notice, and that the plaintiff and J. afterwards, and before the defaults sued for, made it terminable by three months' notice, without the defendant's consent. It was held (*Martin*, B., *dubitante*), that this plea was bad, on the ground that it did not show that the term as to the period of notice was made part of the defendant's contract, and that the alteration alleged *did not in fact materially add to the defendant's risk* (p).

Where the defendants agreed to indemnify the plaintiff against all liability which he might incur in giving a certain bond to the Treasury, and the plaintiff afterwards, in pursuance of a statute passed after the giving of the indemnity, made a payment to the Board of *Trade, to obtain the cancelling of the said [*355] bond, it was held, that the defendants' liability as surety had not been altered by such payment, which was covered by the indemnity, and that the defendants were liable for it to the plaintiff (q).

Moreover, even though a material variation be made by the principal debtor and the creditor in the terms of their original contract, or if the creditor so deals with his principal debtor, as to alter the position of the surety, still the surety is not discharged, if the transaction was with his concurrence (r). But if a surety becomes aware that the creditor is going to give time, or do something else, which, if done without his assent, may discharge him, he is not, it seems, bound to warn the creditor against doing the act (s). Material variation of contract between creditor and principal does not discharge surety if made with his consent.

2ndly, as to the discharge of the surety by a variation which is not in itself material, where the surety has contracted on the faith of the original contract, or has expressly made the terms of it part of his own contract. Effect of variation not itself material if contract between creditor and principal.

The surety is held to have become surety *on the faith* of the original agreement, if notice was given to him of the terms of the contract between the creditor and the Surety dis-

---

(p) *Kelly*, C. B., in his judgment in this case, says: "The authorities cited go to show that we are to look at the terms of the surety's engagement, not at the terms of any agreement between the employer and employed, unless these terms are made part of the surety's agreement, or unless something has been done which, with reference to those terms, substantially alters his position."

(q) *Webster* v. *Petre*, 4 Ex. D. 127.

(r) *Woodcock* v. *Oxford and Worcester Banking Co.*, 1 Drew. 521. See also *Oakford* v. *European Shipping Co.*, 1 H. & M. 182; *Swire* v. *Redman*, 1 Q. B. D. 536; 35 L. T. 470; 24 W. R. 1069.

(s) Per *Blackburn*, J., in *Polak* v. *Everett*, 1 Q. B. Div. 673.

Secondly.
Variation of contract between creditor and surety.
Surety is usually discharged by any variation.
Bacon v. Chesney.

Secondly, let us next deal with the case of the varia-tion of the terms of the agreement originally made between the creditor and the surety.

As a general rule, any variation of the terms origi-nally made between the creditor and the surety dis-charges the surety. Thus, for instance, in *Bacon v. Chesney* (b), it was held that if A. engages to guaran-tee the amount of goods supplied by B. to C., provided *eighteen* months' credit be given, and B. gives credit for *twelve* months only, he is not entitled, after the expira-tion of six months more, to call upon A. on his guaran-tee. Lord *Ellenborough,* in this case, said : "The claim as against a surety is *strictissimi juris,* and it is incumbent on the plaintiff to show that the terms of the guarantee have been strictly complied with. And so, again, where the bond by a surety purported to guarantee the payment of flour (of a specified quality), to be supplied by the obligee in order to enable the principal debtor to execute a contract, and the obligee designedly supplied inferior flour so that the contract was annulled ; it was held, that the obligor was, in equity, entitled to have the bond cancelled (c).

So, too, where defendant guaranteed the payment of gold with which the plaintiff should supply a goldsmith [*359] *for the purposes of his trade, and the plaintiff discounted bills for the goldsmith and gave him for them partly gold and partly money ; and the gold was applied to the goldsmith's trade, but the goldsmith did not indorse the bills, it was held, that the defendant was not liable under his guarantee for the gold so fur-nished (d). To a similar effect also is the well-known case of *Whicher v. Hall* (e). There a contract was made between A., B. and C., whereby A. agreed to let and B. agreed to take the milking of thirty cows at 7l. 10s. per annum, from 14th February, the rent to be paid quarterly in advance, and C. agreed to pay or cause to be paid the said rent. It was laid down by the court that in such a contract C. was a mere surety, and that in an action against him for the rent, A. was bound to prove a *literal* performance of the contract on his part, and that any variation made in such a con-tract by A. and B., without the consent of C., discharges

Whicher v. Hall.

(b) 1 Stark. 192.
(c) *Blest v. Brown,* 3 Giff. 450 ; 8 Jur., N. S. 187 ; 10 W. R., L. C. 569.
(d) *Evans v. Whyle,* 5 Bing. 485.
(e) 5 B. & C. 269; 8 Dow. & Ry. 22. See also *Wright v. San-ders,* 3 Jur., N. S. 504.

the latter, though his risk is not thereby increased. And it was further held in this case, that though it appeared that the alteration as to the mode of using the cows made no substantial difference as to profit or loss, the surety was discharged.

Upon the like principles, also, in *Mills* v. *The Alderbury Union* (*f*), it was decided, that, where a person becomes surety for another for moneys to be received by that other, the surety cannot be made liable, unless such other person individually and personally receive the money; and it has further been decided (*g*), that where a person is surety for another for the due accounting for moneys received by him, he is not liable for the nonpayment of money by that person jointly with another. And, where a person became surety by a *promissory note for a floating balance due to [*360] banker's from a customer, it was held that the surety was released by the bankers crediting the customer with the full amount of the note, without advancing the money at the time (*h*). And so, likewise, on the same strict principle, in *Philips* v. *Astling* (*i*), it was decided that, upon a contract to guarantee a bill for a given sum, the surety is not liable, even to the extent of that given sum, on a bill given for a larger sum. So, too, in *Pickles* v. *Thornton* (*k*), where the defendant in consideration that the plaintiffs would give up their lien on certain goods of Y., and would take the acceptances of Y. for 140*l.*, guaranteed to the plaintiffs payment of the same, and the plaintiffs accordingly gave up to Y. the said goods and took acceptances of Y. for 145*l.*, namely, one acceptance for the sum of 105*l.* and one acceptance for the sum of 40*l.*, it was held that the defendant was not liable even to the extent of 140*l.*

Where, however though there be an *apparent* variation there is *really* no variation of the terms of the original agreement, the surety will not be discharged. Thus, in *Davey* v. *Phelps* (*l*), the facts were as follows: —A surety gave a bond conditioned for the due payment by M. of all sums in which M. should, from time to time, become indebted to the plaintiffs for goods supplied to him by them in the course of their business. The plaintiffs, having drawn a bill upon M. for coals

Margin notes: Surety for moneys to be received by another not liable unless the money is actually received.

When surety stipulates for advance to third person, giving latter credit for a promissory note is no performance.

Surety for bill for a given sum not liable even to that extent if bill given for larger sum.

Pickles v. *Thornton.*

Surety not discharged where no real variation of the contract.

(*f*) 3 Exch. 590.
(*g*) *Mills* v. *Alderbury Union, supra; Bellairs* v. *Ebsworth*, 3 Camp. 52; *London Assurance Company* v. *Bold*, 6 Q. B. 514.
(*h*) *Archer* v. *Hudson*, 7 Beav. 551.
(*i*) 2 Taunt. 206.
(*k*) 33 L. T. R. 658, C. A. See also *Clarke* v. *Green*, 3 Ex. 619.
(*l*) 2 M. & Gr. 300.

supplied to him, discounted the bill, which was dishonoured. M. went to the plaintiffs and telling them
that he wanted 80l., to enable him to take up the bill,
asked them to *lend* him that sum. The plaintiffs thereupon gave him a cheque for 80l., with which, and his
own money, he took up the bill. It was held, that this
[*361] *was not in substance a loan by the plaintiffs to
M. of the 80l., but an advance by them for the specific
purpose of taking up the bill, which, as between the
plaintiffs and M., remained unpaid to that extent ; and
that, consequently, as the plaintiffs might have recovered the 80l. from M. as for goods sold, the defendant
was liable to pay that sum.

(B.) Discharge of surety by creditor taking additional security from principal debtor in lieu of original security.

(B.) *The surety may be discharged by the creditor
taking additional security from the principal debtor in
lieu of original security.*

A creditor discharges the surety if he take a further
security in lieu of the original security; or if he take
a further security of such a kind and given under such
circumstances as to operate as a merger of the original
security (m).

However, a creditor, by taking additional or further
security from the principal debtor, does not discharge
the surety, *unless* he took it in lieu of the original security (n), or unless the additional security operate as a
merger of the original security (o).

Whether a security was taken in lieu of original security is mainly question of fact.

Whether or not a security was taken in lieu of a prior
one, is, to a great extent, a question of fact. However,
where a security was originally given by bond, it was
held that it was not released by the creditor subsequently taking from the principal debtor a promissory
note for the amount due, subject to a general under-·
standing, though not in writing, that the giving of the
note was not to affect the bond (*p*). And, upon somewhat similar principals, it was decided in *Collins* v.
Owen (q), that a bill for the amount of a guarantee, given
by the principal debtor and taken by the plaintiff be-
[*362] fore the expiration *of the time mentioned in
the guarantee, but afterwards destroyed in the surety's
presence, is no waiver of the guarantee.

(m) *Clarke* v. *Henty*, 3 You. & Coll. Exch. Cas. 187; *Boaler* v. *Mayor*, 19 C. B., N. S. 76.
(n) See *Clarke* v. *Henty*, *ubi supra; Gordon* v. *Calvert*, 4 Russ, 581; *Eyre* v. *Everett*, 2 Russ. 381; *Twopenny* v. *Young*, 3 B. & C. 208, 210.
(o) *Boaler* v. *Mayor*, 19 C. B., N. S. 76.
(p) *Wyke* v. *Rogers*, 1 De G., M. & G. 408.
(q) 15 L. T., N. S. 327.

Whether or not a further security is a *merger* of one previously taken is, to a great extent, purely a matter of law. It would *seem* that there is no merger if it be expressly stipulated that the additional security shall be collateral only (r). And at all events, it is quite clear that a security, not under seal is not merged in a specialty security, unless the latter be as extensive as the former and between the same parties (s).

(C.) *The surety is discharged if the creditor volun- tarily discharge the principal debtor without reserve of remedies against the surety.*

Whatever has the effect of discharging the *principal debtor*, will generally discharge the surety also. In such a case the discharge of the principal is an *implied* discharge of the surety (t).

Thus, for example, if a deed of composition with the principal debtor be voluntarily executed by the creditor, the surety will be discharged (u). If, indeed, such deed were made with his consent (x); or if the original instrument of guarantee provided that the composition with the principal should not release the surety (y); or if the composition deed contained a reservation of remedies against the surety (z); then in any of these cases, for *reasons which we shall presently see, [*363] the surety is not discharged.

So, again, a surety was held to be discharged where a composition deed, under the Bankruptcy Act, 1861 (a), was executed by the creditor with the principal debtor, unless it *expressly* reserved the rights of the sureties against the principal debtor (b). And, in such a case, it was held, that the *implied* reservation contained in a reserve of the rights of the creditors against the sureties was not sufficient (c). But in other cases it was

Marginal notes: Whether the original security merges in subsequent one is a question of law. (C.) Discharge of surety by discharge of principal debtor. Voluntary execution by creditor of a deed of composition. Effect of a composition deed under Bankruptcy Act, 1861, on surety's liability.

(r) Per *Keating*, J., in *Boaler* v. *Mayor*, 19 C. B., N. S. 76.
(s) *Boaler* v. *Mayor, supra.*
(t) See *Burke's case* cited 2 B. & P. 62; cited 6 Ves. 809; and also cited 18 Ves. 20.
(u) *Wilson* v. *Lloyd*, L. R., 16 Eq. 60; 42 L. J., Ch. 559; 28 L. T. 331; 21 W. R. 507; *Ex parte Glendenning*, Buck, 517; *Boultbee* v. *Stubbs*, 18 Ves. 20, and observations of Lord *Eldon* at p. 22; *Duffy* v. *Orr*, 5 Bligh, N. S. 620: *Ex parte Gifford*, 6 Ves. 805; *Ex parte Carstairs*, Buck, 560; *Davidson* v. *M'Gregor*, 6 M. & W. 755.
(x) *Cowper* v. *Smith*, 4 M. & W. 519.
(y) *Kearsley* v. *Cole*, 16 M. & W. 128. See also *Davidson* v. *M'Gregor, ubi supra: Keyles* v. *Elkins*, 5 B. & S. 240; *Bateson* v. *Gosling*, L. R., 7 C. P. 9; 41 L. J., C. P. 53; 25 L. T. 570; 20 W. R. 98.
(z) *Kearsley* v. *Cole, ubi supra.*
(a) 24 & 25 Vict. c. 134.
(b) *Hooper* v. *Marshall*, L. R., 5 C. P. 4.
(c) *Ibid.*

(1521)

held that a deed under the same statute was valid, although not containing any clause reserving rights against sureties, unless it were shown that there were sureties, a creditor's rights against whom would be affected by its absence (d).

Effect of execution by creditor, as trustee thereof, of deed of assignment releasing principal debtor.

Where one of several persons, to whom the defendant had given a guarantee, subsequently executed a deed of assignment of the debtor's property, *in the capacity of trustee under such deed*, it was held, that as such deed-operated as an extinguishment of the debtor's liability, the defendant, as surety for the debtor, was thereby *entirely* released from liability under the guarantee (e).

Why release of principal debtor discharges surety.

The reason why a simple release of the principal debtor discharges the surety, is, that it would be a fraud upon the principal debtor to profess to release him, and then to sue the surety, who in turn would sue him (f).

Effect on surety's liability of discharge of principal by operation of law.

But although, as a rule, the discharge of the principal is the discharge of the surety, that is not the case where the discharge does not take place by the voluntary act of the creditor. Where the discharge is effected by the *operation of law*, the surety is [*364] not thereby released. Thus, a surety for a bankrupt is not discharged by the creditors signing the bankrupt's certificate, even after notice from the surety not to do so (g). And in a case decided before the Bankruptcy Act, 1883, which abolishes liquidation proceedings, it was held that the unconditional discharge of a debtor in liquidation did not release his sureties, although they (the sureties) did not assent to, but protested against, his discharge (h). . And in cases under the Bankruptcy Act, 1883, the acceptance or approval of a composition or scheme will not release any person who, at the date of the receiving order, was surety, or in the nature of surety for the debtor. For it is expressly provided that the acceptance by a creditor of a composition or scheme of arrangement shall not release any person who, under the Bankruptcy Act, 1883, would

(d) *Johnson* v. *Barratt*, L. R., 1 Exch. 65 ; *Poole* v. *Willats*, L. R., 4 Q. B. 630 ; 38 L. J., Q. B. 255 ; 20 L. T. 1006 ; 17 W. R. 1009 ; 9 B. & S. 957.

(e) *Teede* v. *Johnson*, 11 Ex. 840.

(f) Per *Mellish*, L. J., in *Nevill's case*, L. R., 6 Ch. App. at p. 47.

(g) *Browne* v. *Carr*, 7 Bing. 508. See also *Langdale* v. *Parry*, 2 Dowl. & Ry. 337.

(h) *Ellis* v. *Wilmot*, L. R., 10 Ex. 10; 44 L. J., Ex. 10 ; 31 L. T. 754 ; 23 W. R. 204 ; *Ex parte Jacobs, In re Jacobs*, L. R., 10 Ch. App. 211. And see *Megrath* v. *Gray*, L. R., 9 C. P. 216.

not be released by an order of discharge if the debtor
had been adjudged bankrupt (i). And such order of
discharge does not release any person who was surety,
or in the nature of surety for the bankrupt (i).

Where the obligee of a surety bond, without the consent of the surety, executed a deed by which the principal debtor was released from his debts, "in like manner as if he had obtained a discharge in bankruptcy,"
it was held, that, although if the debtor had obtained
his discharge in bankruptcy the surety's liability would
have continued, yet, as the. release by the obligee was
his own act, the surety was discharged (j).

Moreover, even in the case of a voluntary discharge of
the principal debtor by the act of the creditor, in order to
release the surety, there must be an actual *legal [*365]
discharge of the principal debtor, and not a mere
intention or contemplation of releasing him. Consequently, where a debtor and his surety, by a fraud, to
which the debtor was a party but of which the creditor
was innocent, succeeded in persuading the creditor to
release the debtor, it was held, that as no consideration
moved from the surety, the release was ineffectual ; and
it was further determined that the creditor was entitled
to be restored to his rights against the surety (k).

*Where no
actual legal
discharge of
principal
debtor,
surety re-
mains liable.*

Where a composition deed, by which the defendant
guaranteed the payment by the debtor (B) of the last
of three instalments, contained a clause that in "the
event of B. being adjudicated bankrupt, or of a conveyance or assignment of his property being made or
required under the provisions of the deed, before full
payment of the composition, the defendant should be released from his guarantee." it was held that the defendant
could only be released from his guarantee by a bankruptcy
of B. procured under the provisions of the deed (l).

Again, although, as a general rule, a voluntary discharge of the principal discharges the surety also, yet
the surety may, by express stipulation in the guarantee, agree to remain liable, even after the discharge of
the principal debtor. And in that case he is of course
not discharged by the discharge of the principal (m),

*Surety may
expressly
agree to re-
main liable
after prin-
cipal's dis-
charge.*

(i) Sect. 18 (15); sect. 30 (4).
(j) Cragoe v. Jones, L. R., 8 Exch. 81 ; 27 L. T. 36.
(k) Scholefield v. Templer, 4 De G. & J. 434 ; 28 L. J., Ch. 452.
(l) Glegg v. Gilbey, 2 Q. B. D. 6, 209 ; 46 L. J., Q. B. 325 ; 35
L. T. 927. And see Hughes v. Palmer, 19 C. B., N. S. 393 ; Webster v. Petre, 4 Ex. D. 127.
(m) Cowper v. Smith, 4 M. & W. 519 ; Union Bank of Manchester v. Beech, 13 W. R. 922 ; 34 L. J., Ex. 133 ; 12 L. T. 499 ; 13
W. R. 922.

since there is then no ground for the presumption that the discharge of the principal was an implied discharge of the surety also (n).

The consent of the surety to the discharge of the principal debtor will also have the effect of preventing [*366] such *discharge operating to release the surety. Thus, the surety is not discharged by the execution by the creditor of a composition deed with his assent (o).

Effect on surety's liability of a covenant not to sue principal. Again, it is clear that a mere covenant not to sue the principal debtor, qualified by a reserve of remedies against the surety, will certainly not discharge the latter (p). And formerly if, after executing a covenant not to sue the principal debtor, the creditor had sued him, such debtor might, it seems, have either brought a cross action on the covenant against the creditor, or have pleaded the covenant by way of equitable defence, since a court of equity would have restrained the creditor from suing the principal debtor by granting an unconditional injunction.

Effect of *release with reserve of remedies against surety. Upon similar principles, although *absolute and unconditional release* of the principal debtor discharges the surety, yet where the release contains a proviso, reserving the rights of the creditor against the surety, the surety is not discharged by it (q). In such a case, the instrument, by the very force of the proviso, is prevented from being a *release* and is cut down to a *covenant not to sue.*

Green v. Wynn. In *Green v. Wynn* (r), Lord *Hatherley* thus explains this doctrine (s): "But the authorities say that if, on the one 'hand, the debtor is released, and on the other hand, all demands against other persons are reserved, then it is inconsistent with the frame and object of the deed to hold that the release is intended to be complete and absolute, as that would make the two parts [*367] *of the deed utterly inconsistent. The release cannot be construed to be absolute, because then no rights would be reserved in any case, and the courts have, therefore, held that such a release is not to be

---

(n) See *Mr. Burke's case*, 2 B. & P. 62; 6 Vesey, 809; 18 Vesey, 20.

(o) *Cowper v. Smith*, 4 M. & W. 519.

(p) *Price v. Barker*, 4 E. & B. 760; *S. C.*, 24 L. J., Q. B. 130.

(q) *Maltby v. Carstairs*, 1 M. & R. 547; 7 B. & C. 735.

(r) L. R., 4 Ch. App. 204—206; 38 L. J., Ch. 220; 20 L. T. 131; 17 W. R. 385.

(s) See also *Currey v. Armitage*, cited 4 C. B., N. S. 221; *Bateson v. Gosling*, L. R., 7 C. P. 9; 41 L. J., C. P. 53; 25 L. T. 570; 20 W. R. 98; *Webb v. Hewett*, 3 K. & J. 438; *Kearsley v. Cole*, 16 M. & W. 128; *Vorley v. Barrett*, 1 C. B., N. S. 225; 26 L. J., C. P. 1.

construed as absolute, *but only as a covenant not to sue.* That being so, the remedy is gone, as between the debtor and the creditor, inasmuch as the creditor cannot sue the debtor; but, as against all other persons, the rights of the creditor are reserved." In accordance with this doctrine, under the following circumstances, a surety was held not to be released:—A deed of arrangement under the Bankruptcy Acts, 1861 and 1869 (*t*), contained a release of the debtor, subject to a proviso reserving the rights of creditors holding securities. The Court held that this operated as a covenant not to sue, and not as an extinguishment of the debt, so as to bar the remedy against the surety, notwithstanding the deed contained an absolute assignment of all the debtor's property and effects to the trustees, and also provisions for enabling them to carry on the trade for the benefit of the estate (*u*).

It *seems,* however, that as a general rule the reservation of rights against the surety, on giving the principal debtor a release, must appear *on the face* of the instrument, and that *parol* evidence of a reservation cannot be given (*x*). The general rule, however, does not appear to be without exceptions. Thus, in one case, the principal debtor executed an assignment of property for the benefit of his creditors containing a release by the creditors, but no reservation was contained of the creditor's rights against the surety. The creditor executed the deed with the privity of the surety, and on the understanding, as shown by the evidence, that his rights against the surety were not to be prejudiced * thereby, [* 368] and under these circumstances it was held that, even assuming that it was necessary that the reservation of remedies against the surety should appear *on the face* of the deed, at all events the omission of such express reservation did not discharge the surety, as the deed was executed with his consent (*y*).

It should also be noticed that though, as a rule, a release to the principal debtor is a release to the surety, yet a release given after the surety has made himself a principal debtor for the amount due has not this effect. This appears to be in analogy with similar cases which have been cited in two previous places. Thus, for principal

Semble, reservation of rights must appear on face of release.

Release of principal debtor after surety has himself become a principal will not discharge.

(*t*) 24 & 25 Vict. c. 134, and 32 & 33 Vict. c. 77.
(*u*) *Bateson* v. *Gosling,* L. R., 7 C. P. 9; 41 L. J., C. P. 53; 25 L. T. 570; 20 W. R. 98.
(*x*) *Cocks* v. *Nash,* 9 Bing. 341.
(*y*) *Ex parte Harvey,* 23 L. J., Bank. 26; *Wyke* v. *Rogers,* 21 L. J., Ch. 611; 1 De G., M. & G. 408.

instance, where the surety has given a security for the debt, the general rule will not apply, but the creditor, notwithstanding the release, will, in the absence of evidence to the contrary, retain his right against the surety. And this is not affected by the fact that the surety has actually paid part of the debt, and the security is for the balance (z).

Effect of release of one of several joint debtors where it is alleged that the remainder are only sureties for him.

Where a bond has been given for payment of money on a certain day by A., B. and C. jointly, and it does not appear on the face of the bond that B. and C. are only sureties, it is no defence to an action on the bond against B. and C. after A.'s death, to plead that A. was the principal, and that the plaintiff had released A.'s executor before bringing the action (a).

(D.) Effect of discharge of one of several sureties by creditor.

(D.) *The discharge by the creditor of a co-surety may, it seems, under some circumstances, discharge a surety.*

It is doubtful whether the simple discharge of one surety without more, under any circumstances, operates as a discharge of the other or others(b). It is submitted, [*369] *that it ought not to do so, for it is settled that the right of contribution is not thereby destroyed (c); and, so far as the decisions have gone on the subject, they are in accordance with, and tend to support, the view contended for. Thus, it has been decided that it is competent for creditors executing a deed of composition with the principal debtor, and certain of his sureties, to reserve their remedies against other sureties (d); and in the very singular case of a release of one co-surety, with a reserve of remedies against the other, it is settled that the surety is not discharged (e). Such a release would seem to operate as a covenant not to sue (f). In the recent case of *Ward* v. *National Bank of New Zealand* (g) it was held that where two or more sureties contract *severally*, the creditor does not break the contract with one of them by releasing the other; the contract remaining entire, the surety in order to escape from liability must show an existing right to

Where sureties severally liable, release of one by creditor does not discharge the rest.

(z) *Hall* v. *Hutchons*, 3 Myl. & Kee. 426.
(a) *Ashbee* v. *Pidduck*, 1 M. & W. 564.
(b) *Ex parte Gifford*, 6 Ves. 805, 807: *Thompson* v. *Lack*, 3 C. B. 540; contra *Evans* v. *Brenridge*, 2 K. & J. 174, 183; *Nicholson* v. *Revill*, 4 Ad. & E. 675; and see *Done* v. *Whalley*, 2 Ex. 198.
(c) *Ex parte Gifford*, supra.
(d) *Ex parte Carstairs*, Buck, 560.
(e) *Thompson* v. *Lack*, 3 C. B. 540. See also *North* v. *Wakefield* 13 Q. B. 536; *Cheetham* v. *Ward*, 1 B & P. 630; *Solly* v. *Forbes*, 2 Br. & B. 38.
(f) *Willis* v. *De Castro*, 4 C. B., N. S. 216; 27 L. J., C. P. 243. And see *Ex parte Good*, *In re Armitage*, 5 Ch. D. 46.
(g) L. R., 8 App. Cas. 755; 52 L. J., P. C. 65; 49 L. T. 315.

contribution from his co-surety which has been taken away or injuriously affected by the release.

(E.) *The surety, as a rule, and subject to certain exceptions, is discharged by the creditor agreeing to give time to the principal debtor.*

If the creditor, without the consent of the surety, enter into a binding agreement *with the principal debtor* to give him further time for payment, the surety will be discharged (*h*). This is the case, even though no *injury could accrue to the surety, for he him- [*370] self is the fit judge of what is or is not for his own benefit (*i*). It is not, however, every agreement or promise made by the creditor which will have the effect of discharging the surety.

In the first place, an agreement by the creditor to give time to the principal debtor will not discharge the surety, and never did so either at law or in equity, unless it be of a *binding* character, and unless made on valuable consideration (*k*). Thus, where a creditor

(E.) Surety discharged by creditor agreeing to give time to principal debtor.

The agreement to give time must be a binding one.

(*h*) *Combe* v. *Woulfe*, 1 M. & Scott, 241; 8 Bing. 156. And see *Lewis* v. *Jones*, 4 B. & C. 506; and note at p. 515. Observations of Lord *Hatherley*, L. C., in *Oriental Financial Corporation* v. *Overend, Gurney & Co.*, L. R., 7 Ch. App. 142, 150; L. R., 7 H. L. 348; 31 L. T. 322; *Samuel* v. *Howarth*, 3 Mer. 272; *Newton* v. *Chorlton*, 2 Drew. 333, 338; *Wright* v. *Simpson*, 6 Ves. 714, 734; *Nisbet* v. *Smith*, 2 Brown, C. C. 578, and note (*a*), 583; *Rees* v. *Berrington*, 2 Ves. jun. 539 a; *Clarke* v. *Henty*, 3 You. & Coll. 187; *Blake* v. *White*, 1 You. & Coll. 620. See note (*a*), p. 515, of 4 B. & C., observations of Lord *Eldon*, in *Hawkshaw* v. *Parkins*, 2 Swanst. 539, 546. Observations of *Tindal*, C. J., in *Browne* v. *Carr*, 7 Bing. 508 515; *Ewin* v. *Lancaster*, 12 L. T. 632; 13 W. R. 857; *Bailey* v. *Edwards*, 4 B. & S. 761; 34 L. J., Q. B. 41. See also *English* v. *Darley*, 2 B. & P. 61; *Moss* v. *Hall*, 5 Exch. 46; *Oakeley* v. *Pashaller*, 10 Bligh, N. S. 548; *Isaac* v. *Daniel*, 8 Q. B. 500; *Davies* v. *Stainbank*, 6 De G., M. & G. 670; *Pooley* v. *Harradine*, 7 E. & B. 431; *Bank of Ireland* v. *Beresford*, 6 Dow. 233; *Archer* v. *Hall*, 4 Bing. 464; *Eyre* v. *Bartrop*, 3 Madd. 224; *Howell* v. *Jones*, 1 C., M. & R. 97; *Greenough* v. *M'Clelland*, 2 Ell. & Ell. 426.

(*i*) *Samuel* v. *Howarth*, 3 Mer. 272. See also on this subject *Polak* v. *Everett*, 1 Q. B. D. 675 *et seq.*; *Home* v. *Brunskill*, 3 Q. B. D. 495. See also per Lord Chancellor *Eldon*, in *Ex parte Glendinning*, Buck, 517, 519. In *Ex parte Gifford*, 6 Ves. 805, 806, and in *Ex parte Wilson*, 11 Ves. 410. Per Lord *Langdale*, M. R., in *Calvert* v. *The London Dock Co.*, 2 Keen, 638, 644; *Blest* v. *Brown*, 8 Jur. 603. But see *Newton* v. *Chorlton*, 2 Drew. 333, 339. And see *Petty* v. *Cooke*, L. R., 6 Q. B. 790, 795; 40 L. J., Q. B. 281; 25 L. T. 90; 19 W. R. 1112.

(*k*) *Blake* v. *White*, 1 Y. & C. 620; *Heath* v. *Key*, 1 Y. & J. 434. Per Lord *Eldon*, in *English* v. *Darley*, 2 B. & P. 61, 62. See also *London Assurance Co.* v. *Buckle*, 4 B. Moore, 153; *Hearn* v. *Cole*, 3 Dow. 459; *Philpot* v. *Briant*, 4 Bing. 717; *Clarke* v. *Wilson*, 3 M. & W. 210; *Badenall* v. *Samuel*, 3 Price, 521; *Brickwood* v. *Annis*, 5 Taunt. 614. Observations of *Pollock*, C. B., and

[*371] knew that the *surety was negotiating a loan for the principal debtor for the purpose of paying off therewith the debt for which the surety was liable, and thus getting rid of such liability, and the creditor made a promise to the debtor, without consideration, to give him further time, and this induced the surety to desist from his attempt to raise the money ; it was held that the surety's liability to the creditor was not discharged (l).

Pleading agreement giving time to principal debtor.

An agreement by a surety to give time to his principal may, however, in some cases be binding, whether it be written or verbal. Formerly, indeed, where the guarantee was under seal, if time were given to the principal debtor, by *parol* agreement, the surety could not set up such parol agreement as a defence at law (m), but was obliged to resort to a court of equity for relief; for, at law, an instrument could only be dissolved by one of equal or superior force (n). Eventually, however, by virtue of 17 & 18 Vict. c. 125, s. 83, such an agreement might have been pleaded to an action by way of equitable defence (o), though, of course, the surety was still at liberty to resort to a court of equity for relief. And now, since the passing of the Judicature Act, the defendant may raise in any court any equitable answer or defence which would formerly have been good by way of answer if the suit had been brought in chancery (p).

Agreement to give time need not be express.

An agreement to give time need not, however, be made in express words in order to have the effect of discharging the surety. If an agreement in effect be a giving of time by an *implied* agreement, it will operate to relieve the suretyship. Thus, for instance, where [*372] *a bond creditor, by agreement with his debtor, takes interest by anticipation on his debt, a court of equity would formerly have restrained an action on the bond, whether brought against the principal or the surety (q). For such an agreement amounts to an agreement to give time, as, by taking interest, the

Channell, B., in *Price* v. *Kirkham*, 3 H. & C. 437 ; *Smith* v. *Winter*, 4 M. & W. 454 ; *Tucker* v. *Laing*, 2 K. & J. 745 ; *Petty* v. *Cooke*, 40 L. J., Q. B. 281 ; L. R., 6 Q. B. 790 ; 25 L. T. 90 ; 19 W. R. 1112 ; *Bell* v. *Banks*, 3 M. & G. 258 ; *Arundel Bank* v. *Labbe*, Chitty on Bills, p. 296.
(l) *Tucker* v. *Laing*, 1 K. & J. 45.
(m) *Davey* v. *Prendergrass*, 5 B. & Ald. 187. Per Lord *Abinger*, C. B., in *Blake* v. *White*, 1 Y. & C. 420, 425.
(n) *Davey* v. *Prendergrass*, *sup.*
(o) Per *Cur.*, in *Woodhouse* v. *Farebrother*, 5 E. & B. 277, 289.
(p) Judicature Act, 1873, s. 24, sub-s. (2). And see *Mostyn* v. *West Mostyn Coal Co.*, 1 C. P. D. 145.
(q) *Blake* v. *White*, 1 You. & Coll. 620.

creditor would be prevented from suing on the bond.
So a creditor who takes a promissory note or bill from
a debtor, who is in default, impliedly gives him time,
since he cannot sue the debtor until the maturity of the
bill or note (r). Likewise the renewal of a bill by the
creditor may operate to discharge the surety, unless
made with the assent of the latter (t). Again, where
the obligee of a bond had placed himself in such a
position with regard to the principal debtor that he
could not demand payment of the bond until a certain
agreement entered into with third parties had been
carried into effect, it was held that this amounted to
such a giving of time to the principal debtor as discharged a surety to the bond (u).

Since, in order to discharge the surety, there must be
a binding agreement by the creditor to give him time,
it follows that mere *passive inactivity*, or omission to
press the debtor, as distinguished from *an agreement*
giving further time, will not discharge the surety (x),
even *when the debtor has become insolvent [*373]
during the time thus suffered to elapse (y). Thus,
when the surety set up, as a defence to an action
brought against him by the creditor, that the latter had
delayed an unreasonable time—to wit, ten years—to
demand payment from the principal debtor, it was held,
in a case decided in Ireland, to be a bad defence (z).
The surety may, however, as we have seen (a), stipulate in his contract that the creditor is not to sue him
until after failure of the creditor's utmost efforts against
principal expressly stipulated for.

Passive inactivity will not discharge surety.

Unless active measures against principal expressly stipulated for.

(r) Croydon Commercial Gas Co. v. Dickinson, 1 C. P. D. 707; 2 C. P. D. 46.
(t) Torrence v. Bank of British N. America, L. R., 5 P. C. 246; 29 L. T. 109; 28 W. R. 329.
(u) Cross v. Sprigg, 2 M. & G. 113.
(x) Trent Navigation Co v. Harley, 10 East, 34; Wilkes v. Huley, 1 C. & M. 249. Per Gibbs, C. J., in Orme v. Young, Holt, N. P. C. 84; London Assurance Co v. Buckle, 4 B. M. 153; Goring v. Edmonds, 6 Bing. 94; Peel v. Tatlock, 1 B. & P. 419. Per Jervis, C. J., in Strong v. Foster, 17 C. B. 201, 215; York City and County Banking Co. v. Bainbridge, 43 L. T., N. S. 732. Per Lord Eldon, in Mayhew v. Crickett, 2 Swanst. 185; Boultbee v. Stubbs, 18 Ves. 20, 22; Eyre v. Everett, 2 Russ. 381; Black v. The Ottoman Bank, 10 W. R. (P. C.) 871; 6 L. T. 620; 8 Jur., N. S. 801; Dawson v. Lawes, 1 Kay, 280; M'Taggart v. Watson, 3 Cl. & Fin. 525. Per Lord Eldon, in Samuel v. Howarth, 3 Mer. 272, 278; Perfect v. Musgrave, 6 Price, 111. Per Lord Cottenham, in Creighton v. Rankin, 7 Cl. & Fin. 325, 346, 347; Shepherd v. Beecher, 2 P. W. 288. Per Lord Eldon, in Wright v. Simpson, 6 Ves. 714, 734. Per Pollock, C. B., in Price v. Kirkham, 3 H. & C. 437, 441.
(y) Trent Navigation Co. v. Harley, ubi supra.
(z) The Belfast Banking Co. v. Stanley, 1 C. L. Ir. 693.
(a) See ante, p. 186.

the principal debtor, and, in such a case, of course, mere passive inactivity on the part of the creditor would discharge the surety (b).

Inchoate agreement to give time will not discharge surety. Again, since it will not discharge the surety, unless it is a *binding* agreement, it also follows that, if an agreement be made to give time to the principal debtor, but such agreement never take effect, the surety is not discharged. Thus, for instance, if such agreement be conditional on the performance of some act by the principal debtor, which the latter omits to perform, as the operation of the agreement is wholly prevented, the surety is not discharged (c). And in a recent *American* case it was held that an agreement by a creditor to accept a certain percentage within a specified time in full of his claim, but containing no stipulation for delay [*874] *or extension, and never complied with, did not discharge a surety for the debt (d).

Agreement to give time will not discharge surety unless made with principal debtor. In the next place, in order to have the effect of discharging the surety, it is necessary that the agreement should be made with the principal debtor himself, and not with a mere stranger. An agreement made by the creditor *with a stranger* to give time to the principal debtor, even though it be binding, and made for a valuable consideration, does not operate as a discharge of the surety (e).

The agreement must also give time to principal debtor himself. Lastly, in order to have the effect of discharging the surety, the agreement with the principal debtor must be an agreement *to give time* to him. If there be no giving of time the surety is not discharged. Thus, under the following circumstances, it was held that there had in reality been no giving of time, and therefore no discharge of sureties. Certain sureties, by the terms of their contract, were not to be liable till demand made on them. The creditors, when a balance was due to them from the principal debtors, took from the latter, without consulting the sureties, a warrant of attorney for the amount due, with a stay of execution if they should discharge the debt by instalments of 100l. a month, and on default, execution was to issue for the whole. It was held that the warrant of attorney cer-

---

(b) *Holl* v. *Hadley*, 2 A. & E. 758; 8 Bing. 156; *Watson* v. *Alcock*, 22 L. J., Ch. 858; 17 Jur. 568; 4 De G., M. & G. 242; *Montague* v. *Tidcombe*, 2 Vern. 518. But see *Musket* v. *Rogers*, 5 Bing. N. C. 728.

(c) *Vernon* v. *Turley*, 1 M. & W. 316; *Badcock* v. *Samuel*, 3 Price, 521. See also *Price* v. *Edmonds*, 10 B. & C. 578.

(d) *Miller* v. *Hatch*, 39 Amer. R. 346 (U. S.)

(e) *Fraser* v. *Jordan*, 26 L. J., Q. B. 288; 8 El. & Bl 303. See also *Lyon* v. *Holt*, 5 M. & W. 250.

tainly gave time, which might have discharged the
sureties if they had been affected by it ; but that here
the sureties' liability, not arising *till demand*, and, previous to the demand, default having been actually made
by the debtors, so that execution might have instantly
issued for the whole debt, the agreement made ·by the
warrant of attorney was at an end, and the sureties
were no ways *injured, as there was nothing [*375]
to interfere with their immediate recourse to the principal debtors (f).

What is a "giving time'' was defined by the Court What
of Exchequer in the case of *Howell* v. *Jones* (g), in the amounts to
following terms:—   a giving of
                                                                                    time.
   "We think it means extending the period at which, *Howell* v.
by the contract between them, the principal debtor was *Jones.*
originally liable to pay the creditor, and extending it by
a new and valid contract between the creditor and the
principal debtor, to which the surety does not assent."
In this case a guarantee was given by the defendant to
the plaintiff, who was a banker, by which the defendant
became responsible for the amount of such cheques one
Bowers might from time to time draw on the plaintiff.
It was contended by the plaintiff that the defendant, as
surety, was not discharged, though the plaintiff had on
one occasion taken *Bowers'* acceptance for the amount
of his balance, inasmuch as, in taking such acceptance,
the creditor was only dealing with the principal debtor
on the original terms of the contract between them.
Bolland, B., in delivering the judgment of the court,
said: "If, however, the creditor continues to deal with
the principal debtor on the original terms of the contract
between them, he cannot, we think, by any length of
credit which he so gives, be properly said to give time
to the debtor.   The time must be given as an extension
of the original credit.   If, therefore, it could be shown,
in fact, that the taking the three months' bill in this
case in *February*, 1828, from the principal debtor was
part of the original contract between the bankers and
Bowers, for which the defendant became the guarantee,
there would be much force in the arguments addressed
to the court on the part of the plaintiffs, that the defendant was bound to know the nature of the contract
*which he guaranteed, and that the course of [*376]
dealing between the bankers and *Bowers* might be

(f) *Prendergast* v. *Devey*, 6 Madd. 124, 126. See also *Price* v.
Edmonds, 10 B. & C. 578 ; *Jay* v. *Warren*, 1 C. & P. 532; *Whitfield* v. *Hodges*, 1 M. & W. 699.
   (g) 1 Cr., M. & R. 97, 107.

properly referred to for that purpose. But, giving them
the full benefit of the argument, it is disposed of by the
facts of the case." And accordingly the court on these
facts held that the defendant was discharged.

Whether time has been given sometimes depends on construction of original contract.
Although the general meaning of the expression
"giving time" is thus defined, it is nevertheless sometimes difficult to say what really was "the period at
which, by the contract between them, the principal
debtor was originally liable to pay the creditor." This
sometimes has to be ascertained from the terms of the
original contract between them. And in such cases the
words used must receive a *reasonable* interpretation.
Thus, in *Simpson* v. *Manley* (*h*), a guarantee ran as
follows: "If you give A. B. *credit* we will be responsible
that his payments shall be regularly made." The question having arisen whether there had been a giving of
time to A. B., it became necessary to decide when A. B.
was, under these terms, bound to pay the creditor. The
court held, that the word "credit" meant a fair and
reasonable credit according to the manner in which A. B.
and the persons guaranteed should deal, and did not
confine the guarantee to dealings according to the strict
customary credit of the trade.

Custom of trade will not justify giving of time to principal debtor.
In other cases, again, the period at which the debtor
becomes liable to pay the creditor is not indicated by any
express agreement between them on the point. And in
such cases the time at which the debtor becomes liable to
pay is the time at which *legal* liability accrues. Accordingly *custom of trade* would not apparently justify
indulgence to the principal debtor (*i*). Thus, evidence
that *according to the custom of the trade* the plaintiffs
delivered coals to N. H. daily, and that at the end
[*377] *of every month he gave a bill payable in two
months, was held not sufficient to charge the defendant
upon a guarantee for the payment of coals to be delivered to N. H. at a credit of two months from the delivery (*k*). On the part of the defendant it was con
tended, that this was a dealing at variance with the
express language of the guarantee, which was for a
credit of two months from the delivery. On the part
of the plaintiffs it was urged, that the delivery, being
according to the custom of the coal trade, which must
have been in the contemplation of the parties at the
time the guarantee was executed, the whole supply of

(*h*) 2 C. & J. 12.
(*i*) *Combe* v. *Woulfe*, 8 Bing. 156; 1 M. & Scott, 241; *Holl* v.
Hadley, 5 Bing. 54; 2 A. & E. 758.
(*k*) *Holl* v. *Hadley*, *ubi supra*.

coals for each month must be considered as delivered
on the last day of the month, which was a delivery within
the terms of the guarantee. The plaintiffs, however,
were nonsuited, and a rule to set the nonsuit aside was
discharged.

It was formerly doubtful, prior to the introduction of
equitable pleas, whether in order to enable a surety to
raise at law a defence, on the ground that time had been
given to the principal, it was necessary to show that the
original contract between the plaintiff and the defendant
was that of creditor and surety (*l*). It was, however,
decided in equity, that the holder of a security was, in
dealing with the security, affected by knowledge acquired after taking the security, as to which of the parties liable on the security was the principal and which
the surety (*m*).

In equity, the defendant's right to relief arose from
the existence of the relation of principal and surety
*between the surety and the principal debtor, [*378]
and from the creditor's actual or constructive knowledge
thereof at the time he took the security; and the fact
that the creditor did not agree to treat the surety as a
surety, did not debar the latter from such relief, and
such knowledge might have been relied upon in a court
of equity, and eventually might have been alleged in
an equitable plea at law (*n*).

These distinctions between law and equity are now
abrogated, and the equitable rule will now prevail when
any conflict arises between legal and equitable doctrines,
as provided by the Judicature Act, 1873 (*o*). However, joint debtors cannot by subsequent agreement
inter se, that the one is to be surety only for the other,
change their position with regard to the creditor, without his assent, and so deprive him of his right to treat
both as principal debtors (*p*). And a creditor who,
after notice of such agreement, gives time to one of

Sidenotes: Former distinctions between law and equity as to right of original contract between surety and principal to be treated as a surety where the contract does not distinguish in express terms between principal and surety. These distinctions no longer exist.

(*l*) *Manley* v. *Boycott*, 2 Ell. & Bl. 46; *Strong* v *Foster*, 17 C. B.
201; *Bailey* v. *Edwards*, 4 B. & S. 761; *Ewin* v. *Lancaster*, 12 L.
T. 632; 13 W. R. 857, and cases there cited; *Lawrence* v. *Walmsley*, 12 C. B., N. S. 799, 807. See also *Taylor* v. *Burgess*, 5 H.
& N. 1; *York City & County Banking Co.* v. *Bainbridge*, 43 L. T.,
N. S. 732.
(*m*) *Oriental Financial Corporation* v. *Overend & Co.*, L. R.,
7 Ch. App. 142; 7 H. L. 348; 31 L. T. 322; *Maingay* v. *Lewis*, 5
Ir. C. L. R. 229.
(*n*) *Greenough* v. *M'Clelland*, 2 Ell. & Ell. 424; and see *Goodman* v. *Litaker*, 37 Amer. R. 602 (U. S.).
(*o*) 36 & 37 Vict. c. 66, s. 25 (11).
(*p*) *Swire* v. *Redman*, 1 Q. B. D. 536; 35 L. T. 470; 24 W. R.
1069.

the joint debtors does not thereby discharge the other
(*q*).

Effect of agreement to give time with reserve of remedies against surety. It may however, happen that all these three requisites to his discharge may exist, that is to say: that there may be a binding agreement: that it is an agreement made with the principal debtor himself; and that it is an agreement to give time; and yet that the surety is not discharged. For there are certain cases in which although all these three requisites exist, it is held, that the surety cannot possibly be affected and is not discharged from his engagement. One instance, and perhaps the most common instance, of this is, where an agreement giving time to the principal debtor is expressly made *with a reserve of remedies* [*379] *against the surety*. For such a reservation prevents there being any discharge of the surety (*r*). The reason for this is, *first*, because it rebuts the implication that the surety was *meant* to be discharged, which is one of the reasons why the surety is ordinarily exonerated by such a transaction; and, *secondly*, because it *prevents* the rights of the surety against the debtor being impaired, the injury to such rights being the other reason why, in ordinary cases, the surety is discharged. For the debtor cannot, where there is a reservation, complain if the instant after paying the creditor the surety enforces his rights against him; and the debtor's consent that the creditor shall have recourse against the surety, is impliedly a consent that the surety shall have recourse against him (*s*). A creditor may, upon giving time to his debtor, reserve any right against the surety without communicating the arrangement to the surety (*t*).

Reserve of remedies should usually appear on face of instrument. In order to keep alive the liability of the surety it must, however, as a rule, appear *on the face* of the instrument giving time that the remedies against the surety are reserved (*u*) Still, it seems that this is not *always* necessary and that, sometimes, such a reserva-

(*q*) *Ibid.*
(*r*) Per *Parke*, B., in *Kearsley* v. *Cole*, 16 M. & W. 128. Per Lord Chancellor *Eldon*, in *Ex parte Glendinning*, Buck, 517, 519 ; *Wyke* v. *Rogers*, 1 D. M. & G. 408; *Boaler* v. *Mayor*, 19 C. B., N. S. 76, 83, 84 ; *S. C.*, 13 W. R. 775 ; *Ex parte Gifford*, 6 Ves. 805, 808. See also *Owen* v. *Homan*, 4 H. L. Cas. 997, 1037 ; *Close* v. *Close*, 4 De G., M. & G. 176.
(*s*) *Webb* v. *Hewitt*, 3 K. & J. 438.
(*t*) *Ibid*; *Kearsley* v. *Cole*, 16 M. & W, 128.
(*u*) *Ex parte Glendinning*, Buck, 517, 520, See also *Boultbee* v. *Stubbs*, 18 Ves. 20, 22; *Overend, Gurney & Co., Limited* v. *Oriental Financial Corporation*, L. R., 7 Ch. 142 ; 7 H. L. 348 ; 31 L. T., 322.

tion may be proved by parol evidence (x). Certainly it may be proved by *parol evidence* that there was a general understanding between the creditor and the principal debtor, that the *taking of a promis- [*380] sory note should not discharge the surety (y).

Another instance in which, although there is a bind- Where the ing agreement with the debtor to give him time, the effect of surety is, nevertheless, not discharged, may also be men- alleged tioned. This is the case where the effect of the agree- agreement to give time is ment beween the creditor and the principal debtor is, to accelerate in point of fact, to accelerate the surety's remedies. surety's Obviously, as against the surety, this does not amount remedies. to an agreement giving time (z). Indeed, besides the cases which have been mentioned, it has been laid down as a general rule, governing all questions of this kind, that a surety is not discharged if his remedies are not interfered with (a); if the agreement is made with his assent (b); or if he subsequently confirms it (c).

Neither does an agreement made with the principal Agreement debtor, after the surety has himself become a principal to give time debtor and subject to a primary liability, discharge the charge surety. Thus, after a decree in equity had been obtained surety who by the creditor against the surety, it was held that no has previ- arrangement giving time to the principal debtor, with- ously become out the knowledge of the surety, would discharge the debtor. latter (d). The creditor "having by the decree estab- lished his right against the estate of the surety, has a right to proceed under it ; and all that follows is in the nature of execution of the decree, and the subsequent dealing with the principal debtor does not operate to discharge the surety from a liability under which he is no longer *as surety*, but under the decree" (e). [*381] And, on the same ground, where by an agreement made with the creditor subsequently to the guarantee, the surety has converted himself into a principal debtor, an arrangement giving time to the original debtor made *after* such agreement will not discharge or effect the

(x) Per Lord Justice *Turner*, in *Ex parte Harvey*, 33 L. J., Bank. 26, 32. And see note (a), 4 B. & C. 515, 516.
(y) *Wyke* v. *Rogers;* 21 L. J., Ch. 611 ; 1 De G., M. & G. 408.
(z) *Hulme* v. *Coles*, 2 Sim. 12.
(a) Per *Blackburn*, J., in *Petty* v. *Cooke*, L. R., 6 Q. B. 790, 795 ; 40 L. J., Q. B. 281 ; 25 L. T. 90 ; 19 W. R. 1112.
(b) *Clerk* v. *Devlin*, 3 B. & P. 363 ; *Smith* v. *Winter*, 4 M. & W. 454 ; *Tyson* v. *Cox*, 1 T. & R. 395 ; *Cowper* v. *Smith*, 4 M. & W. 519 ; *Union Bank of Manchester* v. *Beech*, 13 W. R. 922.
(c) Per Lord Chancellor *Eldon*, in *Mayhew* v. *Crickett*, 2 Swanst. 185, 192 ; *Smith* v. *Winter*, 4 M. & W. 467.
(d) *Jenkins* v. *Robinson*, 2 Drew. 351.
(e) Per *Kindersley*, V.-C., in *Jenkins* v. *Robinson, supra.*

surety. An example of this is afforded by the case of
Reade v. *Lowndes* (*f*). In that case judgment having
been obtained against a surety, he entered into a *new*
arrangement with the creditor (irrespective of the principal debtor), by which execution was not to issue while
he kept up certain policies for securing the debt. It
was held, that by this arrangement the surety became
a principal, and that no subsequent dealing between
the creditor and the principal debtor could annul it.

To what ex-
tent surety is
discharged
by agreement
giving time
to principal.
It is now necessary to consider *to what extent* a
surety is discharged by an agreement giving time to
the principal. In *Bingham* v. *Corlett* (*g*), it was held
that in the case of a continuing guarantee for the price
of goods to be supplied to a person at a specified credit,
if goods are supplied at a longer credit than that stipulated for by the surety, and these goods are subsequently paid for, and *afterwards* other goods are supplied at the specified credit, in respect of which default
in payment is made by the principal debtor, the surety
is liable for this default. In *The Croydon Commercial Gas Co.* v. *Dickinson* (*h*), the facts were as follows :—A principal (with sureties for the performance
of the contract) contracted to take tar from a gas company, and to pay for each month's supply within the
first fourteen days of the ensuing month, unless the
[*382] company *should by writing allow a longer
time for payment. After the expiration of the first
fourteen days of August, the company took a promissory note from the principal for the amount due for
July. Default was made by the principal in payment
of the amounts due in July, August and September.
It was held that the sureties were discharged only as
to the amount due in July, the contract being separable, and the position of the sureties as to the amounts
due for August and September not being affected by
the giving time for payment of the amount due for
July. This decision has been followed in the *Irish*
case of *Dowden* v. *Levis* (*i*). There the defendants
were sureties to the plaintiffs for H. D., on a continuing guarantee for the value of goods to be supplied by
the plaintiffs to H. D. not exceeding 3,000*l.* in all.
The plaintiffs, without the knowledge or consent of defendants, having taken a bill from H. D. at three

(*f*) 23 Beav. 361. ; 26 L. J., Ch. 793.
(*g*) 34 L. J., Q. B. 37 ; 12 W. R. 1030.
(*h*) 2 C. P. D. 46 ; 1 C. P. D. 707; 46 L. J., C. P. 157 ; 36 L.
T. 135 ; 25 W. R. 157.
(*i*) 14 L. R., Ir. 807.

months still current for 45l., on account of a portion of the sum due for goods supplied to H. D., the actual amount due being for goods previously ascertained, it was held that the defendants were not released from liability to pay the balance of the sum due for the goods supplied to H. D. under the guarantee, but were only discharged to the extent of the 45l. for which the bill was taken.

(F.) *The surety may be discharged by the creditor agreeing with the principal debtor to give time to the surety himself.*

It has recently been decided in the case of *The Oriental Financial Corporation* v. *Overend, Gurney & Co (j)*, that if the holder of a security agrees with the principal to give time to the surety, he thereby discharges the surety. Lord *Heatherley*, L. C., said, "If the creditor agrees with the principal that he will not *sue the sureties, the case is stronger than the [*383] usual case of an agreement to give time to the principal, which only involves, by implication, an engagement not to sue the surety. The position of the surety is changed, because it is one thing to lie by and wait before suing the principal, during which time the surety has a right to come in, discharge the debt, and immediately sue the principal, and another thing to engage positively with the principal that time shall be given to the surety, and so tie up your own hands from doing that which would throw the surety upon the principal." Where, however, the creditor, by separate contract with the surety himself, made on good consideration, gives him further time, he is not thereby discharged (k).

(G.) *Another group of cases in which the surety is held to be discharged, by the conduct of the creditor, consists in those cases in which a loss has occurred through the negligence of the latter. Such negligence of the creditor may consist (1) in laches by him; or (2) in the loss by him of securities given for the guarantee debt*

(1,) *The surety may be discharged by the laches of the creditor.*

It is a rule that the surety will be discharged if the creditor omit to do anything which he is bound to do for the protection of the surety, though mere passive

Sidenotes: (F.) Discharge of surety by creditor agreeing to give time to surety himself. (G.) Discharge of surety by negligence of creditor. (1.) By laches of the creditor. Mere *passive* negligence does not constitute laches.

(j) L. R., 7 Ch. App. 142; 7 H. L. 348; 31 L. T. 322.
(k) *Defries* v. *Smith*, 10 W. R. (V.-C. S.), 189.

negligence on his part will not have this effect (*l*). A
good example of this rule is furnished by the case of
Watts v. *Shuttleworth* (*m*).   There it was stipulated in
the agreement between the plaintiff and the principal
debtor, that the plaintiff should insure from risk by fire
the work which the principal debtor was doing for him.
[*384] *The defendant, when he became surety for the
due performance of the work, was informed of this
stipulation. It was held that he was discharged by the
plaintiff's omission to insure. In this case it was also
expressly laid down in terms that in equity, upon a
contract of suretyship, if the person guaranteed does
any act injurious to the surety, or inconsistent with his
rights, or, if he *omits* to do any act which his duty
enjoins him to do, and the omission proves injurious to
the surety, the latter will be discharged.   The following
additional instances of the application of this rule may
also usefully be cited :—Where a person binds himself
by guarantee to indorse any bills which may be given
in part payment of a debt to be contracted by a third
person, the person so binding himself is discharged,
unless a demand be made upon him to fulfill his engagement within a reasonable and convenient time (*n*).

In *Philips* v. *Astling* (*o*), the defendant guaranteed
the payment of a bill by the drawer or the acceptor.
The party who gave this guarantee was not a party to
the bill.   The bill was not presented for payment when
it became due, as it ought to have been ; two days afterwards notice that it remained unpaid was given to the
drawers, but no notice was given to the defendant.
The drawers and acceptor continued solvent for many
months after the bill was dishonoured, and it was not
until they had become bankrupts that payment was
demanded of the defendant.   Under these circumstances, because the necessary steps were not taken to
obtain payment from the parties to the bill while they
continued solvent, the Court of Common Pleas held the
surety, *i. e.*, the person who guaranteed the payment of
the bill, to be discharged.

A broker, when he bought goods for his principal,
agreed for one-half per cent. to indemnify him from any
[*385] *loss on the resale.   It was held that this un-

(*l*) Per *Hannen*, Sir J., in *Guardians of Mansfield Union* v.
Wright, 9 Q. B. D. at p. 688, and per *Cotton*, L. J., in *Carter* v.
White, 25 Ch. Div. at p. 670 ; *Strong* v. *Foster*, 17 C. B. 201 ; 25
L. J., C. P. 106.
(*m*) 7 H. & N. 353 ; 5 H. & N. 235.
(*n*) *Payne* v. *Ives*, 3 D. & Ry. 664.
(*o*) 2 Taunt. 206.

dertaking was discharged when the principal had a fair opportunity of selling to advantage but neglected it, though he was afterwards obliged to sell at a loss (p).

It also appears that where any one gives security for the conduct of another in a certain office, which brings him in contact with persons also in the office, he has a right to expect that these persons will, in all things affecting the surety, conduct themselves according to law and discharge their duties (q). But though this is generally true, yet it cannot avail to discharge a surety who has expressly bound himself for a person's doing certain things, unless it can be shown that the party taking the security has by his conduct either prevented the things from being done, *or connived at their omission*, or enabled the person to do what he ought not to have done, or leave undone what he ought to have done, and that, but for such conduct, the omission or commission would not have happened (r). Thus, in the case of *Dawson* v. *Lawes* (s), a bond was given by two sureties for the faithful discharge of his duties by an official assignee in bankruptcy. Immediately upon his death, by the examination of his books, he was found to be a defaulter to a very large amount. Actions were commenced on the bond against the sureties. One of the sureties sought to restrain the action, on the ground of the negligence of the officials, whose duty it was to examine the assignees' accounts, &c. There did not appear, however, to have been any want of compliance by these parties with the rules and *regulations [*386] in bankruptcy, and the motion for an injunction was refused. It was held, in this case, that to discharge a surety for the due performance of duties there must be, on the part of the obligee, such an act of connivance or gross negligence amounting to a wilful shutting of the eyes to the fraud, or something approximating to it. Again, in the case of *Guardians of Mansfield Union* v. *Wright* (t), where the defendant disputed his liability as surety for a collection of poor rates in re-

Marginal note: Surety may be discharged by conduct of persons towards officer for whose good behavior he is bound.

(p) *Curry* v. *Edensor*, 3 T. R. 524; and see *Mutual Loan Fund Association* v. *Sudlow*, 5 C. B., N. S. 449; 28 L. J., C. P. 108; 5 Jur., N. S. 338.
(q) Per Lord *Brougham*, in *Mactaggart* v. *Watson*, 3 C. & F. 525; *Meir* v. *Hardie*, 8 Shaw & Dunlop, 346; *Montague* v. *Tidcombe*, 2 Vern. 518. See also *Dawson* v. *Lawes*, 23 L. J., N. S. 434, 439.
(r) Per Lord *Brougham*, in *Mactaggart* v. *Watson*, 3 C. & F. 542, 543.
(s) 23 L. J.,N. S., Eq. 434.
(t) 9 Q. B. Div. 683 ; 31 W. R. 312 ; 47 J. P. 228 ; and see *Watertown Fire Insurance Co.* v. *Simmons*, 41 Amer. R. 196 (U. S.).

spect of the sums omitted to be collected, upon the
ground that the loss would not have occurred if the
overseers had looked more diligently into the proceedings
of the collector, it was held that as no negligence was
imputed to the plaintiffs themselves, and they were not
answerable for the conduct of the overseers, the defendant was not discharged from his liability as surety.
Moreover, *Jessel, M. R.*, in his judgment, expressly
states that in his opinion the defence would have failed
even if the overseers had been the plaintiffs.   And it
was held, in a case decided in *Ireland*, that mere negligence, even if gross, on the part of a creditor, unac-
companied by positive acts of concurrence in the defal-
cation of a debtor, will not discharge the surety, and is
no ground of equitable defence (*u*).

Surety for good behavior may require employer to dismiss employed for misconduct. Non-compliance with such request discharges surety.

Where a bond is given for the good behaviour of
another in an office or employment, the surety is entitled to call on the employer to dismiss the employed
if, after the giving of the bond, the employed is guilty
of acts for which he may be dismissed (*x*).   And, consequently, if the employer has placed it out of his
power to comply with this request of the surety, by
continuing the employed in his service, when he ought
to have dismissed him, the surety is discharged (*y*).

Aliter, where power of dismissal vested in third person.

[*387] *But it would seem that the omission by the
creditor to exercise a power of suspension from office,
as distinguished from a power of dismissal, would not
terminate the surety's liability (*z*).

Mere omission by creditor to do something which he is not legally bound to do is not laches.

Upon the other hand, the rule that laches by the
creditor discharge the surety, does not extend to mere
omissions by the creditor to do something, which, although he may have been requested to do it, he is not
by his own promise, nor in any other way, legally bound
to do.   Thus, for instance, in *Shepherd* v. *Beecher* (*a*),
A., on apprenticing his son to B., gave B. a bond for
1,000*l*. for his son's fidelity.   The son embezzled 203*l*.,
which A. paid, but *desired B. not to trust the son any
more with the cash.*   · Notwithstanding this B, did trust
the son again with the cash, and was *negligent* in calling him to account, and he embezzled 1,000*l*. more.
It was held that A. was liable, but not to answer more,
in the whole, than 1,000*l*., *including* the first 203*l*.

(*u*) *Madden* v. *M'Mullen*, 13 Ir. C. L. R. 305.
(*x*) See *ante*, p. 288.
(*y*) *Sanderson* v. *Aston*, L. R., 8 Exch. 73; *Burgess* v. *Eve*, L.,
R., 13 Eq. 450; *Phillips* v. *Foxall*, L. R., 7 Q. B. 666.
(*z*) *Byrne* v. *Muzio*, 8 L. R., Ir. 396, Ex. D.
(*a*) 2 P. W. 288.

The court, in giving judgment, said : "The father having given this bond for his son's fidelity, though there was an embezzlement, and though the father sent this letter to the master, desiring him not to trust the son with receiving cash any longer, yet the father continued bound, *and ought not to have satisfied himself with sending the letter and taking no further care of the matter*, but should have endeavored to have made some end with the master, *and to have got up the bond;* wherefore he must continue liable to answer some embezzlements, unless there should appear fraud in the master."

The surety is not discharged by the mere omission of creditor to give surety notice of misconduct of principal. Thus, in *Peel* v. *Tatlock* (*b*), it was decided that if A. became bound to B. for the honesty of C., who embezzles money, B. may maintain an action on *the guarantee, though three years have elapsed [*388] without any notice having been given of the embezzlement of C. by B. to A. ; at least, if A. was acquainted of the circumstance from any other quarter, and B. does not appear to have industriously concealed it from him, and A. will not be discharged from his guarantee, though B. appear to have given credit to C. for the amount of the sum embezzled. {.Omission to give surety notice of misconduct of principal does not bar creditor's right of action.}

If the guarantee for another's good conduct expressly stipulate that notice of any act of dishonesty committed shall be given to the surety, the omission to give such notice, like the omission to fulfil any other stipulation in the contract, will operate to discharge the surety. •But such a proviso, unless expressly made to extend to acts of dishonesty which occurred on the part of the person employed *before* the guarantee was given, or the employment had commenced, is fulfilled by giving notice of such fraud and dishonesty only as would form the foundation of a claim under the guarantee (*c*). {Unless surety has expressly stipulated that such notice shall be given.}

Neither is an accidental omission to answer an inquiry laches which discharges a surety. Thus, in the case of *Oxley* v. *Young* (*d*), the defendant guaranteed to the plaintiff payment of goods to be supplied to C., upon an undertaking of D. to indemnify the defendant. The plaintiff accordingly informed the defendant that the goods were preparing, and afterwards shipped them for {Accidental omission to answer surety's inquiry is not laches.}

(*b*) 1 B. & P. 419.
(*c*) *Bryne* v. *Muzio*, 8 L. R., Ir. 396, Ex. D., but see *Enright* v. *Falvey*, 4 L. R., Ir. 397, which was not cited to the Court in *Byrne* v. *Muzio, ubi supra.*
(*d*) 2 Bl. 613.

C. without giving notice to the defendant that they were shipped. Afterwards, D. desired to recall his indemnity, upon which the defendant wrote to the plaintiff to know whether he had executed the order. To this inquiry no answer was given by the plaintiff for a considerable time, he having gone abroad in the *interim.* Upon this the defendant, supposing from the silence of [*389] *the plaintiff that the order was not executed, gave up his indemnity to D. It was held that the defendant still remained liable on his guarantee.

Nor creditor's omission to take proceedings which must have proved fruitless.
So,.too, the omission of the creditor to take proceedings which would obviously have a fruitless result does not amount to laches or discharge the surety. Thus, in *Muskett* v. *Rogers* (e), a guarantee given by the defendant was to be void if the plaintiff should omit to avail himself to the utmost of any security he held of W. R., and if anything should prevent the defendant from retaining the proceeds of an execution levied on the property of W. R. It was held, that the guarantee was not avoided by the plaintiff's omitting to put in suit a bill of exchange, drawn by W. R. and accepted by an insolvent still in prison, or by the defendant's being deprived of a part of the proceeds of his execution against W. R., such part being the value of the goods of another person wrongfully taken under that execution.

Or if he neglect at surety's request to sue principal, who afterwards becomes insolvent.
In cases where the guarantee does not expressly stipulate that the debtor shall be sued, before having recourse to the surety, it would seem that a surety is not released by the creditor's neglect to sue the principal upon request, although the principal afterwards become insolvent (f).

The rule laid down in *Watts* v. *Shuttleworth* (g), that an injurious act or omission of the creditor will discharge the surety, was held not to apply under the following circumstances:—A bank granted a letter of credit to a company, and agreed to accept bills drawn upon them by the company in respect of that credit, on the terms that the company should ship tea and forward bills of lading, invoices and policy of insurance on the tea to the bank, and should also draw on B. & Co. bills to be accepted by B. & Co. to an amount suffi- [*390] cient to cover the *amount authorized by the letter of credit. B. & Co. guaranteed the performance by the company of these terms, "holding themselves re

(e) 5 Bing., N. C. 728. See *Holl* v. *Brown*, 2 Ad. & E. 758.
(f) *Smith* v. *Freyler*, 47 Amer. R. 358 (U. S.).
(g) 7 H. & N. 353; S. C., 5 H. & N. 235.

sponsible for the same." The company drew on the
bank, and the bank accepted the bills, but owing to the
failure of the bank after the dates when the bills were
drawn and before they became due, the company shipped no tea, and did not perform any of the terms agreed
on. It was held, that the failure of the bank was no
reason why the company should not have performed its
part of the contract, and that B. & Co. were not relieved from their guarantee (h). It was also expressly
held, that the failure of the bank did not amount to an
injurious act so as to discharge B. &. Co. (the sureties)
within the rule laid down in *Watts* v. *Shuttleworth.*

The recent case of *Carter* v. *White* (i) is a good example of the doctrine that a surety is not discharged
merely by the negligence of the creditor. There a
debtor gave his creditor a bill of exchange accepted by
himself, but with the drawer's name left in blank. The
plaintiff, at the same time, as a surety deposited with
the creditor certificates of stock in a joint stock company as collateral security for the debt. The debtor
died insolvent without the creditor having filled in the
drawer's name. The bill was never presented for payment, nor was notice given to the plaintiff of its non-
payment. It was held, that the surety was not discharged from liability by the omission of the plaintiff
to fill up the drawer's name and to give notice of the
non-payment of the bill to the defendant. It was held,
also, that a bill of exchange, accepted for valuable consideration, with the drawer's name left in blank, may
be completed by the insertion of the drawer's name
after the acceptor's death.

Omission by creditor to render bill of exchange complete by inserting drawer's name, will not discharge surety for its payment.

*In cases where the Crown is in the position of [*391]
creditor and a subject is the surety, the *laches* of the
creditor does not, it seems, discharge the surety, as it is a
general doctrine that *laches* cannot be imputed to the
crown (k).

Semble, where guarantee given to the Crown laches on the part of latter do not discharge surety.

(2.) *The surety is, generally speaking, discharged pro
tanto by the loss, through the fault of the creditor, of
securities received by the creditor from the principal
debtor.*

(2.)Discharge of surety *pro tanto* by loss of securities held by creditor.

We have already seen (l) that a surety is entitled to
the benefit of all the securities which the creditor has

(h) *Ex parte Agra Bank,* L. R. 9 Eq. 725. See judgment of
Bacon, C. J., in this case, at p. 732.
(i) 25 Ch. Div. 66; 50 L. T. 670; 32 W. R. 692; 54 L. J., Ch.
Div. 138; and see *Belfast Banking Co.* v. *Stanley,* 1 Ir. C. L. R.
693.
(k) *The Queen* v. *Fay,* 4 L. R., Ir. 606.
(l) *Ante,* pp. 290 *et seq.*

against the principal. It follows, therefore, that, if the surety be deprived of his benefit by the act of the creditor, he will be discharged to the full extent of the security to which he was entitled (*m*); and, consequently; a creditor is bound to use diligence and care with regard to securities held by him. Thus, for instance, a creditor holding a mortgage for a guarantee debt is bound to hold it for the benefit of the surety so as to enable him, on paying the debt, to take the security in its original condition, unimpaired (*n*). The right of the surety is to have the same security in exactly the same plight and condition in which it stood in the creditor's hands (*o*). This doctrine does not, however, apply to such securities as life insurances. It is not the duty of the creditor on the bankruptcy of the debtor to keep up a policy on the life of the latter. On the contrary, it is his duty to sell and realize such a security (*p*).

Abandon-
ment by
creditor of
execution
against
principal
debtor.

Upon the same principal, again, an abandonment by the creditor of execution against the principal releases [*392] *the surety, because the creditor is a trustee of the execution (*q*). This was also the case when, under the old law, the execution was against the body. So, that a surety was discharged where the creditor, by neglecting the statutory formalities, lost the benefit of an execution under a warrant of attorney, which, according to the agreement of suretyship, he had proceeded to enforce upon a notice by the surety (*r*).

Destruction
of right of
distress for
rent does not
discharge
surety.

A surety, however, is not discharged where by conduct of the creditor a right of distress for rent in arrear is destroyed, as this is not strictly a security held by the creditor in respect of a debt within 19 & 20 Vict. c. 97, s. 5 (*s*).

Security
received from

So, again, a surety has also an equitable right that

(*m*) *Wulff* v. *Jay*, 20 W. R . Q. B. 1030 ; *S. C.*, L. R.; 7 Q. B. 756 ; 41 L. J., Q. B. 322 ; 27 L. T. 118 ; 20 W. R. 1030 ; *Capel* v. *Butler*, 2 S. & S. 457 ; *Straton* v. *Rastall*, 2 T. R. 366 ; *Williams* v. *Price*, 1 S. & S. 581 ; *Strange* v. *Fooks*, 4 Giff. 408 ; 11 W. R. 983. See also *Watts* v. *Shuttleworth*, 7 H. & N. 353 ; 5 H. & N. 235 ; *Ex parte Mure*, 2 Cox, 63.
(*n*) *Pledge* v. *Buss*, Johns. 633.
(*o*) *Id.*,Per *Wood*, V.-C.
(*p*) *Coates* v. *Coates*, 33 Beav. 249. See also *Wheatley* v. *Bastow*, 7 De G., M. & G. 261.
(*q*) *Mayhew* v. *Crickett*, 2 Swanst. 185. See also observations of Lord *Eldon*, in *English* v. *Darley*, 3 Esp. 49, 50 ; 2 B. & P. 61 ; and of *Leach*, V.-C., in *Williams* v. *Price*, 1 S. & S. 581.
(*r*) *Watson* v. *Alcock*, 1 Sm. & Giff. 319 ; 4 De G., M. & G. 242. See also *Wulff* v. *Jay*, L. R., 7 Q. B. 756 ; 20 W. R. 1030 ; 41 L. J., Q. B. 322 ; 27 L. T. 118 ; 20 W. R. 1030 ; but see *The Queen* v. *Fay*, 4 L. R., Ir. 606, 616.
(*s*) *In re Russell*, *Russell* v. *Shoolbred*, 29 Ch. Div. 254.

any security given by a co-surety shall not be wasted (t). **a co-surety**
But it *seems* that this right is the only right which a **must not be**
surety possesses in respect of such a security. **wasted.**

In order, however, to effect a discharge of the surety, **Surety is not**
it must appear both that there has been a loss of secu- **discharged,**
rities, and that such loss was caused by the fault of the **though cred-**
creditor. Thus, where there has not been any actual **itor assigns**
loss at all, but, at most, a transaction which *might* **securities**
possibly have caused a loss and affected the surety's **without**
position, the surety is not discharged; and, and accord- **notice to**
ingly, where a creditor has security upon the equitable **him.**
interests of his debtor and of a surety in a trust
fund, and such creditor assigns the debt, together
with the securities for the same, it is not necessary
*to give the surety notice of such assignment, [*393]
and the assignee does not lose his right against the interest of the surety, though no such notice be given. *Wheatley* **v.**
This is settled by the case of *Wheatley* v. *Bastow* (u). *Bastow.*
In that case, *Turner*, L. J., in his judgment, says,
"This point, so far as I am aware, is wholly new, and
it is certainly of great importance, as it introduces a
new element into the consideration of the cases of principal and surety. In the absence of authority, we can
determine the question only upon principle. It must
depend upon what are the relative obligations of the
creditor, the assignee and the surety arising out of the
relation which subsists between them. The creditor, is
no doubt, under the obligation of preserving the securities which he takes from the principal debtor, for (as
observed by the Vice-Chancellor) the surety may entitle
himself to the benefit of those securities, and, if any of
them be lost by the act or default of the creditor, the
surety may be wholly or partially discharged; *but the
creditor enters into no contract with the surety not to assign the debt or the securities.* The law gives him the
right to assign them, and, if he does so assign them,
the obligation which attached upon the creditor attaches
upon the assignee. The position of the surety is in no
respect altered. The assignee, on the other hand, ac-
quires by the assignment all the rights of the assignor,
and it is difficult, I think, to see how the surety can be
in a better position against the assignee than he was in
against the assignor. The surety, it is said, has the
right to know who is the assignee; but, admitting this
right, the question still remains, is the right of the assignee against the surety destroyed, because the fact of

---

(t) *Margetts* v. *Gregory*, 10 W. R., Ex. 630.
(u) 7 De G., M. & G. 261, 279. 280.

the assignment has not been communicated to him?
On whom does the law cast the *onus* of finding the
[*394] creditor? Generally *speaking, as I conceive,
upon the debtor, but, apart from this consideration, the
surety, if he have no notice of the assignment, may
pay the creditor, and the payment, as I apprehend,
will be perfectly good against the assignee, and, if,
upon the payment being made or tendered, the creditor be required to deliver, and does not deliver any
securites held by him, the surety would, no doubt, be
entitled to relief in this court, and to stay any proceed
ings by the creditor. It is to be remembered in these
cases, that a surety, though a favoured debtor, is still a
debtor, and that he may at any time relieve himself by
paying the debt; and, further, that if notice to the
surety of the assignment of the debt be held to be necessary, serious impediments to assignments by creditors may, in many cases, be created."

Depreciation in value of securities held by creditor does not discharge surety. Neither, of course, is a surety discharged by the mere
fact that a loss has taken place with regard to the prop-
erty given as security. To discharge the surety, it
must appear that such loss was in some way attribut-
able to the fault of the creditor. And, even should a security prove absolutely worthless, whether it was so
originally or whether it became so afterwards, the
surety is not discharged unless the loss or deficiency of
the original and primary security was occasioned by
the act of the creditor (x). Thus, in *March* a trader
assigned all his goods, &c., to A. B., to secure a composition to his creditors, and A. B. became liable for the
payment. The wife of the trader became surety to A.
B. in respect to her separate estate. In *November* the
trader was made bankrupt, and A. B. entered into an
arrangement by which he gave up the goods to the assignee. It was held that the first assignment to A. B.
was an act of bankruptcy, and that the wife's separate
estate as surety was not released (y).

Where surety has become a principal, the loss of securities held by creditor does not discharge him. Moreover, even where there has been a loss, and a
[*395] *loss caused by the fault of the creditor, the
surety is not in all cases discharged. For, in analogy to
a line of cases which have been before alluded to (z), it
was held that where, by subsequent dealings with the
creditor, the surety had converted himself into a principal
debtor, and the creditor *afterwards* took the principal

(x) *Hardwick* v. *Wright,* 35 Beav. 133.
(y) *Ib.*
(z) *Ante,* p. 380 ("Giving Time to Principal.")

(1546)

debtor in execution, and discharged him without payment, he had not thereby released the surety (a).

IV. The fulfilment of the purpose for which the guarantee was given has, of course, the effect of completely discharging the surety. Such fulfilment usually takes place either: (1) By payment made by the principal debtor; (2) By a set-off having arisen between the creditor and the principal debtor; or (3) By payment made by the surety, and accepted by the creditor, in satisfaction of the suretyship's liability. *(IV. Discharge of comcharge of surety by fulfilment of purpose for which guarantee was given.)*

(1.) *The surety is discharged if payment be made by the principal debtor.* *(1.) Where payment is made by the principal debtor.)*

The surety will, of course, be discharged if the debt guaranteed be paid by the original debtor. And if it be only paid in part, the surety will be discharged *pro tanto.*

In the simple case of a payment of the debt being made by the principal debtor, in the ordinary course of business, generally speaking no difficulty or question arises. A surety is, of course, discharged if the principal debtor pay the creditor the amount of the secured debt. A payment made by the principal debtor will not, however, have the effect of discharging the surety unless it be a *valid payment.* Thus, where a creditor accepted money from the principal debtor which he thought, at the time he accepted it, was a good and valid payment, whereas, in fact, the payment amounted to a *fraudulent preference*, and as such was subsequently set aside, it *was held, that the creditor had not thereby [*396] done an act against the faith of the contract with the surety, so as to discharge the surety (b). *(The payment must be a valid legal payment to have this effect.)*

It is, moreover, sometimes difficult to determine whether a particular transaction amounts to a payment by the surety. Thus, in *The Guardians of the Lichfield Union* v. *Green* (c), the defendant executed a bond conditioned to be void if G. *should honestly, diligently and faithfully perform and discharge the duties of his office* as treasurer of a poor law union. One of the duties was to pay out of any money, for the time being in his hands belonging to the guardians, all orders, &c. drawn upon him. G. was a country banker issuing his own notes. On the 28th December the plaintiffs, *(Difficult sometimes to determine whether what has been done amounts to payment. Guardians of Lichfield Union v. Green.)*

(a) *Pease* v. *Lowndes*, 23 Beav. 361.
(b) *Petty* v. *Cooke*, L. R., 6 Q. B. 790; 40 L. J., Q. B. 281; 25 L. T. 90; 19 W. R. 1112; and see *Pritchard* v. *Hitchcock*, 6 M. & G. 851; 6 Scott, N. R. 801; 12 L. J., C. P. 322.
(c) 1 H. & N. 884; 26 L. J., Ex. 140; 3 Jur., N. S. 247

the guardians of the union, drew several orders for money, some of which, to the extent of 95*l*, were on that day presented at G.'s bank, and were paid in notes of the bank. On the 31st December the officer of the union presented other orders, and received 200*l* in notes of G.'s bank. On the same day, the plaintiffs having to transmit money to London, their clerk presented to G. an order for 4*l*. 19*s*. 8*d*., and obtained from him a common banker's draft on a bank in London, which was afterwards dishonoured. G. stopped payment at three o'clock on the 31st December, and on the 1st January was declared a bankrupt. It was held, that the defendant, as surety, was not liable to make good either of the three several sums of money to the plaintiffs, on the ground that, as far as related to the 95*l*, the plaintiffs by retaining it in their possession during the Saturday, thereby conclusively elected to treat the orders as paid, and that the sureties had a right to treat the transaction as payment; and that, as far as [*397] *related to the other two sums, inasmuch as the plaintiffs, instead of claiming their right of being paid in sovereigns or Bank of England notes, thought fit to receive the country notes from G., the obligation of the defendant was thereby satisfied and discharged.

Surety entitled to benefit of all payments obtained from principal, whether voluntarily or by compulsion.

The surety is not only entitled to the benefit of all. payments made by the principal debtor voluntarily and in the usual course of business, but he is also entitled to the benefit of all payments obtained from the principal debtor by process of law or by the realization of securities given by him.

If the creditor makes available any of the securities for the debt guaranteed, the surety is entitled to the benefit of it. So, where the creditor distrained upon goods mortgaged to the surety by the principal debtor, for the *same* debt in respect of which the distress issued, it was held, that the surety's liability was discharged to the extent of the sum produced by the sale of the goods (*d*).

Doctrine of appropriation of payments.

It frequently becomes a question, moreover, whether a payment made by the principal debtor was made on account of the debt guaranteed or in respect of some other matter. Consequently, the doctrine of appropriation, or, as it was termed in Roman law, "imputation," of payments, is one of great importance to sureties. Where, for instance, the principal debtor is indebted to the creditor in *two* sums, and for the pay-

(*d*) *Pearl* v. *Deacon*, 24 Beav. 186; and see *Kinnaird* v. *Webster*, 39 L. T. R. 494; 27 W. R. 212; 10 Ch. Div. 139.

ment of *one* of these *only* a guarantee has been given, and subsequently to the contracting of these two debts, sums of money not sufficient to cover either debt are paid to the creditor by the debtor, the question arises, in respect of which of the debts are these sums paid? The law of England, in regard to the appropriation of payments, is concisely stated by *Tindal*, C. J., in *Mills* v. *Fowkes* (e), in the *following words :—"Ac- [*398] cording to the law of England the debtor may, in the first instance, appropriate the payment, *solvitur in modum solventis;* if he omit to do so, the creditor may make the appropriation, *recipitur in modum recipientis;* but if neither make any appropriation, the law appropriates the payment to the earlier debt." It is necessary to observe that, according to our law, if the *debtor* wishes to appropriate a payment to a particular debt, he must exercise the option *at the time of making the payment* (f). But it is not necessary that the *creditor* who receives the money should make an *immediate appropriation* of it. "The payee may make the appropriation at *any time* before the matter comes to trial, and he is not bound to give notice thereof to the payer" (g).

According to the Roman civil law, however, the creditor, as well as the debtor, had to make the appropriation at the time of payment (h). Also, according to that law, if neither the debtor nor creditor exercised the right of appropriation, the payment was applied to the more burdensome of two debts where one was more burdensome than the other, thus favouring the debtor rather than the creditor (i). If, however, both debts were equally burdensome, then the payment was applied to the earlier debt (k). — Appropriation of payments according to Roman civil law.

An instance of this doctrine of appropriation of payments being applied in case of the surety is afforded by the case of *Marryatts* v. *White* (l). There security was given by a surety for goods to be supplied to his principal. Goods were subsequently supplied, and pay- — The doctrine of appropriation of payments applied where sureties

---

(e) 5 Bing. N. C. 455—461. See further *Clayton's case*, Tudor's L. C., Merc. and Maritime Law, 2nd ed., p. 1, and notes thereto. See also 1 Story, Eq. Jur., Pothier on the Law of Obligations (Evans' ed.), pp. 368—376.

(f) Tudor's L. C., Merc. and Maritime Law, p. 18, and cases there cited.

(g) Tudor's L. C., Merc. and Maritime Law, p. 21, and cases there cited.

(h) Dig., lib. 46, tit. 3, § 1.

(i) Dig., lib. 46, tit. 3, § 5.

(k) *Ibid.*

(l) 2 Stark. 101.

claim benefit [*399] *ments were from time to time made by the
of payments
made by
principal.
principal. In respect of some of these payments, discount was allowed for prompt payment. It was held,
that it must be inferred in favour of the surety that all
these payments were intended in liquidation of the
latter account. In *Kinnaird* v. *Webster* (*m*) the following were the facts :—The sum of 2,000*l*. was advanced
by A. & Co., bankers, to B., a customer of theirs, and
placed by them to the credit of his general current account. A. & Co. took as security for the advance ten
promissory notes to mature during a period of ten
weeks, at the rate of one note per week. C., as surety
for B., gave a written undertaking that if the promissory notes and interest on any of them were not duly
paid he would, upon demand, secure payment of the
same by a mortgage of certain specified property.
Moneys were paid from time to time into B.'s account
more than sufficient to meet the bills if they had been
so applied ; but as the account was at the same time
largely drawn upon it was, when the bills matured,
largely overdrawn. A. & Co. having claimed for a
mortgage upon the property of C., it was held that
A. & Co., having received moneys which they might
have applied in payment of the notes secured by the
surety which had fallen due, were bound to have so applied them, and that the debt was moreover discharged
on the principal of *Clayton's case, ubi supra.* In a
subsequent case this decision was supported upon the
ground that the intention of the parties was that only
if sufficient money was not paid in by the principal
debtor to meet the bills, was the guarantor to be looked
to for payment ? (*n*) Upon the other hand, it has been
held that a payment by the obligor of a bond to the
obligee, to whom the obligor is also otherwise indebted,
[*400] *cannot, without some circumstances to show
that it was *intended* to be made in discharge of the
bond, be so applied in favour of the surety of the
obligor in an action upon the bond under the defence
of payment (*o*). So, also, in the case of *Williams* v.
Rawlinson (*p*), the doctrine of appropriation of payments was held not to discharge the defendant. In

(*m*) 10 Ch. Div. 139 ; 39 L. T. R. 494 ; 27 W. R. 212 ; 48 L. J.,
Ch. 348.
(*n*) *In re Booth, Browning* v. *Baldwin*, 27 W. R. 644, 645 ; 40 L.
T. R. 248.
(*o*) *Plomer* v. *Long*, 1 Stark. 153, and see note (*a*) at the end of
this case. See also *Wright* v. *Hickling*, L. R., 2 C. P. 199.
(*p*) 2 Bing. 71. See also *Kirby* v. *Duke of Marlborough*, 2 M.
& S. 18 ; *Simson* v. *Ingham*, 2 B. & C. 65.

that case the defendant executed a bond conditioned
to secure the plaintiffs, who were bankers, for any sums
which for ten years the plaintiffs should advance on
bills, &c., which T. should from time to time draw on
them, or make payable at their house, and all cheques,
&c., not exceeding 5,000l. in the whole. It was agreed
that this bond should not affect a prior security given
by T. to the plaintiffs. No notice was given to the
defendant by the plaintiffs that T. was indebted to
them 10,000l. at the time the defendant executed his
bond. T., however, saw the accounts every fortnight,
and received the vouchers half-yearly. At the close
of his account, T. was indebted to the plaintiffs more
than 10,000l. ; but, subsequently to the executing of
the defendant's bond, he had paid into the plaintiffs'
bank more than 5,000l. It was held that the defendant was liable to the extent of 5,000l. Best, C. J.,
said, "When the money was paid, nothing was said
as to the account to which it was to be applied, and
if the two accounts were blended, the course of business is to apply the payments to the earlier ; that is
the principal laid down in Clayton's case (q) and confirmed in Bodenham v. Purchas (r), but here the accounts must have been blended, for the defendant's
principal agreed to such an application of his payments;
*his accounts were settled half-yearly, and he [*401]
must have seen that the remittances subsequent to the
bond had been applied to the 10,000l.

The presumption that where a variety of transactions _{Presumption} are included in one general account, the items of credit _{in favour of} are to be appropriated to the items of debit in order of _{appropria-} date, in the absence of other appropriation, may be re- _{tion of items} butted by the circumstances of the case showing that _{items of} such could not have been the intention of the parties _{debit in} (s). It is quite clear that the mere existence of a sure _{may be} tyship does not, in the absence of express contract, take _{rebutted.} away from the principal debtor and creditor those
powers which they would otherwise have of appropria-
ting payments which are not subject to any particular
contract with the surety. S. guaranteed the account
of T. at a bank by two guarantees, one for 150l., the
other for 400l. By the terms of the guarantee, the
surety guaranteed to the bank "the repayment of all

(q) Reported 1 Mer. 572.
(r) Reported 2 B. & Ald. 39. And see Hart v. Alexander, 2 M.
& W. 484.
(s) City Discount Co. v. McLean, L. R., 9 C. P. 692. See also
In re Booth, Browning v. Stallard, 27 W. R. 664 ; 40 L. T. R. 248.

moneys which shall at any time be due from the customer to you on the general balance of his account with
you ;" the guarantee was moreover to be "a continuing
guarantee to the extent at any one time of " the sums
respectively named, and was not to be considered as
wholly or partially satisfied by the payment at any time
of any sums due on such general balance ; and any
indulgence granted by the bank was not to prejudice the
guarantee. S. having died, leaving T. and another executors, the bank on receiving notice of his death, without any communication with the executors beyond what
would appear in T's pass book, closed T.'s account,
which was overdrawn, and opened a new account with
him, in which they did not debit him with the amount
of the over-draft, but debited him with interest on the
same, and continued the account until he went into
liquidation when it was also withdrawn. It was held
[*402] (reversing the *decision of *Bacon*, V.-C.), that
there was no contract, express or implied, which obliged
the debtor and creditor to appropriate to the old over
draft the payments made by the debtor after the determination of the guarantee, and that the bank was entitled to prove against the estate of S. for the amount
of the old over-draft less the amount of the dividend
which they had received on it in the liquidation (*t*).

Doctrine of appropria-tion does not prevent rate-able distribu-tion of dividend on bankruptcy of principal debtor where there is a surety for payment of debt by in-stalments.
The doctrine of appropriation of payments does not
enable a person who, as surety, is the obligor of a bond
for the payment of money by instalments, to have the
whole dividend received by the creditor upon the *whole*
debt, under the bankruptcy of the principal debtor,
applied in discharge of that instalment. Such dividend
can only be *rateably* applied, in part payment of each
instalment as it becomes due (*u*).

(2.) Dis-charge of surety by set-off between principal and creditor.
(2.) *The surety may be discharged by a set-off exist-*
ing between the principal debtor and the creditor.
By the *Roman civil law, compensatio*, or set off,
operated as an *extinguishment* of the debt, *ipso jure* ;
hence it had the same effect as payment, to which it
bore a near affinity, and by its operation the debtor was
liberated from his debt and his sureties from their obligation (*x*). By *English* law, however, a set-off existing between the principal debtor and the creditor is certainly *not* regarded as operating to cause AN EXTINCTION of
the debt between the parties. But where the creditor,

(*t*) *In re Sherry, London and County Banking Co.* v. *Terry*, 25
Ch. D. 692 ; 53 L. J., Ch. 404 ; 50 L. T. 227; 32 W. R. 394.
(*u*) *Martin* v. *Brecknell*, 2 M. & S. 38.
(*x*) Colquhoun's Summary of the Roman Civil Law, par. 1843.

without the consent of the surety, becomes indebted to
the principal debtor in a sum which would amount to a
set-off *in full*, the surety has a *complete* defence against
the creditor, which he might formerly have availed himself of, by *equitable plea*, in an action at law (*y*.)　The
Judicature Act now *enables a defendant to [*403]
raise any equitable answer or defence in any court, that
is to say, anything which would formerly have been
good by way of answer if the suit had been brought in
chancery (*z*).　If the set-off be *partial*, and not complete,
then the surety has only a defence *pro tanto*.

In the recent case of *Bowyear* v. *Pawson* (*a*), an unsuccessful attempt was made to extend the surety's right
of set-off to a case where the sum claimed by the surety
consisted of a share of a debt which the plaintiff owed
to him and another (the principal debtor) who was not
a party to the action.　The facts of the case are as follows :—Action on a covenant to pay all liabilities which
the plaintiff might incur under a deed of assignment
made between the plaintiff and other parties.　The defendant pleaded that the covenant was the joint and
several covenant of himself and one Wilson, and that
before action the plaintiff was indebted to Wilson in an
amount exceeding the plaintiff's claim against the defendant, and that Wilson had assigned the plaintiff's
debt to himself and the defendant as tenants in common in equal shares.　As to one-half of the plaintiff's
claim the defendant claimed to set off one-half of the
debt so assigned, and as to the other half the defendant
said that he was entitled to be exonerated by Wilson,
and to call upon him to contribute in equal shares to
the payment of the plaintiff's claim.　The court held,
that the defence was no answer to the plaintiff's claim
and refused to allow the set-off.

(3.) *The surety may be discharged by payment made
by him and accepted by the creditor in satisfaction of
the suretyship liability.*

Whether a particular payment made by a surety
*operates as an extinguishment of his liability [*404]
under a particular guarantee may give rise to doubt in
cases where the surety is, independently of his guarantee, liable on his own account to the creditor.　In
such cases it is desirable, in order to avoid all question,

(3.) Dis-
charge of
surety by
payment
accepted by
creditor for
him in such
satisfaction.

(*y*) *Bechervaise* v. *Lewis*. 20 W. R., C. P. 726 ; *S: C.*, L. R., 7
C. P. 372 ; 41 L. J., C. P. 161 ; 26 L. T. 848.
(*z*) Judicature Act. 1873, s. 24, sub-s. (3).　And see Wilson's
Judicature Acts, 4th ed. p. 19.
(*a*) 6 Q. B. D. 540 ; 50 L. J., Q. B. 495 ; 29 W. R. 664.
(1553)

for the surety to require his guarantee to be given up to him on his making the payment. On this subject the case of *Waugh* v. *Wren* (b) may be usefully referred to. There a surety guaranteed that certain deeds which had been deposited by his principal with a bank, as security for the amount then due or thereafter to become due from him to the bank, so that the whole should not exceed 2,000l., were good for the amount specified. Afterwards when the principal was indebted to the bank in the amount of 4,000l., the surety paid them 3,000l. and received back the guarantee, his object being, according to his own statement, to liquidate his own engagement and to reduce the debt of the principal. It was held that the payment made by the surety was obviously intended by him to be, and was received in discharge of, the suretyship liability, and not in redemption of the deeds deposited by the principal debtor with the creditor.

V. Discharge of surety by operation of Statute of Limitations. V. Supposing none of the contingencies which have been now enumerated happen to the suretyship, it will, in process of time, like other contracts and rights, become extinguished by the operation of the Statute of Limitations.

A discharge of the surety may take place by the operation of the Statute of Limitations.

In the case of a guarantee *not under seal*, after six years have elapsed from the period at which the surety first became liable to make payment to the creditors, the right of the creditor to compel him to do so will be barred by 21 Jac. 1, c. 16, s. 8. If, however, the guarantee [*405] *antee be under seal, the creditors' rights against the surety will not be barred until the expiration of *twenty years* (c). It is frequently a matter of some little difficulty to determine *when* the right of the creditor to call upon the surety for payment first commenced, and the Statute of Limitations, therefore, began to run. This question must, to a great extent, depend upon the circumstances of each individual case, but the three following decisions may be useful as a guide :—

When the Statute of Limitations begins to run against the creditor. **Colvin v. Buckle.** In *Colvin* v. *Buckle* (d), the defendants gave the following guarantee :—

(b) 11 W. R. 244.
(c) 3 & 4 Will. 4, c. 42, s. 3. For the *general* effect and operation of the Statute of Limitations, the reader is referred to works treating on the law of contracts generally.
(d) 8 M. & W. 680.

"You having expressed some doubt of the propriety of paying Mr. *Gooch* his draft on you for 850*l.* in our favour, we hereby engage, if you will pay us the same, we will reimburse you the amount on demand, with interest, in the event of your finding it necessary to call upon us to do so, *either from the state of Mr. Gooch's pending accounts with your London or Bengal house, or from any other circumstances.*" It was held that the Statute of Limitations began to run against the plaintiffs *when all the facts were ascertained upon which the defendant's legal liability depended,* and that the delay in the adjustment of the accounts between the plaintiffs and Gooch, caused by needless litigation, in which the plaintiffs were engaged, did not prevent the Statute of Limitations from running.

In *Holl* v. *Hadley* (*e*), H. gave the plaintiffs a guarantee for the value of coals to be supplied to N. H., on condition that no application should be made to him (H.) for payment, but "on failure of the utmost efforts and legal proceedings" of the plaintiffs to obtain payment from N. H. Coals were supplied under the guarantee, and remained unpaid for till April, 1820. *At that period H., in consideration of the plain- [*406] tiffs giving N. H. (the principal debtor) "*two years and upwards*" for the liquidation of his then debt, agreed to reserve to the plaintiffs all claim that they might have upon him, H., by virtue of the former security, and "to be bound by the consequence thereof, if, at the expiration of such period," the plaintiffs should not have been paid. N. H. never paid the debt. In *April*, 1824, he went to *France*, but was occasionally in *England*, privately and for short periods, from that time till 1830, when he finally returned. The plaintiffs issued process against him in June, 1826, and continued it till 1830, when they arrested N. H. upon it on his return to England. Soon afterwards he became insolvent. In July, 1828, the plaintiffs commenced an action against H. on his guarantee; that action abated by his death in 1829. Afterwards, in June, 1829, the plaintiffs brought an action upon the guarantees against his executors, who pleaded the Statute of Limitations. Issue was joined on that plea. It was held that, assuming that the first guarantee was incorporated with the second, a reasonable time must be allowed after the expiration of the two years for the plaintiffs to endeavour to obtain payment from H. Nevertheless

Holl v. *Hadley.*

(*e*) 2 A. & E. 758; 5 Bing. 54.

that the plaintiffs, having allowed two years to pass
without proceeding against N. H., after which he went
abroad, had certainly exceeded such reasonable time,
and were barred of their remedy against H. by the
Statute of Limitations in July, 1828.

Hartland v. Jukes. In *Hartland* v. *Jukes* (*f*) the facts were as follow :—
In the year 1855 W. Courtney proposed to open a
banking account with the Gloucestershire Banking
Company, and thereupon he and W. Steward, as his
surety, gave the banking company their joint and
several promissory note for 200*l*., and at the same time
[*407] *a memorandum in writing was signed by them
and delivered by the banking company. This memorandum, in effect, provided that the promissory note was
given as a further and collateral security to the banking
company, for the banking account intended to be kept
by W. Courtney with them, and that it should be held
by them, and that they should be at liberty to recover
thereon to the full amount thereof all the money which
W. Courtney should at any time thereafter become liable for or indebted to the banking company on his banking account. The account was opened, and on the 31st
December, 1855, W. Courtney was indebted to the banking company in 173*l*. No demand of payment was
made, however, nor was a balance struck until 30th
June, 1856, when 194*l*. was due to the banking company on the account. A balance was afterwards struck
every half-year, the banking company from time to
time making advances, and W. Courtney paying money
into the bank with which his account was credited. The
The sums so credited exceeded the value of the promissory note. The account was not closed till February,
1861, when a balance of 161*l*. was due to the banking
company. In March, 1862, the banking company com-
commenced an action on the note against W. Steward's
executors. It was held that the cause of action was
not barred by the Statute of Limitations.

APPENDIX.

An Act to repeal the Guarantee by Companies Act, 1867, and to make other Provisions in lieu thereof. [11th August, 1875.]

WHEREAS by the Guarantee by Companies Act, 1867, the heads of public departments were authorised to accept as security for persons required to give security for the due performance of the duties of an office or employment in the public service the guarantee of a company which complied with the conditions contained in that act, and received a certificate from the treasury as provided by that act:

And whereas it is expedient that the power of the treasury to give such certificate to a company as is provided by the said act should cease, and that the said act should be repealed, and other provision made as hereinafter mentioned:

Be it therefore enacted by the Queen's most excellent Majesty, by and with the advice and consent of the lords spiritual and temporal, and commons, in this present parliament assembled, and by the authority of the same as follows:

1. The Guarantee by Companies Act, 1867, is hereby repealed, and every certificate granted by the treasury to a company under that act is hereby cancelled.

Provided as follows :

(1.) Where a certificate has been given by the employer as mentioned in the said act of the amount due in respect of any loss from the guarantor, such certificate shall continue to have the same effect as provided, by the said act; and,

(2.) All rights and remedies vested in any company under section seven of the said act shall continue to be so vested; and,

(3.) Such remedy, and any investigation or legal proceedings in respect of any such right, loss, or remedy, may be had and carried on in like manner as if this act had not passed.

*2. Where a person holding any office or employment in the public [*410] service is required by law to give security for the due performance of the duties of such office or employment, the treasury may from time to time, if they think fit, by warrant made upon the representation of the head officer of the department in which such person serves, authorise that head officer, in such cases, under such circumstances, and upon such conditions as may be specified in the warrant, to vary the character of the security, notwithstanding that the same may be prescribed by any act or otherwise.

The treasury may from time to time, by warrant made upon the like representation, revoke or vary any previous warrant made in pursuance of this section.

A warrant made in pursuance of this section may apply to any class of persons as well as to any single person.

Every warrant of the treasury made in pursuance of this section shall be laid before both houses of parliament within one month after it is made, if parliament be then sitting, or, if not, within one month after the then next session of parliament.

For the purposes of this section every person who is remunerated out of the consolidated fund, or out of moneys provided by parliament, or out of fines or penalties, or other moneys which otherwise would be paid into the receipt of her Majesty's exchequer, or out of other public revenue, or who holds any public office or employment under the crown in respect of which he is entitled to fees, shall be deemed to hold an office or employment in the public service.

The expression "treasury" in this act means the Commissioners of her Majesty's Treasury.

3. Where the guarantee of any company has before the passing of this act, been accepted as security for any person holding any office or employment in the public service, such guarantee shall continue to be received as security for such person, subject to any power which the head officer of the department in which such person serves may have to require some other security.

4. This act may be cited as the Government Officers (Security) Act, 1875.

INDEX.

(1559)

326 . INDEX.

AGENT—*continued.*

subsequent recognition of agent's act, 159.
agent need not sign as such, 159.
  parol evidence of agency admissible, 159.
where agent signs his own name and that of his principal, he must be
  taken to have signed as a contracting party, 159.
agent need not sign in name of principal, 159, 160.
where agent signs his *own* name, parol evidence when admissible to prove
  agency, 159.
agreement that agent was not to be liable as principal may be pleaded,
  159, 160.
authority of agent countermandable, 160.
agent must have *some* authority, 160, 161.
effect of his signing without authority, 161.
  his liability in such a case, 161.
what class of agents possess implied authority to give a guarantee,
  161—170. *See* AUCTIONEERS; BROKERS; PARTNERS.
del credere agent, what is, 134. *See* DEL CREDERE COMMISSION; STATUTE
  OF FRAUDS.

AGREEMENT,

requisites of agreement, 2—7. *See* CONTRACT OF GUARANTEE.
substitution of new for old, 346—348. *See* DISCHARGE OF SURETY.
variation of terms of, 350—361. *See* DISCHARGE OF SURETY.
parol evidence to explain written agreement, 150, 159, 180. *See* EVI-
  DENCE.
sect. 4 of Statute of Frauds requires *whole* agreement to be in writing, 148
  et seq. See CONTRACT OF GUARANTEE.
  consideration need not now appear in writing, 150 *et seq. See* CON-
    TRACT OF GUARANTEE.
memorandum in writing need not be contemporary with agreement, 173.
  but when it is made there must be a complete agreement actually in
    existence, 173.
to satisfy Statute of Frauds agreement need not be contained in one in-
  ,strument, 173, 174. *See* CONTRACT OF GUARANTEE.
to satisfy Statute of Frauds agreement must be reduced to writing before
  action, 32.

ALIENS,

common law as to contracts by, 16, 17.
Naturalization Act, 1870, effect of, 17.

ALTERATION,

of instrument of guarantee, 340—343.
  rule in *Pigot's case* applies to guarantees, 340, 341.
    semble, immaterial alteration by a party does not invalidate instru-
      ment, 342.
  effect of alteration made with consent of principal debtor, 342.
ground on which discharge by alteration of written instrument proceeds,
  342, 343.
verbal alteration of contract within Statute of Frauds, 347.

APPROPRIATION OF PAYMENTS,

explanation of the doctrine, 397 *et seq.*
right of appropriation in *English law,* 397.
  debtor first right to appropriate, 398.
  if he does not, creditor may, 398.
  if neither does, then law appropriates to earlier debt, 398.
  application of doctrine where sureties claim benefit of payments made
    by principal, 398—400.

(1561)

328   INDEX.

(1562)

(1564)

(1565)

334 INDEX.

(1568)

DEFAULT—*continued.*
surety's liability does not arise until principal debtor has made default,
185 *et seq.*
but he need not be informed of such default, 189.
surety only liable for default guaranteed against, 206.

DEFENCE. *See* DISCHARGE OF SURETY ; FRAUD ; STATUTE OF LIMITATIONS.
verbal guarantee may, *semble*, support, 42.
right of set-off founded upon plaintiff's guarantee, 202.
by principal debtor when sued by surety, 283.
grounds on which injunction formerly granted now available as a, 288.
surety, when sued by creditor, entitled to benefit of set-off which principal
had against latter, 289, 402, 403.
defendant can claim contribution by means of third party notice, 313, 314.
to action for contribution, 311 *et seq.*, 320 *et seq.*
parol dispensation may now be pleaded to action on a deed, 347.
since Judicature Act defendant may raise in any court any equitable answer or defence which would formerly have been good by way of answer
if the suit had been brought in chancery, 371.

DEL CREDERE COMMISSION,
whence phrase borrowed, 134, note (*d*).
nature of, 134 *et seq.*
definition of, 134.
del credere agent not primarily liable, 134, 135.
promise of *del credere* agent, whether within Statute of Frauds, sect. 4 . .
134—142. *See* STATUTE OF FRAUDS.

DIRECTORS,
liability of company on guarantee given by, 170.
where directors guarantee performance of a contract by their company,
which is *ultra vires*, they still remain liable as sureties, 184.

DISABILITY. *See* INFANTS; INSANITY ; MARRIED WOMEN.
promises to be answerable for persons under, 85 *et seq. See* STATUTE OF
FRAUDS.

DISCHARGE OF DEBTOR,
does not always relieve surety, 184, 185.
provision in B. A. 1883, on this subject, 184, 185.

DISCHARGE OF SURETY,
does not follow from discharge of bankrupt principal, 184, 185.
provision in B. A. 1883, on this subject, 184, 185.
even before Judicature Act, regulated by same principles at law and in
equity, 323.
matters invalidating guarantee *ab initio*, 324—344.
fraud, 324—340. *See* FRAUD.
alteration of guarantee, 340, 343. *See* ALTERATION.
failure of consideration, 343, 344.
revocation of contract of suretyship, 344—350. *See* REVOCATION.
by act of the parties, 344—348.
where notice of revocation given by the surety to the creditor,
344—346.
new agreement substituted for original one by mutual consent
346—348.
by death of the surety, 348—350.
surety's death does not affect his *past* liability, 348.
its effect on *subsequent* transactions depends on nature of the guarantee itself, 348, 349.
result of decisions on this subject stated, 349, 350.

22 (1571)

338   INDEX.

(1572)

EQUITY—_continued._

principal debtor was compelled in equity to exonerate surety from liability, 276, 277.

semble, Chancery Division will now give relief in such cases, 276, 277.

doctrine of contribution rests on, 307, 308. _See_ CONTRIBUTION.

same principles always governed discharge of surety at law and in equity, 323.

right of surety to all the equities creditor could have enforced, 297 *et seq.*

fusion of law and, effected by Judicature Act, 307, 378.

EVIDENCE,

parol evidence to prove an executory consideration, 27.

entry in books of plaintiff evidence to show to whom credit given, 108, 109.

written evidence of guarantee must exist before action brought, 32

parol evidence of consideration to explain surety's *written* promise not admissible, 150, 151.

parol evidence of agency, 159.

parol evidence to prove that guarantee is signed by an agent, 159.

written evidence of agent's authority to sign guarantee unnecessary, 159

parol evidence admissible to *charge* undisclosed principal, but not to *discharge* person signing as agent, 159. 160.

parol evidence to connect different papers containing agreement of parties, 174.

parol evidence to explain, not contradict written instrument, 180.

unstamped guarantee cannot be given in evidence, 175. *See* STAMP.

surrounding circumstances may be given in evidence, 180, 181.

surety not estopped by recital in bond from proving no *legal appointment* of principal to office, 205.

parol evidence of agreement giving time to debtor admissible, 371.

whether reserve of remedies against surety may be proved by parol evidence,

in release, 367, 368.

in agreement giving time to principal debtor, 379, 380.

EXECUTED CONSIDERATION,

will not support a guarantee, 26.

sometimes difficult to determine whether consideration is executed or executory, 26 *et seq.*

EXECUTION. *See* CAPIAS AD SATISFACIENDUM.

promise by execution creditor to sheriff's solicitor, 65.

promise to pay if execution against third person withdrawn, 76.

abandonment by creditor of execution against principal debtor, 391, 392.

after surety has converted himself into a principal debtor, 395.

creditor a trustee of execution for surety, 392.

EXECUTOR,

cannot by retainer obtain benefit of verbal guarantee received from his testator, 42, 43.

of principal debtor, when also his surety, may exercise right of retainer, 278.

EXECUTORY CONSIDERATION.

will support a guarantee, 24.

future advance or supply of goods, 24, 25.

future employment of third persons. 25, 26.

sometimes difficult to determine whether consideration is past or future, 26 *et seq.*

when consideration executory, mutuality of agreement may not exist till consideration performed, 25.

(1576)

INTENTION,
concurrence of, necessary to a contract, 2.
definition of, 8.
parties to contract must be capable of forming intention, 7, 8.
to render guarantee binding as such, its language must clearly indicate
intention to incur the liability of a surety, 178, 179.

INTEREST,
when surety liable to creditor for, 209.
surety entitled to recover interest from principal debtor, 281.
surety for a company proving for interest, 281, 282.
bond creditor agreeing by anticipation to take interest on his debt, 371, 372.

INTOXICATION,
contract entered into under, renders agreement voidable, 10, 11.

JOINT LIABILITY,
promise to be jointly liable for another, 83—85. *See* STATUTE OF FRAUDS.

JUDGMENT,
against principal debtor not binding on surety, 181, 182, 197, 273.
summary application for, where writ especially indorsed, 198, 199.

JUDICATURE ACT,
rules under, enable claim upon a guarantee to be enforced by especially
indorsed writ, 198, 199.
rules under, as to joinder of plaintiffs, 199, n. (v).
of defendants, 201.
abolishes restraining of actions by injunctions, 288.
grounds on which injunctions formerly granted now available as a defence. 288.
assigns to Chancery Division jurisdiction to set aside and cancel agreements, 288, 289.
fusion of law and equity effected by, 307, 378.
rules under, as to third party notices, 313, 314. *See* THIRD PARTY.
provision in, as to raising equitable defences, 371.
provision in Judicature Act, 1875, as to administration of insolvent estates
as in bankruptcy, 278.

JURY.
determines whether supply of goods to third person *reasonable*, 24, 25.
when signature to contract not in its usual place, its effect for jury, 171.
to whom credit given is for jury, 97, 101, 104, 106, 107.
for jury to say whether defence by surety reasonable, so as to entitle him
to recover from principal costs of defence, 282.

LACHES,
surety discharged by, 383—391.
mere passive negligence does not constitute, 383.
neglect to insure, against fire, work performance of which guaranteed, 383,
384.
guarantee to endorse third person's bills discharged, if demand to endorse
not made in reasonable time, 384.
when surety for payment of negotiable instrument, but not a party to
it, discharged by omission to present for payment, 188, 189, 384.
surety for solvency of purchasers discharged by omission to sell at good
opportunities, 384, 385.
when surety discharged by conduct of persons associated in office with
principal, 385, 386.
neglect of employer to dismiss dishonest servant, 386.
negligence of employer in calling upon employed to account after notice
not to trust latter, 387.

LACHES—*continued.*
omission to give notice to surety of third person's embezzlement, 387, 388.
when surety has expressly stipulated that such notice shall be given, 388.
accidential omission to answer surety's inquiry, 388, 389.
omission by creditor to take proceedings which would have been fruitless, 389, 390.
omission by creditor to render bill of exchange complete by inserting drawee's name, 390.
semble, where guarantee given to crown, laches on part of latter do not discharge surety, 391.

LANDLORD,
promises to pay rent in arrear if landlord will not distrain, 67—69, 122—125, 146, 147. *See* STATUTE OF FRAUDS.

LEADING OBJECT,
of contract, a test whether sect. 4 of Statute of Frauds applies, 129—142.
See MAIN OBJECT ; STATUTE OF FRAUDS.

LEASE,
bankruptcy of assignee of lease, followed by disclaimer of official receiver, does not discharge surety, 184.

LIABILITY OF PRINCIPAL DEBTOR. *See* DEBTOR.

LIABILITY OF SURETY. *See* SURETY.

LIEN,
promise in consideration of lien being given up, 65, 66, 118 *et seq.*, 130, 131, 143, 144. *See* STATUTE OF FRAUDS.

LIMITATIONS. *See* STATUTE OF LIMITATIONS,

LIMITED GUARANTEE,
sometimes difficult to determine whether guarantee limited in amount is applicable to *whole* debt or *part* thereof, 205—206.
principles regulating this subject, 206.
importance of ascertaining the nature of the liability under the guarantee when principal debtor has become bankrupt, 303, 304.

LORD TENTERDEN'S ACT (9 Geo. 4, c. 14).
sect. 6 cured evasion of sect. 4 of Statute of Frauds, 33, 34.
by sect. 6, representation of character, &c., not actionable unless in writing, 33, 34.
origin of this enactment, 33, n. (*p*).
rule where representations of character, &c., partly *written* and *verbal,* 34.
defendant not liable unless representation false to his knowledge, 34,
but defendant need not benefit by the deceit, 34.
attempted evasion of sect. 6, of Lord Tenterden's Act, 34, 35.
cases within sect. 6 . . 35 *et seq.*
representation of credit of firm of which defendant a member, 36
to whom representation must be made, 36, 37.
signature of representation, 37—39.
liability of company on representation of credit, &c., *signed* by its manager, 37—39.

MAIN OBJECT,
of promise, 129—142. *See* LEADING OBJECT ; STATUTE OF FRAUDS.

MARKSMAN,
mark by, a sufficient signature of agreement within Statute of Frauds, 171.

(1578)

(1579)

NOTICE. *See* THIRD PARTY.
  guarantee sometimes expressly determinable by notice, 344, 345.
  when guarantee silent on the subject, power of revocation depends on nature of guarantee, 345.
  guarantee for person employed cannot be revoked by notice so long as he retains the *status* which he acquired on the *faith* of it, 345, 346.
  when notice of surety's death will revoke guarantee, 348—350.
  creditor may assign securities without giving notice to surety, 392—394.

NOVATION,
  substitution of one debtor for another who is thereby discharged, 90, 91. *See* STATUTE OF FRAUDS.
  conversion of *sole* debt into a *joint* debt, 90, 91.
  acceptance of composition from a stranger in lieu of original debt, 91.

OFFER. *See* ACCEPTANCE.
  to guarantee not binding, 2, 3.

OFFICE,
  promise to be answerable for third person in an office, 204, 205, 207, 225—246. *See* BOND.

OFFICIAL RECEIVER IN BANKRUPTCY,
  disclaimer by, of lease, does not release surety for assignee, 184.

OPERATION OF LAW,
  discharge of principal debtor by, does not discharge surety, 363, 364.
  what amounts to discharge by operation of law, 363, 364.

ORDER OF DISCHARGE IN BANKRUPTCY,
  does not release any person who was surety, or in the nature of surety, for bankrupt, 184, 185.
  provision in B. A. 1883, on this subject, 184, 185.

ORIGINAL DEBTOR,
  where his liability extinguished by guarantor's promise, 89—91. *See* STATUTE OF FRAUDS.

PAROL EVIDENCE. *See* EVIDENCE.

PARTICULARS OF DEMAND,
  surety claiming payment of definite sum by way of contribution must give, 313.

PARTIES,
  to contract of guarantee, 1.
  names of contracting parties must appear in writing, 157. *See* CONTRACT OF GUARANTEE.
  guarantee need not be addressed to other contracting party, 157, 158.
  to action on guarantee, 199—201.
    as plaintiffs, 199, 200.
      joinder of, 199, 200.
        provision in Judicature Rules, 199, note (v).
    as defendants, 200, 201.
      joinder of, 201.
        provision in Judicature Rules, 201.
  signature of one contracting party as agent for other, to memorandum of guarantee, 162.

PARTNERS,
  guarantee addressed to one of several partners, 158.

(1540)

350

SECURITY—*continued.*
effect of primary security becoming worthless, 394.
creditor need not give surety notice of assignment of securities, 392—394.
effect of creditor taking *additional* security, 361, 362.
as to *merger* of original security in inferior security, 361, 362.

SEE PAID,
promise to *see paid*, 104, n (*k*).

SEPARABLE,
where promise is, action is maintainable on part outside Statute of Frauds, 45 *et seq.*
effect of alteration of one of two separate and distinct things, performance of which surety has guaranteed, 358.

SET-OFF,
mere liability under guarantee not formerly capable of being set-off, 202.
but money *actually paid* under a guarantee constituted set-off, 202.
subject of set-off now regulated by Judicature Rules, 202.
equitable defence by surety of set-off in full between principal debtor and creditor, 289, 402, 403.
now available in any Court, 403.

SIGNATURE. *See* AGENT; LORD TENTERDEN'S ACT; PARTIES.
promise to *procure* the signature of another to a guarantee not within statute, 77—79. *See* STATUTE OF FRAUDS.
of memorandum in writing to satisfy sect. 4 of Statute of Frauds, 158—173. *See* CONTRACT OF GUARANTEE.
such memorandum need only be signed by party to be *charged*, 158.
signature by agent, 158—170. *See* AGENT.
where signature to memorandum must be placed, 170, 171.
casual introduction of name in an instrument, 171.
when signature not in its usual place its effect is for jury, 171.
the *kind* of signature to memorandum of guarantee, 171—173.
mark by marksman, 171.
whether signature by *initials* sufficient, 171, 172.
signature without *christian* name, 172.
printed signature, 172.
signature by contracting party as a *witness*, whether sufficient, 172.
whether alteration of draft amounts to a signature, 172.
signature by indorsement of draft agreement, 172.
effect of guarantee drawn up in plural number and signed by one person, 172, 173.
effect of signature by party to be charged of telegraph form accepting offer, 173.
signature of a paper referring to another paper containing terms of agreement, 174.

SOLICITOR,
verbal guarantee of, 41. *See* STATUTE OF FRAUDS.
promise by a defendant to pay charges of plaintiff's solicitor, 60. *See* STATUTE OF FRAUDS.
guarantee addressed to solicitor for plaintiff, 158.
guarantee by one of several solicitors in partnership, 168, 169.

SPECIAL PROMISE,
evasion of Statute of Frauds by treating special promise as a false representation, 33.
remedy applied by 9 Geo. 4, c. 14, s. 6 . . 33, 34. *See* LORD TENTERDEN'S ACT.
what is, 47—49. *See* STATUTE OF FRAUDS.

(1585)

352   INDEX.

(1,700)

Phila. : The Blackstone Pub. Co.